Segmented Labor, Fractured Politics

Labor Politics in American Life

PLENUM STUDIES IN WORK AND INDUSTRY

Series Editors:
Ivar Berg, *University of Pennsylvania, Philadelphia, Pennsylvania*
and Arne L. Kalleberg, *University of North Carolina, Chapel Hill, North Carolina*

WORK AND INDUSTRY
Structures, Markets, and Processes
Arne L. Kalleberg and Ivar Berg

Current Volumes in the Series:

THE BUREAUCRATIC LABOR MARKET
The Case of the Federal Civil Service
Thomas A. DiPrete

THE EMPLOYMENT RELATIONSHIP
Causes and Consequences of Modern Personnel Administration
William P. Bridges and Wayne J. Villemez

ENRICHING BUSINESS ETHICS
Edited by Clarence C. Walton

LABOR AND POLITICS IN THE U.S. POSTAL SERVICE
Vern K. Baxter

LIFE AND DEATH AT WORK
Industrial Accidents as a Case of Socially Produced Error
Tom Dwyer

NEGRO BUSINESS AND BUSINESS EDUCATION
Their Present and Prospective Development
Joseph A. Pierce
Introduction by John Sibley Butler

THE OPERATION OF INTERNAL LABOR MARKETS
Staffing Practices and Vacancy Chains
Lawrence T. Pinfield

SEGMENTED LABOR, FRACTURED POLITICS
Labor Politics in American Life
William Form

THE STATE AND THE LABOR MARKET
Edited by Samuel Rosenberg

WHEN STRIKES MAKE SENSE—AND WHY
Lessons from Third Republic French Coal Miners
Samuel Cohn

A Chronological Listing of Volumes in this series appears at the back of this volume.

A Continuation Order Plan is available for this series. A continuation order will bring delivery of each new volume immediately upon publication. Volumes are billed only upon actual shipment. For further information please contact the publisher.

Segmented Labor, Fractured Politics

Labor Politics in American Life

William Form
The Ohio State University
Columbus, Ohio

Plenum Press • New York and London

Library of Congress Cataloging-in-Publication Data

On file

ISBN 0-306-45031-3

A Division of Plenum Publishing Corporation
233 Spring Street, New York, N.Y. 10013

10 9 8 7 6 5 4 3 2 1

Printed in the United States of America

To
Cathy Sternberg
Nancy Rytina
Steven Rytina
Helen Land

Preface

My curiosity and concern about the working class in America stems from childhood memories of my father, a cabinetmaker, and of my oldest brother, an autoworker, who were passionately involved in the labor movement. Perhaps because they so wanted the working class to achieve greater social and economic justice and because they insisted it was not happening, I became curious to know the reasons why. Without even being aware of it, I began to explore a possible explanation—the internal diversity of the working class.

In my studies of autoworkers (the prototype proletarians) in the United States, Italy, Argentina, and India, I discovered that they seemed to be more divided economically, socially, and politically in the more economically advanced countries—an idea that ran contrary to the evolutionary predictions of my Marxist friends. When I reported this in *Blue-Collar Stratification* (1976), I was surprised that some of them who were committed to an ideology of working-class solidarity attacked the hypothesis because it ran against their convictions.

I decided to explore the hypothesis more fully in the United States. In *Divided We Stand* (1985), I reported the results of my research: strong earnings, status, and political divisions in the working class existed not only in the past but also in the present, magnified by differences in race, gender, and labor union affiliation. But strangely enough, very few studies had examined the organizational behavior of labor in the Democratic Party on the local, state, and national level, and only a few scholars were currently doing research on the topic. To be sure, considerable research had been done in the 1950s and 1960s, but it seemed to contribute little to the understanding of the current scene. Its theoretical approach embraced a conception of social class that seemed inapplicable to the stratification changes in the following decades. An attempt had to be made to address the impact of these changes on current labor practices. The search for answers turned out to be elusive. *Segmented Labor, Fractured Politics* represents an attempt to understand labor's inability to be more effective in political pursuits.

This book is the last of an unplanned trilogy to examine divisions of the working class and its inability to forge a cohesive political strategy. But there is still much to be learned about this topic. I hope that other scholars will pursue it. This work is based on two beliefs: that organized labor is or ought to be interested in the well-being of workers who are not as fortunate as union members, and that labor's legislative agenda cannot be achieved without a more politically disciplined membership.

My debts in writing this book are many, a few of which I acknowledge here. First, I am indebted to the late J. David Greenstone, who wrote *the book* on American labor politics which started me on my quest to see how it had changed since the 1960s. I am very grateful to the labor union leaders, party leaders, and newspaper reporters who graciously agreed to be interviewed. In particular, I appreciate the help of officers of the Central Labor Councils of the AFL–CIO: Daniel Radford in Cincinnati, Richard Acton in Cleveland, and William Rittenhouse in Columbus. Jay Power and Ben Albert in the Washington AFL–CIO were the most helpful in improving my understanding of operations at the Washington headquarters.

I am most indebted to Joan Huber for her help and countless suggestions for improving the manuscript. My conversations with Michael Wallace over the years have enriched my understanding of the way that economic organizations function. Richard Hamilton suggested many ways to improve the manuscript, and he deepened my concern to do more historical research. Craig Jenkins stimulated me in many ways to think about the mysteries of social and political movements. Andrew Newman deepened my understanding of social organization and multilevel analysis. Robert Kaufman and Toby Parcel shared their knowledge of labor market stratification and helped me rethink its bearing on labor politics. Krishnan Namboodiri helped me think about macrosocietal organization and how to study it. Edward Crenshaw gave me ideas about urban organization and how it might affect labor politics. Lauren Krivo and Kent Schwirian guided me to important community research and Verta Taylor shared her ideas on social movement theory and research.

My colleagues in political science, Randall Ripley and Herbert Asher, graciously gave me access to their Ohio surveys of labor union members and the public. Lawrence Herson guided my search into local government relations with organized labor. William Angel shared his experiences in labor–party relations in Lima. James Kweeder at Cleveland State University, Alfred Tuchfarber at the University of Cincinnati, and William Nelson at the Ohio State University shared their insights into the politics in their respective cities.

Charles Tilly's lectures and conversations showed me how I should incorporate widely disparate social phenomena into a single theoretical statement. Daniel Cornfield, Michael Goldfield, and Kevin Leicht helped me rethink labor's relations to the Democratic Party. Raymond Boryczka helped me unravel some mysteries of labor history in urban Ohio. Rick Fantasia's important field work stimulated my thinking on the revitalization of the labor movement. Michael Schwartz provided a counterbalance to my pessimistic views on labor movement revival.

Funds from the Center for Labor Studies, the College of Social and Behavioral Science, and the Department of Sociology at the Ohio State University supported graduate students who helped in the interviewing and data analysis. Jacqueline Keil helped in the interviewing and processed data on labor union legislation and membership. Brian Martin also shared in the interviewing and in the analysis of data from the U.S. Department of Labor and Bureau of the Census. Christopher Papaleonardos recorded interviews and critically responded to my ideas of labor politics. Richard Haller, Joan Arnfield, and Jane Wilson patiently taught me how to solve my confrontations with computers.

William Form

Columbus, Ohio

Contents

PART I CHANGE AND DECLINE

Abbreviations

ABC	American Building Contractors
AFL	American Federation of Labor
AFL-CIO	American Federation of Labor–Congress of Industrial Organizations
AFSCME	American Federation of State, County, Municipal Employees
AFT	American Federation of Teachers
BTC	Building Trades Council
CEA	Columbus Educational Association
COPE	Committee on Political Education
CIO	Congress of Industrial Organizations Committee on Industrial Organizations
CWA	Communication Workers of America
CAP	Community Action Program of the UAW
DNC	Democratic National Committee
DRIVE	Democrats, Republicans, Independents for Voter Education (Teamsters)
EPAC	Educational Political Action Committee
FEPC	Fair Employment Practices Commission
FOP	Fraternal Order of Police
IAM	International Association of Machinists
IBEW	International Brotherhood of Electrical Workers
LCCH	Labor Coalition Clearing House
LLPE	Labor's League for Political Education (AFL)
NEA	National Education Association
NIRA	National Industrial Recovery Act
NLRB	National Labor Relations Board
NRA	National Recovery Act

NAFTA	North American Free Trade Act
OSHA	Occupational Safety and Health Act
OCSEA	Ohio Civil Service Employees Association
OEA	Ohio Educational Association
OFT	Ohio Federation of Teachers
OCAW	Oil, Chemical, and Atomic Workers
PAC	Political Action Committee
PATCO	Professional Air Traffic Controllers Association
PEOPLE	Public Employees to Promote Labor Equality
SEIU	Service Employees International Union
UAW	United Automobile Workers of America
UFCW	United Food and Commercial Workers
UMW	United Mine Workers of America
USW	United Steel Workers of America

I
Change and Decline

1

Explaining Labor's Political Fortunes

Brilliantly but briefly, the U.S. labor movement blossomed in only two decades of this century.[1] Until the New Deal, business and government built a structure that managed to contain the movement. Especially in difficult economic times, business repeatedly beat back labor's threats to become a significant economic and political actor (Gordon, Edwards, and Reich 1982, pp. 122–80). The crisis of capitalism during the long Great Depression created conditions for a new alignment in the political order. The Democratic Party, struggling to forge a majority coalition, appealed to industrial workers, ethnic communities, and liberals for support.

In 1933, after the party elected Franklin Roosevelt and seized control of Congress, the administration searched for novel solutions to end the economic and social crisis. In a relatively short time, legislation that became known as the New Deal made it easier for increasingly restive workers to organize labor unions. The New Deal also included legislation that aided farmers, eased unemployment, and assisted children and the aged.

Activists in the American Federation of Labor seized the opportunity to organize workers in the industrial heartland. A wave of sit-down strikes dramatized organized labor's determination to overcome management resistance. A sympathetic National Labor Relations Board (NLRB) quickly conducted elections and certified the formation of new unions. The series of successful strikes for union recognition rapidly increased union mem-

[1]Throughout this work, unless otherwise specified, the term *labor* refers to unions, organized labor, and the labor movement.

bership. Liberals rallied with labor to form a coalition that they hoped would create a permanent Democratic majority.

The nation's entry into World War II produced an insatiable demand for arms and manufactured goods. Under a no-strike agreement, labor and management temporarily put differences aside. Both industry and unions expanded rapidly. Unexpected postwar prosperity doubled union membership from its pre-New Deal level. Within a few years, labor had organized almost half of the urban labor force and gained an undreamed of measure of economic security, status, and political influence. At the time, few thought that they would look back to this period as labor's Golden Age.

Unexpectedly in 1947, a conservative coalition in Congress passed the antilabor Taft-Hartley Bill, which restricted union practices and permitted states to enact right-to-work laws. This convinced even conservative craft-union leaders that they should strengthen their political organization and buttress the Democratic Party, following the industrial unions' example. Progress toward this goal was slow. In 1952, a resurgent Republican Party, supported by many union members, elected (and then reelected) a popular general, Dwight Eisenhower. Union membership continued to grow as the labor force expanded, but the unionized became a shrinking portion of it. In 1960, the Democrats elected Kennedy, and in 1964, Johnson. Most labor leaders, reassured that Eisenhower represented a temporary Republican interlude, assumed that the liberal coalition would hold.

Four years later, in 1968, the nation's political complexion changed. The Vietnam war, the civil rights movement, and the women's movement split the labor-liberal coalition, exposing deep cleavages in the Democratic Party. Labor's political machine, COPE (Committee on Political Education), remained dormant during the 1972 McGovern–Nixon race. Public confidence in labor dwindled as Republicans seized the political initiative. In the ensuing two decades, the Democrats elected only one president, Jimmy Carter in 1976. Economic recessions, industrial restructuring, declining union membership, unsympathetic Republican administrations, and ideological splits within and between labor and the Democratic Party eroded the liberal–labor coalition and labor's influence on it. Even Clinton's victory and Democratic control of Congress in 1992 did not assure labor leaders that their legislative goals would be passed. Labor had lost much influence on the party even though labor remained the party's major source of money and support.

What transformed labor's political influence? Why did it happen? Typically, scholars have thought of labor's political fortunes as part of a larger conflict with business over shares of the economic pie, in short, as class theory. Some form of that theory has been used for so long and with so many subtle shades of ideology that its effectiveness in explaining the transformation in labor politics is now dubious. This book approaches the question with a theoretical framework that emphasizes the central impact of external societal changes, economic and organizational changes that have made labor's static political apparatus increasingly ineffective. In this chapter, I note some major shortcomings of class theories of labor politics. Then I discuss the class theory that was most promising three decades ago when Greenstone (1969) first formulated it. After evaluating its current applicability, I propose an alternative, segmentation theory, which may better explain changes in labor politics, especially since the 1960s.

CLASS THEORIES

Most explanations of labor politics in Europe and the United States have used some form of class theory, in which classes are conceptualized as groups with different economic interests and relationships. Politics is considered a form of class conflict to control governmental influence on distributional issues. Because inequalities persist, class theories at first seemed adequate for scholars and reformers to explain why some groups fail to get their fair share of economic and political resources. But the theories have confronted problems when applied to different societies and situations. Scholars of various ideological and methodological proclivities have modified the theories to suit their purposes. Other scholars have modified the modifications, with the result that the plethora of class theories have had little in common (Parkin 1979). It is therefore difficult to select a class theory that is the most appropriate for the analysis of labor politics. Therefore, I focus on some general features of Marxist theories.

Marxist-type class theories have a number of common features. Table 1.1

Table 1.1
Contrasting Class and Segmentation Theories

Item	Class	Segmentation
Unit of analysis	Class	Determined by research
Class–union link	Increasing	Uncoupled
Class and union growth	Increasing	No trend
Class and union homogeneity	Increasing	Decreasing
Income distribution	Disagreements	Polarization
Class–union solidarity	Increasing	Decreasing
Intergroup conflict	More class conflict	Sporadic conflict
Class–Party ties	Growing	Contingent

contrasts them with segmentation theory, which is discussed in greater detail later. Class theories posit the objective social reality of class and class relations and they are the fundamental units to be used to explain politics. Segmentation theory makes no assumption about the basic explanatory unit because it changes according to political problem, time, and place. The unit may be an occupation, an interest group, an institution, a sector, a region, or something else.

In research on union politics, class theory assumes that unions are class actors; their activities have consequences for class struggles. Unions will grow and, along with the parties they sponsor or affiliate with, attract an increasing segment of the working class. Segmentation theory uncouples union and class relations because classes are rarely unified actors. Unions are organizational actors, and they place higher priority on their own interests than on those of groups with which they have an affinity. Moreover, the growth of unions, union-linked parties, and classes is historically contingent, not inevitable.

Early class theories assumed that unions would lose their occupational distinctiveness as the growing working class became more homogeneous through the evolutionary expansion of manufacturing. Differences between union and nonunion workers would decline with class homogenization and increasing union and class solidarity. In contrast, segmentation theory claims that evolutionary trends toward an increasingly differentiated economy stimulate the formation of unions with more diverse occupational, industrial, or sectors characteristics. The increasing diversity of unions and the other groups with which they interact politically, magnifies their problems of arriving at political consensus (see Table 1.1).

Class theories do not agree on the future of working-class affluence under capitalism. It may gradually increase as the class becomes better organized or decrease as a result of capitalist exploitation. Segmentation theory forecasts a more polarized income structure, with the unionized becoming more affluent according to their strength, while unorganized unskilled workers become poorer or richer depending on market conditions.

For union–party relations, class theories project a tendency for unions and parties to merge and the gradual evolution of successful class parties. Political class conflict therefore increases. Segmentation theories project increasingly amorphous, tenuous, and contingent links between unions and parties because both become more diversified in their interests and alignments. Thus, while class theories project increasing class conflict in party relations, segmentation theories predict an increasingly fluid bargaining field.

Segmentation theorists claim that class theorists have raised many questions that they have not resolved. How many classes are there: two, three, four, twelve? How many class fractions? Are classes real or nominal categories? Can classes act politically? What parts of the working class constitute the "real" proletariat? Is organized labor a class, a class segment, or an interest group? Do class actors (e.g., labor unions) statistically represent the classes they claim to act for? Are classes in perpetual conflict, or do they accommodate? These questions do not arise in segmentation theories because class is not mandated as the unit of analysis. If these basic questions about class have not been resolved after a century and a half of research, then class is of limited use in political analysis (van den Berg, 1989, p. 165).

Class theories inadequately explain political change, especially changes in labor politics (Wilson 1979, p. x; Clark, Lipset, and Rempel 1993). Part of the difficulty arises from lack of agreement on whether organized labor *is* a class or whether it *represents* a class, a class segment, or simply itself (see Table 1.1). Especially in America, labor's occupational composition has continually changed. The unionized, always a minority of the working class (however defined), never represented its occupational makeup; union members have remained a relatively privileged sector of workers in selected industries (Form 1985, Ch. 6). By contrast, in Scandinavia, almost all employees, from laborers to skilled, white-collar, managers and professionals, belong to labor unions. Lumping these diverse and sometimes competing occupational groups into one class makes the concept almost meaningless.

Class theories of labor politics find it hard to explain why labor-oriented parties that control governments often fail to secure stable public acceptance. Even where labor is strong and incorporated into government policymaking, it has trouble maintaining public support, especially when it enacts legislation favorable to its traditional constituency (Cameron 1984, pp. 170–4). In moderating their political program to appeal to the "middle class," labor politicos often lose the loyalty and support of union members.

A satisfactory theory should be able to explain labor politics in all mature industrial capitalist nations that have democratic polities, whether labor is strong or weak politically. The class theory that comes closest to this goal is Greenstone's *Labor in American Politics* (1969). It has two great merits. First, it is empirical, based on hundreds of interviews with Detroit, Chicago, and Los Angeles labor leaders actively working to influence political parties and government. Such empirical studies are rare (Masters and Delaney 1987b). Most literature on labor politics consists of commentary embedded in a class framework; authors have not talked to and observed labor activists or study their political organizations. In contrast, studies based on interviews with labor leaders typically focus on industrial relations or labor–management bargaining, not external politics. Greenstone's (1969) second strength is his comparison of the utility of class and pluralist (interest-group-bargaining) theory. He also used organization theory to help overcome some of the simplicities of class theory.

Greenstone conducted his field research in the early 1960s when union members were primarily white male manual workers earning middle-range incomes. Like others, he assumed that labor's political interests flowed from its class position. His examination of labor politics in three large metropolitan centers and in Congress convinced him that labor's interests had broadened from representing certain occupational groups to representing the interests of all consumers as a class. However, Greenstone did not, perhaps could not, anticipate that structural changes in the economy would alter labor's "class" composition, and that changes in the political parties would alter labor's relations to them and other interest groups, including the consumer "class." Segmentation theory, which I develop below as an alternative to Greenstone, retains a stratification perspective because the organization of inequality does not coincide with class organization. Segmentation theory takes into account structural changes in the economy and society that have altered the patterns of stratification. The stratification perspective is also retained because my personal beliefs pervade this work. I believe that labor is or ought to be concerned about the well-being of workers who are less fortunate. To be strong, labor must focus equally on the welfare of union and nonunion workers alike. For this reason, it must engage in politics and achieve a modicum of political discipline.

SEGMENTATION THEORY

Segmentation theory deals with the problems of coordinating huge entities like institutions, sectors, strata, or society. It holds that individual groups generally place their interests above those of the groups with which they interact, creating problems of intergroup coordination. The theory could also be called *coordination theory* on the grounds that interdependent complex institutions (like labor and political parties) require considerable coordination to integrate for common action. The problems of segmentation or coordination vary in time and place, but segmentation problems expand as societies expand and become more complex (Hawley 1978, p. 791).

Segmentation theory synthesizes and modifies two theories that have long histories: economic segmentation theory, an expanded version of dual economy theory, and organizational segmentation theory, an application of parts of Durkheim's and Michels's theories of organizational growth and change. Segmentation theory attempts to explain how economic *and* organizational segmentation processes interact and magnify the problems of arriving at consensual politics.

Segmentation theory deals especially well with problems dealing with labor politics. It holds that (1) national and international economic changes have greatly diversified labor's occupational composition, political interests, and behavior; (2) changes in community and political organizations have effectively weakened and divided labor's political organizations, and (3) these changes have made labor less capable than its competitors of revising its political mobilization techniques to overcome its divisions.

All labor movements in industrialized democracies have internal divisions, but the American movement has been most divided and decentralized (Zolberg 1986). Ideally, segmentation theory should account for labor's political divisions both where organized labor is a minority of the labor force, as in the United States, Great Britain, and France, and in countries where it represents almost all employees, as in Scandinavia. The theory should also explain variations in labor solidarity and divisions over time.

Operationalizing segmentation–coordination processes is difficult. The forces that increase diversity, heterogeneity, and specialization among interdependent organizations may under some conditions either increase or decrease the costs of coordinating collective action (Olson 1965). It is difficult to determine when rising diversity in an institution such as labor raises the cost of collective action beyond the possible benefits of independent action (see Chapter 12).

No theorist, to my knowledge, has formally combined economic and organizational segmentation theories to explain current labor politics. However, in the Preface to the second edition of *The Division of Labor in Society*, Durkheim (1893) sketched a general theory that combined the evolution of economic *and* social organization in industrializing societies to explain how increasing *economic* specialization and *organizational* division of labor at first undermine societal ethics, consensus, and cooperation. Under these conditions, interdependent groups must invent organizational forms (ideally, occupational corporations) to deal with the social, economic, and political problems of their members, and to work with other corporate bodies to attack common problems. Durkheim thought that to remain effective, these organizations should remain outside government.

In pondering the costs of societal segmentation, Durkheim predicted that harmonious arrangements rather than class conflict would solve the problems raised by rapid economic and social change. His predictions about the dominant role of occupational corporations (such as labor unions) in members' lives have not been fully realized, but his insights into the linkage of economic change and occupational politics remain useful. Few social scientists have systematically built on Durkheim's theory of occupational politics, but since the 1960s, they have begun to explore the political consequences of economic segmentation.

To identify sources of current segmentation in labor politics, I chose a few illustrative studies from an enormous literature. I refer first to those that show how changes in the economy diversified labor's occupational and industrial composition and then its politics. Second, I select a few studies that illustrate how changes in labor's internal organizations and labor's organizational environment (management initiatives, party relations, and urban ecology) fragmented its political operations and consensus. Third, insights from both sources are used to sketch the evolution of labor politics in the West and in the United States, which is the primary concern of this work.

ECONOMIC SEGMENTATION

Galbraith (1967) and Averitt (1968) early observed that the economic structure of advanced capitalism had become segmented into corporate and entrepreneurial sectors, or center and periphery. The corporate center or sector contains a few large, stable, oligopolistic, capital-intensive firms that are unionized and engage in long-term planning, train their employees, and organize their markets. The periphery sector contains many small, nonunionized, labor-intensive, competitive firms that do not engage in planning and employee training and are subject to the vicissitudes of the free market. Averitt noted that core firms produce goods for government but did not examine how this might affect their own and their unions' politics (Wallace and Kalleberg 1981, pp. 81–92).

Doeringer and Piore (1971) and Gordon (1972) held that labor markets are segmented into primary and secondary types. In primary markets, workers are educated and skilled, paid higher wages, have careers in internal labor markets, and tend to be unionized. Secondary markets contain less-educated and lower-skilled workers, pay lower wages, experience high labor turnover, and are less unionized. Participants in primary markets work in core firms that produce goods for government and are more involved in politics. Workers in periphery and secondary markets are more apathetic politically. Many sociologists, noting that both sector and market dichotomies oversimplify reality, have elaborated more sophisticated theories of sector and market stratification (see Berg 1981). However, despite the plethora of studies based on the improved theories, no one has systematically elaborated how labor unions in different sectors and markets vary in their political organizations and political behavior (see articles in Berg 1981).

Gordon et al. (1982, pp. 2–4) developed a historically based theory of economic segmentation. They noted three stages in the development of the working class, labor–management structures, and labor markets. In the stage of initial proletarianization, from 1820–1890, wage labor became predominant in the manufacturing sector, and skilled workers controlled production. In the second stage, from the 1870s to World War II, the period of homogenization, mass-production manufacturing created a class of semiskilled workers, a competitive labor market, and a system of supervision where work was subjugated to machine or assembly-line pacing. In the third or segmentation stage, from the 1920s to the 1990s, internationalizing of the economy, the computer revolution, and other changes not only stratified sectors and labor markets but segmented them further by sex and race. These fissures weakened the working class and the labor movement, a condition that will endure until a new type of economy emerges and labor devises new organizational solutions to its problems. Again, the authors failed to amplify how sector and market segmentation affect the politics of labor and its individual unions.

However, a few sociologists have suggested how different economic sectors and work environments affect the political orientations of workers and their unions. Interviewing automobile workers in four countries that varied in their economic development, I found that the more developed the economy, the more the workers varied in their income, social status, and political ideology (Form 1976, Ch. 12). In the more advanced societies, workers, especially the skilled, wanted their unions to improve working conditions and to avoid politics and broad working-class issues. A later study (Form 1985, Ch. 9), noted that American manual workers were stratified economically, socially, and politically—by skill level, economic sector, income, and ascriptive characteristics. A survey of studies of the politics of union locals revealed deep cleavages between officers and rank and file over union political involvements. These studies considered workers' orientations to internal union politics, but not the politics of the unions themselves. This book, the third of a trilogy, completes my analysis of working-class politics.

Apostle, Clairmont, and Osberg (1986, p. 905), in a study of Canada's Maritime Provinces, found that government relations and the political behavior of firms and their workers differed by economic sector. Low-wage marginal firms in secondary markets were dependent on government social welfare policies (e.g., the minimum wage), and their workers had little interest in politics. Central-core-like firms had business and economic ties with government. Their unionized workers displayed considerable interest in politics even though their party identification varied more than that of other employees. Firms between these poles were least involved with government; their workers lived in a conservative political ambience. The three economic sectors did not differ in local political involvements. Again, this suggestive study did not examine the impact of economic segmentation on union politics.

Perhaps the most imaginative study of the economic sector's relation to labor politics was Sabel's (1982) research on the political dynamics of workers and unions in Germany, France, and Italy. He found most theories, including class theories, inadequate because they dismiss important variations in employees' work environments, occupational diversity, and political concerns. Sectoral dualism emerged as a political as well as an economic response to changes in which both labor unions and management participated. Occupational strata and unions in Renault and FIAT automobile factories responded differently to political and technological changes. The Emilia-Romagna in Italy was evolving a third sector based on independent subcontracting in the textile industry. Here, new political arrangements were changing relations between workers, owners, parties, municipalities, and unions.

ORGANIZATIONAL SEGMENTATION

While economic and technological changes can diversify or consolidate the work organization and politics of workers, unions, and management, organizational changes can also have parallel effects. Here I note some sources of organizational segmentation in labor movements, which are political institutions that suffer the instabilities of all democratic institutions (Lipset 1960). Thus, both the internal organization of the labor movement and its relations to its organizational environment must be examined for their effects on politics (see Form 1990b).

All historical studies of labor movements have shown that they evolved from simple to complex institutions (e.g., Bauman 1972). Mature movements comprise small and large unions (internationals) typically based on industry, which, in turn, comprise many subunits or locals. Labor movements have struggled historically over the extent to which they should be coordinated hierarchically or should be permitted to remain relatively autonomous (Windmuller 1974). Whatever the solution, cooperation has typically been impeded by barriers between members and officers (Michels 1911), between the unions in communities (Greenstone 1969, Ch. 3), between factions within unions (Lipset, Trow, and Coleman 1956), between locals and their national organizations (Marcus 1966), between national union federations, between ideologies of federations (Mills 1948), and between federations and political parties (Tilly 1984). Thus, organizational segmentation of labor is based on autonomy, hierarchy, locality, technology, factionalism, ideology, and external politics. Barriers to political consensus within and among unions also arise from the social heterogeneity of their members based on skill, wealth, gender, education, ethnicity, race, and religion (Form 1985). The more these features coincide (e.g., gender compounded by race), the greater the potential political segmentation.

Like all organizations, unions must interact with organizations in their external environment (e.g., industries, businesses, other unions, parties; Hodson and Sullivan 1990, Part 3), and organizations that monitor them (government agencies such as the NLRB; Goldfield 1987, Ch. 9). Changes in labor's external relations come about by changes in technology, industrial relations, relations to other unions, government agencies, political parties, and other groups. The more turbulent this organizational environment, the more labor as a whole experiences difficulties in arriving at consensual politics (Aldrich and Marsden 1988; Emery and Trist 1965).

THE EVOLUTION OF SEGMENTED LABOR POLITICS

Segmentation theory does not explain the rise of organized labor and its political programs (see Marks 1989 for a current treatment of that problem), but it does address the organizational problems that emerge as labor movements grow. In fact, segmentation theory has been applied to other organizations and institutions in industrializing countries. The problem of order, how a complex society coordinates large and changing interdependent organizations, has a long history in sociological theory. Kerr et al. (1960), Form (1979), and others have considered the problem in the evolution of the labor movement as a whole. The following sketch focuses more narrowly on evolving political problems of labor. It is not a social history of the labor movement, but an effort to apply the insights of three theories of segmentation: Durkheim's (1893) theory of the effects of increasing organizational density in society, Michels's (1911) theory of organizational oligarchy, and Piven and Cloward's (1977) theory of social movement institutionalization. Combined, the theories help explain why, in industrializing societies of the West, labor confronted changing patterns of intra- and interunion divisions as it interacted with political parties and other groups to advance its political agenda.

When labor unions were first organized in the West, they were led by workers who sought to control the use of their labor in order to wrest higher wages and better working conditions from employers. These goals were advanced more rapidly when governments were forced to recognize labor unions as legitimate participants in the economy and polity. Unions sought governmental protection (or freedom from it when the government restricted unions as in the United States) for the right to organize, strike, and engage in politics. In short, economic gains and security were enhanced when employer bargaining was supplemented with political action to obtain governmental protection and welfare benefits. To the extent that unions were successful, they overcame internal divisions and built integrating institutions.

Nations varied in the extent to which unions successfully combined economic bargaining and political action (Sturmthal 1973; Marks 1989). Obviously, more gains were realized as more workers were unionized and as more voters came to support working-class parties or goals. The more success labor achieved on both fronts, the more it confronted two persistent organizational problems: establishing and maintaining internal discipline, and gaining reliable support from sympathetic groups and voters. Success in both arenas inevitably produced a more socially heterogeneous union membership and more heterogeneous political alliances.

Maintaining discipline in both the economic and the political market became persistent concerns. Social differences among union members (occupation, industry, earnings, religion, region, and ethnicity) were so important in Europe that separate and competing unions and federations were organized. As Windmuller (1974) summarized matters, Sweden developed three major labor associations based on occupation. France, Italy, Germany, Belgium, and Switzerland developed one major federation and two or three smaller ones, based mostly on religion and political ideology. The United States at various times had one or more federations based on occupation, industry, or sector, as did Great Britain.

Parallel processes occurred in the political arena. Early labor-oriented parties were small, whether sponsored by unions or by parties, and they focussed on class objectives. Most of those parties died. In the more successful ones, the more they grew, the more heterogeneous their constituencies became, and the more party leaders worked to maintain a working-class focus (see Bauman 1972, Chs. 4, 5). Inevitable compromises with diverse interest groups diluted, delayed, or modified the original class programs.

When labor-oriented parties first appeared, occupational structures were relatively simple. Most urban workers had few skills, and the skilled minority tended to take over positions of leadership (Marks 1989, p. 49). Even though unionized workers in the manufacturing sector never became a majority of the labor force anywhere, early labor-oriented parties attracted relatively homogeneous working-class voters who were attracted to labor's social welfare agenda.

Technological changes, beginning with the industrial revolution, drastically transformed the occupational, industrial, and social composition of the labor force. Three major technological shifts (mechanical, chemical, and electrical) in the nineteenth and early twentieth centuries significantly changed labor force occupational composition (Knapp 1976, Ch. 10). Thereafter, the majority of employees in advanced industrial societies were employed in white-collar and service industries. The original manual working-class sector declined, while higher-status occupations expanded. White-collar, technical, managerial, and professional occupations grew, diversifying the social class mix of the labor force. As Durkheim (1893) pointed out more than a century ago, problems of social solidarity, cohesion, and morale grow with specialization and diversity, that is, with increasing segmentation.

Labor unions confronted a dilemma. When they expanded into new occupations and industries, membership became more socially diversified, increasing the problem of internal integration. Union failure to expand in growing economic sectors threatened the unions' political influence. Thus, after the 1960s, the unionized sector of the American labor force declined at the same time that its membership became more diversified and better represented the labor force's occupational, industrial, racial, and gender composition. Similar trends in some European countries magnified labor's problems of sustaining political consensus when it was most needed to stem growing political threats (Touraine 1986, p. 173).

Rarely noted, these changes paralleled segmentation tendencies inside labor's formal organizations, exacerbating them. Michels's (1911) iron law of oligarchy dealt primarily with cleavages in mature labor movements: Labor officials tended to remain in office and develop interests and goals different from those of the membership. Officers became more involved with political parties, more conservative, and more removed from the economic and shop floor problems of union members. At the same time, like other growing institutions, labor's organizational structure grew and became more specialized to deal with its widening external contacts with parties, newspapers, educational institutions, and social welfare and government bureaus (see Marks 1989, Ch. 3).

These interorganizational networks developed a life of their own. As

Durkheim observed, organizational interdependence grows with organizational density, impeding the ability of individual organizations to change the system. The process of linking the labor movement to other social institutions, especially *incorporation* into government entities (Regini 1992), tended to constrain and sometimes modify labor's original working-class objectives. Yet, as part of the state's administrative apparatus (as in Scandinavia, Belgium, and Germany, unlike in the United States), labor was able to defend workers from the worst effects of economic and political change (Cameron 1984, pp. 164–5). Goldthorpe (1984) perceptively noted that the very process of incorporation encouraged economic dualism and its stratifying impact on the working class.

Unable to secure such a legal niche, American labor nonetheless penetrated the local community associational network to some degree, including municipal commissions, welfare, and voluntary organizations. However, it remained more exposed to attacks by business groups and unsympathetic parties when they attained power. Whether formally incorporated into government or informally incorporated into the community's associational network, many critics defined labor leaders as a privileged elite and part of the system. In the United States, this declining confidence in labor leaders grew with rising inflation in the late 1960s and the 1970s. As elsewhere, the American public became increasingly critical of the self-interest apparent in the informal social contract between big business, big labor, and big government (Lipset and Schneider 1983, Part II). Parallel redefinitions of labor's power also occurred in Europe.

Social movement theory also points to sources of potential segmentation that parallel those observed by Michels. In its early phases, the labor movement displayed the militant features of protest movements. Over time, the very success of movements encourages their institutionalization. Full-time administrators devise organizational solutions to recurrent problems. Rank-and-file members cede decision making to officers, cease attending meetings, and become detached from the organization. Officers devise ways to stay in office, defend their organizational practices, and stifle protests (Piven and Cloward 1977, pp. 155–61). Members begin to define these activities as "politics," as an inevitable consequence of holding office. In labor, when officers tried to mobilize members for political action during the 1970s, they encountered apathy or resistance. In Great Britain, for example, the majority of manual workers opposed union links to the Labour Party just before its rise to power in 1974 (Weakliem 1993). By 1979, labor's social contract with government to control wages had collapsed, as had the Labour government itself (Regini 1984, p. 138). In 1993, the Labour Party limited the number of votes assigned to labor in the party

(*Wall Street Journal* 1993). Similarly, in the United States, despite the informal social contract between big labor, business, and government, in 1974 almost half of union members thought that unions had too much power (Lipset and Schneider 1983, p. 206).

Expectedly, to overcome disenchantment, officers felt they should educate members on the importance of politics and party loyalty. They had to become informed about labor's historic struggles to achieve wage gains, recognition, and political influence. Officers spoke of the need to revive early labor-movement fervor (see Chapter 14). But the new generation of officers themselves had had little personal experience with the close relations between the officers and the rank and file in the early movement. In sum, creating a political organization within the labor movement (as in the United States), or jointly with a party (as in Great Britain and Sweden), or as an arm of a party (as with the Communists in France and Italy) confronted labor with complex problems of union–party coordination.

The above scenario is complicated by the fact that the parties themselves did not escape fragmentation tendencies. Class parties experienced problems of sustaining a class program when they tried to attract a majority of voters, some of whom identified with other classes (Hindness 1971). Tired of internal party struggles to attain their goals, some groups decided to sever party ties and engage in independent action as an interest group or lobby, thereby weakening the party. Just as labor confronted the problems of integrating its diversifying membership, parties confronted equally difficult tasks of integrating labor and other groups in a stable coalition. Schisms deepened as two interdependent but internally fragmented institutions, labor and the party, bargained to maximize individual and common goals.

Thus, the liberal–labor–class coalition began to crumble in the American Democratic Party in the late 1960s, and a similar breakup began in Britain's Labour Party and other European parties. Some groups became less class- and labor-oriented as they pursued their special interests (e.g., racial or gender equity, preserving the environment, consumer protection, and social security). Sometimes groups accumulated sufficient resources and followers to form a separate party (e.g., the Green Party in Germany and the Social Democratic Party in Britain), to become a party faction (e.g., the Black Caucus in the U.S. Democratic Party), or to abandon the party to become an independent lobby (e.g., the National Organization for Women). In short, groups in or outside labor felt they could do better without the restraints of the liberal–labor–party coalition. Parties found it increasingly difficult to respond to the fragmentation in the rising social movement industry (McCarthy and Zald 1987, p. 21).

CONSOLIDATION AND SEGMENTATION IN AMERICAN LABOR POLITICS

The fragmentation processes described above apply to the American labor movement with some modifications. American labor has generally been more divided than labor in the the rest of the West (see especially Regini 1984, pp. 124–31). Never an integrated movement or institution, it was and remains a loose cluster of autonomous internationals (see Tannenbaum 1965, p. 711). Therefore, the research task is concerned less with explaining segmentation in labor politics than with explaining *variations* in it.

Below, I briefly describe the major stages in the development of the American labor movement in terms of forces that tended to consolidate or segment its political apparatus. I conclude, in parallel with Stinchcombe's (1965, p. 145) observation, that at each stage a set of similar unions invented a political organization that had distinctive political objectives that survive to this day. As a consequence, four sets of unions in today's labor movement encounter difficulties in integrating their political machines to pursue a common political agenda. Much of this book illustrates the difficulties in local, state, and national politics.

Prior to the Civil War, workers often tried to organize local unions and consolidate them into larger federations. Most of the unions were organized around trades (thus, trade unions), and their linkages to each other and the major parties were weak. Neither the unions, the federations, nor the party links endured for more than a few years. Product and labor markets were usually local or regional; local unions could not accumulate the resources to sustain long strikes, especially during depressions. Moreover, the unions were too small to contribute substantially to political parties organized around the stronger agricultural and commercial interests (Ware 1935, Chs. 6,7). It is hardly appropriate to refer to a labor movement in this era because unions had not developed stable ties with one another beyond the community.

Not until after the Civil War, which speeded the integration of the economy, especially in the North, did a national labor federation emerge that lasted more than a few years. The Knights of Labor, established in 1869, endured for about thirty years. It grew as an amalgamated craft–industrial-type federation with a broad political agenda. Importantly, in 1885 it won a major strike in the railroad industry, one of the few national industries. Social, economic, and political differences in the organization were many, and the highly centralized hierarchy could not bridge them because of its policy of admitting all occupational groups, including the crafts, unskilled industrial workers, the professions, and even employers.

Nor could the Knights agree on an organizing or political strategy. Internal conflicts, better-organized employer associations, competition with national craft unions in the American Federation of Labor (AFL), and economic adversities had killed the organization by the end of the century (Daugherty 1941, pp. 328–31). In short, the Knights were too segmented locally to be integrated effectively by a central organization.

In 1886, a number of strong national unions organized the AFL on the principle that strong unions could endure only with members who had a natural affinity for organization: the crafts. The AFL set ideological and party politics aside and concentrated on economic bargaining. It engaged in ad hoc politics, supporting or opposing individual candidates according to their behavior toward the unions. Unlike the Knights, the AFL minimized the problem of coordinating a socially heterogeneous membership by concentrating on crafts that tried to establish monopolies in local labor markets. The AFL recognized only one union in a craft or industry and granted local unions and their internationals enormous autonomy. The "problem" of coordinating the movement was contained by limiting locals' occupational and social heterogeneity. Political factionalism among unions was contained by letting them work out ad hoc political arrangements (voluntarism) that suited their special interests, not those of the working class. Many relatively well-paid craft unions could accumulate sufficient resources to weather long strikes and economic depressions.

Although AFL membership fluctuated with economic prosperity, it grew during World War I and the postwar years. By 1920, it represented about 16 percent of the nonfarm labor force, about the same as today. The subsequent depressions reduced membership to about 9 percent in 1930, just before the New Deal (Reynolds 1974, p. 368). Thereafter, as described below, the labor movement grew and changed enormously. However, the political formula that the AFL had forged had became so ingrained in many unions that they largely retained it, with the consequence that a fault line survives to this day in the labor movement.

Labor movement growth after 1932 was made possible by a change in the nation's political environment. The U.S. Constitution had created a federal system with separation of powers, the most decentralized polity of any Western nation (Lowi 1943). Business, government, and labor remained largely separate realms, and they seemed incapable of cooperating to break out of the Great Depression of the 1930s. After the Democrats took control of the federal government in 1933, Franklin Roosevelt launched the New Deal, a series of legislative remedies designed to overcome the reluctance of business, labor, and government to cooperate in the economic crisis. Among the remedies was legislation to restrain the historical business–government alliance that impeded union organizing. In the new political environment, the depressed AFL labor movement began to grow. Thus, *external* changes in labor's political *environment* permitted it to prosper despite its divided and decentralized structure (Form 1990b).

The expansion of the labor movement had to occur in the manufacturing sector, whose employees were largely unskilled and semiskilled manual workers. Despite opposition from many craft unions, in 1935 a Committee on Industrial Organization within the AFL undertook the task of organizing these workers with the resources contributed by small amalgamated unions and the United Mine Workers (Daugherty 1941, p. 343). Within two years, 32 unions with 3 million members joined the CIO. After suspending the unions for violating its commandment of not organizing more than one union in an industry, the AFL began an organizing drive of its own (Daugherty 1941, pp. 343–47). Bitter jurisdictional fights and fruitless negotiations ensued. In 1938, the expelled unions created their own federation, the Congress of Industrial Organizations (CIO). Although both the AFL and the CIO grew during World War II as labor and management agreed not to strike, they remained deeply divided in organizing and politics after the war (Mills 1948).

The political conflicts had their origin in the AFL's Nonpartisan League, launched in 1936 to keep the Roosevelt and prolabor Democrats in office. Policy controversies in the league convinced many AFL leaders that it was dominated by the CIO, so the AFL withdrew from the league in 1938 (David 1951, p. 105). More active in supporting Roosevelt and the Democratic Party than the AFL, more ideologically liberal, and more determined to influence national social welfare policies, the CIO launched its Political Action Committee (PAC) in 1943. Originally a way of coordinating political fund raising, the PAC soon took on the character of a party within the Democratic Party, a vote-getting machine with its own agenda for the party (Calkins 1952, p. 10). The AFL created a similar but more cautious organization, the Labor League for Political Education (LLPE). When the two federations amalgamated in 1955, they melded their political units into the Committee on Political Education (COPE). COPE's effectiveness, as described below, depended on the cooperation of its member unions. But the ex-AFL and ex-CIO unions retained their political orientations and styles, marking a fault line in COPE that persists to this day.

Even so, the two prosperous decades after World War II (1945–65) represented the summit of labor unity inside and outside the party. Thereafter, turbulent changes in the economy reduced union representation in the labor force, increased labor's internal diversity, and reduced its influence in the Democratic Party. After 1968, the Vietnam war, the civil rights movement, the women's movement, and other events increased party factionalism, fragmenting the earlier liberal–labor–party coalition and reducing labor's dominant position in it. In short, changes in labor's *external political environment* largely accounted for its explosive growth during the New Deal, its postwar consolidation, and its policy of party involvement. Changes in labor's *external economic and political environment* a generation later reduced its numbers, exacerbated its divisions, and weakened its political influence. Acting more like an interest group than a social movement, labor politics began to drift back toward its pre–New Deal pattern.

Yet labor experienced two favorable outcomes in the 1960s that partly compensated for its membership losses after the 1970s: the rise of public sector unions and the expansion of service sector unions. Without these unions, membership today would be lower than in the AFL heyday of the 1920s. In 1962, by executive order, President Kennedy gave federal employees the right to organize. Soon after, many states passed laws permitting government employees, including teachers, to organize. The explosive growth of government and teachers' unions created two of the currently largest labor unions; the National Education Association (NEA) and the consolidated American Federation of State, County, and Municipal Employees (AFSCME). Other public sector unions also grew (e.g., the Fraternal Order of Police, the Fire Fighters, and independent unions in various government bureaus).

These public sector unions increased organized labor's economic, social, and political diversity. As explained later, they differed in many ways from the ex-AFL and ex-CIO unions. Public sector unions operated in a stable, growing, and protected labor market. Their members included a wider range of occupations, from professionals to unskilled laborers. Although not formally incorporated into the state, their political focus was on government, a fact that legislators could not ignore. Their economic resources were larger and more secure than those of most unions, large enough to forge political organizations that could cooperate with COPE or ignore it with impunity. Those inside COPE (e.g., AFSCME), not aligning on either side of the AFL or CIO divide, developed distinctive organizational styles. Unions outside COPE (the NEA, the police, and the fire fighters) operated effectively without it. In short, public sector unions differed enough from the ex-AFL and ex-CIO unions to constitute a third division within the labor movement.

Finally, as manufacturing jobs contracted rapidly after 1970, clerical and service occupations grew. Many new workers entered the labor force to satisfy the rising demand for retail clerks, hospital attendants in the expanding health industry, janitors in the large urban office complexes, clerical workers in the insurance industry, employees in the hotel industry, and so on. Many of these new jobs paid little more than the minimum wage and were part time. But when organized and combined with the existing unions, they offered workers more security, health insurance, and other benefits than the nonorganized sector. Women, blacks, and immigrants filled many of these positions. Two strong unions became among the largest in the AFL-CIO: the United Food and Commercial Workers (UFCW) and the Service Employees Industrial Union (SEIU), their growth an heroic achievement in an era of union decline.

As we shall see, UFCW and SEIU developed a quite different political apparatus and style. The occupational mix in their industries was larger than that in the craft, the industrial, and perhaps even the public sector unions. They included many poorly educated women from racial and ethnic minorities working in small and often widely scattered locations. The difficulties that officers encountered in educating the membership for political action exceeded those in other unions. This situation produced a politically active officer corps that was inclined to embrace liberal politics somewhat similar to that of the ex-CIO unions but without political support from local officers or rank and file—a true Michelsian solution. The political style developed in response to this situation constitutes the fourth divide in the labor movement.

To conclude, four union groups evolved at different times in different economic sectors, becoming politically segmented and developing political styles that were hard to meld into a single coherent political organization. Given the movement's decentralized history, a high degree of uncoordinated, competitive, and even conflictual politics may be expected to continue. The problems that labor faces in aggregating inside and outside interests are problems that segmentation theory can inform. The research challenge requires the investigator to specify the structural sources of segmentation, identify the cleavages that policymakers must bridge, and specify the organizational inventions needed to forge a working consensus. This is a formidable and challenging task.

OVERVIEW

This book is divided into three parts. Part I examines a class theory of labor politics, changes in labor's class composition, and changes in labor's political and organizational environment from 1960 to 1990. Part II examines labor's political organization and activities in detail in selected cities and at the state level. Part III considers labor politics at the national level: its changing relations to the Democratic Party, its record in Congress, and the possibility of the labor movement's renewing itself. Finally, I evaluate the adequacy of segmentation theory. A brief overview of each chapter follows.

Chapter 2 reviews Greenstone's (1969) class theory of American politics, raising questions about its current adequacy. Greenstone asserted that labor politics had shifted from protecting employees at work to advancing their interests as a consumer class. Then he portrayed three patterns of labor's relations to the Democratic Party: dominating it in Detroit, accommodating to the party machine in Chicago, and remaining disorganized in the disorganized Los Angeles environment. Finally, he examined labor's involvement in Congress to advance the interests of labor as a part of the consumer class. Evaluating Greenstone's analysis, I suggest that it may not hold today because the basic political ingredients have changed, namely, the class composition of organized labor, party organization, and the liberal–labor coalition.

Chapter 3 examines labor's changing place in the nation's stratification system from the pre–New Deal era to the present. It compares organized labor and the national labor force in occupation, industry, race, gender, and earnings. As membership declined, labor became more heterogeneous and more representative of the labor force. This resulted in new political problems for labor, new political cleavages, and different relations to the political parties and interest groups.

Chapter 4 discusses societal change in party organization and residential patterns that altered the organizational environment of labor's political machine. The erosion of the Democratic Party's political machines confronted labor's political machine, COPE, with new problems. Increased use of television, increased control of the political campaign by professional managers, and the rise of machines controlled by individual candidates called for operational change in COPE, as did the suburbanization of union members and the growth of African-American political machines. In short, change in parties, electioneering, demographic and city residential patterns, and new social movements created a new organizational environment to which COPE had to respond. Without innovative solutions, rising divisions between labor, the parties, and other interest groups were bound to grow.

Chapter 5 focuses on the importance of local community politics in state and national politics. I found that, contrary to prevalent theory, local politics is alive and well in metropolitan America; labor's deep involvement is necessary to its political success. The political unreliability of union members in local and national elections turns out to be labor's main political weakness. Unlike business, labor has neglected local politics between state and national elections, a central deficiency of COPE.

Part II examines local labor politics in detail. Chapter 6 presents a historical profile of business, labor, and politics in three Ohio cities, each with a different economic, labor, and political tradition. Political and economic changes in Cleveland, Columbus, and Cincinnati were found to have different effects on labor's response to political parties in local, state, and national elections. I report on the labor–party relations as perceived by Democratic and Republican Party leaders, leaders of COPE, officials of unions outside COPE (Teamsters, Auto Workers, National Education Association, police), and officers of the largest unions in COPE. I also examine how officials of locals of the same union perceived local politics and labor's place in it. In each city, labor developed a different political pattern.

Data in Chapter 7 reveal that the Democrats' success in Cleveland did not rest on labor–party unity. Despite the fissures between them, success was based on the historical political loyalties of major segments of the population.

Chapter 8 analyzes labor's attempt to improve labor–party cooperation in Cincinnati and describes the difficulties of overcoming the traditional political loyalties of the rank and file.

Chapter 9 describes how labor and the Democratic Party in Columbus accommodated to the historical domination of the Republican Party in local, state, and national politics.

Chapter 10 compares the three cities for the ways that labor and the party tried to aggregate their constituencies. Little evidence was found to support the survival of the 1960s pattern of Democratic machine politics in Chicago or a labor-dominated Democratic Party in Detroit. The internationals' inability to persuade the locals to support their political objectives was traced to the different ways that locals accommodated to the dominant local political culture. Thus, an important ideological cleavage within labor emanates from its response to local political cultures.

Chapter 11 analyzes COPE's organizational effectiveness from the rank-and-file perspective during the 1988 gubernatorial race in Ohio. The political behavior and attitudes of union and nonunion respondents are compared for each city, as reported in a opinion survey. A comparison of the officers' reports of their political efforts with members' evaluation of them exposed the political cleavages within labor and between labor and the community.

Part III analyzes labor's relations to the national Democratic Party and the Congress. Labor's decision to back the Democratic Party in the 1930s was based on New Deal legislation that protected it and on the promise of future party support. Labor soon found that it had to bargain with party leaders to preserve its influence and past gains.

Chapter 12 examines labor–party bargaining from 1933 to 1992 in the selection of presidential candidates and development of party platforms. The application of segmentation theory proved useful in charting labor's varying influence, exposing cleavages within labor in its dealing with the party, disagreements among party elites, and labor's changing relation to interest groups in the party. A theory of sunk investments helped explain labor's persisting party loyalty, despite rebuffs.

Chapter 13 describes the relations between the national, state, and local COPEs, between the national COPE and unions outside it, and how labor's Washington lobbyists try to link their work to COPE's electoral efforts. Segmentation theory again proved useful for examining the changing liberal–labor coalition in Washington. I compare the extent to which COPE, the Americans for Democratic Action, and the Consumer Federation of America agreed in their ratings of the performance of individual Congress members over a twenty-year period. Then I examine the bills that COPE selected from 1947 to 1992 to evaluate the performance of members of Congress. The content of the bills is compared for issues dealing with unions, class, consumer, general-welfare, and foreign affairs. The issue mix grew over time in a context of increasing concern about trade union matters, supporting the evolutionary theory of organizational segmentation.

Chapter 14 describes how successful social movements institutionalize, how they change objectives, and how they lose vigor. Can labor recapture its earlier social movement dynamics? The evidence suggests that militant unions have not consolidated their protests into a sustained social movement and that organizational reforms in COPE have met with limited success. To become more powerful politically, labor must recruit new members, increase productivity, and reorganize COPE to take into account post-1960s changes in its organizational environment.

2

Can a Class Theory of Labor Politics Be Saved?

J. David Greenstone's *Labor in American Politics* (1969) provides the most sophisticated class theory of labor politics available today. This chapter describes his theory, his method of testing it, and the theory's main strengths and weaknesses. In subsequent chapters, I examine the validity of some of his main hypotheses in contemporary local, state, and national politics. Then I compare the fruitfulness of his class and my segmentation approach to labor politics.

Greenstone completed most of his fieldwork by 1962 and supplemented it in 1965. The data apply to a period when labor was much stronger than today and its mix of internationals was quite different. When the book was reprinted in 1977, Greenstone wrote a new introduction that reviewed labor politics in the eleven years after his original fieldwork in 1965. During that time, labor and the party had split over the Vietnam war, the civil rights movement, and other issues. Yet Greenstone concluded that no fundamental changes had occurred in labor's political style, its relations to the Democratic Party, and its place in the stratification system.[1]

More than three decades have passed since Greenstone did his fieldwork. Since then many changes have taken place in American society and in American labor that may bear on the current validity of Greenstone's

[1]Graham K. Wilson, a British social scientist, also examined U.S. labor politics in *Unions in American National Politics* (1979). Because he thought that class analysis was not useful in the study of labor, he ignored Greenstone's stratification concerns. He completed his fieldwork in 1977 at about the time of Greenstone's second edition; the two books may be usefully compared for their conclusions. Both seem to have ignored the impending decline in labor's membership and in its influence in the Democratic Party.

conclusions. In this chapter, I present his major conclusions and evaluate their initial plausibility.

LABOR IN THE STRATIFICATION SYSTEM

As a political scientist writing in the 1960s, Greenstone was interested in two issues that were being widely discussed: (1) the adequacy of pluralist theory as opposed to a class theory of labor politics and (2) the "aggregation process," or the ability of parties to accumulate and coordinate the interests of various groups.[2] He concluded that pluralist theory could not account for labor's attachment to the Democratic Party because the alliance between the two after the New Deal foreclosed bargaining between them. In Chapter 12, I challenge this thesis and examine their bargaining over 60 years, from 1932 to 1992.

Although Greenstone concluded that a stratification approach was superior to pluralism in explaining labor politics, he also considered Marx's class theory inadequate in two areas. It did not explain labor's pluralistic politics before or during the New Deal, when labor behaved primarily as an interest group. And contrary to Marxist theory, the New Deal and the Democratic Party mobilized the heterogeneous and apathetic mass of industrial workers and made them a political force in the party. This process was opposite to Marx's assumption that the working class actively mobilizes itself to support labor or socialist parties.

Greenstone concluded, however, that in the post-1928 era the relations between American labor and the Democratic Party developed in parallel to the labor–party relations that had appeared earlier in Europe. Although a viable labor or social democratic party did not emerge in the United States, industrial growth had disorganized workers' lives. Outraged by the lack of governmental concern for the welfare of workers, labor unions joined liberals to demand social welfare legislation along the lines promoted by social democratic parties in Europe (pp. 77–9). By the 1960s, labor's role in the Democratic Party represented "a partial equivalence" to the social democratic-party–trade-union alliances in Western Europe. That is, American labor's electoral and lobbying efforts, its factional influence in the party, and its welfare-state policy goals were similar to those of labor in Europe. In addition, American labor had organized and coordinated the social welfare demands of unorganized lower-status groups, an activity typically attributed to political parties (pp. 361–2).

[2]Greenstone's writing often contains unspecified and ambiguous strings of concepts (e.g., "pattern of welfare-state flow channels") that make clear summary difficult.

Unlike many European labor leaders, middle-class liberals and even the most class-conscious union members in the Democratic Party did not reject capitalism. Moreover, the political realignments of the New Deal era gradually moderated the demands of competing groups in the Democratic Party, including labor. Thus, many AFL unions retained their pluralistic approach to politics, and rural and southern Democrats remained politically conservative. In this atmosphere, labor's loyal support of the party caused it to soften its 1930s working-class demands. By the mid-1960s, a new pattern of "postproletarian" class relations had emerged (p. 80).

LOCAL LABOR–PARTY RELATIONS

Greenstone described how these shifts in labor–party relations evolved in three very different cities: Detroit, Chicago, and Los Angeles (see Chapters 3–5). Labor's welfare-state demands, especially after the merger of the AFL and the CIO in 1955, had to be accommodated differently in each city. Labor confronted different problems in each city: in Detroit, it had to confront the problem of how to play its dominant political role; in Chicago, it confronted the problem of how to respond to the dominant patronage machine of the Democratic Party; in Los Angeles, it confronted the problem of how to respond to the pervasive disorganized political scene.

When the United Auto Workers (UAW) entered politics in the 1940s, they revived a feeble non-issue-oriented Democratic Party in Detroit and in Michigan. Once labor decided to become politically active, the dominance of the automobile industry in Detroit permitted the CIO to dominate the Democratic Party there. Eldersveld's (1964, p. 113) classic study of party behavior in Detroit showed that, in 1956, 73 percent of the Democratic precinct leaders in Wayne county were union members. The UAW also dominated the AFL-CIO's political machine, COPE. It relied heavily on its own congressional district organization, and not on union personnel, to recruit election workers. Thus, COPE's strong grass-roots electoral organization in working-class neighborhoods was relatively independent of the Democratic Party.

COPE's electoral efforts increased Democratic Party voting turnout by 15 percent. UAW leaders were so effective in promoting their social welfare goals in the party that sympathetic Democratic governors and legislators were elected from 1940 to 1956. In no other metropolitan area or state did labor so dominate the party as in Detroit and Michigan. Yet, even under these most favorable conditions, labor's influence on the party and in politics declined in both city and state. Labor never dominated the party in Detroit as much as the Democratic machine dominated Chicago politics. Even at its zenith, labor lost all mayoral elections in Detroit between 1937 and 1961. The nonpartisan ballots, good-government norms, low turnout by low-income voters, charges of labor domination of the party, and the personal popularity of some candidates limited labor's influence. Unwilling to affiliate with the merged AFL-CIO, former AFL unions endorsed candidates different from COPE's. As UAW leaders became part of the Democratic party elite, they moderated their social welfare demands and compromised with other interest groups, accommodating to the conservative party drift. Aided by their superior electoral skills, a white backlash, and divisions among the Democrats over the Vietnam war and other issues, the Republicans regained control of state government.

In Chicago, labor confronted the problem of how to deal with patronage in the party. Chicago's political structure differed from Detroit's in two important ways. First, the Democratic Party had a strong centralized political machine. It had viable ties in local ethnic neighborhoods, served as a quasi-welfare organization, accumulated large patronage resources, and developed workable relationships with AFL unions and business. Second, the Chicago Federation of Labor, dominated by the building trades, protected its narrow interests and tried to curtail independent political activities on the part of other unions. For seven years, from 1955 to 1962, it delayed the merger of the political machines of the AFL's LLPE and the CIO's PACs into COPE (p. 99).

Although no single union dominated Chicago, the UAW and the United Steel Workers (USW) were large and financially strong. First, with the CIO's PAC and later with COPE, they challenged the Democratic Party machine but never developed sufficient organizational or financial resources to control it. Party loyalists knew more about voters in the neighborhood, convinced them that COPE workers were outsiders, brokered the interests of local groups, and protected the unions with the police and in the courts. However, the unions had sufficient resources to engage in precinct work, and they wrested control from the party in two suburbs where it was weak. The UAW and the USW had to rely on their own staffs and not on the weak COPE district organization to recruit electoral workers.

Cooperation between the party and the unions was most successful in national elections, where local interests were muted. While the party reduced COPE's capacity to channel working-class demands (unspecified), it did not resist all such efforts. Over time, COPE's alliance with middle-class and good-government liberals somewhat weakened the party machine, and liberals were elected to state and national offices. In sum, COPE first fought the machine and then accepted a junior partnership in it and in the Democratic Party. Again, this process moderated the party's social welfare concerns.

In Los Angeles, weak class organization, the absence of strong civic organizations, and a general lack of social cohesion resulted in a disorganized political situation. An earlier reform movement which had installed a merit system and cross-party filing in the primaries had the effect of weakening party machines and reducing voter interest and turnout. In this environment, Republican upper-middle and upper-income groups gained control of government, established an open-shop antiunion regime, and brokered the interests of competing groups (pp. 142 ff.).

The local CIO unions in the auto and steel industries were not large enough to play a dominant party role. Historically, ex-AFL unions, like the Mechanics, the Ladies' Garment Workers, and the building trades, had been under constant attack. After the Wagner Labor Act was passed in 1935, these unions expanded rapidly and became very active politically, strongly backing the Democratic Party and joining CIO unions to press for social welfare legislation. In 1958, labor reinvigorated COPE and strongly backed the party to fight Republican threats to pass right-to-work laws. The referendum was soundly defeated, Democrats gained control of the state, and they abolished cross-filing primaries and other laws that had favored the Republicans.

Although labor generally remained loyal to the Democratic Party, labor's own political organization had become fragmented and less effective. The liberal coalition of party, labor, and other interests fell apart. Individual unions pursued their independent interests and would not commit their resources or yield their authority to COPE. Some unions became entangled in continuing controversies over party leadership and other problems. Episodically, unions would unite and provide leadership in critical contests (pp. 163–66), but rank-and-file political apathy remained a constant concern. In short, Los Angeles politics lacked the cohesion provided by a dominant union in Detroit or the discipline provided by a party machine and active industrial unions in Chicago. In Los Angeles, neither the party, COPE, or their joint organizations coalesced into an effective working relationship. Consequently, labor's social welfare demands declined. Greenstone contended that the Los Angeles pattern resembled that of the nation as a whole.

Greenstone observed that the relations between labor and the party varied with the inducements that COPE and the dominant unions offered their campaign workers. COPE's success in congressional elections in all the cities depended on their resources, attitudes, and political priorities.

Electoral success depended on the extent to which labor and the party together aggregated the interests of other groups. Examining how groups modified their ideological positions, Greenstone concluded that Michels's theory (bureaucratic growth makes parties more conservative) is oversimplified. Rather, over time, organizational growth amplifies and exaggerates the dominant ideological position (p. 137).

LABOR AND POSTPROLETARIAN CLASS POLITICS

Greenstone's explanation of labor's role in creating the welfare state and affecting the course of the Democratic Party underlies his class theory of labor politics. American labor traditionally separated its electoral and lobbying arms. In Congress, it could act boldly like any other interest group in pursuit of trade-union objectives, but as a member of the Democratic team, it could cooperate with other interest groups to strengthen the party. How labor pursued its own objectives and how it worked with other interest groups for working-class legislation defined its class politics.

To ensure a favorable Congress, labor provided resources to elect liberal legislators even where it was not strong, as in the conservative South. Neither traditional interest-group nor Marxist class theory fully explain how labor became involved in a range of legislative issues. For some equity or class issues, such as educational and tax reform, legal details were so complex that labor let the party organize the support or opposition. On exclusively trade union legislation, such as repeal of the Taft-Hartley Act, labor pressured party influentials and the administration, which successfully resisted it. On still other bills, ex-AFL unions would revert to job protectionism, playing the pluralistic political game, and leaving ex-CIO unions to pursue welfare-oriented class politics.

On some general welfare legislation, such as minimum wage, Medicare, Social Security, civil rights, and fair employment, labor collaborated with the party to aggregate the support of other groups. Where the expression of naked party interest might embarrass the party, as in reapportionment legislation, labor inconspicuously assumed the aggregating role, hoping to thwart the accusation that it dominated the party. Understandably, unions were less pluralist on class and welfare-state issues (p. 336), justifying their support for such legislation not on the basis of self-interest but because it benefited those who tended to vote Democratic. In short, labor operated neither as a class party nor as a conventional interest group, but as an organized constituent interest of the Democratic Party (p. 352). To account for labor politics in a fully industrialized (postproletarian) society, an alternative theory was needed that integrated elements of class and pluralist theories (p. 371).[3]

Marxist theory combines economic and political conflicts to explain class behavior. Considering this theory too restrictive, Greenstone turned to Ralf Dahrendorf's (1959) thesis that the basic class division of industrial society lies not between those who own property and those who do not but between those who have authority in organizations and those who do not. However, unlike Dahrendorf, Greenstone thought that economic class relations cannot play a subordinate role. The basic class division in American society is between economic authorities (owners and managers) and economic nonauthorities (wage earners and the nonemployed). Class conflict emerges between the economic authorities in their role as producers and the economic nonauthorities in their role as consumers. He concluded that unions pursue trade union objectives at the workplace and,

> with the decline of working-class unity, unions can be relevant for united class activity in politics only by pursuing their members' role interests as consumers rather than as workers.... A primarily political or economic explanation of class conflict has limited heuristic value in explaining contemporary American politics. Rather, contemporary politics may come to focus on the content of change—that is on the quality of social life. (pp. 374–5)

Substantively, *quality* refers to such issues as truth in advertising, pollution control, conservation, aid to education, fair packaging, rent subsidies, reapportionment, Medicare, aid to education, and public power.

Class conflict in industrial society remains primarily in the workplace because economic authorities (bosses) traditionally ignore the consequences of their production decisions in the lives of their workers and others. Beginning with the New Deal, government policies began to deal with such class concerns (e.g., sales opposed to income taxes). Class conflicts involved struggles over government policies that favor one class over another. Moreover, the state itself increasingly became an autonomous actor capable of tilting its influence toward coalitions organized by either of the two classes or their segments. During the New Deal, coalitions among the economic nonauthorities exercised considerable political authority. Since then, coalitions have shifted back and forth toward one class or another. Knowing labor's role in fashioning these coalitions inside and outside the party is critical for understanding American class politics.

This extended summary of Greenstone's work was necessary to evaluate its validity both for the early 1960s, when it was first outlined, and for

[3]Greenstone's scenario closely resembles what traditional pluralist theory would predict. This issue is discussed at the end of the chapter.

the present. I summarize the reception that Greenstone's work received when it first appeared and then evaluate its original contribution. Parts II and III of this book systematically test Greenstone's hypotheses on community, state, and national levels.

EVALUATING GREENSTONE'S THEORY

Greenstone's book did not receive the attention it deserved when it first appeared in 1969. Since he attacked received wisdom, the reviews were not particularly enthusiastic. Yet the book nicely balanced theoretical and empirical work on an important topic that sociology and political science were studying. Greenstone was well versed in the theory of both disciplines. He appreciated Marx and proposed to modify his theory to fit contemporary industrial society. He exploited Max Weber's theoretical insights into the autonomous role of the state in decision making and Durkheim's insights into the impact of organic solidarity on the politics of occupational and other groups. He also used Michels's organizational theory to interpret the behavior of labor unions, political parties, and legislatures. And he added a structural-ecological component—the size of political units—to these theories in order to explain organizational behavior. Most directly, he adapted Ralf Dahrendorf's modifications of Marxism to build his own theory of class conflict in a postproletarian society. Unfortunately, the major sociological journals—*American Sociological Review*, *American Journal of Sociology*, and *Social Forces*—did not review the book.

Although sociologists have studied pluralist theory (see Lipset 1960b),[4] political scientists have developed it more fully. Greenstone melded aspects of pluralist and Marxist class theory, and he applied his amalgam to the struggles within labor and the Democratic Party, as well as to the struggles between the two. Although some reviewers (Laslett 1972) thought that he did not reject pluralism firmly enough or that he belabored the inapplicability of Marxist theory to American labor (Blantz 1970), they did not evaluate Greenstone's attempt to blend the two traditions.

Greenstone engaged in substantial fieldwork, interviewing over 300 labor activists to uncover urban variations in labor's involvement in the Democratic Party. He also analyzed labor's electoral efforts at precinct, county, city, and congressional district levels, and he examined labor's lobbying activities in Congress. The study of labor politics from the local to the national level is indeed a rare and important undertaking, and I intend

[4]Surprisingly, Greenstone never referred to Lipset's works, which he closely paralleled in attempting to integrate the theories of Marx, Tocqueville, Weber, and Michels.

to follow Greenstone's lead in this book. In short, Greenstone examined a wide range of issues and made good use of the available literature. Above all, he kept the theoretical questions in focus while examining evidence. In all, Greenstone's work was a formidable achievement.

Most reviewers of Greenstone's books did not refer to empirical research to support their criticisms. Thus, Laslett (1972) claimed that Greenstone did not prove that labor had basically changed the Democratic Party, that labor's influence in the party paralleled that of labor on European social democratic parties, that his class model worked as well as Dahrendorf's, and so on. Others blamed Greenstone for what he did not do: examine workers' support for the party before and after the New Deal or their support for Eisenhower or Governor Wallace. McFarlane (1971) faulted the author for not examining labor's lobbying in local government, while Vogel (1970) regretted that Greenstone had not compared labor's party involvement with that of ethnic and other groups.

While all of these criticism may have substance, research monographs are rarely exhaustive. Yet one may reasonably ask whether Greenstone could have reached more reliable conclusions had he adopted a more systematic research design. Apparently, he kept interviewing informants until he was satisfied that he had uncovered the basic pattern. But he did not report how he sampled his labor informants and their unions. Nor did he provide data on the offices they held, their role in COPE, their political disagreements, and related matters. Greenstone sometimes compared the politics of ex-AFL and ex-CIO unions, but he neglected disagreements *within* both camps. Similar observations may be made about his analysis of the Democratic Party. In short, his informal qualitative methods did not provide nuanced answers to several questions.

Greenstone's conception of class was ambiguous and perhaps simplistic. Apparently, the class of "economic nonauthorities" included almost everyone except owners and managers: 90 percent of the labor force, the nonemployed, the retired, housewives, and others. Presumably, the class is equivalent to the consumer class that labor represented in its "postproletarian politics" (never defined). He did not examine the amount or importance of political differences within the huge consumer class or its major segments: union members, unorganized manual workers, the poor, and the nonpropertied middle class (see Form 1985, Ch. 6). He used the term *class* in two senses: the "working class," which has specific goals in work organizations, and the "economic nonauthorities class," which includes many other groups that may have different political objectives from those of the "working class." Did labor represent both classes in the Democratic Party? Did labor act for both classes in its lobbying efforts? Was there any conflict between the two? Did economic authorities have any identity or influence in the Democratic Party? Nor did Greenstone refer to the class of economic authorities in his analysis of community politics. There he focused on the welfare-state interests of labor, a more narrow conception of consumer-class politics.

Although all research efforts are necessarily limited, Greenstone's conclusions would have been enriched had he confronted intraclass conflicts, however class was defined. Greenstone did not neglect conflict as he described the difficulties that labor had experienced in trying to aggregate different interest groups. These descriptions differed little from a straightforward application of pluralist bargaining theory. While he was reluctant to give that theory full credence, he also seemed unwilling to analyze the aggregating process in class terms. Thus, by not confronting internal class conflicts in the context of aggregation theory, he could not explain how and why certain groups overcome or fail to overcome their differences.

In an important sense, segmentation theory as developed in the previous chapter and Greenstone's aggregation theory may be viewed as approaching similar problems from opposite directions. Segmentation theory starts with the tenet that intergroup and intragroup political cleavages are structural, increasingly exacerbated by social change, while aggregation theory implicity assumes that different interests can be aggregated by the resort to sophisticated strategies. Greenstone was presumably committed to a class approach to the aggregation process, but he failed to explain how competing groups in a class are brought together and whether their class cohesion is increasing or decreasing. He did point to working-class cohesion during the New Deal, its subsequent fading, and the rise of consumer-class politics as *the* form of postproletarian politics. However, he failed to develop a theory of conflict within and/or between the working class, the consumer class, the noneconomic authorities, the parties, or other classes.

Perhaps all of these concerns could be brushed aside if Greenstone's main conclusions remain valid today, especially those dealing with labor's relations with local Democratic Parties and labor's class role in national politics. Most of Greenstone's empirical work dealt with labor–party relations in the community, and only in the final chapter did he examine labor's class role in national affairs. With respect to relations in the community, we may ask whether his observations hide important struggles within labor and the party, and whether they hold after 30 years. With respect to national legislation, we may ask whether labor still focuses as much on consumer-class issues or on issues of importance to unions alone.

Greenstone did not prepare readers for his conclusions about consumer-class politics because he rarely referred to consumer issues while analyzing city and state politics. There he emphasized union, welfare-state, economic-equity, and party-control issues. Yet, in his final chapter, which deals with congressional legislation, consumer-class issues become labor's main concern. Possibly, he meant to include working-class, welfare-state, equity, union, and quality-of-life issues as consumer-class issues. Yet he took care to treat them separately.

Since consumer-class politics are key to Greenstone's analysis, three issues about it must be confronted. First, how are consumer issues identified? Importantly, Greenstone analyzed legislation that COPE selected as important (p. 392), not legislation selected by consumer lobbies. He classified COPE's issues as labor, consumer, working-class, pluralist, and mixed, but he did not specify the criteria for distinguishing them.

Second, how important are consumer issues to the rank and file? Labor lobbyists in Washington may rank consumer issue high, while members may consider other issues (race relations, taxes, or gun control) more important. Historically, the most salient issues for the rank and file have been jobs and wages. This suggests two possible sources of political cleavage in labor: (1) differences in issue salience between officers and members as posited in Michels's iron law of oligarchy and (2) differences in issue salience among unions in different economic sectors, as posited by economic segmentation theory (e.g., expansion or contraction of defense industries or government).

Third, what is the relation between labor, consumer, and other interest groups in American politics? If consumer issues are also working-class issues, then other disprivileged groups (racial minorities, poor women, Hispanics, and others) should join labor's fight for consumer legislation and vice versa. Does this, in fact, occur, or do groups generally take advantage of free rider opportunities? Do strictly union issues have relevance to consumers as a class, broadly defined? Does labor sustain a consumer-class program in the face of inconstant support from other "consumer-oriented" groups? In short, the research question is whether Greenstone's vision of labor's place in consumer-class politics is sustained in contemporary American society.

In the following chapters, I examine four major areas that bear on Greenstone's work. The first deals with the working class. While he did not examine labor's socioeconomic composition, he frequently referred to it as a working-class stratum. I examine the occupational social class composition of labor from the 1930s to the 1960s, and then compositional changes from 1960, when Greenstone did his fieldwork, to 1990. In later chapters, I examine whether these changes in class composition altered labor's politics. Second, I raise the question whether Greenstone's community typology of union–party relations applies to contemporary urban reality. The three Ohio cities I selected for study better represent variations in urban patterns than Greenstone's three cities. Third, I explore the changing roles of labor and the party in aggregating interest groups for the party from the 1930s to the 1990s. Fourth, I analyze labor's congressional activities for the extent that they pursue consumer-class goals, trade union goals, and traditional working-class goals. I begin by examining changes in the social class composition of labor.

3

Labor as a Changing Social Class

Greenstone's (1969) thesis held that labor's consumer interests increasingly took precedence over its earlier concern with its economic well-being. Labor now speaks both for its members and for all consumers as a class. This thesis raises questions about class similarities and differences between union members and consumers. Where labor unions have organized most of a nation's labor force as in Scandinavia, union officials can justifiably claim to speak for the nation's workers and consumers. But labor officials often make this claim even when union members are not representative of the nation's consumers. Thus, U.S. labor leaders routinely state that their political aims are not selfish but are designed to help the working class, the middle class, and consumers in general. Labor's opponents question this claim and insist that labor has become a smaller special interest group that speaks only for itself.

Union leaders can neither deny that union membership as a percentage of the labor force has been shrinking since the 1950s nor that the actual number of union members declined in the 1980s. Yet a shrinking labor movement can conceivably become more representative of the nation's labor force, as segmentation theory predicts (Chapter 1). In that event, paradoxically, as labor becomes more representative, it may also become more divided, reflecting the political divisions within itself and the nation. It is therefore important to assess labor's representativeness because the answer may illuminate political questions. Accordingly, this chapter examines four trends in the United States by comparing, first, change in the occupational class composition of organized labor and the labor force from 1935 to the present; second, change in the gender and racial composition of organized labor and the labor force; third, change in the earnings of union members and the labor force since 1970; and last, change since the 1930s in the relative size of the internationals, the primary actors of the labor movement.

OCCUPATIONAL CLASS SHIFTS

The occupational class composition of union members and the labor force are compared for three periods: (1) before the 1935 spurt in union membership; (2) from 1936 to 1970, the period of growth; and (3) from 1971–1990, the period of decline. The three occupational classes are defined as follows: (1) Lower-working class: unskilled and semiskilled manual and service workers; (2) upper-working class: skilled and clerical workers; and (3) middle class: technical, professional, and managerial employees. The occupational composition of the labor force in 1935 is estimated by averaging Census data for 1930 and 1940.

Before the New Deal

From its beginnings, organized labor never matched the U.S. labor force in occupational composition. The high point in labor membership before the New Deal was in 1920, when it made up almost 19 percent of the nonagricultural labor force (Filippelli 1990, p. 139). By 1935, at the beginning of the New Deal, membership had fallen to 12 percent. Unfortunately, accurate data on organized labor's occupational and other characteristics are not available for this period. My estimate is that perhaps 70 percent of union members were upper-working-class skilled or craft workers compared to only 14 percent of the labor force (see Table 3.1). Only 5 percent of union members were upper-working-class clerical workers, compared to 21 percent of the labor force. About a quarter of union members were lower-working-class unskilled and semiskilled manual and service workers, compared to almost half of the labor force. While 17 percent of the labor force were professionals and administrators, almost none were organized. Altogether, 27 percent of the labor force were white-collar employees in professional managerial and clerical occupations (U.S. Bureau of the Census 1961, p. 74). Thus, organized labor vastly overrepresented upper-working-class skilled workers, approximately represented the semiskilled, and substantially underrepresented unskilled laborers, service, and white-collar workers.

The Mature Period

Union membership increased rapidly after 1934, when the National Industrial Recovery Act gave unions some legal protection to organize.

Table 3.1
Class–Occupation Composition of Union Members and Nonfarm Labor Force for 1935, 1970, 1990 (Percent)[a]

	1935		1970		1990	
Occupational and class levels	Union	Labor force	Union	Labor force	Union	Labor force
Middle class						
Professional and technical	—	17	9	18	25	30
Upper working class						
Clerical	5	21	14	27	18	29
Skilled	70	14	25	15	18	12
Lower working class						
Low-skilled and service	25	48	52	40	39	29
Total	100	100	100	100	100	100

[a]U.S. Bureau of the Census (1961); U.S. Department of Labor (1972, 1992).

The CIO primarily but also the AFL organized many semiskilled and unskilled manual workers and a few white-collar workers. When the Great Depression had begun, first- and second-generation southern and eastern European immigrants had made up the bulk of unskilled and semiskilled manual workers in manufacturing. The first CIO members differed little from other industrial workers in ethnic and occupational status. From 1870 to 1935, the manual occupations had become more mechanized and wage differentials had narrowed, homgenizing the class of manual workers (Gordon et al., 1982, p. 100).

The situation changed drastically, especially after World War II. The unionized in heavy industry steadily gained wage advantages over and sometimes at the expense of the unorganized in other industries (Kahn 1978). European ethnic neighborhoods in many cities decayed as upwardly mobile second and third generations moved to middle-class suburbs. Growing numbers of blacks from the South and Hispanics from Mexico, Puerto Rico, and the Caribbean area, as well as Asiatic immigrants, moved into the decaying neighborhoods. Filling the demand for low-skilled labor, they became the new lower class. By the late 1960s, they made up about 20 percent of the labor force and more than a third of all manual and service workers (Roberts 1984, p. 26). Employed in the low-wage unorganized sectors, in economic downturns they suffered un- and underemployment rates double those of the organized labor force.

By the 1970s, organized labor had become more representative of the labor force in all three occupational classes; 52 percent of the unionized compared to 40 percent of the labor force were in unskilled and semi-skilled lower-working-class jobs. About 40 percent of both union members and the labor force were in upper-working-class occupations, but the unionized still included a higher proportion of skilled and a lower one of clerical employees than the labor force. Only about a tenth of union members, compared to a fifth of the labor force, were in middle-class occupations (see Table 3.1). In this era of growth, labor more closely reflected the relative size of the lower and the upper working classes. In short, by the 1970s, American manual workers had become economically and socially stratified. The unionized, first mobilized by the New Deal, experienced upward economic mobility. Urban migrants, who appeared a generation later, were impoverished.

In the 35 years between 1935 and 1970, labor had organized some workers in all major occupational strata (see Table 3.2). The occupational structure of the labor force itself had changed drastically. By 1970, white-collar workers had grown from 38 to 45 percent of the total, and manual and service workers had shrunk from 62 to 55 percent (U.S. Bureau of the Census 1975, p. D 182). White-collar workers made up 25 percent of the unionized and 62 percent of the unorganized. The semiskilled made up 34 percent of the organized, but only 13 percent of the unorganized. Craftsworkers now represented only 26 percent of the organized and 11 percent of the nonorganized; service workers, 8 and 10 percent respectively. Thus, at the end of the decade in which Greenstone completed his fieldwork, the proportion of organized manual and clerical workers combined substan-

Table 3.2
Occupational Composition of Union and Nonunion Full-Time and Part-Time Workers for 1970, 1983, and 1990 (Percent)[a]

	1970		1983		1990	
Occupational level	Union	Nonunion	Union	Nonunion	Union	Nonunion
Professional	7	20	15	12	18	13
Technical	[b]	[b]	2	4	3	4
Managers	4	15	4	11	4	13
Clerical	13	20	13	19	15	18
Sales	1	7	3	12	3	13
Crafts	26	11	20	10	18	10
Operatives	34	13	24	10	20	10
Transport	7	2	8	3	8	4
Others	27	11	16	7	12	6
Laborers—Nonfarm	7	3	7	4	7	4
Service	8	10	11	15	12	14
Total	100	99	99	97	100	99

[a]U.S. Department of Labor (1972, 1985, 1992).
[b]Not available.

tially exceeded that of the unorganized, but managerial and professional employees remained largely unorganized. Importantly, organized manual workers earned mean annual incomes that were 64 percent higher than those of the unorganized; the advantage was probably only 20 percent for clerical workers (Form 1985, Ch. 6).

The Period of Decline

From 1935 to 1945, the organized proportion of the labor force had nearly tripled, from 12 to 35 percent. Union numbers continued to grow from 1945 through the 1970s because the labor force was expanding, but the percentage of the organized declined steadily until the 1990s, when it stabilized at about 17 percent, close to the 1920 level. In 1970, manual workers (craft, operatives, and unskilled laborers), the backbone of the labor movement, made up almost 70 percent of the organized. By 1990, they had become a minority of 45 percent (see Table 3.2). Expectedly, the losses were heaviest among semiskilled factory operatives, but the skilled also fell proportionally. Oddly enough, the percentage of unorganized manual workers in the labor force grew slightly.

While the proportion of manual workers among the unionized declined 22 percent from 1970 to 1990, that of technical and professional workers increased 14 percent; the percentage of the unorganized fell slightly (see Table 3.2). Aided by the NEA's unionization of teachers, professional workers were overrepresented among the organized by 1990. Unionization also increased among service workers, making the union and nonunion representations about equal at 12 percent. Clerical workers grew equally in both groups, so the union percentage remained 13 percent shy that of the unorganized. In short, occupational changes among the unionized over 20 years made them increasingly like the nonunionized; all differences narrowed except for that of managers and sales clerks.

The occupational shifts reflected changes in industrial sectors.[1] From 1970 to 1990, manufacturing workers declined from about 26 to 19 percent of the labor force, while service workers grew from 26 to 32 percent. Employees in business and the professions rose from about 18 to 25 percent (*Statistical Abstract of the United States*, 1991). In contrast, the percentage of union members in manufacturing fell from 44 to 25 percent, and in service from 12 to 8 percent (see Table 3.3). While the labor force in construction

[1]Annually, the U.S. Bureau of the Cenusu, *Current Population Survey*, provides the Bureau of Labor Statistiscs with data on the characteristics of organized and unorganized workers. All the data reported here are dericed from this source. Unfortunately, the Bureau has changed its definitions of industrial and occupational groups over the years, making precise comparisons difficult. However, rough comparisons are useful.

Table 3.3
Industrial Composition of Full-Time and Part-Time Union and Nonunion Workers for 1970, 1983, and 1990 (Percent)[a]

	1970		1983		1990	
Industrial sector	Union	Nonunion	Union	Nonunion	Union	Nonunion
Agriculture	[b]	1	[b]	2	[b]	2
Mining	1	1	1	1	1	1
Construction	11	5	6	4	6	5
Manufacturing	44	22	30	20	25	19
Durable	29	12	18	11	16	11
Nondurable	16	10	12	9	9	8
Transportation	15	5	12	4	12	4
Trade	10	22	9	23	8	23
Wholesale	2	4	2	5	2	4
Retail	8	18	7	18	6	19
Service	12	37	8	24	8	26
Finance	[c]	[c]	1	8	1	8
Forest and fishing	[c]	[c]	1	[b]	1	[b]
Public administration	6	6	32	14	39	13
Total	99	99	100	100	101	101

[a]U.S. Department of Labor (1972, 1985, 1992).
[b]Less than 1 percent.
[c]Included in service category.

stabilized at 5 percent, it shrank from ll to 6 percent in the union sector. The nonunion percentage in transportation remained essentially unchanged at 5 percent, while in the unionized sector it sank from 15 to 12 percent.

The proportion of the ununionized in public administration remained almost constant but exploded from 6 to 39 percent in the unionized sector. Without this gain, the organized labor force in 1990 would have returned almost to its pre–New Deal level of 12 percent. Unions declined most where they had earlier had their greatest strength: the manufacturing centers of the Middle Atlantic, East North Central, and Pacific states (Troy and Sheflin 1985, pp. 7–15). Declining union representation in manufacturing, transportation, construction, trade, and service had made organized labor somewhat more representative of the nation's manual labor force.

In sum, by 1990, unionized workers resembled the entire labor force in class composition more than ever before. The greatest changes occurred in middle-class occupations, now 25 percent of the unionized and 30 percent of the labor force. This 5 percent difference also appeared in the upper working class: 36 percent of the unionized and 41 percent of the labor force. The proportion in lower working class occupations declined to 39 percent for the unionized and 29 percent for the labor force.

GENDER AND RACE CHANGES

Greenstone's 1960s data made few references to women, in part because they constituted only a small portion of the unionized. In 1970, more than four-fifths of the unionized were men compared to about three-fifths of the unorganized. By 1990, women had increased their union representation to 37 percent, but they almost equaled men among the nonunionized.

In 1970, blacks made up about 12 percent of both the unionized and the labor force. By 1990, they had increased slightly among the unionized and declined slightly among the nonunionized. Hispanics made up 6 percent of both groups in the 1980s, increasing slightly in both in the following decade. In sum, organized labor had become more representative of the major minorities but remained much less so for women.

CHANGES IN EARNINGS: 1970–1990

Many observers claim that labor's recent membership decline has eroded its bargaining strength, thus weakening its economic and political appeal to American workers. To be sure, many unions have been forced to give back part of their previous gains. Two-tier wage systems have been introduced where new workers start at a lower wage scale than previously hired workers. The number of union victories in NLRB elections declined after the 1970s, and many downward wage adjustments have been made over the life of major collective bargaining agreements (Goldfield 1987, Ch. 5; *Washington Post* 1987, p. H-1). Yet few researchers have systematically compared union and nonunion earnings over the period to asses the *relative extent* of labor's losses. It is important, therefore, to establish whether the earnings of organized labor have fallen more than those of the unorganized. If not, labor can still appeal to workers on economic if not political grounds. Fortunately, the Bureau of Labor Statistics has gathered systematic data on union and nonunion earnings since 1970. Most of the comparisons below report the median annual earnings of full-time workers for 1970, 1983, and 1990.

In 1970, union sector earnings were significantly higher than nonunion earnings in all industries, except for mining, manufacturing, and wholesale trade (see Table 3.4). The advantages were more than 14 percent in construction, nondurable goods manufacturing, trade, and the services. Then, from 1970 to 1983, the unionized improved their earnings advantages over the nonunionized in every industrial category except mining. They bettered their 1970 position 14 percentage points or more everywhere. In the following seven years, from 1983 to 1990, the unionized maintained their earnings advantage in every industry except finance.

Table 3.4
Ratio of Union to Nonunion Median Annual Earnings for Full-Time Workers by Industry[a]

Industry	1970	1983	1990	1970–1990
Mining	.94	.93	1.06	.12
Construction	1.54	1.74	1.60	.04
Manufacturing	1.01	1.16	1.14	.13
Durable	.94	1.13	1.08	.14
Nondurable	1.14	1.22	1.17	.03
Transportation	1.08	1.15	1.19	.11
Trade	1.19	1.46	1.31	.12
Wholesale	1.02	1.15	1.08	.06
Retail	1.19	1.67	1.05	−.14
Service	1.15	1.58	1.11	−.04
Public administration	1.07	1.24	1.21	.14
Finance	NA[b]	.95	.95	0
Forest and fishing	NA[b]	1.49	1.49	0

[a]U.S. Department of Labor (1972, 1985, 1992).
[b]NA = not available.

Although they lost some of their 1983 gains everywhere except in mining and transportation, their 1990 advantages remained higher than in 1970, except for retail trade and the services. Thus, union membership losses since the 1970s apparently did not seriously erode the earnings advantages of workers still covered by union contracts.

An occupational analysis reveals that, over the two decades, union members in the professions lost their advantage over the nonunionized and increased their advantage by only 3 percent among managers. The 11 percent advantage of unionized technical workers in 1983 increased slightly by 1990, while the 30 percent advantage among clerical workers in 1970 increased by 10 percent over the twenty years. Organized sales workers had slightly higher earnings than the unorganized in 1970; the 14 percent advantage of the organized in 1983 declined somewhat by 1990 (Table 3.5).

For all levels of blue-collar workers, the large and decisive union advantage in 1970 remained for the next twenty years. In general, the lower the skill level, the greater the union earnings advantage in 1970. Thus, unionized craftsworkers earned 17 percent more than the nonunionized, but clerks earned 30 percent more, operatives about 39 percent more, and unskilled laborers and service workers more than 50 percent more. In the ensuing two decades, operatives, craftsworkers, and service workers

Table 3.5
Ratio of Union to Nonunion Median Annual Earnings for Full-Time Workers by Occupational Groups[a]

Occupations	1970	1983	1990	1990–1970
Professional	1.06	.95	.99	−.07
Technical	−[b]	1.11	1.13	+.02[c]
Managers	.98	1.01	1.02	+.03
Clerical	1.30	1.40	1.39	+.09
Sales	.94	1.14	1.01	+.07
Crafts	1.17	1.39	1.39	+.22
Operatives[d]	1.39	1.61	1.55	+.16
Transportation	1.43	1.54	1.44	+.01
Others	1.30	1.55	1.50	+.20
Nonfarm laborers	1.51	1.76	1.58	+.07
Service	1.52	1.68	1.73	+.21

[a]U.S. Department of Labor (1972, 1985, 1992).
[b]Included in the professions.
[c]Base is 1983.
[d]Includes nonfarm laborers for 1983 and 1990.

increased their advantage by an additional 20 percent, while laborers increased theirs by 7 percent.

From 1970 to 1990, sex earnings differentials in the union sector were smaller than in the nonunion sector. Thus, in 1970, union women's earnings were 64 percent of men's in the union sector compared to 58 percent in the nonunion sector. In 1990, the ratios were .83 and .71, respectively. Thus, the gap closed by 19 percent in the union sector and 13 percent in the nonunion sector. Importantly, earnings in this period increased about threefold for unionized and twofold for nonunionized women. Male income rose twofold in the union sector but only 160 percent in the nonunion sector. The rate of increase for black and other women was the same among the unionized, while in the nonunion sector, the increases for African-American women were slightly higher. The situation for black males improved slightly more than for white males in both sectors.

Union and nonunion earnings also differed in range or spread. Data in Table 3.6 report the earnings advantage of each occupational level over service workers, the lowest earners. At all levels, the earnings spread is greater for *nonunion workers*; the higher the level, the larger the spread. The highest union earnings are less than 50 percent higher than the lowest, compared to the 200 percent range in the nonunion sector. The very large earnings advantages of the nonunion professional, technical, and managerial levels undoubtedly reflect the abysmally lower wages of unorganized

Table 3.6
Ratio of Median Annual Earnings of Occupational Groups to Service Workers for Fully Employed Union and Nonunion Employees, 1970, 1983, and 1990[a]

	1970		1983		1990	
Occupations	Union	Nonunion	Union	Nonunion	Union	Nonunion
Professional	1.50	2.15	1.34	2.38	1.46	2.54
Technical	—[b]	—[b]	1.28	1.94	1.31	2.01
Managerial	1.64	2.52	1.50	2.52	1.47	2.50
Clerical	1.11	1.30	1.15	1.38	1.10	1.37
Sales	1.12	1.80	1.13	1.68	.97	1.67
Craft	1.42	1.85	1.49	1.80	1.40	1.75
Operatives[b]	1.13	1.23	1.20	1.25	1.11	1.24
Transportation	1.33	1.41	1.38	1.50	1.27	1.53
Others	1.06	1.23	1.12	1.22	1.06	1.22
Laborers	1.11	1.12	1.18	1.13	1.01	1.11
Service	1.00	1.00	1.00	1.00	1.00	1.00
(Range)	.64	1.52	.50	1.52	.47	1.54

[a]U.S. Department of Labor (1972, 1985, 1992).
[b]Included in the professions.

service workers. In general, the advantages of union over nonunion earners remained stable over the twenty-year interval, except for nonunion technical and professional employees, who increased their advantages.

These data show that *nonunion employees work in environments where incomes are less equal but lower than in the union sector.* Perhaps nonunion workers feel less underpaid because most of them earn a great deal more than the lowest paid in their sector.

SHIFTS AMONG THE INTERNATIONALS

Economic, social, and legal changes from 1930 to 1990 altered the relative size of labor's internationals, which, as we will observe later, changed the policies of the labor movement as a whole. Tracing changes in the size of the internationals is hazardous because some unions merged while others changed their names when they organized workers in other industries. Although data are hard to come by, still other unions changed their sector mix in response to changes in the economy. Thus, the Electrical Brotherhoods (IBEW), which represented both manufacturing and construction workers, suffered heavy losses in the construction industry in the 1970s and 1980s, while the Communication Workers of America (CWA), which represented manufacturing and service sector workers, suffered larger losses through the automation of telephone services.

In 1930, the United Mine Workers (UMW) was by far the largest union in the AFL (see Table 3.7). Five of the fifteen largest unions were in the building trades (Carpenters, Electricians, Painters, Hod Carriers, and Brick Layers), and four were in transportation (Teamsters, Railroad Clerks, Street Railroad Employees, and Railroad Carmen). Only three of the largest fifteen were in manufacturing (Machinists, Ladies' Garment, and Typographical).

By 1960, about the time that Greenstone (1969) gathered his data, the Teamsters had replaced the Miners as the largest union. Mechanization of mining and increased consumption of oil plummeted the Miners from the largest to seventh in size. Six of the largest unions were now in manufacturing: Steel, Auto, Machine, Electrical, Ladies' Garments, and Clothing. Whereas Steel (USW) and Auto (UAW) unions did not appear in the 1930 list, they ranked second and third in 1960, followed by the Machinists (IAM). Also, two clothing unions appeared in the 1960 list. Four or five construction unions were still among the top fifteen (Carpenters, Hod Carriers, Operating Engineers, and part of the IBEW), but four unions in the services appeared among the top fifteen largest (Retail Clerks, R. R. Clerks, Meat Cutters, and Hotel Employees). The IBEW, now in sixth place, included electricians in the building trades and factory workers in electronics manufacturing.

Changes from 1960 to 1991 were equally dramatic. The decline in manufacturing reduced membership in some industrial unions, while service sector growth speeded mergers and organizing within it. Now seven of the fifteen largest unions were fully in the service sector, three fully in manufacturing, and three in construction (Carpenters, Laborers, and Operating Engineers).[2] CWA and IBEW had members in two sectors. Foreign imports of textiles and apparel undercut the industries as well as the membership of the two clothing unions and removed them from the list of the top fifteen, while steel and automobiles imports lowered the Steel Workers' (USW) position from second to eleventh place and the UAW from third to fifth. Even after a merger, the Machinists (IAM) dropped from fourth to eighth place.

Changes in state and federal laws that eased the organizing of government workers speeded unionization of that sector. The unions that merged into AFSCME were not among the top 15 in 1960, but the union's growth had made it the second largest by 1991. The Retail Clerks and the Meat

[2]The list does not include the teachers' union (NEA), which surpassed the Teamsters as the largest in the country with 2.1 million.

Table 3.7
Rank of American Labor Unions by Size: 1930, 1960, 1991[a]

1930	1960	1991
1. Miners	1. Teamsters	1. Teamsters[b]
2. Carpenters	2. Steel Workers (USW)	2. Government (AFSCME)[b]
3. Electrical Workers	3. Automobile Workers (UAW)	3. Food and Commercial (UFCW)[b]
4. Painters	4. Machinists (IAM)	4. Service Employees (SEIU)[b]
5. Hod Carriers	5. Carpenters	5. Automobile Workers (UAW)
6. Musicians	6. Electrical (IBEW)	6. Electrical (IBEW)
7. Teamsters	7. Mine (UMW)	7. Teachers (AFT)
8. R. R. Clerks	8. Garment, Ladies (ULGW)	8. Mach. and Aerospace (IAM)[b]
9. Street R. R. Employees	9. Hotel and Restaurant	9. Carpenters[b]
10. Brick Layers	10. Hod Carriers	10. Communications (CWA)
11. R. R. Carmen	11. Clothing Workers (ACWA)	11. Steelworkers (USW)
12. Machinists	12. Retail Clerks	12. Laborers
13. Typographical Workers	13. Meat Cutters	13. Operating Engineers
14. Letter Carriers	14. R R and Steamship Clerks	14. Hotel, Restaurant
15. Lady Garment Workers	15. Operating Engineers	15. Postal Workers

[a]Sources: *American Labor Year Book* (1931); U.S. Bureau of the Census, *Statistical Abstract of the United States* (1962, 1992).
[b]Mergers

Cutters, merged and new workers were organized to form the third largest union, United Food and Commercial Workers (UFCW). Most surprising, the unions that merged to form the Service Employees International Union (SEIU) organized health and custodial workers to make it the fourth largest. The American Federation of Teachers (AFT), not listed in 1960, became the seventh largest union in 1991. Six of the fifteen largest unions in 1991 had grown, at least in part, by mergers. Moreover, the UAW, the USW, and the CWA, which were almost "industrially pure" in the 1960s remained among the largest only by recruiting members in other industries.

Seven of the largest unions on the 1991 list did not appear as identifiable unions on the 1960 list, and six on the 1991 list had undergone mergers. The two clothing unions on the 1960 list did not make the 1991 list, while the two government unions (AFSCME and Postal Workers) in 1991 were not on the 1960 list. Shifts among the largest unions produced a more representative and occupationally more diverse membership.

Since unions in different industrial sectors have different political interests, changes in the sector representation of the internationals undoubtedly affected labor politics. The eight construction and transportation internationals in the 1930s were noted for a nonideological job-conscious political style. In the 1960s, the seven large internationals in manufacturing pressed for a broad working-class agenda, while the construction unions remained dedicated to their political style. In the early 1990s, the six service sector unions in government, teaching, commerce, and health and custodial services grew to prominence. They, too, developed their own agenda. In brief, the sector mix of internationals in the 1990s differed widely from Greenstone's mix in the 1960s. The present mix probably represents a wider range of political interests than at any previous time in labor's history. This subject is examined in Part III.

SUMMARY

In response to economic and industrial changes in the United States since the 1930s, organized labor became more representative of the labor force. From its original core of mostly skilled workers, labor organized more lower-skilled manual and service workers as well as more highly educated white-collar and professional workers. While union members today do not precisely represent the labor force in occupational and industrial composition, unions have organized workers in all major areas. Labor has also organized blacks in proportion to their representation in the population, but women, Hispanics, Asiatics, and workers in the highest and lowest income groups remain less organized.

The changes in the composition of unionized labor did not all result from changes in its organizing policy. The declining representation of low-skilled manual workers probably resulted from industrial restructuring of the economy, while the growth of public sector unions was a partial response to labor's pressure for legislation that made organizing easier in the sector. During the period under review, more than 3,000,000 teachers, firefighters, police, and others became unionized but outside the AFL-CIO.

Most of the workers who lost unionized jobs in declining industries probably suffered earnings losses, but the remaining union members and newly recruited ones retained most of the traditional union advantages in earnings and fringe benefits. Thus, labor markets remained economically segmented. Although unionized workers earn more than the non-unionized workers almost everywhere, union earnings are more compressed. Scholars have not determined whether this situation has social-psychological and political consequences.

The above analysis demonstrated that organized labor, by becoming more representative of the labor force, also became more internally diversified in its industrial, occupational, gender, ethnic, and other characteristics. Whether this diversification increased labor's difficulties in achieving policy consensus and concerted political action will be pursued in later chapters. The question is complicated by the fact that, as labor changed, its political environment also changed. Both internal and external changes affected labor's ability to devise and implement a political program. The following chapter examines labor's turbulent organizational environment, especially from 1960 to 1990.

4

Labor's Changing and Turbulent Environment

Before the New Deal, the fortunes of the American labor movement were shaped primarily by the labor market and management's efforts to contain union growth. Union membership began to climb in the twentieth century, reaching a peak of 19 percent of the nonagricultural labor force in 1920. The Great Depression caused membership to sink to 12 percent in 1932, just before the New Deal. Then, under the protection of the NLRB, membership soared to an all-time high of 36 percent in 1945. It began to decline almost unnoticed for a decade but thereafter dropped steadily to about 17 percent in 1990 (Kochan, Katz, and McKersie 1986, p. 31; U.S. Bureau of the Census 1990, p. 418). Despite the early percentage decline, the situation looked promising for 40 years because from 1930 to 1970 membership continued to grow from 3,401,000 in 1930 to 21,248,000 in 1970. Then it leveled off for a decade and declined to about 17 million by 1990.

When Greenstone (1969) completed his field research in the mid-1960s, union membership was still growing, and labor's political clout was widely acknowledged. At that time, few analysts anticipated that in the next three decades membership would stagnate and then rapidly decline. Perhaps not causally related, the public's approval of labor also declined from 70 percent in 1961 to 55 percent in 1981 (Lipset and Schneider 1983, p. 203). Public confidence in business and government also fell. As Hamilton (1972, Chs. 8, 9) anticipated, the political transformations under way in both the working and middle classes would have long-term consequences. This chapter describes three changes in labor's environment since the 1960s that weakened its political influence: changes in the economy, the organization and conduct of politics, and community demographic and ecological structure. In consequence, labor's political position differs considerably from what Greenstone described in the 1960s.

CHANGES IN THE ECONOMY

Union membership was unevenly distributed in the nation's economy in the 1930, being highly concentrated in mining, the crafts, and rail transportation. When the New Deal made organizing easier and manufacturing employment expanded during World War II, union membership increased rapidly, especially in the manufacturing centers of the East and Midwest. Since the 1960s, massive changes in the economy have reduced membership in those regions, changing the occupational mix of the membership (see Chapter 3).

From 1960 to 1990, the proportion of workers employed in agriculture declined while remaining stable in construction, transportation, and public administration. In response to technological changes and foreign competition, the labor force in manufacturing fell 10 percent, from almost 30 to less than 20 percent, while the services increased from 25 to 38 percent (Hodson and Sullivan 1990, p. 173). Scholars mistakenly concluded that the United States has been losing its edge in competitive productivity. However, in absolute output, manufacturing dominance continued to increase in the United States. Its productivity remained the highest of any nation in the industrialized world and its rate of increase from 1960 to 1985 was higher than that of any nation except Japan, whose rate was barely higher (Baumol 1990).

Nonetheless, the impact of these changes in the American economy was strongest in the highly industrialized regions where union representation was the highest. Thus, in the Great Lakes region, manufacturing lost 3.4 percent of its workers in 1970–1979 and 16.4 percent in 1979–1985. In lakefront cities, the losses for the same periods were about 40 percent and 36 percent, respectively (Sassen 1990).

Occupational shifts were as profound. From 1960 to 1990, white-collar employment grew 13 percent, from 43 to 56 percent of the labor force, while blue-collar employment declined from 38 to 28 percent. Agricultural employment fell 5 percent, while service work increased 3 percent (Hodson and Sullivan 1990, p. 256). Sassen (1990, p. 476) demonstrated that these changes eroded earnings in manufacturing and raised them in other sectors, producing greater earnings inequality.

These labor force changes had an even greater impact on organized labor because unions were concentrated unevenly in industries, occupations, and regions. In the 1960s, employees were most highly organized in the transportation–communication–utilities sector at 75 percent; by 1990, it sank to 33 percent. In 1960, 71 percent of construction employees were organized; in 1990, 21 percent. In 1960, half of the workers in manufacturing were union members; in 1990, 22 percent. In 1960, trade and services each had 10 percent of its workers organized; in 1990, 7 percent. But in government, the organized proportion rose from 10 percent in 1960 to 37 percent in 1990 (Bok and Dunlop 1970, p. 44; U.S. Bureau of the Census 1990, p. 419).

The reduction in manufacturing employment itself would have explained much of the decline in union membership, but a 28 percent drop of union coverage in manufacturing exacerbated the trend. Even more substantial drops in coverage occurred in transportation, construction, and mining even though employment there remained rather stable. Obviously, management's deunionization drive accelerated the loss of union membership caused by industrial shifts in the economy (Sexton 1991, Ch. 13). The growth of union membership in government, education, and the services did not make up for membership losses in other sectors.

Data in Table 3.4 reveal how these changes altered the size of the internationals. In the 1960s, the five largest unions in order were teamsters, autoworkers (UAW), steelworkers (USW), machinists (IAM), and carpenters. In 1991, the National Education Association (NEA) was largest, followed by the Teamsters, government employees' union (AFSCME), foodworkers (UFCW), service employees (SEIU), and autoworkers (UAW). In 1960, the second largest five were the electrical workers (IBEW), miners (UMW), hotel and restaurant workers, garmentworkers, and laborers. In 1991, the second five were IBEW, Teachers (AFT), IAM, Carpenters, and Communication Workers (CWA). The manufacturing and building trades unions lost heavily while the white-collar and service unions gained dramatically. Later I explore how these compositional changes affected labor's political potential.

Union membership has always been unevenly distributed regionally. In the 1960s, five states accounted for half of the total membership: New York, California, Pennsylvania, Illinois, and Ohio. New England, the Middle Atlantic states, and the Midwest accounted for the bulk of the membership, while the South and the Southwest were least unionized (Estey 1967, p. 10). With the flow of manufacturing and people out of the "frostbelt" to the West, South, and Southwest, union density declined in its traditional areas of strength. By 1990, although union density had increased in the West to almost match that of the Northeast and the Midwest, it had changed only marginally in the South and Southwest. Nowhere did it rise fast enough to make up for decline in Midwest and East (Goldfield 1987, pp. 139–44). In sum, as union membership fell, it became slightly more evenly distributed regionally, but not enough to augment labor's political influence anywhere.

PARTY AND POLITICAL CHANGES

After 1960, changes in the conduct of parties, public confidence in them, and changes in political campaigning affected labor's political performance. Since labor was deeply involved in the Democratic Party, its changes affected labor's position in it. In his study of political change from 1952 to 1988, Wattenberg (1990, pp. 19, 37) demonstrated that parties and politics had become steadily less salient to many voters. They saw fewer differences between parties and preferred to vote for candidate rather than party. Declining party loyalty encouraged split voting and voting for one party's presidential candidate and the other party's congressional candidates. Although vote splitting most often occurred in local elections, the practice grew in state and national elections. Surveys since 1952 reveal that voters increasingly identified themselves as independent or neutral, or as nonvoters. At all levels of age and education, voters were less able to verbalize what they liked or disliked about the parties, but they began to segmentalize their views concerning the president's and the party's performance (Wattenberg 1990, p. 70).

Meanwhile, party organization and behavior changed. Before the New Deal, parties tended to be run by local political machines and "professional" politicians. Parties played an important role in aggregating groups around a few vaguely defined issues or values, selecting candidates for office, raising campaign funds, organizing the campaigns, mobilizing citizens to vote, monitoring party behavior in legislative bodies, and distributing political favors (Schlesinger 1968). While party legislative discipline has always been weak in the United States, during and after the New Deal, at least at the federal level, the president and his party enforced a measure of discipline. The party also played a role in mediating relations between citizen and government.

All these party functions weakened after the 1960s. Wattenberg (1990, p. 78) observed that party-line voting in Congress declined from 60 percent under Franklin Roosevelt to 40 percent under Jimmy Carter. Further, the party's ability to name candidates for office deteriorated as candidates entered more primaries to secure support before the party conventions. In 1952, Adlai Stevenson won the Democratic nomination for president without entering a single primary. In 1958, only 15 states held primaries; by 1978, 39 states held them (Cantril 1991, p. 117). The spread of primaries weakened bonds between candidates and party.

Since 1952, voters have increasingly felt that a particular candidate's attractiveness, not the party stance, influenced their choice. Several factors have contributed to the candidate's increasing importance. The weakening of urban political machines meant that the candidates had to assume more responsibility for supervising campaigns. New York City had 700 party clubs in 1932, 156 in 1975, and hardly any by the late 1980s (Piven 1990). Moreover, the machine's declining organizational and financial strength forced the candidate to assume a larger role in fund raising. Declining patronage reduced precinct workers' motivation to mobilize the vote. In response, candidates relied more on the mass media to influence potential voters. The ability of radio, TV, and mass advertising to reach larger audiences further reduced the already limited political dialogue between party volunteers and voters (Bennett 1991). In order to attract voters from all parties, candidates stressed their personal views rather than their party affiliation. This moderated ideological differences between the parties and favored a middle ground. Although the trend may have supported moderates within organized labor, it probably reduced the motivation of liberals to engage in party work.

Mass media costs escalated as candidates competed for viewer and listener attention. Candidates spent more and more time raising campaign funds, a traditional party function. By 1960, campaign management had become both a profession and a business; candidates began to employ experts rather than rely on the loosely organized party to manage their campaigns (Nachmias and Rosenbloom 1980). Ironically, political action committees (PACs), invented by organized labor in the 1940s to raise funds for the party, were later effectively adopted by candidates and other interest groups to aggregate individual contributions into large campaign chests. This increasingly shifted candidates' obligations from the party to those who had contributed to their PACs.

The rise of congressional campaign committees also weakened parties. Members of Congress collected funds and directed their use to the campaigns of particular incumbents whom they wanted reelected (Nachmias and Rosenbloom 1980, p. 185). While this tactic helped secure threatened seats in Congress, the committees behaved like PACs that were not responsible to the party.

As business and other interest groups organized more PACs, labor's earlier fund-raising advantage eroded, even though its total political expenditures did not decline. Although unions lost more than a million members in the private sector between 1970 and 1987, their total receipts, adjusted for inflation, increased by an estimated 10 percent. But since membership dues could not, by law, be used to support political candidates, labor PACs had to collect more voluntary contributions ("hard money") from members, union staffs, and other sources. Receipts between the 1980 and 1988 election cycles increased impressively, by $31.5 million, or 89 percent (Bennett 1992).

Berry (1984, p. 74) reported that, between 1960 and 1980, the number of PACs in Washington exploded; 600 PACs were registered in 1974 and 3,400 in 1982. Forty percent were sponsored by corporations, which raised a third of all PAC money spent by congressional candidates. From 1974 to 1982, PAC funds rose from $12.5 to $83 million. Saltzman (1987) reported that corporate contributions in 1971–1972 were 47 percent of labor's; a decade later they were 136 percent larger. In 1982, labor organized 350 PACs, while corporations and industrial associations launched 2,100. For the congressional election, corporations, business, and other groups raised $87 million, of which labor furnished $21 million (Rehmus 1984).

Although business does not always back Republican candidates, corporate PACs that contributed more than $25,000 to candidates in the 1980 election gave 64 percent of their contributions to Republicans (Clawson and Neustadtl 1986). Also, in 75 percent of the races, one candidate received at least nine times as much money as the other. In races pitting liberals against conservatives, the conservatives received 92 percent of PAC funds. The data clearly point to labor's losing its battle with business and other groups to raise campaign money.

These data do not reflect the large nonmonetary contributions that labor makes to the party and the candidates in the form of volunteer campaign services. I know of no study that compares the parties in volunteer services, such as making telephone calls, planting signs, and checking on registration and voting. To some extent, these services can be bought, and this is the trend. Here again, business has more funds at its disposal. My interviews with labor leaders revealed that the number of political volunteers had declined along with the membership, and only rarely was the loss restored by the hiring of election workers.

Finally, party leaders experienced more difficulties in brokering the interests of various groups. The most important groups to assert autonomy were African Americans, women, and Hispanics. Each pressed for more convention delegates, more patronage, and more candidates for office (Ulaner 1991). The erosion of citywide political machines quickened as blacks and Hispanics displaced them in cities and states where they were a large plurality or majority (Nelson and Merano 1977; Zax 1990).

Other single-interest groups, which earlier had sought party support, now established independent lobbies and PACs. Organized labor once played a leading role in aggregating liberal groups in the party. But these groups began to compete with organized labor for party influence, forcing labor to take on the appearance of a special-interest group. In turn, voters began to evaluate parties in terms of their special rather than their common interests. Labor, probably more than any other group, suffered from changes in party organization and behavior. In short, all these trends accord with the predictions of segmentation theory. Turbulent social movements external to the party, such as the civil rights and women's movements, pressed their demands on the party, weakening the traditional brokering functions of labor and party leaders. Segmentation tendencies outraced the ability of party leaders and labor to aggregate interest groups and build enduring coalitions.

IMPACT OF COMMUNITY CHANGES

Since World War II and especially after the 1960s, migration from the central cities to the suburbs has magnified COPE's difficulties in operating an effective political machine. Before the war, both industrial and craftsworkers tended to live fairly close to their places of employment. Union headquarters and party clubs were also located in working-class neighborhoods. Factory employees and artisans often shared bonds of residence, ethnicity, religion, race, and kinship (Mackenzie 1973, Ch. 7). To an extent, union and party officials could link into these work plant and neighborhood networks (Kornblum 1974, Chs. 5, 6; Shostak 1969, Ch. 12).

The melding of work and neighborhood politics was far from complete. Large industry was not heavily unionized before the New Deal. Many eastern and midwestern city neighborhoods were segregated along ethnic, religious, and racial lines. Management often exploited these divisions to discourage unionization. One of the CIO's greatest achievements was to persuade workers to submerge separate identities to advance common economic interests. Cooperating in union affairs at work had a political spillover in the neighborhoods. The spatial concentration of workers' homes and workplaces from about 1935 through 1955, the period of fastest union growth, facilitated party and union cooperation. In these two decades, many community studies of labor documented the importance of political activities (see the extensive bibliographies in Form and Miller 1960 and Seidman et al. 1958). The rapid decline of such studies after 1955 reflects labor's declining ability to link factory and neighborhood politics.

Greenstone (1969) studied labor–party relations in Chicago, Detroit, and Los Angeles in the early 1960s just as this era was coming to a close. By 1960, the majority of union members had moved out of the central cities. Greenstone did not examine the overlapping bonds of unions, parties, workers, and ethnic groups in the neighborhoods of his cities, but fortunately, other students did. Kornblum (1974) described how the United Steel Workers (USW) overcame strong ethnic and racial barriers in Chicago's South Side neighborhoods where the steel mills were located. Multiethnic and racial contacts among workers in the mills and in the union became the basis for cooperating in the Democratic Party in the neighborhoods. Today, the steel mills, multiethnic neighborhoods, and union–party networks are gone (Geoghan 1992, Ch. 5).

Sheppard, Kornhauser, and Mayer (1956) also described how ethnic groups and UAW members were concentrated in neighborhoods around Ford, Chrysler, and General Motors plants in Detroit, and how the UAW coordinated local party work. Today, all these plants have moved out of Detroit and few ethnic neighborhoods survive. And Choldin (1985, pp. 374–7) reported that even Los Angeles was earlier segregated into relatively homogeneous ethnic areas which contained most of the economic and social facilities that residents needed. Although residues of such integrated neighborhoods persist, metropolitan decentralization and suburbanization after World War II rapidly separated residence, workplace, and politics, complicating COPE's political mobilization efforts.

Human ecology postulates that the more physically dispersed the interdependent units of a community become, the more energy must be expended to coordinate them (Hawley 1981, p. 11). While efficient transportation and communication facilities reduce the time, energy, and money needed to overcome spatial barriers, the reduction is never to zero. Each member in a system calculates the cost of participation; increasing numbers increase total participation costs. Effective labor politics requires the articulation of four units that may be spatially separated: residence, workplace, union, and political party. The more physically dispersed, the greater the coordination costs.

Residential suburbanization exploded in the United States in the early 1970s when beltways were constructed around major cities (Muller 1981, p.170). As early as 1960, 63 percent of the total U.S. population already lived in metropolitan areas, and almost half of it lived in the suburbs. Only 30 years later, by 1990, 75 percent of the population resided in metropolitan areas, 60 percent of it in suburbs (Choldin 1985, p. 361). While prewar suburbs tended to house higher-income groups, postwar suburbs also housed lower-income groups, blue-collar workers, African Americans, and clerical and technical workers (Logan 1976).

Although residential suburbanization outpaced the decentralizing of manufacturing, sales, and clerical services, suburban job growth was impressive. Kasarda (1980) estimated that by 1970, a quarter of century after World War II, the central cities had lost 1.1 million manufacturing jobs, while the suburbs had gained over 4.2 million. Schwartz (1980) reported that between 1960 and 1970, the central cities lost 828,000 blue-collar jobs but gained 485,000 white-collar ones. The suburbs, in contrast, gained a million blue-collar jobs and two million white-collar jobs. Similar trends occurred in other industries. Muller (1981, p. 134) estimated that from 1960 to 1980, 75 to 90 percent of the newly created jobs were in the outer ring of metropolitan centers.

These trends affected the residential distribution of union members. Election surveys of the National Opinion Research Center revealed that in the early 1960s, 60 percent of union members lived outside the central city; by the late 1980s the figure had risen to 73 percent. Importantly, a decline in voting as well as a decline in voting for Democrats accompanied the suburbanization of union members.

The suburbanization of workplaces greatly lengthened workers' job travel paths. Early industrial decentralization lengthened round trips between central city and suburb; later decentralization lengthened the distance from one suburb to another on beltways (Kowinski 1980). Today, fewer than a third of the workers who live in suburbs commute to the central city. Since few main arteries connect suburbs, intersuburb commuting has become the major traffic problem (Shannon, Kleniewski, and Cross 1991, p. 155). In large metropolitan areas, the average automobile round trip from home to work is about 20 miles (U.S. Bureau of the Census 1978). Commuting time may be more important than distance. Hawley (1981, p. 11) estimated that a sixty-mile radius around a city center represents an hour or more of travel time by auto, the maximum commuting time for the vast majority of workers. In rush-hour traffic, a ten-mile trip often requires a half hour or more. Drski (1985) observed that congestion is no longer limited to central cities. Suburbs increasingly suffer traffic congestion that freeway systems do not and cannot handle. While relatively few workers have traditionally attended union meetings, suburbanization has worsened the problem.

Neighborhoods vary in the density of social bonds and networks. Ward leaders traditionally had access to dense neighborhood networks based on work, kinship, ethnicity, and religion. Greenstone (1969) reported that COPE had access to such networks, especially in Detroit and Chicago. As suburbanization weakened these networks, COPE's electoral problems probably mounted. Since no longitudinal studies have explored this question, the evidence presented below is largely inferential.

In general, the more mobile a population, the harder it is for individuals to maintain local networks. Residential mobility has shown no signs of abating since the 1960s. To the extent that residential duration deepens neighborhood bonds (Hunter 1974), they probably have declined with rising mobility. People maintain some local ties by visiting and telephoning, especially with kin. But moving into new areas lowers participation in local voluntary associations, at least in early years. Shopping for daily consumption items increasingly occurs in large shopping centers outside the neighborhood. Overall, the secular trend points toward declining neighborhood bonds, especially among adults.

Neighborhood social homogeneity and overlapping memberships generally produce more durable social bonds than participation in unrelated organizations. While the socioeconomic homogeneity of neighborhoods has not changed noticeably in recent years, other neighborhood characteristics have. Before World War II, neighborhoods in eastern and midwestern cities were integrated by overlapping kinship, ethnic, racial, and religious bonds. Neighborhoods occupied by first- and second-generation European ethnic groups have declined in number, and although suburbanization has not completely destroyed ethnic neighborhoods, intermarriage between ethnic and religious groups has lessened neighborhood solidarity (Bleda 1979; Alba 1981, 1990). Especially noteworthy has been the decline in local ethnic clubs and churches.

These trends are less strong in African-American neighborhoods. The urban concentration of blacks has increased since 1960. By 1990, blacks were a majority in a dozen cities, including Atlanta, Baltimore, Birmingham, Detroit, Gary, Newark, New Orleans, Richmond, and Washington. In several other cities, their numbers were large enough to make them a major force in local politics. Obviously, neighborhoods in these cities vary in socioeconomic characteristics and social cohesion. However, in both cities and suburbs African-American residences have remained highly segregated (Massey and Denton 1987).

African-American neighborhoods generally display denser organizational and interpersonal networks than white neighborhoods because segregation forces residents to spend more of their social life in the area (Warren and Warren 1977). In segregated neighborhoods, the church is an important institution, and residents tend to patronize local groceries, services, and recreational facilities. Political parties seek leaders who have contacts with these local organizations and their members. Since blacks overwhelmingly favor the Democratic Party, politicos can largely ignore Republican competition, but they must expend considerable effort to mobilize apathetic residents to vote because many of them see no connection between their condition and politics.

Black neighborhoods' denser social ties may appear to be exceptionally favorable for the Democratic Party and COPE, but important obstacles stand in their paths. Although African Americans are more highly unionized than whites, blacks hold relatively few union offices, and only a few profit from working for COPE. Wilson (1987, p. 7) claimed that since the 1950s and 1960s, blacks in central cities have been deprived of the crucial leadership they need to mobilize residents to attain important services. Central-city ghettos have been deprived of many middle-class and professional leaders who have moved to more attractive neighborhoods. The above scenario, with some modifications, also applies to cities where Hispanics are concentrated in large numbers. In sum, metropolitan changes since the 1960s have probably raised obstacles to united political action by lower-status groups. The changes include increased residential mobility, growing separation of work and residence, longer job travel paths, heightened racial cleavage, and loss of neighborhood associations such as political clubs, ethnic and religious organizations, and union halls.

As part of the community, labor unions have been adversely affected by these changes. The decline in manufacturing and its suburbanization have hampered the conduct of union business. Union meeting halls were traditionally located close to the workplace, often in the neighborhoods where their members lived. Meetings were generally held in the evening after dinner. My interviews with local union officers revealed that, as industry decentralized, union meeting halls were typically relocated closer to the plants. Officers wanted to be housed near them to be able to attend quickly to grievances and other problems. Union meetings could be held immediately before or after work shifts, so that members would not need to make two trips in one day. No union in my research chose to locate a hall at a point equally accessible to the residences of its members. Some unions held joint meetings of incoming and outgoing shifts, which marginally increased participation.

In response to declining membership, some unions became general unions, organizing any occupation or industry that seemed ripe for it. Locals can tolerate a limited amount of member diversity, but a point arrives when it is better to split locals into more homogeneous units. This practice results in smaller locals and fewer contacts among them. Obviously, rising member heterogeneity, the downsizing of locals, and increases their number complicated the task of coordinating locals for political work.

REVISITING GREENSTONE'S CITIES

Did the societal changes reviewed above alter union–party relations in the cities Greenstone studied? The limited evidence suggests that they did. Greenstone concluded that in reviving the Democratic party, the

Detroit UAW successfully aggregated a coalition up to 1970. The union's liberal ideology gradually became less intense as the union assumed more responsibility for party welfare. While the UAW could not dominate Detroit politics, it maintained some party discipline with support from blacks, but it exerted more substantial influence on state party and politics.

Buffa's (1984) review of UAW politics in Michigan from 1972 to 1983 revealed important swings in the union's party influence. As the automobile industry and the majority of its white members moved out of the central city, blacks became the majority in an increasingly impoverished Detroit. In 1967, the city experienced a devastating race riot. By 1973, blacks had taken over the Detroit Democratic Party and had elected Coleman Young, the first black mayor. They reelected him for five successive terms.

In 1967, the UAW withdrew from the AFL-CIO, splitting labor in Michigan. Yet, up to 1972, the UAW had maintained a dominant influence in the state Democratic Party and thereafter assumed a leadership role in it (Buffa 1984, p. viii). But the party could not win elections without the support of the white blue-collar workers in the Detroit suburbs. The UAW and the party refused demands by Detroit blacks for a set quota in the party's central committee. Young and the black leaders in the UAW then bolted the party. In 1978 they backed Milliken, the victorious Republican gubernatorial candidate, whose help was needed to revive Detroit's economy. Milliken became the first Republican governor to win in Wayne country in 30 years (Buffa 1984, p. 255). Black leaders boycotted the Democratic Party for two years, charging that it was dominated by an antiblack UAW-Jewish coalition (Buffa 1984, p. 262). Finally, in 1982, blacks ended their boycott as they, the UAW, the AFL-CIO, and the Michigan Education Association agreed to back James Blanchard for governor, a white candidate from a blue-collar Detroit suburb (Buffa 1984, p. 269). In short, after the 1960s, racial splits in the uneasy coalition of the UAW and the Democratic Party altered the influence and strategy of both groups, which hardly resembled the scene Greenstone described for the postwar era up to 1960.

In Greenstone's Chicago, the Democratic Party machine was buttressed by a system of patronage in ethnic neighborhoods and by support from the traditional AFL unions that the party protected. COPE's electoral apparatus was no match for the Daley machine, and labor was forced to accept a junior partnership in the party. Cooperation between the two was stronger in national politics, where local patronage was not at stake.

As in Detroit, white ethnic suburbanization after World War II slowly tilted the city's racial balance toward blacks. By the end of Richard J. Daley's twenty-one-year reign in 1976, the machine was showing signs of crumbling. Racial tensions in the schools, public housing, and government increased. The machine proved less able to deal with charges of corruption, racial disturbances, antimachine reform groups, and challenges by aspiring black ward leaders. Daley's death in 1976 left the party with no successor who could handle the city's mounting administrative difficulties and rising racial tensions. The crumbling party machine enabled Jane Byrne to become the mayor in 1979 (Hirsch 1990, pp. 76–84).

Soon after, Byrne joined Republicans in attacking the ex-mayor's son, Richard M. Daley, in his run for state's attorney. He decided to challenge her in the 1982 mayor's race. Harold Washington, a leading black politician, also entered the race and won, becoming the city's first black mayor. For the first time in 50 years, Chicago's Democratic machine had been defeated (Hirsch 1990, p. 85). Although conflicts between white ethnics and blacks in the city council created an almost ungovernable situation, Washington was reelected in 1986 and appeared to have the party machine under control. His death a year later destabilized his organization, making it possible for the younger Daley to become mayor.

In sum, between 1960 to 1990, the Chicago Democratic Party machine had crumbled in response to rising fiscal problems and racial and ethnic tensions. It was partially rebuilt along racial lines only to crumble once again. It was then shakily rebuilt in an uneasy coalition. During this period, union members were also split along racial and ethnic lines. While COPE continued to play an active role in state and national politics, it could not mediate racial conflicts within the party or in city affairs. The young Daley patched together a workable relationship with black leaders without much help from organized labor. Pinderhughes (1987, p. 260) concluded that the earlier pluralist pattern of Chicago politics had changed, especially when it involved racial issues.

Greenstone (1969) characterized the 1960s political situation in Los Angeles as disorganized. The earlier liberal coalition between labor, Democratic Party leaders, and other interests had fallen apart. Unions pursued their separate interests and would not yield authority to COPE. They would unite episodically, only to split again and follow their earlier pattern of pluralistic politics. COPE ignored local class or social welfare issues but pursued them in state and national politics.

Although racial and ethnic tensions were rapidly rising in the city when Greenstone studied it, he did not examine their political implications even briefly. In the 1977 introduction to the second edition, he ignored the 1965 race riots in Watts and their effect on local politics. Yet, by 1973, Tom Bradley had been elected as the city's first black mayor and served for twenty years in five successive terms. Regalado (1991) claimed that, as part of the liberal coalition, labor played a major role in electing and reelecting

Bradley. After 1969, the overwhelming majority of local labor leaders and union members voted for Bradley, who successfully organized a coalition of blacks, liberal Jews, labor, and business persons interested in downtown development.

Compared to previous mayors and to the situation that Greenstone described, Bradley appeared to be prolabor, but his support was spotty and inconsistent. He maintained a hands-off policy in the struggle between businesses and the janitors' union (SEIU) but urged downtown businesses to remain neutral in the certification election of the union in the downtown restaurants. Bradley supported labor's program to assist needy Mexican immigrants whom the unions wanted to organize, but he also managed to antagonize four public-sector unions. He also strongly supported downtown business development. Toward the end of his regime, only 40 percent of the union leaders approved of his policies (Regalado 1991, pp. 91–93).

Bradley's regime came to an end late in 1993 when a Republican coalition convinced voters that a change was necessary to meet the city's dire financial problems caused by the recession. Richard Riordan, a white Republican business man was elected mayor against the opposition of blacks and most labor leaders. However, he attracted perhaps 40 percent of the Hispanic vote and a majority of the Anglo vote. In short, Bradley's coalition was as much a creature of his own making as that of the Democratic Party. His twenty-year regime provided some order and stability to the otherwise fluid and disorganized situation that Greenstone described. Liberal racial and labor causes attained a degree of respectability not previously permitted in the traditionally antilabor city. Although Bradley's regime came to an end, Los Angeles politics had changed considerably after 1970.

This overview of Greenstone's three cities 30 years after he completed his fieldwork supports the view that labor–party relations were basically restructured. The UAW's party dominance in Michigan and Detroit was severely challenged, the Daley party machine had fallen in Chicago, and the disorganized pattern of labor–party relations in Los Angeles had attained a degree of stability previously unknown. All three cities experienced declines in manufacturing, rapid suburbanization, the rise of racial politics, changes in the mix of internationals, and new cleavages within and between the Democratic Party, COPE, and labor. Analyzing trends in Chicago's Cook County and Los Angeles County from 1960 to 1980, Weiher (1991, p. 113) concluded that municipal boundaries increasingly explained racial, occupational, and political segregation in the metropolitan areas. The trends had proceeded even farther in Detroit's Wayne County.

CHANGING PATTERNS OF LABOR VOTING

A partial analysis of union member voting between 1960 and 1990 points to a weakening of labor's political influence. In the 1964 presidential election, the National Opinion Research Center reported that 83 percent of union members voted. The proportion drifted down to about 75 percent in 1988. While 68 percent of union members voted for the Democratic presidential candidate in 1964, in the ensuing twenty-four years to 1988, a majority voted for the Democratic candidate only in 1976.

Data from the National Election Surveys also reveal a trend of weakening labor influence. Between 1964 and 1980, the difference between union and nonunion members who supported Democratic candidates for president fell from 20 to 11 percent; union members increasingly voted like nonunion members. By 1960, the majority of union members resided outside the central cities of metropolitan regions. Between 1964 and 1980, the percentage living inside the central city steadily drifted downward from 42 to 33 percent. Expectedly, suburban residence weakened union member support for Democratic presidential candidates because the suburbanites were predominantly whites. In every presidential election between 1960 and 1992, union members living in central cities more strongly supported the Democratic candidate than did members in the suburban ring. In 1960, 48 percent of both central-city and non-central-city union members voted for the Democratic candidate. In 1980, 48 percent of central-city unionists voted Democratic compared to 31 percent of non-central-city unionists.

CONCLUSIONS

The economic, political, and community changes that occurred in the 30 years after Greenstone gathered his data were large, and they severely impacted COPE's operations. Losses in union membership did not reduce labor's political expenditures, because dues were raised and member contributions to politics rose. However, a larger membership would have given labor even more financial and political resources. Importantly, labor membership losses were largest in the liberal Democratic states of the Midwest and the East, and the rising membership of the government and services unions could not compensate for this loss.

The suburbanization of union membership occurred simultaneously with the challenge of blacks to control urban Democratic parties. The growth of general unions and the rise of service sector unions made labor more heterogeneous, adding to the problem of building political consensus. The declining salience of political parties and the conservative drift in the country and the Democratic Party raise doubts that a larger labor movement would have basically altered the flow of politics. National leaders probably maintained their liberal agenda, while many party and union members joined the conservative drift. This cleavage may have reduced members' confidence in their unions. By 1980, only 13 percent of union members thought that their unions were doing an excellent or good job, 54 percent ranked the performance as fair to good, and 33 percent as fair to poor (Lipset and Schneider 1983, p. 205).

While the party and labor had historically supplemented one another in aggregating supporters, they seemed to have lost some of their glue as more single-interest groups emerged in the party. The growth of candidate-dominated political machines and independent PACs undermined the tenuous discipline of the Democratic Party. Very likely, COPE was also exposed to similar divisions that undercut its party influence (see Part II).

The turbulent environment of labor after the 1960s undoubtedly reduced COPE's ability to influence its members, the party, and the public. Fundamental to this loss was COPE's declining ability to keep members interested in local politics and its failure to keep local political networks intact. Building strong local political organizations, as we shall see, is basic to successful political action. Yet most labor leaders whom I interviewed considered local politics much less important than national politics. In the next chapter, I examine this neglected area of labor politics.

5

All Politics Is Local*

Despite lapses, American labor has committed itself to support the Democratic Party. To ensure the party's success, labor has built its own voter mobilization organization in COPE. Party loyalty and discipline are the sine qua non for success of both the party and labor. Party success rests on the ability of leaders to convince their followers that the party will make a difference in their daily lives. To be maximally successful, the party stresses that it should win in all elections, local, state, and national. Yet, while local government is closest to voters, turnout in local elections is low; it is highest in national elections. Despite the pivotal importance of local politics in building party discipline, getting out the vote is the toughest problem that party and labor leaders face. The unreliability of the labor vote for the party reflects labor's inability to build a sturdy and effective political machine. The machine can operate successfully in state and national elections only to the extent that it can mobilize voting in local elections.

This chapter examines the importance of local politics for labor and its neglect by both labor leaders and students of labor politics. The chapter then reviews and evaluates class and pluralist theories of labor politics and develops a segmentation theory that may better account for it. The lessons learned provide a backdrop for evaluating labor's political operations in three metropolitan communities: Cleveland, Columbus, and Cincinnati.

STUDIES OF LOCAL LABOR POLITICS

Despite their obvious importance, only a few social scientists in the last three decades have examined labor's local political efforts, perhaps

*Attributed to the late former House Speaker Edward "Tip" O'Neill.

because labor itself has neglected the topic. A survey of fifteen urban sociology texts published between 1975 and 1990 turned up very few references to labor unions and even fewer to their role in local politics. Ten texts did not even index "unions," "COPE," or "labor politics." Of the five that did, only one referred to an empirical study. Two authors indicated that not much is known about labor politics, and two stated that local politics is no longer an important feature of urban life.

Although political science has a long tradition of studying urban government and politics, a review of ten texts revealed that none referred to empirical studies of labor participation in local politics. They devoted most attention to the forms of city government, taxation and fiscal crises, the role of ethnic and racial groups in city politics, relations of cities to state and federal governments, and the erosion of local political machines.

When describing party machines, no text referred to COPE and its relations to the Democratic Party. While some authors observed that municipal unions' wage demands strain city budgets, they did not examine how unions exert political influence to extract wage benefits. In discussions of downtown urban development, some texts mentioned that craft unions favor it but failed to note that other unions have opposed it in favor of other projects. In analyzing state and federal sources of urban finance, the texts ignored labor's role in influencing that legislation. In short, references to labor's local politics were based on casual and unsystematic observations.

The neglect of labor politics in sociology and political science texts reflects the paucity of current empirical research in an area in which interest was once moderately high. From about 1945 to 1970, social scientists studied community decision making, community power structures, and how cities responded to federal programs to attack problems of urban decay, racial conflict, unemployment, inadequate education, unequal employment opportunity, and poverty. Organized labor was involved in all of these programs. Form and Miller (1960), Adrian (1960), Walton (1966), Rose (1967), Clark (1968), and Hawley and Svara (1972) examined literally hundreds of studies that referred to the local political activities of business, labor, and other groups. While they concluded that labor was not the most powerful actor in community decision making, they did describe many situations in which labor was deeply involved.

Case studies of community power structures and decision making declined after the mid-1960s when the Johnson administration began the War on Poverty. The federal government sponsored research to examine the effectiveness of its programs to reduce urban poverty and racial discrimination. National surveys of many communities and their compliance with federal programs (see, for example, Aiken and Alford 1970) replaced case study analysis. As subsequent administrations reduced federal funds for these programs during and after the Vietnam war, community evaluation research came almost to a standstill, which explains the virtual absence of references to labor's role in community politics in current social science texts.

THEORIES OF COMMUNITY POLITICS

Researchers in community and labor politics can be roughly divided into two camps: class theorists and pluralists. I describe each briefly and then offer segmentation theory as a substitute for both.

Class Theory

Class theorists, primarily structuralists and neo-Marxists, took the position that business interests dominate community decision making. Labor, part of the working class, has limited power and plays a subservient role. Recent class theories hold that local politics is declining in importance because basic decisions are being made at the state and national levels and, once made, imposed on local communities. Big capitalists in conjunction with big government dictate local decisions.

Gottdiener (1987) and Katznelson (1981) have worked out an elegant theory on the decline of local politics but have not conducted longitudinal supportive studies in different types of cities for different types of issues. Gottdiener claimed that city politics has withered because large corporations in cooperation with state and federal governments make the decisions that affect local economies and local politics. Local governments depend so much on the well-being of corporate business that no division can exist between their interests and the public's. Cities cannot act autonomously because they so depend financially on state and federal governments to solve problems of race, crime, poverty, housing, and urban decay.

Two tiers of control constrain local politics. First, government infrastructure, embedded in law and the U.S. Constitution, guarantees capitalist domination and persistence. Second, corporations, the state, and citizen groups determine how local governments will redistribute their economic resources. Metropolitan areas are so fragmented by deep "trenches" (Katznelson 1981) among local governments, social classes, and religious, ethnic, and other groups that they cannot cooperate to solve their problems. Local political culture withers as citizens, responding to their powerlessness, become apathetic about local government.

One major local government function remains: regulating the use of space through zoning laws and building codes. However, the several governments in metropolitan areas are too divided to plan for coherent growth. Beholden to the landed interests, they are not free to implement zoning ordinances fairly and rationally. Sharing Gottdiener's (1987) views, Logan and Molotch (1987) claimed that some labor unions support the efforts of local capitalists to change zoning laws. Together they force cities to build "growth machines" that provide business with good profits and construction unions with a steady flow of employment. Other unions support government efforts at taxpayer expense to attract industries that expand membership. Coopted by business, labor cannot and will not unite for the welfare of the working class.

Adherents of the powerless-city thesis note that municipalities hire many union members as teachers, police, firefighters, garbage haulers, and clerical workers whose interest in local politics is limited to protecting their jobs. Union survival is increasingly jeopardized by growing urban fiscal crises (Gottdiener 1987, p. 258) because unions are convenient scapegoats for the high cost of government. To court public favor and arouse antilabor sentiments, city officials undercut unions by subcontracting city services to lower-wage private providers and by fomenting service disruptions. Where unions are absent or weak, government officials and business organizations appeal to employers to locate plants in their cities by offering tax abatements and by emphasizing their community's favorable business climate.

These observations conform to much of what is known about recent urban trends. That the country's legal framework is compatible with the dominant system (capitalism) is obviously true, a structural reality that exists in all nations. This truism is neither a theory nor a finding. Metropolitan areas do embrace many municipalities which do not cooperate; cities do depend on corporations (and others) for tax revenues; and corporations do ask for tax abatements. Some growing cities do develop downtown growth machines. Construction unions do favor urban growth. Zoning and planning are often steeped in politics. Cities and businesses have engaged in antiunion drives. Cities have become somewhat dependent financially on state and federal government.

If there were no exceptions to these themes, research on urban politics would be pointless because everything would be predictable. However, exceptions are abundant. Some community functions and services are predominantly local: education, housing, crime control, zoning, public utilities, parks, welfare, and public health. Federal and state governments are moving many functions back to local governments (Waste 1989, p. 134), forcing cities to find solutions to their financial crises. Unions have convinced governments to deny tax abatements to business. Even with strong business opposition, municipal unions have shown a strong survival capability. And citizens have voted down many growth machine projects.

The extent of exceptions to business–state domination of communities is unknown and should be determined by research. Proponents of the powerless-city thesis are overly inclined to interpret all decisions as elite manipulations. Thus, the corporate cooptation of local groups to increase profits is taken as evidence of capitalist domination, but union extraction of concessions from local government is not interpreted as a working-class victory. Local politics is more complicated: conflicts occur both between and within classes and interest groups. In short, class theories of the powerless and functionless city are elegant and clear, but they do not substitute for systematic empirical research on a representative set of local issues.

Pluralist Theory

Pluralists insisted that the conclusions of class theorists were overdrawn (see Dahl 1961). Local decision making is important in its own right and has its own dynamics which are not determined by a national pattern of class dominance. The arenas largely under community control include education, zoning, property taxes, amenities, and utilities. Moreover, decision making is issue-specific; each type of issue involves different groups, including labor, that enter into temporary alliances to fight for or against particular goals. There are no permanent class alliances of winners or losers. Decision-making patterns vary widely in response to the type of local economy and the residents' social composition. Thus, politics in middle-class suburbs differs from that in manufacturing cities.

Pluralists who study urban government do not mistakenly think that it has little independent power and that urban politics are unimportant. Pluralist theory is not as elegant as class theory because it emphasizes voluntary individual and organizational action in specific situations. Pluralists do not like to generalize about power because they see too many contingencies: It depends on the issue, the situation, and the participants, to say nothing of other factors.

Kweit and Kweit (1990, pp. 210–2) illustrated this hesitancy to generalize about unions' local politics. Union leaders ignore local politics because they believe that most legislation that bears on labor's bread-and-butter issues is enacted at the state and national levels. Moreover, unions vary so much in their social, economic, and political interests that engaging in local politics divides them into opposing camps, a condition to be avoided at all costs. Union leaders realize that the public regards labor as a special-interest group, and engaging in politics only increases public antagonism.

These observations may not stand up to empirical test. Obviously, many union leaders do not ignore local politics. Unions in industries with local markets, like construction, know that local politics matters, and they engage in it actively. While unions differ, they share some social, economic, and political interests, and they engage in local politics when these are threatened. Like leaders of many other interest groups, union leaders are aware of public antagonism toward them, but this does not prevent their involvement in local politics.

Segmentation Theory

The third position on local politics, segmentation theory, brings together some aspects of class and pluralist theory. It holds that local politics are related to state and national politics in indirect, complex, but knowable ways that need to be charted by research. Local politics are neither as tightly constricted as class theorists claim nor as loosely structured as pluralists claim. Five sets of community organizations make up complexes or sectors that typically furnish the main actors in local decision making: labor, business, government, parties, and citizen groups (Form 1954). These sets of organizations often act together but may split on some issues.

Predictably, different combinations of organizations in each complex become involved in controversies or alliances with groups in other complexes in selected areas of decision making. These actors reappear often enough in selected sets of issues to constitute structured contests of local decision making. Thus, some groups are regularly involved in a cluster of issues that focus on education, for example, while others are involved in issues revolving around urban growth and development. A pattern of wins and losses may become discernible over a series of issues, but the pattern is rarely permanent because the participants, their resources, and the external environment change. The organization–issue mix in local politics conditions the mix in state and national politics and vice versa.

Many large and powerful groups ignore local issues even if the issues may affect them in the long run. Thus, the *decision to participate* is in itself a basic ingredient of local political influence because barriers to participation can be overcome over time. Segmentation theory does not ignore stratification in the community but recognizes that bargaining often occurs, even between actors with unequal resources. Marxists are correct in insisting that dominance patterns exist in most communities that tend to conform to institutional inequalities in societies. Business generally has more material resources than labor, but neither business nor labor is always interested in the same issues or tightly united in local politics.

Domination in one arena of urban life (e.g., industrial zoning) does not necessarily extend to others (e.g., residential zoning). All organizations are not always interested in the same economic issues (e.g., raising taxes for education or lowering them through tax abatements for business). In certain games, some unions, businesses, and newspapers align against other unions, businesses, and newspapers. Downtown development is an example, as our case studies will show. The frequency, conditions, and consequences of intergroup contests must be determined empirically. Some groups may cooperate, compete, and fight one another simultaneously on different issues.

Multilevel political analysis challenges class theory's purely logical generalizations. The influence of the federal government and national organizations on local counterparts is reciprocal. Generalizations must be regularly reexamined because modern social structures constantly change. As Norton Long (1958) suggested, urban politics may be studied as an ecology of games whose structure varies from city to city (Waste 1989, p. 7).

This variation provides ample room for analyzing labor's place in local urban politics. Labor, like business, government, and voluntary associations, is internally divided on the types of local issues in which to become involved. As an often reluctant and timid player in community politics, labor has failed to capitalize on its potential influence.

THE CASE FOR LOCAL POLITICS

Downplaying the importance of local politics violates massive evidence that all politics have a local dimension in democratic nations. Marxist theory emphasizes the importance of the local cell to the national party, and pluralist theory also emphasizes the dependence of state and national parties on local parties for material and organizational resources.

Segmentation theory emphasizes the two-way nature of the relationship, how local parties affect national ones and vice versa. The theory profits from Simmel's (1950, Part 3) insight that in complex settings, the ability of centers to dominate local units depends at least in part on the cooperation of the subordinates, a situation that gives them some influence over superordinates. Local units are not passive puppets of central authorities, especially when the center lacks the resources to discipline the periphery. This interdependence presents researchers with a methodological challenge: to determine why and how much local and national party units depend on each other.

Business, labor, government, parties, and citizen groups are all built on local units. National unions are composed of locals, literally situated in local communities. Even the largest national firms, whether locally or absentee owned, are embedded in local labor markets to which employers and unions must adjust. And both must respond to local governmental functions and regulations, which, in turn, are linked to larger governmental units. Political parties parallel the structure of governments, with organizations at the local, state, and national level. Finally, almost all voluntary associations are built on local units. The range of these groups is very large, and they are often tied to or related to the other four large actors. Their influence in local politics cannot be ignored.

In the United States, these five sectors do not relate to each other in a uniform way at the local, state, national, and international level. The five sectors are briefly described with respect to local community involvement.

THE BIG FIVE POLITICAL ACTORS

Labor

Unions vary in the extent to which their internationals dominate their locals. The typology of unions proposed for this study (craft, industrial, governmental, and service) may vary in systematic ways as we later observe. Some highly centralized internationals (e.g., the Teamsters) exert considerable authority over locals, while others (e.g., the Carpenters) have almost no central control. Still others (e.g., the auto workers) exhibit continuing tension between local and national authorities.

The unions' political arms or PACs display equally diverse patterns. While most AFL-CIO internationals belong to COPE, their participation in local, state, or national politics varies. At one extreme, the UAW operates its political apparatus independently of COPE. Its Community Action Program (CAP) works alone at local and state levels, and coordination with COPE is only nominal at the national level. The Teamsters also retain an independent political arm (DRIVE). Other unions not in the AFL-CIO (e.g., police, firefighters, teachers) operate political organizations that also vary in degree of centralization.

Locals' political obligations to their internationals also vary. Even in highly centralized unions, locals may retain the money they raise for politics and spend it in the community, while locals of highly decentralized unions (like some of the building trades) send all locally raised political funds to their internationals, which may return part or all on request. In sum, the looseness in labor's political organizations gives locals plenty of room to engage in community politics. And as noted later, local officials exploit such looseness to launch community, state, and national initiatives that may be unrelated or even contradictory.

Of course, members of municipal unions readily see the importance of local politics. About 43 percent of government workers were organized in 1990. About 60 percent of them worked for local governments, making up about one-tenth of the local labor force. Along with one or two adult members of their families, they may constitute up to 30 percent of the registered voters, a political force that municipal officeholders cannot ignore. Their wage and other demands involve them directly in local politics. They regularly endorse candidates for local office and campaign to elect them.

All strikes attract community attention. Long strikes, especially by large unions, so adversely affect a local economy that ultimately government and business leaders pressure them to settle the disputes (see Form and Miller 1960, Ch. 4).

Finally, labor participates directly in several local institutions (e.g., school apprentice training programs, mayor's commissions, and United Way), as well as on boards of many community organizations. I know of only one study that systematically canvassed all of the labor and business participants in a community's institutional structure, including its voluntary organizations (Form and Sauer 1963). Labor's extensive organizational network can be activated in local politics. In short, on self-interested grounds alone, labor should be intensively involved in local politics.

Business

In 1986, 80 percent of U.S. employees worked in six million enterprises with fewer than 500 employees. These firms furnished 73 percent of the national payroll (U.S. Bureau of the Census 1990, Table 870). Small and middle-sized firms find it difficult to escape some community involvement. No single organization like the AFL-CIO links these businesses on local, state, and national levels. Although the chamber of commerce resembles COPE, businesses tend to organize along industrial lines and vary in local, state, and national political involvement.

Since all business firms pay local taxes, they are interested in local government, if only in monitoring tax legislation. Even large profitable corporations seek property tax abatement from governments in making locational decisions. While executives of large firms rarely seek local office, they take steps to ensure that politicians will be sympathetic to their business needs (Clelland and Form 1969). In contrast, many small proprietors and professionals seek elective office; few union members do.

Many local businesses seek government contracts. Local government budgets seem small compared to state or federal budgets, but they are not trivial. In 1987, 28 percent of all government revenue was spent by local governments, and 62 percent of the total ($254 billion) was raised locally (U.S. Bureau of the Census, 1990, Table 476). Because much of the revenue ($410 billion in 1987) is spent locally, it is an important source of income for local business. Candidates for local, state, and national offices seek funds for their campaigns from local businesses and therefore maintain contact with them. Finally, more than labor, business is directly involved in local education, government, and a host of voluntary associations (Form and Miller 1960, Chs. 11, 18). With such deep involvement in local politics, labor would be foolish to allow business to completely dominate the local political platform.

Government

Researchers disagree on whether government is a passive instrument of contending interests or an actor with independent interests. Traditionally, Marxists have argued that government is a tool of capital, while mainstream social scientists have argued that it tends to be a neutral broker of competing interest groups. Skocpol and Amenta (1986) and others have asserted a view long held in history and political science that governments have their own interests; officials play roles in policy formation and execution that can be as strong as or stronger than those played by private interest groups.

Gottdiener (1987) and others have proposed a related position called *state managerialism*. Governmental bodies, bureaus, and commissions become involved in some policy issues and avoid others. Sometimes governments advance their interests in cooperation with other groups, sometimes alone. Kweit and Kweit (1990, p. 114) claimed that government bureaucrats have become a new urban political machine that, like a party machine, dispenses benefits under the mask of helping others.

Among the participants in local politics, government officials are most dependent on the community. Firms and unions can move elsewhere. Local governments can expand, contract, merge, or die, but they cannot move. Form (1954) early observed that government, like labor and business, is not a single interest group, but a cluster of organizations with common and special interests. Individual governmental units cooperate, compete, or form alliances with nongovernmental groups to attain their objectives. Like other participants in the political game, government officials have invested their lives in local government, and they seek support from local groups. These investments and relationships need to be empirically explored.

The full range of local government involvement in politics cannot be examined here, but a few illustrations reveal the emptiness of claims that local government is powerless and issueless. Critics who claim that local governments are dependent on state and federal revenue fail to examine how municipalities individually and collectively organize to obtain such funds, mobilizing local business, labor, and citizen groups to pressure state and federal government to provide more revenue for local government. It is naive to assume that local government officials, awaiting handouts, are passive servants of higher powers.

A rich research literature documents how local communities have competed with each other for federal funds for urban renewal, slum clearance, housing, downtown development, affirmative action, crime control, and related projects. This movement, called *creative federalism*, peaked from 1960 to 1968 (Kweit and Kweit 1990, p. 147). It was succeeded by a countermovement, the *new federalism*, which sought to reduce the "dependency" of local government on federal funds. The power of local communities to stem this movement is documented by rising federal and state revenue, albeit at a slower pace. During the new federalism period, from 1976 to 1985, intergovernmental revenue to cities climbed in constant dollars from about $22 to $36 billion (U.S. Bureau of the Census 1986, p. viii). Cutbacks in federal and state funds were not uniform across agencies. Police, firefighting, housing, and other services resisted cutbacks most successfully, demonstrating that intergovernmental bargaining continued despite decreasing rates of state and federal funding.

Research on how local governments attract state and federal funds is replete with disputes about who "really" has the power. For example, Dahl (1961) argued that New Haven's success in attracting more federal funds than other cities was due largely to the efforts of city officials, who sparked a coalition of business and other groups to pressure federal agencies. Domhoff (1978), using Dahl's and other data, concluded instead that this success was due to the efforts of a tight local business elite.

Despite the controversies, several findings emerged from the voluminous research on the topic. In a critical study of 582 cities that applied for federal funds for urban renewal, Aiken and Alford (1970) found that localities varied enormously in the amount and speed of attracting funding. The most successful "applications" came from cities with the widest participation by leaders of business, labor, government, and politics, typically from older cities that measured high on ethnicity, manufacturing, unionization, Democratic vote, voter turnout, and housing needs. City officers had accumulated extensive knowledge and experience on how to coordinate the pressure of diverse local groups. Although these findings are dated because cities change, they underscore the role that city officials play in mobilizing local networks to exert pressure on federal authorities.

Researchers may reasonably ask what resources governmental bodies have to bargain with other groups, resources comparable to the wealth of business and the votes of organized labor. The first, and probably most important, resource is their supervision of agencies that spend vast sums of money. As with business and labor executives, city officials' influence grows with the size and resources of local government. City employees form a pressure group to keep the funds flowing.

Government officials' second resource is their expertise in mobilizing private organizations to press for larger municipal budgets. Contrary to their public rhetoric, many organizations want large, well-financed local governments. Municipal labor unions, such as the Fraternal Order of Police, Firefighters, and AFSCME, want to preserve and extend governmental services. Teachers have an investment in well-financed school systems. Many businesses and unions support higher taxes for street construction, building maintenance, and improved financial, legal, health, and other services. The growth of government budgets has a multiplier effect on employment and business similar to the growth of private-sector employment.

Governmental employee associations (unions and associations of teachers, police, and firefighters), business, and citizen organizations that depend on government have relatively few contacts with one another, but they are symbiotically dependent because they feed from the same trough. Government officials have a unique resource: the opportunity to coordinate symbiotically dependent interests into a coalition to press for more taxes or increased local revenue from state and federal sources. Like old-time political bosses, government officials claim that they help private citizens to achieve the common good.

Government officials' third resource, little recognized, is their professional associations: the National League of Cities, the International City Manager's Association, and the U.S. Conference of Mayors. These associations maintain central offices and staffs and publish journals to inform members of how to maximize the welfare of local governments. They hold national conventions to discuss common problems, and they present research data to legislators on legislation needed to solve city problems. These organizations have considerable influence on federal urban policy, especially when Democrats control the presidency and the Congress (Stokes 1973, p. 254). But even under Republican administrations, the professional associations mobilize a formidable presence that Congress must consult in considering urban legislation.

Finally, only governmental officials can claim that they are disinterested and civic-minded, still important virtues in the United States. To be politically effective, labor cannot ignore the critical importance of local government in the intergovernmental network.

Parties

Downplaying the role of parties in community politics is a mistake. Strong national parties cannot prosper with weak local units. The national Democratic Party was so confident of its strength after World War II that it neglected local units, while the Republican Party rebuilt its local units and began to prosper. Both parties must sustain local incentives to attract and hold volunteers. Local political machines provided incentives in the past, but many scholars maintain that reforms undermined and weakened them.

The reform movement attacked corruption and introduced structural changes in the form of city government, such as the introduction of the city-manager and commission forms, civil service, and nonpartisan and at-large elections. Since only a few commission-type cities survive, the following discussion focuses on manager–council and mayor–council forms. The manager–council form tilts decision-making power toward the manager, thus weakening the mayor and the council. About 35 percent of cities today have this form of local government (Kweit and Kweit 1990, p. 105). Shifting power to the manager does not guarantee that all jobs will be covered by civil service. The proportion varies from city to city. Patronage jobs are still available, and the party still plays a role in filling them. Research has not determined how many patronage jobs are needed to keep a local party viable.

About 55 percent of cities have mayor–council governments, with either a weak or a strong mayor. In the weak type, power is typically decentralized to the council, and the party exerts influence through traditional machines. In the strong-mayor type, where authority and accountability focus on the mayor, party influence is weakened. Yet, compared to the manager–council type, the parties are stronger, the elections are partisan, small wards rather than large districts predominate, and some patronage persists. This pattern is more widespread east of the Mississippi in cities with more blue-collar workers and labor union members (Waste 1989, p. 15).

Wolfinger (1972) early explained why party machines did not disappear with reform movements. Patronage probably expanded during the New Deal, as did government spending and governmental power to regulate, control, and supervise industry. At the same time, the exodus of the affluent to the suburbs left the central cities poorer and poorer, and federal funds poured in to help the cities meet mounting problems. This gave the party a needed niche in locating hundreds of young people for temporary summer jobs on city playgrounds and in federally funded projects. The party could help poor and immigrant groups seeking welfare support to penetrate government bureaucracies. Local businesses that wanted information about state and federal agencies to prepare bids for goods and services consulted party leaders.

The local party is still important in identifying candidates for office in all levels of government. Candidates still need money to win elections. Officeholders still enact legislation that helps party benefactors. The party still provides volunteers with meaningful social involvement in important local activities. And the party still provides a repository of information on voting performance in various city neighborhoods, information that candidates need for campaigning.

In evaluating the importance of parties, scholars may be using criteria that have less significance today than formerly. The reforms that once appealed to middle-class voters may no longer be relevant. Most voters are interested not in direct patronage benefits, but in indirect benefits that emanate from favorable legislation. Party leaders can influence legislative bodies to pass such legislation. Republicans have been more successful than Democrats in helping constituencies identify a relationship between party success, economic ideology, and self-interest.

Ultimately, party viability rests on the persisting importance of local issues. Only the blind do not see the crushing problems of today's cities. The reform movement did not prevent new local issues from arising. A good case can be made that cities are more issue-ridden today than in the past. The reform movement was initiated by business interests to solve local problems as they saw them. But as Waste (1989, pp. 129–45) cogently argued, two related problems emerged after reform: problems brought about by new constituencies entering the political arena and problems arising out of the reforms themselves.

Progressive Era reforms called for at-large electoral districts to reduce the patronage associated with ethnic ward machines. Today, racial and ethnic underrepresentation in local councils and bureaus is defined as discriminatory and calls for the reinstitution of ward representation. Paradoxically, the reforms that undermined ward politics only revived it in another form. Similar reverses are evident in other areas of urban life: the socialization and subsequent privatization of municipal services; the creation of commissions to monitor business, followed by business capture; and so on. To conclude, labor can hardly expect to be influential in party affairs without becoming deeply imbedded in local party politics.

Citizen Groups

Organized citizen groups are brought into community decisions, depending on the issue: residential, educational, religious, racial, ethnic, and others. It would be a mistake to ignore their influence. The literature is replete, for example, with illustrations of middle-class residential groups succeeding in fending off the attempts of business groups to change zoning ordinances, or of racial groups succeeding in demanding a share of city contracts, of religious groups closing businesses which they define as immoral, and so forth. In fact, local governments sometimes encourage local groups to take action in defense of their self-interests. In short, it is a gross error to assume that business, labor, parties, and government always or usually have their way. The matter must be resolved by empirical research.

FIVE GROUPS IN INTERACTION

The interpenetration of public and private spheres in local government has been underresearched. Oddly enough, two otherwise opposing perspectives agree that local politics is diminishing in importance. Traditional historians have argued that the reform movement reduced the influence of local party politics and citizens' interest in it (e.g., Burnham 1982). Because citizens could not influence local government, they became politically apathetic and inactive. Marxists and other "elite" theorists have argued that large business and state and federal governments dominate local government, making it powerless and functionless. Therefore, citizens became uninterested in government and withdrew from politics.

Yet the above review of the behavior of local business, labor, government, parties, and citizen groups revealed that they are still interested in the alleged corpse. Therefore, the continuing involvement of these groups in local politics must be explained by research. Some geographers and political scientists argue that almost all economic and political activity is grounded locally: state and national structures must be built on local geographic units (Cox and Mair 1988), big government and big business dominate changes in local government, and reforms to prevent economic interests from influencing political institutions do not stick (Wolfinger 1972).

Most nonpartisan systems become partisan, at least in part. Mayors create new agencies, appoint members, and exempt them "temporarily" from civil service rules. Unanticipated emergencies call for immediate action, and city administrators are "forced" to waive open bidding on contracts. Police and other municipal employees "endorse" officials who run for office. Racial and ethnic groups demand "their share" of municipal employment. Exceptions to zoning ordinances are made to permit the city to grow. The list is limitless.

Local property taxes do not increase automatically. They are often engineered by government officials with the cooperation of local interest groups. Although education and municipal taxes are separated, the process of funding education is profoundly political. In 1986, 40 percent of $65 billion for public elementary and secondary schools was raised locally (U.S. Bureau of the Census 1990, Table 209). Drives to raise local and state taxes for education have been initiated by employees of school boards and by teachers and their unions.

While the politics of urban growth is widely acknowledged, many researchers have oversimplified class explanations of it (Logan and Molotch 1987, p. 82). No advocate of the urban growth machine thesis has sampled a range of land use and zoning decisions in different types of cities over a period of time and kept track of who won, who lost, and the proportion of wins or losses. Case studies cannot substitute for systematic longitudinal research.

Problems of interpreting evidence are not easily resolved. Simply because business elites press for urban growth does not signify that they have coopted all groups. Other groups may have parallel interests. Feagin and Parker (1989, p. 80) revealed that half of the pension funds of 192 unions was invested in four banks that had real estate interests, and that the local building trades typically supported business plans for downtown development. Yet some unions have opposed the trades when business threatened to build factories that employed nonunion workers.

These illustrations point to a rational self-interest model of politics. The fact that groups cooperate does not necessarily signify that all have been coopted, unless any action that does not oppose business is defined as cooptation. Importantly, researchers rarely keep track of business losses. Empty downtown office buildings, bankruptcies, and deserted downtowns suggest that this is a mistake. Union members do not lose when their officers invest pension funds in profitable banks. When building trades support downtown development, unemployment may decrease as well as taxes. There is no necessary loser. Tax abatement to attract business may subsidize a business just as tariffs on foreign-made automobiles subsidize auto makers and workers, both at public expense. Are increases in low-wage jobs preferable to rising unemployment? Are antipollution and pro-environment coalitions always defeated by pro-growth coalitions? Does a tax abatement for one business increase the taxes on other local businesses? These kinds of questions which remain unanswered call for systematic research.

IMPLICATIONS

I have tried to signal the importance of local politics to business, labor, government, and parties. In this work, the importance of local politics to labor is highlighted. Some labor leaders believe that local politics are unimportant, and that they should invest their resources in state and national campaigns. Others think that local politics matter but do not understand how local, state, and national politics are related. In the above discussion, I have tried to specify the number and importance of the relationships to the main political actors of the community. For labor, they are especially important. Policies set by top AFL-CIO leaders cannot be implemented if they are not transmitted to the locals and their importance explained to the membership. Likewise, if the political ideas at the local level are not communicated to national officials, they lose a feeling for their political base, as Michels emphasized. The flow of political communication upward from the local to the national and the flow from the national to the local are critically important in the formation and implementation of any policy. The absence of information flow or the filtering or distortion of information as it flows up or down the hierarchy is critical in any policy matter, and especially important in the implementation of political policies. In democratic polities, the success of policies ultimately depends on the willingness of the rank and file to follow top leadership. For this reason, this research places heavy emphasis on local politics.

Greenstone (1969) identified three urban patterns of union–party relationships based on an area's industrial, governmental, and political characteristics. In Chapter 2, I showed that these patterns no longer apply because city characteristics have changed. I next examine current union–party relationships in three Ohio cities whose industrial, governmental, and political characteristics vary considerably, probing whether changes in metropolitan organization since the 1960s call for a reinterpretation of labor's place in American politics.

II

Labor Politics in Three Cities

6

Economy, Politics, and Labor in Three Cities

Cincinnati, Cleveland, and Columbus were chosen for study not only because they were accessible but also because they were appropriate for the research problem. Greenstone selected Detroit, Chicago, and Los Angeles because they were large and their patterns of union–party relationships differed. He did not consider the extent to which the relationships might depend on the structure of the metropolitan economy. When Greenstone gathered his data in the early 1960s, the Detroit metropolitan region, a specialized automobile manufacturing center, was the country's fifth largest with almost four million inhabitants. The Chicago area, with six million inhabitants, was second largest. The Los Angeles area, third largest, contained almost six million people. Both Chicago and Los Angeles were world trade cities, centers of vast hinterlands.

No three cities can adequately represent all of the nation's cities in economic, political, and labor–party relationships. Conspicuously absent in Greenstone's and this study are southern cities, where unions are weakly represented. Greenstone's cities were among the nation's largest. The Ohio cities are not as large, but they better represent balanced institutional patterns of national metropolitan areas. Each city represents a different type of regional center, neither national nor subregional in scope (see Noyelle and Stanback 1984, pp. 4, 56). Contrary to popular belief, midwestern cities conform to no single pattern. Cleveland is a diversified center located in the industrial belt that stretches along the Great Lakes. Columbus is a large and prosperous white-collar service center. Cincinnati is in between. For each city, I sketch a brief history of the economy, the governmental and political structure, and the trade union patterns in order to provide a context to interpret the labor politics.

Cleveland, Columbus, and Cincinnati, popularly known as the Three Cs, lie on a diagonal from northeast Ohio to the southwest corner: Cleveland on Lake Erie in the northeast, Cincinnati on the Ohio River to the southwest, and Columbus in the center. Cincinnati's Ohio River location favored early commercial and industrial growth (see Figure 6.1). Its population of almost 300,000 before the turn of the century made it Ohio's largest city until Cleveland overtook it in 1900. Columbus, the state capital, was then only a third their size. By 1950, industrial expansion made Cleveland grow to more than 900,000; Cincinnati approached 500,000; and

Figure 6.1. Congressional Districts (Ohio) of Cleveland, Columbus, and Cincinnati areas.

Columbus, 376,000. But by 1990, Columbus was largest, with a population of 633,00. Cleveland had declined to its 1905 level of 505,000, and Cincinnati, to its World War I level of 364,000.

However, the Standard Metropolitan Statistical Area (SMSA) tells another story because the boundaries of Cincinnati and Cleveland, but not Columbus, were set by 1960. Cleveland's SMSA is still the largest with 2.2 million; Cincinnati's SMSA is 1.5 million, and Columbus's SMSA is 1.3 million (see Table 6.1). By 1990, the Cincinnati and Cleveland SMSAs had more than four times as many people as the central city; the Columbus SMSA had only twice as many.

In sum, by 1990, Columbus was the nation's eighteenth largest city; Cleveland ranked twenty-third; and Cincinnati, forty-fifth. However, Cleveland's SMSA population ranked fourteenth; Cincinnati's SMSA, twenty-third; and Columbus's, twenty-ninth.

CINCINNATI

Although Easterners first settled the area in 1788, Cincinnati did not become a busy river port until the steamboat's arrival in 1811. The growth of the machine industry began with the building of steamboats. The upstate canal system was linked to the Ohio River at Cincinnati in the 1830s, and railroads fanned from the city into Ohio, Kentucky, and Tennessee in the 1840s. Commerce and industry grew rapidly; the city had more than 100,000 inhabitants by 1850 (see Table 6.2). By 1860, the value of Cincinnati's manufactured goods was highest in the nation after New York City and Philadelphia (Boryczka and Cary 1982, p. 38). In 1880, the city became

Table 6.1
Size and Rank of the Three Cs
and Their Metropolitan Areas in 1960 and 1990[a]

	City		Metropolitan area	
	Thousands	Rank	Thousands	Rank
1960				
Cleveland	876	8	1,909	11
Cincinnati	503	21	1.268	17
Columbus	471	28	755	33
1990				
Cleveland	506	23	2,202	14
Cincinnati	364	45	1,526	23
Columbus	633	18	1,345	29

[a]U.S. Bureau of the Census, *Population* (1960, 1990).

Table 6.2
Changes in Population (Pop.), Foreign Born (FB), and Blacks (Bl) for the Three Cs, 1840–1990[a]

	Cincinnati			Cleveland			Columbus		
Year	Pop. (000)	FB %	Bl %	Pop. (000)	FB %	Bl %	Pop. (000)	FB %	Bl %
1840	46		2	6		1	6		9
1850	115	47	3	17		1	18		7
1860	161	46	4	43	45	2	19		5
1870	216	37	6	93	42	1	31	24	6
1880	255	28	8	160	37	1	52	18	6
1890	297	24	4	261	37	1	88	14	6
1900	326	18	4	382	33	2	126	10	7
1910	364	16	5	561	35	2	182	9	7
1920	401	11	8	797	30	4	237	7	9
1930	451	8	11	900	26	8	291	5	11
1940	456	6	12	878	20	10	306	4	12
1950	504	4	16	915	15	16	376	3	12
1960	503	3	22	876	11	29	472	2	16
1970	453	2	27	751	7	38	540	2	18
1980	385	3	34	574	7	44	565	3	22
1990	364	3	38	505	6	47	633	3	23

[a]Sources: U.S. Bureau of the Census, *Population* (1840–1990).

a leading center for the manufacture of clothing, steel, machines, and wagons and for meatpacking. Except for the Great Depression of the 1930s, the city grew about 10 percent a decade until 1950. In 1960, Cincinnati's balanced economy led all cities in the production of machine tools, soaps and detergents, and playing cards. The city was also a leading producer of clothing, chemicals, cosmetics, furniture, building materials, jet engines, organs, and automobile parts (see Table 6.3).

Suburbanization was already well under way in 1880. By the 1960s, the city's population had peaked. An arc of thirty suburbs and satellite cities enclosed it on the north and east and on the south across the Ohio river in Kentucky. Townships west and southeast of the city resisted incorporation (U.S. Bureau of the Census 1960).

The original settlers migrated from south and east down the Ohio River. The earliest immigrants were primarily German, secondarily Irish and British. Later, some migrants came from Italy and eastern Europe. Appalachian whites poured into the city after World Wars I and II. By 1840, 3 percent of the population was black; by 1910, 25 percent; and by 1990, 38 percent.

Table 6.3
Occupational and Industrial Composition of the Three Cs SMSAs, 1960 and 1990 (%)[a]

Occupations	Cincinnati 1960	Cincinnati 1990	Cleveland 1960	Cleveland 1990	Columbus 1960	Columbus 1990
Managerial	8.7	10.3	7.8	14.8	8.9	15.9
Professional/technical	12.5	18.4	12.0	17.8	14.5	18.6
Sales	8.7	12.1	8.6	11.1	8.4	14.7
Administrative/clerical	17.6	20.9	17.5	16.1	19.2	16.5
Private household	2.5	.7	1.9	1.1	2.4	—
Service	9.3	12.0	9.0	12.6	9.7	10.7
Farming	.8	1.1	.3	1.3	.8	.7
Craft	14.5	9.5	16.0	10.9	14.0	9.1
Operatives/transportation	19.9	10.2	21.7	10.5	17.4	8.7
Laborers	5.3	4.8	5.2	3.8	4.6	5.2
Total	100.0	100.0	100.0	100.0	99.9	100.1
Industry Manufacturing	34.9	20.4	27.7	22.2	25.4	14.9
Durable goods	19.7	10.9	18.0	15.1	18.3	9.4
Nondurable goods	15.2	9.5	9.7	7.1	7.1	5.5
Nonmanufacturing	65.1	79.6	72.1	77.8	74.5	84.9
Construction	4.2	4.7	4.1	3.2	4.5	4.3
Transportation, public utilities	7.3	5.3	6.0	4.5	6.0	4.2
Trade—whole./retail	22.2	25.8	21.2	24.8	22.2	26.2
Services	18.4	31.1	28.1	32.6	20.7	32.2
Government	12.9	12.6	12.7	12.6	21.1	18.0
Total	99.9	99.9	99.8	99.9	99.9	99.8

[a]*Monthly Labor Review*, State of Ohio (1960, 1990).

Almost from the time of earliest settlement, the city leaders sought to develop the cultural amenities of large eastern cities: museums, libraries, a first-rate symphony, universities, and good restaurants. By the middle of the nineteenth century, Cincinnati was dubbed "The Queen City of the West." In line with its big-city status, Cincinnati later hosted major-league baseball, football, and basketball teams.

The city's population began to decline in the 1950s. By 1990, it had lost more than a third of its inhabitants. Especially on the east side, many whites moved to the suburbs as blacks moved out from the urban core. A shrinking population and tax base eroded city services. Housing decayed rapidly in areas close to the central business district. Local business leaders then launched a movement to beautify the river front and rebuild the downtown. A park, a baseball stadium, and other facilities were built along the river. Downtown, around Fountain Square, an impressive complex of interconnected office buildings, hotels, shopping centers, banks, and parking ramps was constructed. An aggressive campaign brought much business to a new convention center.

From 1960 to 1990, the SMSA labor force grew by two-thirds. Major employers included Proctor & Gamble (detergents and soap), General Electric (jet engines), and General Motors (automobile parts). However, a national trend in restructuring after the 1960s painfully transformed the local economy. In 1988, GM closed its automobile plant in Norwood, a satellite community surrounded by the city. Other employers cut back or failed, reducing employment by 15 percent, mostly in fabricated metals, machinery, electrical machinery, and automobiles. Employment in nondurable goods manufacturing also declined in all industries except printing, which grew slightly, and chemicals, which expanded notably. Service sector employment increased 12 percent; construction, retail and wholesale trade, and finance grew modestly. These changes increased white-collar employment, especially for professionals, technicians, managers, and sales and clerical workers. The number of semiskilled operatives and transport employees shrank by almost half. The number of craftsworkers declined somewhat less. These reductions, the largest in the city, occurred where union membership had been most heavily concentrated (see Table 6.3).

Government and Politics

Cincinnati has long been a Republican stronghold. Early in the twentieth century, the Republican Cox–Hynicka machine dominated local politics. According to Zane Miller (1968), George Cox's machine, in silent partnership with the Democratic Party, had penetrated business, government, and the courts. Cox eventually lost power but later regained it. Machine politics persisted until the mid-1920s, when reformers convinced the electorate to change the system drastically. Reformers, capturing the city government, instituted the city manager plan (Miller and Tucker 1990, pp. 91–3). They hired a professional manager to administer city departments, installed a merit civil-service system, and instituted a nine-member council elected at-large by nonpartisan proportional representation. The mayor, typically the highest vote-getter, was selected by the council, but his functions were largely ceremonial.

The party system did not disappear. Reformers from both parties organized a Charter Committee (a party) to select candidates for local offices. The weakened Democrats made a tenuous alliance with the Charterites. Essentially, a two-party system emerged: the Charter-Democratic alliance and the Republicans. They continually attacked the system of proportional representation as not representing neighborhood and subcommunity interests. Miller and Tucker (1990) described the events that led to the return of ward representation on the council and the emergence of a three-party system.

In response to Republican charges, the Charterites developed a master plan in 1925 that recognized both local and metropolitan interests. Some slums were cleared, and public housing was constructed during the Great Depression, largely for blacks on the west side (Davis 1991, p. 122). In 1948, a second master plan proposed solutions for both metropolitan and subcommunity problems, including riverfront and downtown redevelopment and slum clearance, public housing, and neighborhood conservation to stanch the hemorrhaging of population to the suburbs. High-speed highways were designed to facilitate intersuburban traffic and central-city access. In the 1960s, the Republican-dominated council implemented the part of the plan dealing with highway and downtown development. The parts calling for urban redevelopment and the preservation of subcommunities that would become self-sufficient in educational, health, recreational, and commercial services were only partially implemented. The resulting controversies deepened neighborhood cleavages and demands for a less centralized political structure.

According to Straetz (1958), Charterites and Republicans traditionally presented voters a balanced ticket with candidates from the main ethnic groups (Germans, "Americans," and Irish), the main religions, a black male, a white woman, and perhaps a labor union member. These groups remained split in their ideas about urban redevelopment, and the council could not resolve its disputes. To stem exodus to the suburbs, city officials urged all neighborhood groups to become more involved in planning and implementing the city plan, which had the unanticipated effect of reviving neighborhood identities along ethnic, class, racial, and religious lines, submerging community and metropolitan concerns.

In 1954, some Democrats decided to revitalize the party by decentralizing organization and decision making to the wards. Ward clubs were reactivated to raise funds and select precinct leaders for the party's central committee, which then chose the party leader and determined party policies. The plan to weaken central party control struck a responsive chord among activists in the black wards and among young liberals in other wards and the suburbs, thereby undermining the coordinating role of the subcommunity councils that the master plan envisioned.

The Republicans finally succeeded in eliminating proportional representation in 1957. The new system retained nonpartisan at-large elections, but now the nine candidates who received the most votes (not one-ninth plus one as in the old system) became the council. Many voters who supported the change feared that proportional representation would ultimately result in the election of a black mayor. The Democratic Party, abandoning its alliance with the Charterites, submitted a separate slate of candidates. Predictably, in this three-party system, embittered relations between Democrats and Charterites permitted Republicans to seize control of the council in the 1960s.

Although Republicans rehabilitated much of the downtown and riverfront areas as described above, they did not succeed in building cohesive subcommunities as envisioned in the master plan. To be sure, some historic downtown areas were preserved: the Union Terminal area on the west side and the Lyle Park and Mount Adams districts on the east side. Federal funds from the Economic Opportunity and Model Cities Acts in the mid-1960s financed some public housing, largely for blacks, in the near west end. However, half of the residential area was converted to other uses, and three-quarters of its original population, both black and white, was dispersed (Davis 1991, Ch. 8). The threat to bulldoze more houses for parking near the Crossley baseball field in the west end precipitated a four-day race riot in the black ghetto near the city center in 1967. Neighborhood politics had mobilized both whites and blacks, stalling the implementation of a coherent plan for urban development.

In 1969, capitalizing on discontent with the Republicans for favoring downtown development over neighborhood interests, Charterites and Democrats successfully renewed their coalition and dominated the council from 1973 to 1985. However, the Republicans maintained their grip on the county government. Since the Democrats could not elect a council majority by themselves, they and the Charterites annually alternated in naming the mayor. During this alliance, two black Charterite mayors were appointed: Kenneth Blackwell and Ted Berry. But none of the three parties could develop a coherent program, nor could they discipline their candidates, who increasingly built their own electoral organizations. Unendorsed Democrats ran as Independents, Charles Luken ran as an Independent Democrat, and the Charterites even endorsed some Republicans for county contests. Yet the coalition and the Republicans remained more-or-less united in their efforts to develop the downtown and rehabilitate some neighborhoods.

The city's shrinking tax base exacerbated conflict over the distribution of expenditures. Neighborhood and other groups forged separate alliances to get what they could. In the 1985 election, the poor Over-the-Rhine area north of the city center and the heavily white, lower-middle-class Catholic areas in the western hills mobilized against what they perceived as threats to local control. The election resulted in an all-male council evenly split between the two parties and one Charterite. Unable to agree on a mayor, three Republicans and two Democrats formed a "conservative coalition" to support the interests of the Over-the-Rhine and western hills districts. They selected "Democrat" Charles Luken, son of Tom Luken, as mayor. The conservatives opposed gay rights, abortion, and pornography. While they tried to rehabilitate areas of the city, shrinking federal grants and conflicts between tenants, property owners, and planners stalled the work (Davis 1991, Ch. 10). The disarray of the Democratic party continued, and the council was unable to shape a majority coalition after the following election. The feuding led to a separation of the city and the county party organizations. Later, two leaders were named cochairs of the county party. Regional planning declined as neighborhoods and suburbs continued to press for their special interests (Miller and Tucker 1990, pp. 101–4).

By 1991, the Democratic Party had partly repaired itself. It appointed the popular Tom Luken, former member of Congress, to head the party. He organized a vigorous campaign. For the first time, Democrats won a majority of city council seats while the Charterites elected two council members and the Republicans only one. After a wait of fifty years, the Democrats elected their first county auditor. Surprisingly, the two blacks who had been previously appointed to fill council vacancies were elected.

In 1987, the voters approved a referendum that the mayor would be the council candidate who garnered the most votes. In 1992, Dwight Tillery received the most votes and became the first elected black mayor of Cincinnati. In the same election, the citizens approved a referendum that limited council members to four terms. A number of council members soon decided to run for other public offices. They resigned and were replaced by appointed members. In a year, five vacancies called for the appointment of new members, leading one observer to conclude that council was playing "musical chairs."

In this turbulent environment, the parties experience difficulties making policy and disciplining members. Unless these weaknesses are overcome, Cincinnati may experience the end of local party politics, the aim that the Charterites have sought to achieve since the 1920s. Yet nobody seems happy with the status quo. Even though party politics remains strong on the county, state, and national levels, party loyalty seems to be weakening.

Labor in the Queen City

The first trade union in Ohio, the Typographical Society, was established in Cincinnati in 1825; and the first citywide labor association, in 1836. The association perished in the depression that followed but was revived in 1843 (Boryczka and Cary 1982, pp. 17–18). In the 1840s, unions were organized in response to specific crises. They sponsored some successful strikes, then weakened or disappeared. Rapid industrialization in the 1850s stimulated union militancy, especially in the skilled trades. Although strikes erupted almost weekly (Boryczka and Cary 1982, p. 73), the union movement almost disappeared in the depression of 1857–1858. During the Civil War, several locals combined to form a General Trades Assembly. They won some important strikes but could not survive the depression of 1873–1878.

A string of riots ignited during the 1870s, sparked by racial, religious, nativist, and labor disputes. National media dubbed Cincinnati the "Queen City of Mobs." In the 1880s, the Knights of Labor grew rapidly in Ohio, especially in Cincinnati. In 1884, the Great Cincinnati Riot erupted, allegedly led by workers to protest massive political corruption. This hardened the city's image as mob-ridden. In 1886, 18,000 workers, 20 percent of the workforce, took part in a failed strike for an eight-hour day. The skilled trades demanded that the Knights change their program and tactics. Differences proved irreconcilable, and the trades decided to disaffiliate. With skilled trades from other cities, they met in Columbus on December 10, 1886, and created the American Federation of Labor, which eventually replaced the Knights (Boryczka and Cary 1982, pp. 127–8).

The next year, the United Labor Party held its convention in Cincinnati. Craft, building, and manufacturing locals united to form one of the strongest branches of the party in the country. It fought a local coalition of Republicans and Democrats to capture several seats on the city council and the board of education. Although the party died two years later, a strong socialist party emerged with the growing union movement during World War I. The ensuing depression and postwar red scares weakened both the party and the union movement.

Under the protection of New Deal legislation, Cincinnati unions began to prosper in the late 1930s and 1940s. Although unions organized more rapidly in the state's larger auto and steel centers, Cincinnati's UAW and USW locals became the city's largest. Several other industries were successfully unionized, but labor was never able to organize Proctor & Gamble, the city's largest employer. Except for the very active role that Cincinnati unions played in defeating the 1952 right-to-work referendum in Ohio, they remained rather complacent thereafter.

As elsewhere, union membership in the city declined rapidly during the 1970s and 1980s. When GM closed its Norwood plant in 1988, the UAW lost its local preeminence. However, the American Federation of Teachers (AFT) retained representation rights in the school system, and AFSCME gained strength after 1983, when the Democratic legislature enacted laws permitting government workers to organize. The communication workers (CWA) and steelworkers (USW) began to organize other industries to recoup membership losses, while the service (SEIU) and food (UFCW) workers gained members with the expansion of the service sector. In 1990, leaders of the AFL-CIO Central Labor Council decided to take a more active role in rebuilding the Democratic Party, an experiment examined later in detail. In short, the history of labor in Cincinnati showed that it was capable of resurgence and of importantly influencing the politics of an essentially conservative community.

CLEVELAND

Cleveland, situated on Lake Erie at the mouth of the Cuyahoga river, was platted in 1796. It grew very slowly until 1825, when the Erie Canal opened a water route east to the Atlantic. When the canal system linked Lake Erie to the Ohio River in 1830, Cleveland had only 6,000 inhabitants, compared to Cincinnati's 46,000 (see Figure 6.1). But after 1855, when the Soo Canal linked Lakes Michigan and Superior to Huron and Erie, Cleveland's population more than doubled for four consecutive decades, reaching almost 100,000 in 1870. By 1900, its population of 382,000 made it the state's largest city, surpassing Cincinnati. In 1930, Cleveland's population peaked at 900,000 but then declined about 10,000 people a year to 505,000 in 1990, about 56 percent of its 1930s peak.

Cleveland's boundaries were fixed by 1950, when the city was surrounded by a circle of suburbs and satellite cities. In 1990, the SMSA reached almost two million, over twice the city's peak population in 1930. The regional economy now embraces four populous counties (U.S. Bureau of the Census 1960, 1970, 1980).

Cleveland's early growth was largely commercial because its water transportation system linked Great Lakes shipping to eastern and midwestern canal systems. Later, the city became an important hub in the national railroad system. As a water transfer point for lumber, copper, and iron ore, and as a rail hub for oil, farm products, and coal, the city inevitably became a major industrial center. The Civil War stimulated the growth of iron, machine, and chemical manufacturing. The first openhearth steel furnace was built in Cleveland; there J. D. Rockefeller built the largest oil refinery in the world (Barloon 1987, pp. 360–2).

Although the Great Depression slowed industrial growth, World War II unleashed an unparalleled burst of productivity that continued until the 1960s. Manufacturing was diversified, including steel and aluminum production, machine tools, hardware, vehicles, petrochemicals, electronics, and airplane parts. The city became headquarters for four hundred medical and industrial research centers. In addition, more than a dozen universities and colleges located in the area, and the city hosted major league teams in baseball, football, and basketball. Benefactors gave the city an impressive array of cultural facilities, including a fine symphony orchestra, a ballet company, museums, and libraries. Before World War II, construction began on an impressive mall that would link the city center to the lakefront and to a campus of universities, museums, and cultural institutions. Despite some signs of urban decay, boosters felt that the city would continue to grow in greatness.

Almost from its first settlement, Cleveland was a magnet for European immigrants. In 1860, just before the Civil War, 61 percent of the workforce was foreign-born, mostly British, German, and Irish. A second immigrant wave, mainly from eastern but also from southern Europe, arrived late in the nineteenth and early in the twentieth centuries. As late as the 1930s, more than a third of the labor force was foreign-born, and more than a third were children of one or two foreign-born parents. After World War I, immigration slowed, but it accelerated after World War II, especially from Eastern Eruope (see Table 6.2).

African Americans made up less than 5 percent of the city's population up to 1925. The Great Depression and World War II attracted blacks to the city as European ethnics vacated low-skill jobs and climbed the occupational ladder. In 1950, blacks made up 16 percent of the population, increasing almost 1 percent a year until 1990, when they made up almost half. Ethnicity and race have always been important in civic and union affairs.

After World War II, the area's economy, population, and politics changed rapidly. Although the metropolitan labor force grew 25 percent from 1960 to 1990, manufacturing employment slipped more than 15 percent (see Table 6.2). Over four-fifths of the decline occurred in the durable-goods sector: metal production and fabrication, including vehicles, machinery, and electronic equipment. No gains occurred in construction, transportation, wholesale trade, and government, but small gains appeared in retail trade and finance. The largest gains were in services: lodging, business, recreation, and health, expanding the nonmanual labor force from 46 to 60 percent. The number of managers almost doubled, that of professional-technical workers grew by 50 percent, and that of sales workers increased substantially; the number of clerical workers declined slightly.

These changes devastated blue-collar employment, especially after 1970. Craftsworkers, typically the last to be released in hard times, shrank from 16 to 7 percent of the labor force, while operatives declined from 22 to 11 percent. These industrial and occupational shifts were more severe in the city. Industrial union membership fell drastically, as did the wages of ex-manufacturing workers.

Although Cleveland's economy appeared robust up to 1970, it had showed signs of deterioration by 1955. The Cuyahoga River roughly stratifies the city economically. The central business district and adjacent industrial areas lie east of the river, and the more affluent area, to the west. Influential business organizations have traditionally favored the west side and have allowed the east side to deteriorate.

Richardson (1987) traced this economic divide back to the beginning of the century. During the economic boom of the 1920s, east–west strains eased, but the Great Depression revived them. The influx of African Americans into segregated eastern neighborhoods led to overcrowding, housing deterioration, and erosion of city services. The city experienced difficulty in raising taxes or obtaining approval of bonds to make improvements. Operational deficits were common. World War II and the Korean War temporarily restored prosperity. From 1920 to the late 1950s, the suburbs repeatedly rejected referenda for a regional government. Many observers warned that the city's housing stock, its downtown, and its services were deteriorating, but government and business leaders were slow to attack the problems.

From 1950 on, Cleveland's finances and city services deteriorated more rapidly. Although the city built highways to facilitate suburban access to the city center and movement around the suburban ring, displaced families increased housing congestion and deterioration, especially in the black ghettos. The exodus of more than 300,000 inhabitants to the suburbs in the late 1970s and the departure or closing of manufacturing firms depressed tax revenues. The central shopping district decayed as suburban malls flourished. Although a bond issue was passed in 1957 to improve the port's access to St. Lawrence and Atlantic commerce, improvements in the decaying east side were delayed. Federal urban renewal and housing grants were insufficient to brake the deterioration of housing, schools, and city services.

In 1967, a week of rioting, fires, and vandalism broke out in the overcrowded Hough district. Large losses in life and property brought a call for action. Carl B. Stokes, the young African-American mayor, instituted some reforms. In 1972, the state backed a city bond issue to raise revenue; federal revenue-sharing money poured into the city's coffers. However, as long as the city's revenue structure remained unchanged, not enough could be done to visibly improve the city's depressed and unkempt appearance. In the 1977 local election, tax abatement for downtown business development was approved, even as the deterioration of nearby neighborhoods continued unabated. The crisis came to a head in 1978, when the city defaulted on its debts and lost its favorable bond rating. The city-owned electric power company could not pay its debt to a private utility. Voters finally passed a measure to increase city income taxes by 50 percent, temporarily easing the fiscal crisis.

In 1979, Republican mayor George Voinovich began to reshape the city's financial structure, reorganizing city offices and reducing expenses. A tax referendum was passed that enabled the city to reduce its debt and make capital improvements. In the following year, banks agreed to refinance city debts. In 1983, the city's improved financial situation permitted it to reenter the national bond market (Campbell 1990, p. 129). However, the unemployment rate still hovered around 15 percent, twice the national rate, and the educational system continued to erode, although signs of improvement began to appear.

In the late 1980s, business and civic leaders launched their plan to rebuild the city center. The Mid-Town corridor restored a deteriorated fifty-block area with attractive commercial and industrial establishments. The bleak industrial flats on the near west side and the warehouse area were transformed into an attractive shopping, office, and residential district. The inner harbor area was rebuilt with recreational facilities, new hotels, office buildings, and convention facilities. Local foundations, universities, and the city cooperated in improving nearby neighborhoods. New industries began to move into the area. Cleveland, looking up, began to have a new look (Campbell 1990, pp. 130–1).

Politics and Government

Before the Civil War, Democrats and Whigs had equal success in governing the city. After the war, the Republican Party dominated local politics until 1900. Then the Democrats gained dominance until World War I, but Republicans were able to elect the mayor until 1941. In 1920, the Real Estate Board and the Citizen's League convinced voters to adopt the city manager plan. Both parties managed to circumvent it, and the Republicans still maintained their grip on the mayor's office. The Democratic Party remained deeply divided, but in 1940, the popular Ray T. Miller managed to unite ethnics and blacks behind the party, which was able to control city government through the 1950s. However, suburbanization continued to weaken both parties and internal struggles in the Democratic Party festered (WRHS 1987).

Traditionally, mayors from both parties were Protestant businessmen or professional men of British or German ancestry. Not until 1941, when Democrat Frank J. Lausche was elected mayor, did a descendant of more recent (Slovenian) immigrants win a top political office (Campbell 1990, p. 109). However, as early as 1920, the city council began to change in ethnic composition. A few council members from new immigrant backgrounds, as well as blacks, were elected. By 1930, the council's ethnic composition matched that of the wards (Richardson 1987, p. 775). Lausche operated outside the Democratic Party organization throughout his political life. When he became governor of Ohio in 1945, Thomas L. Burke, an Irish-American Democrat, defeated his Republican rival to become mayor for eight years. Burke built a freeway system into and around the city, but his administration neglected the central-city housing crisis.

In 1953, Anthony Celebrezze, an Italian-American, won the mayor's race as an Independent Democrat and remained in office for four terms. He worked effectively with the white ethnics on the council. His administration improved the harbor facilities and attracted $140 million in federal grants to improve housing in four predominantly black neighborhoods. However, these efforts could hardly keep up with the housing and educational deterioration caused by the swelling influx of blacks and Appalachians. Blacks protested this state of affairs but could do little about it (Campbell 1990, p. 112).

When Celebrezze left Cleveland in 1962 to become a cabinet secretary in Washington, Ralph Locher, a Rumanian of Swiss-Austrian parents, was named mayor. He was elected mayor in the following year with strong white ethnic support. Although he expanded seaport and airport facilities and mediated a struggle within the plumbers' union over admitting black apprentices, blacks turned against him because they felt he had not improved their employment opportunities, housing, and educational facilities. By this time, blacks were more than a third of the population, the largest single constituency. But they did not gain an equitable share of power in the council or the party. The Hough riots of 1967 galvanized them into political action.

Carl B. Stokes, an African-American legislator, had earlier run for mayor as an Independent Democrat and was defeated. When he challenged Locher in the 1967 primary, he had the backing of the business community, middle-class liberals, blacks, and funds that Congress of Racial Equality (CORE) had received from the Ford Foundation. Although Stokes did not have organized labor's support in the primary (Weinberg 1968, p. 131), he overwhelmed Locher. In the regular election, he received AFL-CIO endorsement but little material support except from the Teamsters (Nelson and Merano 1977). He narrowly defeated his opponent to become the first black mayor of a major American city. Stokes managed to release HUD (Housing and Urban Development) funds that had been frozen during Locher's regime, and he raised city income taxes. He also improved blacks' access to city employment, education, and welfare, as well as street repair and water purity. The Glenville "shoot-out" in 1968 was a tragic confrontation between black militants and police that ended in seven deaths. In the aftermath, Stokes was unable to raise city taxes again or pass critically needed legislation. Although he was narrowly reelected in his 1969 campaign against Republican Ralph Perk, he and the council engaged in seemingly endless battles in the face of mounting problems (Campbell 1990, p. 121).

Disillusioned by lack of party support, Stokes organized the Twenty-first District Caucus in 1970 independent of the Democratic Party. His brother Louis was the member of Congress from the district, and Carl named him chair of the caucus (Stokes 1973, p. 243). The caucus successfully fought the party and dominated it in the primaries and in local and state elections.

Stokes decided not to seek a third term as mayor in 1973. Ralph Perk, the Republican who had become the representative of white ethnics, ran for mayor. Stokes inadvertently split African Americans and Democrats by backing both an Independent Democrat who had skipped the primary and the candidate who won the Democratic primary. In the three-way contest, Perk was elected the first Republican mayor in over thirty years. He managed to cool racial strife and still retain white ethnic loyalty. By transferring some utilities to the county and borrowing funds, he postponed a financial crisis. He won two terms as mayor. The Democratic Party was in disarray, with the Twenty-First District Caucus exercising its independence and with turnovers of party chairpersons. Perk was confident of winning another term in 1977. He entered a nonpartisan primary and was defeated by an Independent Democrat, Dennis Kucinich. The new mayor rapidly alienated a number of groups. His feisty style, his inability to work with the police union, and his failure to confront neighborhood issues led to a recall vote, which was narrowly defeated.

Yet Kucinich decided to run for reelection in 1979 because he was certain that he had ethnic support and the backing of Stokes and the black community. The Republicans selected George Voinovich to run for mayor. An experienced campaigner, he attracted widespread ethnic, business, and labor backing. While Kucinich garnered 45 percent of the African-American vote, he lost the solid support of white ethnics. Voinovich was elected by a clear majority (Campbell 1990, p. 128). Quickly reordering Cleveland's affairs, he successfully ran for office twice more, again with labor and business support. In 1981, the council's size was reduced from thirty-three to twenty-one. After ten years in office, Voinovich successfully ran for governor of Ohio, this time without labor support (see Chapter 11).

Meanwhile, ex-School Board President Arnold Pickney, Congressman

Louis Stokes, and Council President George Forbes struggled to control the Twenty-First District Caucus and the Democratic Party. In the tangled political situation, Forbes attracted business support to build his machine in the African-American community. He backed Republican Voinovich for mayor and convinced many blacks to support him. As Forbes distanced himself from the black community and alienated many whites, Michael White, a sophisticated black politician, entered the race for mayor as a Democrat in 1990. With the support of the newspapers, business, blacks, and some labor unions, he was elected. Although blacks constituted the majority in ten of the city's twenty-one wards, they still lacked the unity they had had under Carl Stokes and could not control the Democratic Party.

Briefly, the Republicans had elected the mayor for twenty-five years up to 1940; the Democrats, for the next thirty years to 1970. Both have occupied the office about equally since then. During its somewhat longer dominance of the council, the Democratic Party has been as often fractured as united. Independent Democrats have been more successful than party faithfuls in getting elected. On the other hand, the Republican Party seems to have been more united but less appealing to voters. The role of labor during this period will be examined later, but it, too, appears to have been as split politically as the Democratic Party.

Organized Labor

Harrison's (1987, pp. 604–6) brief overview of labor in Cleveland notes that several unions were founded before the Civil War but few survived. In the postwar period, turbulent strikes were not uncommon, but they typically failed. Ten unions banded together in 1873 to form the Industrial Council of Cuyahoga County. A violent strike against Standard Oil launched by the coopers' union in 1877 became a general strike which lasted three days. It was finally broken by the National Guard cavalry summoned by the governor. Another large strike flared in 1882 at the Cleveland Rolling Mills. Management broke it by hiring Polish and Bohemian immigrants as scabs. However, the union movement continued to gain strength and won between 70 and 80 percent of its strikes between 1881 and 1886, when the Knights of Labor launched a major membership drive.

The AFL craft unions challenged the Knights, and by 1900, the AFL had become the dominant labor organization. Employers resisted union growth by recruiting workers from the large and readily available immigrant population. However, the prosperity initiated by World War I stimulated union growth and the acceptance of black members. Soon after the war, the AFL tried to organize the steel industry, but employers broke the bitterly contested strike. In a counterattack, the employers then launched the American Plan Association (APA) to promote the open shop. Although the APA was largely successful, a few strong craft unions managed to survive through the Great Depression.

When the Democrats captured control of the Congress in 1932 and passed protective labor legislation, Cleveland's union membership soared (Boryczka and Cary 1982, pp. 203–10). Reflecting the national pattern, AFL unions fought CIO growth. The CIO expanded much more rapidly than the AFL in the mass-production industries of steel, automobile, chemicals, rubber, and oil. A pattern of internal labor strife was set.

The 1936 sit-down strike of auto workers at Cleveland's Fisher Body plant sparked sit downs at Flint's GM plants and in the Akron rubber factories. In 1937, the Steel Workers Organizing Committee (SWOC) launched a long and bitter strike at Little Steel, which the employers finally broke with the help of the National Guard. Also in 1937, the AFL and the CIO violently confronted one another in organizing the garment industry. The state ordered mounted police to make a path for AFL workers to break the strike of the CIO's International Garment Workers' Union (IGWU). CIO sympathizers, mainly from the UAW and the SWOC, entered the fray to support the IGWU. In the end, the IGWU won recognition in two of the four plants.

While turbulent union–management relations and interunion tensions eased during World War II, immediately thereafter CIO unions were torn by ideological strife. Mounting tensions between the United States and the USSR spilled over into union affairs. Communists had played an important role in organizing the CIO unions and held important union offices. Many Catholic union members and workers of eastern European ancestry united to expel communists from the labor movement, urging the Cleveland Industrial Council to repudiate endorsements of alleged communist candidates for the school board and other offices. The unions split again in 1948 over endorsing Harry Truman or Henry Wallace as Democratic candidates for the presidency. Where communist leaders could not be dislodged from office, as in the United Electrical Workers (UE) and the Mine, Mill, and Smelter's Union, the CIO expelled them and then began a drive, largely successful, to replace them with new CIO unions. Internal labor strife subsided for two decades.

Three important trends radically transformed the union scene in the 1970s and 1980s. First, many union members moved to the suburbs and satellite cities such as Parma and Garfield Heights. Cuyahoga County COPE experienced increasing difficulty in accommodating the diverse political concerns of Cleveland and suburban members. Large suburban locals contested city locals' dominance of COPE. Second, the civil rights movement and federal legislation mandating equal opportunity for blacks and women forced recalcitrant ex-AFL unions to accept them as members and officers. Ex-CIO unions experienced similar problems to a lesser degree. As African Americans became labor's largest minority, racial and ethnic antagonisms of the wider community spilled over into union affairs, including COPE's relations with the Democratic Party. Third, union membership declined somewhat faster in ex-CIO than in ex-AFL unions, while public-sector and service unions grew, altering the political balance among the major unions. In short, Cleveland's tumultuous labor history paralleled many of the conflicts of the Democratic Party.

COLUMBUS

Ohio became a state in 1803, and Columbus, in Franklin County, was chosen as capital in 1812 because of its central location. When the governor arrived in 1816, the town had 700 inhabitants. It had only 2,000 by 1830, when it was linked to the canal from Cleveland to Portsmouth on the Ohio River (see Figure 6.1). When the railroads reached Columbus in 1850, its population of 18,000 was about the same as Cleveland's but much smaller than Cincinnati's 115,000. During the Civil War, Columbus became a major Union Army headquarters, a military training center, and the site of a prison for Confederate soldiers. As a junction of five railroads, the city became a commercial center of a rich agricultural region. Ohio State University was established at the city's edge in 1870. Manufacturing began to expand as the city tapped the coal and iron ore resources of southeast Ohio (Hunker 1958, p. 39). By 1890, Columbus had developed robust carriage, foundry, and shoe industries. Using assembly-line techniques, 1,000 employees turned out one carriage every eight minutes. The rolling mills daily produced over one hundred tons of steel rails. In 1900, the city's population of 125,000 made it the state's third largest but still one-third Cleveland's and Cincinnati's size (Foster 1990, pp. 8–12).

World War I had little impact on manufacturing, but the postwar boom expanded the city's commercial and governmental sectors. By 1930, Columbus's balanced economy enabled its 300,000 inhabitants to weather the Great Depression somewhat better than most cities. During World War II, the federal government located a Curtis-Wright airplane factory locally, which employed 25,000 workers. After the war, other manufacturers were attracted to Columbus because they could hire qualified workers released from declining aircraft production (Hunker 1958, p. 58). Durable-goods manufacturing expanded as new plants were built by General Motors,

Westinghouse, Timken Roller Bearing, and Lustron. Columbus also became the headquarters of several large banks, insurance companies, and fast-food chains (e.g., Bank One, Nationwide Insurance, Bordens, Wendy's, White Castle, and Rax Restaurants). By 1965, the city's population of half a million had overtaken Cincinnati's but lagged behind Cleveland's.

Like other midwestern cities, Columbus suffered a relative decline in manufacturing from 1960 to 1990, but unlike theirs, its unemployment remained low because educational, governmental, and business services expanded rapidly. Thus, the area suffered little from deindustrialization. By 1985, the city's population surpassed Cleveland's. Clerical, technical, and professional workers in information- and computer-dependent enterprises were attracted by Columbus employers such as the State of Ohio, Ohio State University, seven major insurance companies, Chemical Abstracts, Batelle Research Institute, the Defense Construction Center, AT & T Network Systems, and CompuServe. In 1990, no manufacturing firm was among the area's twenty largest employers.

After 1960, the Columbus population grew because, in 1955, the city made annexation a precondition for providing city water and sewage. Unlike its sister cities, Columbus grew to surround most of its 1960 suburbs. In less than twenty-five years, the Columbus SMSA labor force grew 2.2 times compared to 0.6 for Cincinnati and 0.2 for Cleveland. While all three SMSAs suffered a percentage loss in manufacturing, Columbus actually gained 22,400 manufacturing employees, Cincinnati lost 6,600, and Cleveland lost 88,300 (U.S. Department of Labor 1965–1988). From 1965 to 1988, manufacturing employment in the Columbus SMSA fell from about 25 to 15 percent of the labor force (see Table 6.3), mostly in fabricated metals and machinery. Increases occurred primarily in professional services and secondarily in trade, finance, insurance, and real estate. The proportion in government employment actually fell 3 percent.

From 1960 to 1990, the number of manual workers in the Columbus SMSA fell from more than a third to less than a quarter of the labor force, while the number of white-collar workers rose proportionately. Almost a fifth of all workers were managers, professionals, and technicians in 1960; by 1990, they made up more than a third. Sales and clerical workers increased their proportions slightly, while the members of craft and operative workers declined somewhat more (see Table 6.3).

Columbus always had a smaller percentage of foreign-born inhabitants than its sister cities. At the Civil War, almost half of Cleveland and Cincinnati residents were foreign-born, compared to perhaps a quarter in Columbus (Table 6.2), a disparity that has persisted. After World War II, Columbus attracted many Appalachians to work in the manufacturing sector. Today, the ethnic mix is predominantly British and secondarily

German. Up to 1940, Columbus had relatively more African-American residents than its sister cities. After World War II, blacks increased more rapidly in Cleveland and Cincinnati (Table 6.2). Today, almost a quarter of Columbus residents are blacks, compared to a third in Cincinnati and half in Cleveland. The Columbus figure would be higher except for the continuing annexation of predominantly white areas. A tenth of the Columbus SMSA is black, compared to a fifth in Cincinnati and Cleveland.

Government and Politics

Columbus became a Republican stronghold after the Civil War, and only five Democrats were elected mayor thereafter (Egger 1975). The first was George Peters, a lawyer, elected in 1881 along with a black councilman. Then, in 1887, Philip Bruch, a druggist, was elected. In 1907, another lawyer, Dewitt Badger, became the Democratic mayor. In 1914, citizens voted to abandon ward representation for the council and instituted a nonpartisan ballot with at-large representation. Predictably, voting dropped sharply in the lower-income wards (Martin 1991), and Republicans retained dominance.

In 1932, in the midst of the Great Depression, Henry Worley, a liberal Democrat, a carpenter, and organmaker, was elected mayor. His liberalism angered Republicans, who rallied to defeat him roundly in 1936 just as Democratic strength was peaking nationally in support of Roosevelt and the New Deal. Republicans maintained control until 1954, when Democrat M. E. Sensenbrenner became mayor. A moderate with wide business, labor, black, and newspaper support, he was reelected until 1959. After a four-year absence, he became mayor again from 1964 to 1972, when Republican Tom Moody defeated him.

Sensenbrenner held the post longer than any other mayor. His administration was responsible for the successful annexation policy of city growth. No Democratic mayor has been elected since Sensenbrenner, although Democrats have dominated the council for more than 25 years. A Democrat held the congressional seat from 1931 to 1939, but Republicans have held it for the last half-century.

Today, both mayor and council agree that urban growth and development are their primary concern, followed by education, crime, and neighborhood services. Most of the issues are tinged variously with a racial dimension. An analysis of newspaper reports since the Sensenbrenner era shows that while urban development has not been disputed, disagreements have arisen on how to finance it. Most groups want Columbus to grow and become as visible nationally as Cleveland, Cincinnati, Indianapolis, Pittsburgh, or St. Louis. All groups want big-city amenities:

major league athletic teams, sports arenas, up-scale shopping centers, ethnic restaurants, gentrified neighborhoods, an airport hub, an outstanding symphony orchestra, an opera company, a ballet corps, and a convention center.

Citizens point with pride to city progress, stressing that Columbus is not only larger than Cleveland and Cincinnati but also has a more pleasant ambience. They concede that Columbus's wealthy families have not been as generous in supporting cultural amenities. Therefore, the city must attract business, industry, and residents to provide the income to increase amenities and make the city more nationally visible. Jerry Hammond, a black council member for 16 years and an outspoken critic of Republican mayors, addressed the Columbus Metropolitan Club on his appointment to a state government office: "All city issues lead back to growth policies and the leadership provided by the mayor."

The city has worked closely with the chamber of commerce to promote downtown growth and attract new business. A perusal of newspaper files over 20 years reveals that the city has steadily supported downtown development. Thus, it bought land for a downtown mall, Capital Square South, and lent it to a development corporation for five years. The city then paid $1.5 million to relocate utilities for the mall. A bed tax on hotels and motels was levied to provide $2 million for the Columbus Convention and Business Bureau. The city provided $13.4 million to improve the Convention Center. Nationwide Insurance paid $20 million to beautify the site of the new Convention Center in exchange for paying no real estate taxes for 20 years. A $7.1 million project to build a freeway from the city center to the airport was proposed and later passed. A $29.5-million bond referendum was authorized, but defeated, to build a downtown indoor sports arena; $4 million was appropriated to improve the Brewery District near the downtown center; and $25,000 was appropriated to maintain the brick streets nearby in gentrified German Village. The city gave $750,000 to the sponsors of Son of Heaven, a Chinese art exhibit, to make up for its losses. The exhibit was held in the vacated Central High School located on an 18-acre plot downtown by the Scioto River. The board of education later sold the property to the city for $13.5 million, an alleged bargain. It may become the new site of the Art Museum or the Science and Industry Center. Ford Dealers asked the council for $200,000 (not approved) to continue the annual Columbus 500 auto race through the downtown city streets.

The city offered tax abatements to attract new business and support the expansion of local business. The council approved a $9.5-million tax abatement for LTV Steel and Sumitomo Metal Industries of Japan, an offer that was not accepted. The city debated spending $5.5 million to provide road access to a new $2-billion northside shopping center. The area was not annexed, and the offer was withdrawn. The council first considered offering The Limited Corporation a tax exemption of $19.4 million for its local expansion and later approved a smaller exemption. Bank One was offered a tax abatement to build another facility in the area.

The city spent undetermined sums for an international floral exhibit (Ameriflora) to celebrate the five hundredth anniversary of the discovery of America. A newspaper publisher later covered part of the debt. A proposal offering new home builders a tax abatement was roundly defeated, but the city offered firms inducements to gentrify German Village, Victorian Village, and the Brewery District near the central city. While Democrats, both white and black, were more inclined than Republicans to limit these ventures, a biparty council majority generally approved of them.

The seven-person council has been divided on racial issues. From 1975 to 1992, blacks typically held two seats. As the majority, the Democrats normally selected the council president, who appointed committee chairs. Yet developers often gave to the campaigns of the mayor, who appointed the chair of the zoning commission, who was usually a Republican. Blacks concentrated on the community services committee, which dispensed local funds, federal grants-in-aid, and patronage. Jerry Hammond and Ben Espey, two recent black council members, kept race issues alive before the council.

Hammond's legal right to sit on the council was challenged because he had committed a felony in his youth. When he came to his first council meeting, 2,000 blacks appeared at city hall to demonstrate support. Hammond quickly became an influential member. He sponsored an ordinance requiring the city to grant 10 percent of its contracts to minority-owned businesses. The council resolved to do no business with banks that had South African connections. The mayor was asked to investigate cases of alleged police brutality against blacks. As council president, Hammond appointed a Democrat to chair the zoning committee, and he chaired the community services department himself.

The city has been heavily committed to community services. In 1988, it subsidized thirty-eight social service agencies that provided job training, medical, legal, and health services to the poor, mostly blacks. The council annually appropriated almost $2 million for six neighborhood health centers and matched federal funds for housing, job training, and crime control. In 1987, the city gave the health department $500,000 to fight AIDS and an equal amount to the shelter board to house the homeless. In 1990, $400,000 was appropriated for antidrug and antialcohol programs.

Black council members constantly reminded the city that the fire and police departments were not recruiting African Americans in proportion to their local number. A $150,000 fund was appropriated to recruit blacks over a two-year period. The examining board was asked to change its written examination standards for blacks. In response to insufficient recruitment efforts, black firefighters brought a successful class-action suit against the city. Black fire and police personnel organized themselves separately from the unions. The mayor appointed a special committee on civil rights to review the adequacy, relevance, and integrity of police records. The city filed suits against court-ordered "quotas" for firefighters and city contracts. Although it lost both cases, the struggle continued. A white police officer was recently charged with using excessive force against a black university student. Although the court found him innocent, the department ordered that he undergo a two-year rehabilitation, program which the Fraternal Order of Police challenged.

Blacks have submitted referenda to supplement the at-large system of council elections with ward representation, aimed at increasing the number of blacks on the council. These referenda were defeated in 1968 and 1975 despite their endorsement by the Democratic Party. Conservative Democrats on the council stalled further action. Racial divisions have pervaded issues dealing with education and crime. Blacks have long felt that the educational system was segregated, disadvantaging black students. When certain districts were annexed to Columbus, students were permitted to continue enrolling in suburban schools. A discrimination suit filed against the board of education in the early 1970s resulted in a federal court order to equalize educational opportunity through busing. Blacks charged that school superintendents evaded compliance. To prevent white flight and to meet criticisms from blacks, the board of education established specialized "alternative schools." During the long turmoil of firing superintendents, suits, and countersuits, many upper-middle-class residents moved to the suburbs in search of more stable school systems. Recently, residents of predominantly black areas demanded more neighborhood control of schools.

City officials are determined to maintain quality schools to attract affluent residents. The city has established and funded thirteen area commissions that encourage residents to communicate concerns about zoning and education directly to the city. Whether this system will exacerbate or reduce racial hostilities is not yet clear.

Big-city status brought Columbus big-city problems. While the rates of serious crimes have not reached Cleveland's level, they top Cincinnati's. The city attained notoriety as a center of drug distribution, and police regularly conduct drug raids with FBI assistance. Residents, especially in the black community, periodically call for more police protection. The police chief has claimed that the police academy lacks funds and facilities to train larger cohorts, but the black community and others have insisted that the police are reluctant to train more black applicants.

Despite their numerical majority in city and county, Democrats have not agreed on how to confront major issues. Party leadership has been episodic and weak. The Mayfield machine was well organized in the 1950s and 1960s when it managed Sensenbrenner's reelections, but subsequent party leaders have not maintained the organization. Having lost much middle-class support, the party has relied more heavily on labor unions, blacks, and white liberals.

The party system plays a visible local role. Nonpartisan at-large elections do not obscure party rivalry. While party leaders minimize the importance of patronage, enough of it exists to attract party workers. The city budget is large, and local businesses actively compete for contracts. The executive directorship of the county Democratic Party is a full-time position. A recent director served as council member, council secretary, head of the council research office, a U.S. Department of Labor official, and a representative on the county board of elections and also ran twice for Congress.

Council members have access to patronage. They appoint the city clerk, city treasurer, legislative assistants, and employees of the council research office. They provide access to jobs emanating from federal programs in the city, local recreational programs, and neighborhood nursery centers. They serve as conduits to city agencies for neighborhood groups that seek better city services. They control the city council's public relations fund, become involved in awarding nonbid contracts to local business, and make final decisions on rezoning disputes and the hiring of consultants. The presidency of the city council is a highly influential office, and competition for it is keen. Council members have been selected by the governor to fill vacated assembly and senate seats and to serve in state agencies. Ex-council members have been offered employment opportunities in local business. The city funds many private social service and cultural organizations. In short, personal and organizational patronage is large enough to attract many people to work for the parties.

The city confronts a wide range of issues important to citizens and groups, including labor unions. Yet the Democratic Party often lacks organization and vitality. In 1987, it gathered too few signatures to put a mayoral candidate on the ballot. In 1993, the party leader resigned. Over the protests of African-American political influentials, the executive committee named a successor who had been a Republican and a recent Independent.

Organized Labor

Before the Civil War, Columbus unions would collapse almost as soon as they were organized. The war tended to stabilize the labor situation. In 1866, a series of strike losses led the unions to form a citywide trade assembly, even before Dayton and Cleveland. In the 1877 depression, a railroad strike stirred a rash of protest strikes throughout the state. In Columbus, they resulted in a riot that caused millions of dollars of business and property losses (Boryczka and Cary 1982, pp. 74–78). Columbus hosted the National Labor Reform Party in 1872, the Ohio Workingman's Party in 1877, and the founding of the American Federation of Labor in 1886.

Several craft unions gradually established themselves in the city. Violent confrontations with business were few, although in 1910 the National Guard was summoned to break a long strike of the Street Railway Employees' Union. Soon after World War I, AFL leaders launched a weekly paper "to combat the Bolshevik menace and the IWW" (Boryczka and Cary 1982, p. 161). Metal fabrication industries and unions grew during the prosperous 1920s, but the Great Depression stunted union growth.

Under the protection of New Deal legislation, the AFL's Committee on Industrial Organization launched a strong organization drive. Unlike in other industrial centers, the early growth of industrial unions in Columbus did not divide the AFL. However, when the Columbus Federation of Labor supported the CIO strikes of mine, rubber, and auto unions in 1937, AFL leaders complained to AFL president William Green, who then revoked the local federation's charter. When the AFL evicted the CIO unions in the following year, Columbus CIO locals disaffiliated from the AFL. The expansion of the metal industries during World War II rapidly increased CIO membership. The Curtis-Wright airplane plant added 16,000 new UAW members, and the expanding steel industry doubled USW membership. White-Westinghouse growth made the local electrical union (IUE) a powerhouse.

Columbus CIO unions also grew during the post–World War II decade. Yet the AFL, rather than the CIO, invaded the "red" United Mine and Mill local in 1949 and also became the bargaining agent at American Zinc Oxide. The struggle against communists in CIO unions was not as brutal in Columbus as in Cleveland. When the AFL and the CIO merged nationally in 1955, leadership disputes among the CIO unions (the UAW, the USW, and the IUE) delayed it three years in Ohio (Vantine 1992). In the 1960s, ex-AFL unions in particular resisted compliance with fair employment legislation, but with less lingering bitterness in Columbus than elsewhere. Union membership continued to expand locally but declined thereafter in the major CIO unions almost as rapidly as it had grown. U.S. Defense Department cutbacks steadily reduced the employment of airplane workers at Rockwell International. A long strike and a national boycott at Borden's reduced the size of the local Amalgamated Clothing Workers' Union. Declining employment in the auto and steel industries shrank UAW and USW membership precipitously, and the closing of the White-Westinghouse plant almost erased the IUE. A growing service sector cushioned local unemployment but did not stem the decline in the number of union members and in labor's political strength.

Membership decline was eased in 1983 when the Democratic governor, Richard Celeste, kept his promise to permit public employees to organize. AFSCME and the Ohio Civil Service Employee's Association (OCSEA) membership soared in state and local government. Membership fell in the building trades, but the steady construction of state office buildings and at the university cushioned the decline. Federal deregulation of transportation reduced Teamsters membership, but again local prosperity slowed the decline. Outside the AFL-CIO, teachers, police, and firefighters organized and became important political actors. As elsewhere, membership in the United Food and Commercial Workers (UFCW) climbed, but unlike elsewhere, service employee (SEIU) membership fell rapidly. While union membership declined notably in Columbus, labor remained large and rich enough to exert considerable political muscle if it so decided. Yet Columbus had a fairly strong labor tradition, and while it faltered in the 1980s, membership and resources remained substantial.

COMPARING THE THREE Cs

The above accounts do not provide rich data on labor's local political involvements partly because labor leaders preferred not to publicize them. Their modesty about their influence in the Democratic Party reflected their desire to avoid being accused of dominating it. In the following chapters, I examine labor's local party activities and influence in detail. Here, I briefly compare their local settings.

Clearly, the three cities differ enough in their economic, political, and labor systems to illustrate many of the political problems that labor confronts today. Columbus's economy recently experienced the most growth, especially in the service and white-collar sectors. Cleveland, more than Cincinnati, retained its durable-goods manufacturing sector, but Cincinnati's economy recovered more rapidly by diversifying. Unsurprisingly, per capita income was substantially lower and more polarized in the Cleveland area because of the city's high poverty rate and suburban affluence (Herson and Bolland 1991, p. 417). Educational differences between the city and its ring were also largest in Cleveland. Unemployment has always been highest in the Cleveland area and lowest in Columbus.

While racial cleavages are prominent in the three cities, they are broadest and deepest in Cleveland, least in Columbus, and moderately high in Cincinnati. Racial segregation in city and outer ring has always been highest in Cleveland and lowest in Columbus (Choldin 1985, p. 247). Since 1940, segregation has declined steadily in Columbus and Cincinnati but has remained stable in Cleveland. Residential areas of blacks are most clustered, closest to the central business district, and most concentrated in Cleveland (Massey and Denton 1987). Yet racial issues in education are as visible in Columbus as in Cincinnati and Cleveland.

Both Cleveland and Cincinnati have more blacks involved in local and national politics than Columbus, probably reflecting areal differences in their numbers rather than the openness of local political systems. European ethnic politics is most pervasive in Cleveland and least so in Columbus, again reflecting ethnic groups' relative size. In sum, by such indicators as income, education, unemployment, race, and ethnicity, the Cleveland area is most polarized and Columbus least polarized.

For over sixty years, from 1931 to 1992, the three Cleveland congressional districts elected only Democrats to Congress with one exception: One district elected a Republican from 1955 to 1961. In contrast, in sixty years, Columbus's congressional districts elected only one Democrat for one term. Historically, both Cincinnati districts elected mostly Republicans, but since 1977 one district has consistently elected Democrats. In county elections, both Columbus and Cincinnati have been strongly Republican, while Cleveland has been Democratic. Both Columbus and Cleveland have the strong-mayor type of government, while Cincinnati has the city manager form. Columbus has typically had a Democratic council and a Republican mayor. In Cleveland, both have traditionally been Democrats, but recently, some Republican mayors have been elected. Until 1993, the Charterites on the Cincinnati council prevented either party from gaining a majority and naming the mayor.

Cleveland Democratic Party leaders have been less effective in local politics (Hadden, Masotti, and Thiessen 1967) than in state and national elections. After 1941, the party generally did not endorse Democrats for mayor when they first ran for office. Democratic Party leadership, traditionally unstable in Cincinnati, has recently has shown signs of stability. In Columbus, party leadership has been weak for several decades.

Cleveland's decentralized ward politics fostered permanent conflict within the council and between it and the mayor, weakening governmental effectiveness. Although neighborhood political identity is weaker in

Cincinnati, it is much stronger than in Columbus. Tripartite party coalitions with a strong city manager have permitted Cincinnati government to function effectively, while weak party salience in Columbus has enabled some mayors to exert strong leadership.

Union density is highest in Cleveland, lower in Cincinnati, and lowest in Columbus. Industrial unions are likely to exert more influence in Cleveland politics than other unions. Service-sector unions have the edge in Columbus. Cincinnati's pattern is balanced. In Cleveland, labor and the Democratic Party display a symbiotic relationship, enduring one another in uneasy embrace. In Cincinnati, labor's vacillating party influence has lately stabilized and grown. Labor's party stance in Columbus has been indecisive, often divided.

In sum, political patterns in the Three Cs, much like those in the nation, represent variations around the Los Angeles pattern that Greenstone characterized as fluid and disorganized. The most important national changes since 1960 are well represented in the three areas: changes in the economy, changes in party organization and political campaigning, changes in the organization of metropolitan regions, and changes in union strength and composition. The three regions have also been confronted with a wide range of race, class, economic, and political issues that have appeared in the nation. While no three cases adequately represent the entire nation, the three cases selected here represent a wide middle range. The following chapters describe in detail the patterns that have appeared in each city.

7

Cleveland

Banking on Tradition

In the following chapters, I analyze the organization of labor politics in three Ohio metropolitan areas. Because the areas differ in economic, political, and social characteristics, labor and the political parties tend to confront different problems in coordinating their electoral efforts. The chapter focuses on the parties' relations to major constituencies, the relations of COPE, labor's political arm, to member unions and other unions not in COPE, and the party–labor system that emerges at election time. As indicated elsewhere, the evaluation of labor's performance rests on two personal beliefs: that the labor movement is interested in its welfare as well as in that of other workers not so fortunate, and that for the attainment of working-class welfare, a modicum of labor political discipline is essential.

The Democrats' steady electoral successes in Cleveland and Cuyahoga County point to a strong party to which labor makes an important contribution. The party–labor link in Cuyahoga County is crucial to party's control of state government. If the Democratic plurality tops 150,000 in Cuyahoga County, Democrats normally dominate the legislature and elect the governor; if not, downstate Republicans win. In low-turnout elections, Democrats usually gain control of the House of Representatives while Republicans gain control of the Senate and elect the governor. In presidential elections, Ohio has followed national trends. From 1932 to 1992, Ohio supported the successful candidate in all elections but one: It chose Dewey over Roosevelt in 1944. In congressional elections over the same sixty years, no Republican candidate won the city's electoral district; 80 percent Democratic majorities were typical. Democrats won the seats about 60 percent of the time in the two districts outside the city in Cuyahoga County.

From 1931 to 1970, when Ohio permitted counties to be split to form state house and senate districts, Cuyahoga County Democrats won about 90 percent of the contests. After 1970, electoral districts had to be drawn along county lines. Democrats still maintained their advantage, but won only 70 percent of the county's state senate races. Democrats have also won the majority of countywide elections. In city elections, the council has typically had a Democratic majority. Republicans elected the mayors before 1940, and Democrats, between 1940 and 1970. Democrats have held a slight edge since 1970.

What have been the sources of Democratic Party strength and how much has organized labor contributed to it? To answer this question, I interviewed 100 informants, read documents, and made observations of my own.[1] Making generalizations required subjective judgments. Although I may state few reservations in making conclusions, they should be taken as provisional constructions of what I thought was going on.

After discussing the general problem of the relations of labor and the Democratic Party, this chapter describes seven activities: (1) Democratic Party efforts to coordinate the interests of its main constituencies: ward leaders, elected officials, labor, and the African-American and white caucuses; (2) Republican Party efforts to appeal to the same constituencies; (3) COPE efforts to aggregate the interests of its member unions; (4) the political efforts of three bodies outside COPE: the UAW, the Teamsters, and the Building Trades Council (BTC); (5) the political activities of eight large unions in COPE which, with the UAW and the Teamsters, include the bulk of organized labor; (6) the efficacy of labor's political "machine"; and (7) the efficacy of the labor–party system. The chapters on Cincinnati amd Columbus that follow conform to the broad outline of this chapter.

Over the years, labor and the Democratic Party tried to coordinate their electoral organizations during election campaigns. Unsurprisingly, they encountered problems because they differed in structure, objectives, constituencies, and resources. The party is a cluster of caucuses or interest groups that include the black community, ward organizations, organized labor, financial backers of the party, candidates' electoral organizations, and political influentials in local, state, and federal government. Labor's political organization (COPE) and the political organizations outside it are also a loose cluster of unions that operate somewhat independently. Melding party and labor organizations into an effective electoral machine is

[1]See Appendix A for the problems I confronted in obtaining the data. Unless otherwise indicated, the data reported for the three metropolises were largely drawn from the interviews with labor, party, and other informants.

fraught with difficulty because they often disagree on issues; their efforts and concerns vary in local, state, and national elections; issues change over elections; and the involvement of other groups in the party coalition changes constantly.

The party–labor electoral machine is amorphous, unstable, and changing. It has no central command structure; member cooperation is purely voluntary and therefore ephemeral and opportunistic. The few patterns that carry over from one election to another tend to become routinized, reducing opportunities to accumulate organizational expertise. Since class interests, however defined, cannot be coordinated in this loosely structured electoral system, segmentation theory is better suited than class theories to analyzing how this system works.

THE DEMOCRATIC PARTY AS A COORDINATOR

In November 1990, George Voinovich, former Republican mayor of Cleveland, won the gubernatorial election. Democratic Party leaders were trying to explain their defeat. Visiting Democratic Party headquarters in Cleveland about a week after the election, we found three bleak half-empty rooms in an old building in a transitional area near the central business district. The executive director and a secretary worked in two dismal, poorly furnished offices. Of one hundred offices I visited during the research, perhaps a half-dozen were smaller or less well furnished.

The structure of the Cuyahoga County Democratic Party is standard. The party chair was elected by the 750-member executive committee, 350 of whom were selected by the party itself and 400 of whom were elected in the precinct primaries. Party affairs were run by the smaller operating committee, where ward leaders, candidates, and others jockeyed for control. The party's appointed full-time executive director was also a ward leader.

The most influential party actors were the ward leaders, who ran the Democratic clubs without much concern for the central party. The party chair did not become deeply involved in ward affairs because he could not control the bulk of the ward patronage. The most visible source of patronage, about 200 jobs on the county board of elections, were filled by precinct workers loyal to the ward leaders. Patronage was funneled mainly through networks among ward leaders and elected officials at various levels of government. These networks, once dominated by white male ethnics, were being invaded by African Americans and women. Several informants observed that more money was being raised for local and state campaigns than for presidential ones. If true, patronage, privilege, and access may be larger than party leaders and others acknowledged. City government alone employed more than 9,000 workers and collected over $700 million in revenue. While informants observed that patronage was small, unimportant, and declining, each mentioned a different source: offices of the mayor, auditor, judges, sheriff, board of elections, temporary non-civil-service jobs, temporary job vacancies, emergency federal programs, and others. I estimated that the number of temporary and permanent patronage appointees was over 500.

Links between ward leaders and city council members were more important than ward links to party officers because council members, with access to some patronage, could influence the quality of city services in the wards. Between ward and party organizations, two informal coalitions competed for dominance in party decision making: the African-American and white "caucuses."

The black caucus was formally organized as the Twenty-First Congressional District Democratic Caucus in 1970 (see Chapter 6). In the early 1990s, Mayor Mike White was its leading influential; Louis Stokes, Forbes, and others were also recognized. At times, the caucus was torn by conflict. For example, Forbes had earlier forged a personal machine that had divided ward leaders and the party, backing Republican Voinovich, who was twice elected mayor. Such divisions dampened political interest in the black community, lowered registration and voting, and reduced the caucus's influence in the party even though it sometimes held half of the executive committee seats. Michael White had slowly rebuilt the machine. Even though leadership contests had weakened the caucus, it was still strong enough both to elect Mike White as the city's second black mayor and to contest labor's influence in the Democratic Party. As the proportion of African Americans in the city grows, the caucus, if unified, may soon dominate the party's operating committee, reduce the influence of ward leaders, and centralize party control.

White ward leaders did not have a formal caucus, but they met informally to consider candidates for local, state, and national offices and discuss party matters. The ability of candidates, both white and black, to run for office as Independent Democrats without party sponsorship underlined the weakness of the central party. Candidates increasingly attracted the larger proportion of campaign funds for TV and radio spots and did not funnel them through the party. Even candidates with party sponsorship ran their own campaigns. The party provided printed materials, funding-raising advice, and a meeting place for volunteers. It raised about $100,000 annually, mainly by sponsoring expensive dinners. An observer concluded,

> In effect, there are twenty-one independent party organizations represented by twenty-one ward clubs. Other organizations get formed when candidates challenge the incumbents. The county party suffers from extreme factionalization.

Although consistent party success and Republican weakness in most wards permitted factionalism to survive in the party, the Republicans had recently won some elections by exploiting Democratic divisions. Democratic Party leaders typically paid little attention to electoral outcomes in suburbs and outlying municipalities because city registration drives paid dividends, whereas county drives sometimes increased Republican turnout. Expectedly, party leaders rarely took stands on issues that divided their constituencies (e.g., tax abatement and subsidizing the Gateway development project; see Chapter 6). Neither did they tip the balance in controversies over candidate selection. Their obsessive neutrality perpetuated the splits.

With some notable exceptions, party activists and spokespersons for major constituencies agreed that the party was poorly organized, had ineffective leadership, and had performed poorly. It was an assembly of interest groups without a strong central office. Without personally attacking party officers, observers commented that officers had less influence on party affairs and political outcomes than any constituencies: ward leaders, black leaders, financial supporters, elected officials, candidates for office, and organized labor.

Party leaders disliked commenting on the sources of party funds. They acknowledged receiving small contributions from officeholders and party regulars, larger ones from Jewish leaders, and the largest share from labor. Yet union members occupied only a quarter of the seats on the executive committee and African Americans about half. Labor leaders resented this situation and blamed party leaders, who minimized the disagreements with labor and insisted that relations were cordial and cooperative. They noted that the UAW (not COPE) had supported the party chair's reelection and that labor, the party, and the candidates had cooperated in the county coordinated campaign, reducing duplication in sample ballot distribution, making phone calls, and participating in other activities.

Party leaders allowed that labor groups would have more party influence if they were not so divided over candidates. Thus, in the 1990 gubernatorial election, the Pipefitters and the Ohio Federation of Teachers supported the Republican, Voinovich. Even more unions had supported him twice for mayor, but then they asked members to support his Democratic opponent, Celebrezze, for governor. Such shifts undermined party discipline. More important, labor had not developed a strong ward presence, especially in the African-American wards. Blacks remained especially suspicious of the building trades, which had resisted accepting black apprentices. Black party leaders observed that union members preferred white Republicans over black Democrats. In short, labor did not elicit sympathetic support from the party's most important interest groups.

Local party leaders hesitated to analyze local Democratic weaknesses, preferring instead to explain why the *state* party had lost the gubernatorial election. They explained that the Republicans had built a superior campaign organization, collected more money, and even managed to obtain support from the pastors of the black churches. Although Democratic ward organizations performed better than in previous elections, at best they could increase Democratic turnout only 4 percent in a close race, not enough to offset a huge Republican advantage in television advertising. Finally, the dispersal of white ethnic groups in the metropolitan area diluted their party loyalty. The party's future had to depend increasingly on party harmony, good organization, and a higher voter turnout in the black community.

THE REPUBLICAN PARTY

Republican headquarters, a large and well-furnished suite in the heart of the business district, contained a bright conference room, computers, wall maps, and pleasant work space for volunteers. A pianist at the entry played classical music. The former party chair, who had served full-time for twenty-three years, had been replaced recently by two part-time co-chairs. Experienced professionals, they supervised the executive director and staff. Although the party was not as well funded and staffed as in Columbus and Cincinnati, its officers expected early improvement.

Cleveland Republicans acknowledged that "the demographics" or the local ethnic and racial mix tipped the scales against them. For 260 county elective offices, the party therefore recruited only a few white and African-American candidates whom they identified as "winnable." The party provided seed money and consulting, training, and campaign services. Party leaders were also devising new ways to increase the Republican turnout of blacks and ethnic groups. The recent election of Republicans Perk and Voinovich for mayor proved that this was possible. After Kucinich's disastrous administration, Voinovich, who had always maintained strong ties with some influential blacks, asked the Black Ministers' Alliance to back his race for mayor. Grateful for their decisive support, he increased black representation in city offices and directed a greater flow of city contracts to African-American businesses. When Voinovich ran for governor, he again asked for and received support from the Black Ministers' Alliance. The ultimate test of the Republican strategy would be a victory for a Republican African American.

Some Republicans thought that their party's main challenge was to build a strong ward organization to attract union members, as it had done to attract white ethnics and African Americans. The current party chairs realized that labor had a more effective electoral organization than the Democratic Party and that labor had to become very upset with the Democrats before it would back Republicans. Voinovich's election as mayor and governor had shown that labor's solidarity could be broken. Former Republican chairs had not held meaningful dialogues with labor, but the new leadership was courting unnamed unions with Republican affinities. Undoubtedly, some unions, like the UAW, would remain beyond reach, but means could be devised to fracture labor's allegiance to the Democratic Party.

COPE, ITS SATELLITES, AND THE DEMOCRATIC PARTY

COPE was designed to develop labor's political resources and help maximize its potential political influence. Success, never realized, depended on full cooperation between the Democratic Party and its main constituencies. Splits within labor, especially at the local level, had long impeded this goal. COPE, the UAW, and the Teamsters now operated separate political organizations. Because COPE supervised the largest political organization, I examine it first.

Over the years, COPE had found that monitoring politics in Cuyahoga County's several municipalities had become increasingly difficult. It therefore organized separate COPEs for the southeast and southwest regions. The two COPEs coordinated the political work of almost two hundred locals, a formidable task because many communities had no central labor bodies. The southwest COPE included thirteen municipalities; the southeast COPE, seven. The communities differed in occupational, racial, ethnic, and union composition and also in political concerns. The building trades and the steel workers (USW) were most active in the southwest COPE; the UAW, which was not in COPE, was most active in the southeast. Cleveland's COPE was supposed to coordinate the work of its two regional bodies. Even with three COPEs, some county areas were not being monitored. Many (perhaps the majority) of union members did not live in the community where they worked.

The operations of the three COPEs were almost identical. All had screening committees to evaluate candidates for office, using questionnaires that asked for positions on important labor and consumer issues. Sometimes the candidates were interviewed. Acceptable ones were endorsed and recommended to the next higher level of COPE. Regional COPEs sent recommendations for local, state, and national offices to the county COPE, which almost automatically approved all endorsements for local offices. Recommendations for other offices were sent to the state COPE for approval. Regional COPEs did not endorse candidates in party primaries and routinely backed previously endorsed incumbents unless their records had deteriorated seriously. Consequently, other groups in the party dominated the candidate selection process.

Some time before elections, each local union sent members' names, addresses, and phone numbers to the county COPE, which transmitted them to state or national COPEs. Lists were merged, individual names were reordered by zip code or electoral district and returned to county COPEs. These lists were used to make contact with members. Obviously, the lists did not include members of unions not in COPE (UAW, Teamsters, NEA). Moreover, perhaps a third of the persons listed were no longer union members or were given incorrect addresses or phone numbers. The local COPE (not individual locals) would then send members printed material about the election. COPE also organized phone banks to remind members to register and vote. Members could also receive election materials from their locals, internationals, and the Democratic Party.

As elections approached, COPE volunteers might send union members literature, sample ballots, lapel buttons, yard signs, and bumper stickers. The amount budgeted for these activities was small ($1,000 for COPE southeast and $1,700 for COPE southwest). Regional COPEs typically raised no funds, but locals sometimes solicited funds that were sent to candidates and internationals or were used to make contact with nonunion members. COPE gathered no data on contacts with members, but a 1992 survey revealed that coverage was far from complete (see Chapter 11).

Cleveland's COPE, the state's largest, was responsible for the political education of 180,000 members. With limited and shrinking finances, it focused largely on transmitting national and state COPE recommendations to locals, conducting joint projects with locals (phone banks, political rallies), and arranging contacts with the Democratic Party. COPE was designed not to centralize operations but to coordinate locals' work. It organized meetings for volunteers, mostly officers and a few activists, to instruct them on how to conduct registration and voting drives at work sites and in neighborhoods and how to operate phone banks on election day. Occasionally, it sent campaign literature to the locals for dissemination. Because of lack of funds, COPE no longer distributed its candidate endorsements to all union members.

Finally, to avoid duplication, COPE was mandated to cooperate with the UAW and the Teamsters (e.g., share membership lists and information on endorsed candidates). However, neither side systematically consulted the other. COPE officials were reluctant to evaluate these efforts because they felt powerless to change them. But COPE did take umbrage when the UAW or the Teamsters endorsed different candidates or took positions different from those hammered out within the AFL-CIO. While the three organizations mostly endorsed the same candidates, the press publicized the exceptions. No consultation took place among the three bodies after the election.

Before elections, COPE selected screening committees, provided representatives for the Democratic Party's executive committee, and coordinated work with the party, like distributing literature to both union and nonunion voters. The law permitted this practice because the party, not labor, paid for the publications. In addition, the party gave labor the precinct lists of registered Democratic voters. In the party's executive committee, labor took part in decisions on finances, election of officers, and naming of candidates for primaries and regular elections. Outside regular party meetings, labor rarely made contact with other groups about party matters.

Although labor was a key party player, COPE leaders described relations with the party as one of "mutual toleration." Grievances were long-standing. As the party's largest financial supporter along with the Jewish community, labor felt it did not receive adequate recognition. It claimed it had only 20 percent of the five hundred seats on the party's central committee, rather than the 25 percent reported by the party. Other constituencies received more seats (e.g., the ward leaders and the African-American caucus). Recently, a labor member had occupied one of two Democratic seats on the board of elections. When he was forced to vacate the seat, the party refused to fill it with another labor representative. Since labor had no interest in the patronage but wanted better access to voter information available at the board, the party's decision was interpreted as a test of influence and "a put-down of labor." Party leaders defended the decision to give the seat to an African American because he would use the patronage to strengthen the party. The conflict undoubtedly involved personal antipathies and strained the atmosphere of party meetings.

Labor criticized the party for poor organization and inactivity. The party no longer distributed a preelection ballot. It did little except hold dinners to raise money at election time. It monitored the largest pool of Democratic voters in the state, but it did not exert proportionate influence in the state party. Nor did it resolve disputes. Thus, in a recent primary for state senator, COPE endorsed one candidate, Mayor White endorsed another, the party made no endorsement, and the mayor's candidate won. This victory for the black caucus publicly revealed it to be more influential than COPE or the party. Since party leaders did resolve or balance differences, labor felt it had to assume the burden of mediation. In short, labor politicos resented party leaders because labor demanded no patronage, operated a more effective electoral organization, and played the mediator role, and yet its contributions were undervalued or unrecognized.

COPE experienced other difficulties in the party. COPE had insufficient presence in the wards to challenge ward leaders and too few volunteers in suburban communities. It did not train enough members in the Twenty-First District Caucus to offset suspicions that labor still blocked blacks from influential positions in unions and party. Labor leaders brushed these charges aside as past misunderstandings with no current relevance.

COPE's efforts to aggregate groups in the party were also impeded by labor's internal divisions. The UAW operated alone because it had the resources to demand recognition as a major party player. Teamster strategy (see below) did not call for party recognition. COPE and the UAW generally agreed on issues and candidates and remained suspicious of the Teamsters' behind-the-scenes self-serving agenda. The Ohio Educational Association wanted labor support on school issues but would not share its membership list. At times, COPE members were less cooperative than the unions outside it. Thus, the pipefitters backed Republican gubernatorial candidate Voinovich. On the Gateway and stadium projects, labor was bitterly divided. The UAW opposed tax abatement; the building trades and COPE backed it strongly.

COPE sometimes played a passive rather than a coordinating role in the labor community. Individual unions had to seize the initiative on different issues. On construction issues like Gateway, the building trades initiated calls to other unions for support; on the community-college and school-levy-millage issues, the American Federation of Teachers (AFT); on municipal services, the laborers, firefighters, or police; on health and social services, AFSCME; and on judges' appointment, COPE depended on the Bar Association's recommendations.

COPE's leaders diagnosed some of its weaknesses: the exodus of its strongest (largely white) supporters to the suburbs, which also increased electioneering costs. Although declining membership had reduced COPE's operating funds, the decline of volunteers was more serious. Fewer were willing to work for candidates, operate phone banks, and update lists of union and party members, forcing COPE to resort to the unheard-of practice of hiring others to perform these tasks. Nonvoting, especially among younger members, was increasing, except in the black wards, where it fluctuated widely. Sometimes voter turnout was low in areas with high union and party membership.

Labor could not match Republican funds for TV advertising, which, unionists thought, could influence 25 percent of voters to change their minds. Labor activists also found it hard to build consensus on important political issues even in heavily blue-collar suburbs. Nonpartisan races had reduced voter interest, and the race factor had "complicated things." To rebuild interest, COPE leaders felt they had to convince members that some political issues were more important than others, that jobs and health care mattered more than divisive issues like abortion, gay rights, gun control, and school prayer. As a COPE official said, "This organization is a political election committee, not a political education committee. If we did a proper education job, there wouldn't be a need for an election committee."

LABOR'S BIG THREE OUTSIDE COPE

I now examine three labor organizations outside COPE: the UAW, the Teamsters, and the Building Trades Council (BTC). The interviews with these units follow the same themes as interviews with the eight major unions that follow. Table 7.1 provides member characteristics of the ten unions, *provided by informants* or *estimated* by the interviewers.

United Auto Workers

When the UAW and the Teamsters reaffiliated with the AFL-CIO in Ohio, they elected to remain independent of COPE in local and state politics. Both were strong economically but polar opposites in political philosophy. If COPE, the UAW, and the Teamsters could agree and work together, they could visibly augment labor influence in the party and nation. While the Teamsters and the UAW obviously valued their autonomy, they did not want to be accused of weakening labor's political influence. How they justified their stance and how they cooperated with COPE were important research concerns.

The UAW's equivalent of COPE was its Community Action Program (CAP). While COPE was organized on a community basis, CAP was organized regionally. Region 2 of the UAW included 50,000 members in northeast Ohio and northwest and north central Pennsylvania (see Table 7.1). Although the majority of members lived in Ohio, CAP could not ignore politics in the Pennsylvania communities. Region 2 operated six Ohio CAP councils, of which Cleveland's was largest. Its CAP clearly had

Table 7.1
Characteristics of Cuyahoga County Unions as Reported by Informants, 1991–1992

Union	Members	Check-off (%)	Blacks (%)	Democrats (%)
Auto workers (UAW)	8,000	25[a]	35	80
Steel workers (USW)	12,000	25[a]	40	75
Communications (CWA)	7,000	5[a]	30	60
Teamsters	25,000	80[a]	10	65[a]
Building trades (BTC)	16,000	—	10	80[b]
Electricians (IBEW)	1,800[c]	50	10	55
Carpenters	8,000	5	10	80[b]
Government (AFSCME)	5,000	—	50	75[a]
Teachers (AFT)	5,000	—	15	65
Service (SEIU)	6,800	40	60	95
Food (UFCW)	15,000	—	60	70

[a]Guessed.
[b]Reported, but unlikely.
[c]For the construction local; total IBEW, about 3,500.

enough resources and members to be taken seriously by the Democratic Party and its candidates. Although it could not match COPE's membership and resources, CAP duplicated COPE's screening committees, phone banks, registration drives, and volunteer organizations.

The regional decline of manufacturing had reduced UAW membership by a third or more. Yet CAP did not reduce its staff because the UAW had maintained CAP's income by negotiating a voluntary political "check-off" clause in contracts with Ford, Chrysler, and General Motors. Although CAP raised little additional cash or "hard" money at election time, check-off funds and contributions from from staffs, officers, and activists were large enough (perhaps $200,000 or more annually) to attract candidates, who were pressed to endorse the UAW's strong working-class, welfare-state philosophy. More forcibly than any union, the UAW presented its philosophy in its chief publications, *Ammo* and *Solidarity*. It also published several attractive pamphlets written in clear, straightforward prose that explained the union's positions on issues such as health care insurance, consumer legislation, taxes, unemployment, drugs, race relations, minimum wages, and laws bearing on union political action. The union also furnished locals with well-designed handbooks on how to build a political education program, inform workers on issues, improve communication with members and the public, and influence legislators. CAP councils also published newsletters and papers. However, much of this literature failed to reach members because most locals did not buy it.

Officers of Cleveland locals, reluctant to be interviewed, repeatedly referred me to state CAP council officials and union lobbyists. More than officers of other unions, UAW local officers were informed about local politics, but they were even better informed about state and national issues. Local CAP Council leaders, who shared the international officials' political ideology, strongly urged their members to support liberal candidates for office. The UAW Congressional District Action Committees also urged local officials to communicate UAW views to legislators. These efforts' success was undetermined. Local CAPs routinely supported liberal candidates and issues, but their efforts were limited by scarce resources and volunteers.

Cleveland's UAW leaders thought that the local Democratic Party was moderately effective mainly because it had many more precinct workers than did labor. However, the party and COPE sometimes supported causes (like tax abatement) that ran counter to the interests of the average worker. Also, the party lacked cohesiveness, a coherent program, and inspired leadership. African Americans and ethnics operated their own political machines and did not cooperate with the party. UAW officers regarded CAP as the party's strongest supporter but complained that the candidates that CAP helped to elect became conservative in office and avoided the union. Emphasizing its consistent liberalism, UAW leaders kept reminding other unions that the UAW had not joined COPE in supporting Republican Voinovich for mayor, and that the UAW had fought tax abatement and the Gateway project almost alone.

CAP officials claimed that they did not want to dominate the party but make it more liberal. They lamented their lack of progress. A few threatened "to start playing hard-ball politics," but no one had devised a workable strategy to make the party more liberal. Unwilling to admit that the UAW was partly responsible for the fragmentation of labor and the party, they refused to join COPE on the grounds that it was incapable of disciplining its locals to support endorsed candidates. In contrast, UAW locals rallied behind CAP-endorsed candidates, whatever their previous reservations.

UAW activists identified the building trades and the Teamsters as UAW ideological opposites who supported assured winners without regard to ideology. The communication workers (CWA) were regarded as almost as liberal as the UAW. Although AFSCME had some liberal elements, it would not join the UAW in a liberal coalition because AFSCME would not forget past organizing disputes. Liberals in the United Food and Commercial Workers (UFCW) were too occupied with internal problems to work with the coalition. AFT leaders were too self-serving and aloof, except when they needed help on millage issues. Ethnics and blacks were too preoccupied with internal squabbles. UAW leaders perceived many local political cleavages and did not comprehend why other groups in labor and the party were not as liberal as the UAW. In short, the UAW's sense of running a superior, more liberal, more populist organization limited its aggregating role in the party and labor. Some activists endorsed a doomsday scenario: A worsening economic and political situation would eventually convince others to join a UAW-led liberal coalition.

The Teamsters

The Teamsters' Joint Council included 57,000 members in northeast and central Ohio, down from 75,000 in the last two decades. With about 25,000 members in the Cleveland area, the Teamsters were larger, richer, and as politically active as the UAW (see Table 7.1). Only a few Teamster locals in the construction sector participated in COPE; the others participated in the Teamsters' PAC, DRIVE (Democrat Republican and Independent Voter Education). DRIVE, the nation's largest PAC, netted $10.5 million in the 1989–1990 election cycle. Joint council officers thought that most Teamsters were "Democrat-minded" but not automatic party supporters. According to a high official, "Party identification is the last thing we look at in a candidate. You know that, contrary to most unions, we backed Voinovich [for governor]. He's had good experience, and we expect him to do well. We'll see."

Unlike most union officials, Teamster officers were not discouraged about the local or state political scene. They drew a self-portrait of a tough, competent, strong, nonideological union well able to look after its interests under any conditions. They did not complain about declining membership, lack of resources, or lack of volunteers. The union maintained its level of political spending simply by raising contributions and dues. Confident that their members were politically active, the Teamsters seemed as intensely involved in politics as the UAW.

Teamster leaders placed as much importance on political action as any union in this study, and they were confident that their political education program was superior to any union's. They acknowledged that the union was highly centralized, but they insisted that stewards played a pivotal role in members' political education. Steward training emphasized politics and "the need to communicate its importance to members on a one-to-one basis." The Teamsters' political credo embraced two principles. First, politics is central to preserving and increasing the number of Teamster jobs; whatever promotes economic growth anywhere (business, government, welfare, education) promotes Teamster jobs. Second, politics costs money. To protect their jobs and make more money, members must make political contributions. The steward must convince members to take part in the political check-off and to contribute to political campaigns. Not surprisingly, check-off participation and political contributions were highest in the nation.

Like the UAW, the Teamsters saw little advantage in belonging to COPE. Not only were their screening committees, registration drives, and phone banks more efficient, Teamsters did not have to spend energy confronting their "philosophical differences" with COPE. An officer explained:

> Too many people in COPE look whether there is a "D" or an "R" after the candidate's name. There's where we differ. We do not have an automatic party response. We want to know how the candidate stands on *our* issues and how they behaved in office. So, we do not have an automatic endorsement for incumbents. We screen both on the primary and regular elections. And we keep track of them *after* the election. When the campaign is over, we give them a period of grace ... maybe 60 days. Then we ask them to come through. We keep an eye on them all the time. We're not bashful. We want the dividends for our support. After election, the work really begins.

The Teamsters were almost alone in not complaining about a decline in volunteers, claiming that they had little problem in attracting hundreds of volunteers to operate phone banks and attend rallies. Isolation from COPE and CAP caused the Teamsters little concern. They acknowledged that the UAW and the building trades were strong politically, but the Teamsters saw little need to join them even when they all agreed on policies. The Teamsters rarely took the lead in confronting community issues. They took no stand on the Gateway project because their members were split on beverage "sin taxes" that were part of the package, but the Teamsters supported other unions that promoted tax abatement for new businesses. In short, the Teamsters avoided operating in the limelight, preferring to make quiet contacts with government officials and legislators.

The Teamsters strongly criticized the Democratic party for its inability to devise a coherent program. Yet about 80 percent of Teamster endorsements were of Democrats; 20 percent were of Republicans. The Teamsters regarded their own electoral organization as superior to those of both political parties because more than 75 percent of the candidates they endorsed were elected, exceeding either party's rate. Thus, even though organized labor was becoming weaker politically, the Teamsters felt they were holding their own.

The Teamsters' analysis of local labor politics ran contrary to their philosophy and practice. They insisted that labor should be more *united* to forge a coherent agenda. Something was wrong when Democrats controlled both houses of Congress and yet could not pass an anti-striker-replacement bill. Moreover, the debilitating contest for leadership among the unions partially accounted for labor's weaknesses. According to a Teamster:

> Labor should learn from business. It meets, talks over common problems, gets an agenda, and acts. It knows how to win. Labor should do likewise. Labor should be more visible and vocal. It should not be ashamed of acting in its self-interest and being accused of being big and successful. Big business does not apologize for being in favor of business, so labor shouldn't apologize for being prolabor.

In short, by acting independently, the Teamsters contributed to a divided labor movement. To realize the proposals they made to improve labor politics, the Teamsters would have to abandon their current practices.

The Building Trades Council (BTC)

The BTC's fifteen unions included about 30,000 members, the majority in Cuyahoga County. Membership had slowly declined from 35,000 in 1970 largely because of the loss of the residential construction market and the failure to train a sufficient number of apprentices. Each trade sent a representative to the BTC, which "coordinated" collective bargaining, job practices on and off building sites, and political activities.

The BTC operated independently of COPE even though its member unions belong to it. The BTC duplicated most COPE functions, namely, screening candidates, raising money to support candidates, and mobilizing voters. Duplication was justified on grounds that the building trades had "different" (local) interests, whereas most unions in manufacturing and in the services had interests "outside the community."

The building trades have been more decentralized than other unions because their labor markets are inescapably local. State and national bodies have established policies that permit local bodies to determine most of their own affairs. Thus, the state BTC can overrule the recommendations of local BTCs only by a two-thirds majority; even then, locals can and do follow their own inclinations. Similarly, unions that belonged to a local BTC have felt free to deviate from its decisions. The BTC raises cash contributions for political campaigns, while member unions use dues or "soft" money for political education. Most BTC money was spent on local and state elections, rarely for national contests. About fifteen times a year, the Council published *The Cleveland Citizen*, the state's oldest operating labor paper.

Although the BTC was supposed to articulate its political stands with COPE, it sometimes acted independently. State and local BTC leaders became irritated with COPE for not supporting the BTC strongly on the prevailing wage issue (paying union wages on all government construction). The BTC therefore led the fight and withheld support from COPE on other matters. But even BTC members sometimes refused to follow its recommendations. In 1990, the pipefitters in the BTC backed Republican Voinovich for governor even though the BTC endorsed his opponent, Celebrezze. While the state BTC was more active in politics than its local bodies, both functioned primarily as redistribution agencies. The BTC did not operate phone banks or distribute political literature because the individual trades did so. The BTC might propose a door-to-door campaign, but member unions were expected to implement it. The BTC bought yard signs, and the individual unions distributed them if and how they saw fit. This loose, decentralized structure undoubtedly resulted in an uneven coverage of the membership.

The BTC's officials claimed that its members were overwhelmingly Democrats, a claim that officers of the individual trades did not support. They reported that half or more of their members, especially younger ones, had no party preference or political interest. Most officers of locals and activists nearing retirement age were uninclined to spend much energy educating new members in politics. When they did, they stressed community participation. Thus, the BTC received federal funds to conduct minority training programs. It held a seat on the chamber of commerce's labor advisory board, composed of labor, owners, and contractors who made plans to attract construction to the area. The board strongly supported the Gateway project and tax abatement for downtown construction. It took a firm stand against the "shortsighted" UAW position, proclaiming that the UAW would support tax abatement were automobile jobs at stake.

In sum, the BTC, the Teamsters, and the UAW together represented about 20 percent of area union members. In ideology, the Teamsters represented pure job-conscious unionism, the UAW represented social unionism, and the BTC tilted strongly toward the Teamster pattern. COPE vacillated in a compromise of its member unions but tilted toward the UAW pole. The insistence of the UAW, the Teamsters, and the BTC on supporting separate political organizations exacerbated the segmentation of local union politics.

THE BIG EIGHT UNIONS IN COPE

The carpenters and the electricians (IBEW) were the largest unions in the BTC, and they also belonged to COPE. How did they play their dual membership role? Although both unions had factory and construction locals, I concentrated on construction ones in the BTC. Membership in both unions had declined since the 1970s but leveled off recently. Neither union had achieved its targeted representation of black members and seemed satisfied with about 10 percent. Officials estimated that a majority of their members were Democrats but that they had little political interest. The officers themselves thought that politics were very important, and they supported the international and its PACs.

The Carpenters

The carpenters had recently been reorganized. Five locals in the greater Cleveland area, 10,000 members in all, had been consolidated into one district. About 7,000 lived in Cuyahoga County (see Table 7.1). Perhaps because the carpenters relied heavily on state and national officers to coordinate local PACs, local officers seemed out of touch with members. One said:

> To give you a statement on our political orientation, I should say that we are nonpartisan. In fact, one of our recent surveys showed overwhelming support for a labor party. I'd say that about 95 percent of our members are Democrats. Our members have a pretty good awareness of politics. They're smart. Our paper, *The Ohio Citizen*, comes out once a month. We try to use the paper as a means to politically enlighten our members. We flood them with the issues.

Yet officers admitted that local political involvement was restricted by insufficient funds. Locals raised very little money at election time. About 5 percent of the members (officers?) participated in the political check-off. The local ritualistically bought tickets to BTC-sponsored annual dinners for favored incumbents. Most of the money that the carpenters raised in the state, about $40,000 per election, went to their state PAC. Money that the staffs contributed by political check-off went to the national PAC, the Carpenters' Legislative Improvement Committee. Although the carpenters also sent representatives to COPE's screening committee and phone bank operations, they were apparently not otherwise involved. A few officers and activists took part in activities like screening committees, phone banks, yard sign distribution, and canvassing.

Cleveland's carpenters belonged to the state and county growth association, organized to attract developers to the Cleveland area, and to the midtown corridor group, which was planning to rebuild the city center. Apart from paying membership dues in these organizations, the carpenters left the work and leadership to business. Membership was thought necessary to maintain rapport with business and to ensure that employers would hire union labor and pay "prevailing wages." The carpenters considered the pipefitters, rather than the IBEW, to be the most politically active union in the BTC. Outside the BTC, the Teamsters were thought most effective, but how they exerted their influence remained obscure. The UAW was also considered influential but also the most disruptive of labor harmony, especially on the Gateway project.

The carpenters thought that the local Democratic Party lacked leadership, but "dollar for dollar" it did as well as the Republicans. The national party also had inept leaders because they had failed to dissuade many union members from voting for Republican presidents Reagan and Bush. Labor was also unable to discipline its members, but our informants did not know what labor should do to build discipline. Like many others, they supported a doomsday scenario: If labor continued to be buffeted by business and government, it would be driven to unite and fight back. In short, like the IBEW, the carpenters' sense of meaningful politics was derived from its almost exclusive preoccupation with local construction issues. Unlike the IBEW, the carpenters' sense of the larger political scene was one of powerlessness and despair, reflecting its loose, decentralized, and inactive organization.

The Electricians

IBEW locals in the Cleveland area had about 3,500 members. The local I examined had 1,800 members (Table 7.1). It took its political work seriously. About half of the members participated in the political check-off, raising $8,000–$10,000 in voluntary contributions in the last election cycle (see Table 7.1). A third went to the international; the remainder went to local politics. Officers insisted that raising money was no problem and that its six-member staff recruited enough volunteers to perform the needed political work. Although the union cooperated with both COPE and the BTC, it worked mainly through the BTC and traditionally followed its recommendations. In line with customary practices, the IBEW conducted its own registration drives (i.e., not through the BTC or COPE), door-to-door electioneering, phone banks, and political advertising.

IBEW officials thought that they had organized a political education program superior to that of most BTC unions, which carried out assigned tasks ritualistically. The IBEW acknowledged that the UAW and the Teamsters were also politically effective and that some disagreements with the UAW (Gateway, tax abatement) were unbridgeable. The IBEW was interested in advancing government and nonresidential private-sector construction. It loaned money from its pension funds, probably at lower interest rates, to local builders who employed only union labor. Admitting a penchant for pursuing their own special interests, IBEW leaders understood that the UAW and the Teamsters were pursuing their "natural" interests by not joining COPE.

IBEW activists had become somewhat disillusioned with the local Democratic Party in recent years. While the party chair was prolabor, he failed to respond sufficiently to labor's concerns. Even though the party depended on labor support, it sometimes endorsed candidates unacceptable to the building trades. In response, the IBEW did not hesitate to endorse Republican mayors Voinovich and Forbes as well as Republican judges. In the future, IBEW would pull away from the party even more unless it supported more candidates who had labor support. In sum, the IBEW's political involvement was job-centered. Its leaders believed that such activism on a national scale would cure most of labor's weakness.

The Steel Workers

The USW and the UAW were the largest industrial unions in the Cleveland area. Unlike the UAW, which was centralized along regional lines, the USW's District 28 contained 128 locals in northeast Ohio, each plant with its own local. Reflecting racial and residential composition in the Cleveland area, about 40 percent of the 23,000 members were black (Table 7.1). The union had lost half its members since the 1970s, but steel workers still earned high wages. In the 1960s, many members moved to the suburbs, but they generally retained their party identification. About three-quarters were still Democrats, and surveys revealed that 60 percent voted in the recent gubernatorial election. Like the UAW officials, those in the USW held strong liberal working-class views.

The USW was restructuring its political education program because its officers knew that many members did not follow their voting recommendations. Members needed more information on why the union favored some candidates over others. The USW committed 5 percent of its budget to political education and it raised some "hard" money during campaigns. The union also held district and state legislative conferences to educate activists on issues that should be communicated to members.

The USW participated in all three regional COPE bodies and screened no candidates independently. However, it published literature, conducted registration drives, and operated its own phone banks. All the staff were expected to "walk the precincts" on Election Day in door-to-door canvassing. USW officers felt that their electoral work was equally effective among African-American and white members. Theirs was the only union to coordinate voter registration drives with the blacks' Twenty-First District Caucus.

USW leaders felt an ideological affinity to the UAW, which, they believed, was the most politically effective union in the region. Yet the USW supported tax abatement as a job-creating mechanism, while the

UAW had opposed it because it shifted tax burdens to the poor. USW officers thought their union was almost as strong politically as the UAW and that COPE would be much stronger with the UAW in it. If the union joined COPE, the two unions could make COPE more liberal. Other unions with strong programs included the communication workers (CWA), the clerks (UFCW), and AFSCME. While the building trades influenced the outcome of some local issues, they appeared unable to "see the big picture on the state and national level."

USW officials regarded the local Democratic Party as too divided "regionally." Westside Democrats were interested in consumer matters; the Twenty-first District Caucus, in party control; and white ethnics, in retaining patronage and resisting African-American political control. While blacks had almost half the seats on the party executive committee, labor was given only 15 percent. Therefore, it could exert little influence even though it provided most of the party's income. Yet the USW remained loyal to the party and hoped gradually to increase labor's influence in it. In short, USW officers were politically active, were abreast of the local political scene, recognized their problems, and knew what to do about them.

Communication Workers

The CWA included four locals with about 7,000 members in several different industries. The local selected for study had 4,200 members, 80 percent in the telephone industry. Over half were women; 30 percent were African Americans (Table 7.1). The locals recently joined to form a city council for legislative action. Perhaps a third or more of the local's technicians and skilled workers were Republican; clerical workers and operators, mainly African Americans, were Democrats. Officials estimated that about 60 percent of the members were Democrats, the lowest estimate for any union in the area. Union officers were very disturbed about members' political apathy and conservatism. Only 50 volunteers (40 of them staff members) had worked at the polls on Election Day.

The officers concluded that members did not follow union recommendations because they received too little information on issues and candidates. To improve matters, the union was planning a "grass roots mobilization drive." Officers planned to have fifteen-minute weekly conversations with each member in order to convince them that their concerns would become the basis of political action. To obtain management's acceptance of the program, the union proposed that it could also conduct such conversations with workers to explore their ideas on how to improve productivity and morale.

Executing this plan would require much more money for political education. The local was already spending about a third of its million-dollar budget on political education and nearly a tenth on publications. This proportion exceeded that of any union in this study. Even so, the results were disappointing because members did not read the materials. Older workers, especially, had little commitment to the union. Therefore, the officials planned to identify younger members who were willing to run for local offices such as school boards. Those who succeeded might become committed to a lifetime of involvement in union politics.

Despite feelings of inadequacy, the CWA staff was more involved in political education than most union officers. All the CWA officers were deputy registrars, and they had made contact with all members to get them to register. The local had recently convinced 3,000 members to write to their legislators urging them to support a bill that prohibited employers from replacing striking union members with unorganized workers. A month before the gubernatorial election, twelve activists in the public-sector local conducted a door-to-door canvass in areas where many members lived. The local also operated fifty phones on Election Day, in addition to working on COPE's phone bank.

The CWA had withdrawn from COPE in 1989 over a series of controversies. Martin Hughes, a former CWA district leader, had been president of the Cleveland AFL-CIO. Although he was convicted of misusing CWA dues for political purposes, the central body continued to support him. Charging that COPE was dominated by old conservative white males who refused to retire, the union helped organize a "change slate" made up mostly of women and minority candidates, but none was elected. Tensions with COPE intensified, and the union stopped paying its per capita dues to the central body. A CWA-UAW coalition backed victorious Mike White for mayor, while COPE backed Forbes, the loser. Finally, realizing that its tactics would not change COPE, CWA leaders recommended that the union rejoin COPE and work for change from within. They agreed to accept the recommendation of COPE's screening committee, and they linked CWA's phone bank operations to COPE's.

CWA officers thought that the UAW had the most effective political program because it reached all members, including retirees. CWA's own reputation was thought to be better than it deserved. Yet, its political program was stronger than any of the building trades, the AFT, and the UFCW. On the local level, the police and the firefighters, though crippled by racial tensions, were also considered effective. The CWA's strained relations with AFSCME harked back to a jurisdictional dispute to organize state government workers, which the CWA lost. Nonetheless, AFSCME was admired for its ability to promote member interests despite lack of interest in working-class issues. The CWA's relations with the IBEW were also tense because the IBEW had tried to organize CWA electricians in the telephone industry. The CWA local was the only union in this study that had made contact with the AFT to visit schools and teach students about the importance of unions. The CWA refused to work with the Teamsters, whom they regarded as too conservative to be considered a union.

Despite past differences with COPE, AFSCME, and IBEW, CWA officers thought that divisions within labor were few and not serious. Thus, the union's disagreements with the IBEW had not damaged the CWA's relations with the other building trades. The UAW's battles with COPE and the building trades on tax abatement had to be put in context; the parties agreed on 50 to 75 percent of the issues. Most informants in this study considered this rate of agreement as unacceptably low!

CWA also discounted splits in the Democratic ranks among African Americans, white ethnics, and labor. The union member on the party's executive committee estimated that labor held 15 percent of the seats, the lowest estimate of any union in this study. However, the USW's devotion to the Democratic Party was not complete. It had backed Republicans Voinovich and Douglas for mayor on grounds that the Democratic Party failed to address labor concerns. In frustration, some CWA leaders had once considered joining other "progressive" unions to create a third party, a suggestion stoutly resisted by members earning $50,000 to $80,000 a year. However, a rapidly deteriorating economy was now threatening industry earnings. If the industry succeeds in lowering wages, members might be aroused to push for "genuine" political change.

CWA officers felt that the confused political situation and the industry's uncertain future called for a reappraisal of the union's relations with management. The CWA had often pressed the grievances of undeserving members. Continuing this practice in the face of management's need to improve productivity and lower labor costs might provoke management to try to break the union. Members should therefore cooperate with management to increase productivity but should stoutly resist any effort to split workers from the union. In sum, CWA's officers were very worried about the union's political ineffectiveness. They had considered several plans to improve it, but some of them seemed unworkable. They wanted to create a liberal coalition within COPE, but past juridictional disputes with other unions and the resulting strains impeded progress. Uncertain of the steps to be taken, they remained determined to overcome members' complacency.

Government Workers

AFSCME's 100,000 Ohio members belong to three affiliates: OPSE (Ohio Public School Employees), OCSEA (Ohio Civil Service Employees), and AFSCME Ohio Council 8 (primarily municipal, county, and state university employees). The Cleveland Region of Council 8 included 8,000 members in four northeastern Ohio counties (the majority living in Cuyahoga County), making it the area's fifth largest union (Table 7.1). The largest of the twenty-six locals were in the County Hospital System, the State Department of Human Services, and Metro Health Service. These units contained professional, clerical, manual, and service workers. The president of the Cleveland region, a woman, estimated that perhaps two-thirds of the members were women and about half were African Americans. Because some municipalities made residence a requirement for public employment, most members lived in cities.

The great majority of AFSCME members were Democrats. Because their livelihood depended on public funds, members were more interested in politics than most unionists. In particular, they were anxious about the funding of their agencies and the erosion of local and state government services. Unlike most unions, AFSCME experienced little difficulty in recruiting volunteers for registration drives, fund solicitation, and phone bank operation. Occasionally, precinct canvassing was undertaken. In these grass roots efforts, AFSCME's volunteers considered their performance superior to COPE's.

While participation in political check-offs varied by local, large contributions were raised at election time and sent to the state PAC, PEOPLE (Public Employees Organized to Promote Labor Equality). State legislative action committees monitored state policies, studied candidate records, and monitored local issues. AFSCME screened candidates for state and local office independently of COPE and followed the incumbency rule of not rescreening satisfactory incumbents. A spate of publications informed members of the union's position on local issues and candidates. For example, AFSCME targeted two major issues: levies for health and human services and the Cuyahoga Community College. Members quickly recognized the importance of these issues, and many volunteered to work for their passage.

AFSCME conducted its political work both with and without COPE, thus reaching its members and the broader labor community. AFSCME officers considered the UAW's political organization best in the area, equal to its own. Labor would be much stronger politically if the UAW and the Teamsters would join COPE and adopt AFSCME's policy of combining cooperation and independence. The AFT, another government union, did not inculcate an appreciation of the labor movement in members, even though the AFT sought labor support to help pass school levies.

As in most unions, AFSCME leaders felt that the Democratic Party did not respond to labor's interests. The party depended on labor for money and volunteers but did little to involve it in party decisions. Party leaders mistakenly thought that labor's interests were narrow and did not understand that its primary concern was the welfare of "working people." Thus, party leaders were responsible for the party's declining appeal. To reverse the tide, the party needed to pursue issues with broad appeal, such as national health insurance. In the long run, labor's program could be advanced only by education, by convincing teachers to carry the message that promoting labor's welfare promoted the general welfare. In sum, AFSCME operated a sophisticated political organization to advance its self-interests. It cooperated with COPE but had not developed a strategy to extend labor's influence in the party.

Teachers

Cleveland's AFT signed its first collective bargaining agreement in 1964. By 1990, it represented 5,000 county teachers and had as many members as AFSCME (Table 7.1). But AFT members were conservative and became involved in local issues that had little party relevance. A recent survey revealed that two-thirds were nominal Democrats who did not strongly identify with any party. The union's legislative priorities focused on the educational issues set at the national conventions. State and local units were expected to implement them.

AFT locals conducted workshops on political education and raised "hard money" that was sent to the Washington office, which then disbursed it to favored congressional candidates. The Ohio Federation of Teachers (OFT) sent its locals a plethora of publications, newspapers, pamphlets, and manuals which dealt with its political issues. AFT contributed to the state COPE, but the latter did not become involved in local school board races, tax levies, and millage referenda. In the past, the Cleveland AFT used COPE's screening committee for school board elections, but in 1991 AFT created its own committee to screen for a wide range of offices. The local also operated phone banks at election time. Although AFT endorsements were often the same as COPE's, in 1991 the AFT backed Republican Voinovich for governor.

AFT's political targets were as narrowly job-centered as those of the building trades: funding for education and Head Start funding, career ladders for teachers, peer options for locals, and school choice vouchers. Cleveland's AFT did not ask COPE to support these issues. For school levies, the AFT made direct contact with other groups (e.g., business, the African-American community, and churches). Although the AFT and the Ohio Educational Association (OEA) tried to coordinate efforts to increase state funding for education, they often split on other issues. The OEA rather than the Republican Party seemed to be the AFT's main opponent. Both unions sent delegates to the National Democratic Convention. Together, they constituted the convention's largest occupational group. Contact with AFL-CIO members at conventions was limited largely to educational issues.

While AFT officials were aware of the political influence of other Cleveland unions and the issues that divided them, the AFT rarely engaged in partisan issues. Its officers were aware of Democratic Party cleavages, but they avoided taking sides or forming coalitions even on educational issues. AFT officers thought that the party was losing popular support because it had become too "rigid" (liberal) ideologically, while voters were more concerned about the quality of individual candidates. In short, the AFT, like the Teamsters, played a separatist game in COPE and in the party in pursuit of its job interests. Making loose and temporary commitments was seen as the best strategy to promote teachers' welfare.

Food and Commercial Workers

A majority of the 29,000 members of UFCW Local 880 in northeast Ohio lived in Cuyahoga County. Over half were women and African Americans who worked in food-processing plants, groceries, bakeries, and pharmacies. Officers estimated that a substantial majority of the local's Cleveland members were Democrats (Table 7.1), but elsewhere they divided evenly among the two parties and independents. However, everywhere they were politically apathetic and did not understand how politics could affect their well-being.

Although the local's leaders said they were interested in politics, they had not established a political education committee, nor did they include politics in steward training. The local's newsletter dealt almost exclusively with internal union matters. Small sums of money were raised by the active ballot club. The union sent a delegate to COPE's scanning committee, although the union disapproved of COPE's incumbency rule. Otherwise, the union did not engage its members in politics. At election time, UFCW's large staff of forty-five to fifty operated phone banks from its three offices in the area.

UFCW local officials had strong opinions about local politics even though they seemed detached. They disapproved of UAW and Teamster policy not to join COPE but then indicated that the two unions had a strong political program and that it cooperated with COPE in the "United Labor Agency." No other informants mentioned this agency; on the contrary, they indicated that UAW cooperation with COPE was informal and accidental. The UFCW admired AFSCME's strength in state politics and its ability to mobilize its members politically. The building trades were regarded as locally influential despite their internal divisions.

In the interviews, UFCW informants knowledgeably discussed local issues important to members, especially tax rates and zoning. Yet the union took no stand on tax abatement, the issue that aroused such passionate controversy in other unions. However, the UFCW backed Gateway because it promised to create jobs. Contrary to almost all other informants, UFCW officers thought the local Democratic Party very strong, even though it had become conservative and rejected candidates appealing to labor. Labor did not expect to dominate the party, but it deserved more representation in party committees. When asked what should be done to increase public sympathy for labor, UFCW officials thought that labor education in the schools was the best strategy.

In short, UFCW politics was left to state and national officers and to the union's full-time lobbyist in Columbus. Here, the union met with some success. Recently, it had defeated a legislative proposal to limit the picketing of food stores and successfully resisted the governor's attempt to privatize state liquor stores, which were organized by the union. In sum, the UFCW, a large union in the growing service sector, had failed to develop a political education program of interest to its largely African-American members. The officers embraced a liberal rhetoric, but they gave little thought to implementing it.

Service Workers

The president of the Service Employees International Union (SEIU) was a third-generation member. The local had 8,000 members; 85 percent lived in the county, 65 percent in Cleveland. The union's amalgamated structure had four divisions: public employment, health care, building services, and industry. Almost two-thirds of the members were African American, most of them women (Table 7.1). More than a third worked in part-time jobs in janitorial and cleaning services. Membership in the local declined during the early 1980s and leveled off in 1990.

Almost all SEIU members identified themselves as Democrats, but few showed interest in politics. The local's political education program was minuscule. Its political education committee had one member; its only function was to make sure that members received the publication of the state central body, which listed its candidate endorsements for state offices. Locals were asked occasionally to participate in letter-writing campaigns to legislators with reference to particular bills. Otherwise, the local undertook no political work independent of COPE. SEIU officers surprisingly claimed that about 40 percent of the members participated in the political check-off and that small additional sums were raised at election time.

SEIU officers favored the Gateway project and tax abatement for downtown development. Following COPE's lead, they supported Republican Voinovich for mayor and then supported Celebrezze against Voinovich for governor. Officials were either uninformed or unwilling to examine racial issues in Cleveland politics. Although the SEIU's membership was predominantly African-American, its white officers made no contacts with the Twenty-first District Caucus. They supported COPE's endorsement of Forbes for mayor against the successful black Democratic candidate, Mike White. Predictably, reflecting COPE's position, SEIU officers expressed dissatisfaction with the local Democratic Party; they blamed COPE for not putting more pressure on the party to back labor causes.

Although aware of the liberal ideology of the international's officers, local officers were detached from local politics. Thus, they were aware of the UAW's working-class stance; of the BTC's sole interest in promoting local construction; AFSCME's progovernment growth policies; and the Teamsters' isolation from the labor movement. They knew that the SEIU was the nation's third largest union, that it ranked twenty-sixth in raising PAC money, and that their international was committed to national health insurance, civil rights, equal opportunity, and other liberal goals. Yet, the local did little to inform members about these issues. In short, both the UFCW and the SEIU, as the largest unions in the expanding service sector, seemed detached from local politics, the political issues that affected their black members, and their internationals' political goals.

EVALUATING THE LABOR–PARTY POLITICAL SYSTEM

Given the divisions within the Democratic Party and its constituencies, it is remarkable that the party had won so many elections. Ward leaders, ethnic groups, racial groups, and unions had developed their political organizations. Party leaders could not coordinate them because each group wanted to retain its base of influence. Union officials felt that, given their contributions to the party, labor was underrepresented in party committees and its interests were neglected. African Americans had more members than labor on the party's executive committee, but they also represented more voters.

Labor seemed as fragmented as the party. Its three major electoral organizations (the UAW, the Teamsters, and COPE) were not coordinated. AFSCME, some BTC trades, and the teachers did not fully cooperate with

COPE, sometimes deviating from its candidate endorsements and public stands. Most unions in COPE and the BTC spent more money pursuing their individual objectives than supporting umbrella organizations. Yet none of labor's political organizations systematically monitored community *issues* important to some or all members. Informants rarely mentioned racial equity, taxes, city services, housing, health, welfare, education, transportation, crime, and public safety. COPE was designed to monitor these issues but did not, possibly because its officers made no serious effort to probe members' political concerns. The effectiveness of the labor–party system deteriorated as each became more divided and less concerned about local community issues.

APPLYING SEGMENTATION THEORY TO LABOR

The theory of union segmentation grouped unions into four types. How did the politics of each type differ? The ex-CIO unions most retained the New Deal working-class orientation, the UAW with élan and the USW with remnants of élan, while the CWA was struggling to revive it. Among the ex-AFL unions, the Teamsters most preserved a job-oriented tradition. The building trades were close behind, but the IBEW tilted toward the CIO pattern. Among the public sector unions, the teachers fitted comfortably into the AFL job-oriented pattern, while AFSCME had devised a two-pronged approach: formal solidarity with COPE and sector-oriented unionism. UFCW and SEIU, as new service unions, had the least developed programs. While their internationals espoused working-class politics resembling that of the ex-CIO unions, their local officers seemed incapable of articulating or implementing it. Thus, the theory of union political segmentation has preliminary support.

The ten unions, the main actors in labor's political system, may be classified in terms of their relationship to COPE. The UAW and the Teamsters were not part of it. The BTC unions (e.g., the carpenters and the IBEW) were coordinated, if at all, by the BTC rather than by COPE. But the BTC itself was decentralized and depended completely on the willingness of members to cooperate. They often did not. AFSCME and the teachers (AFT) retained a measured distance from COPE. Altogether, six of the ten major unions were outside or peripheral to COPE. The communication workers (CWA) had recently returned to COPE and begun to cooperate, while the steel workers (USW) remained steadfastly committed to COPE. The clerks (UFCW) and service workers (SEIU) were solidly in COPE, but their political programs were weak. In sum, labor's segmented political system was tenuously coordinated.

The political behavior of the ten unions varied considerably. The UAW probably had the most centralized and best financed organization. It focused on issues important to the poor, African Americans, and manual workers and consistently pursued their issues in local, state, and national affairs. The Teamsters' political organization was the best financed, and as strong and centralized as the UAW's. It was as job-oriented as the UAW was class-conscious, as secretive as the UAW was open. The political objectives of the Teamsters, carpenters, teachers, and electricians were job-oriented, while those of the UAW, USW, and CWA were oriented to race, class, and union issues. AFSCME's public rhetoric supported the liberal wing of labor and the party, but it committed most of its resources to advancing its interests in the government sector. The leadership and members of SEIU and UFCW was disposed to support liberal social welfare goals, but their involvement in COPE and Democratic Party affairs was small and ritualistic.

The major political division of the ten unions ran along a job-versus-social-welfare axis. The split roughly paralleled the unions' race composition and the members' party disposition. Although the unions' exact racial makeup is unknown, blacks ranged from 10 to over 60 percent (see Table 7.1). In the job-oriented unions (the building trades, the Teamsters, and the teachers), blacks made up less than 20 percent of the members. These unions also had the lowest percentage of Democrats. The social-welfare-oriented unions all contained more blacks, from 35 to 60 percent, and, with the exception of CWA, a higher percentage of Democrats. All of the local officers interviewed were white. No union office was located in an African-American neighborhood; and only the USW had developed contacts with the Twenty-first District Caucus. In short, the unions were split along several lines: occupation, cooperation with COPE, political objectives, racial composition, and support of the Democratic Party.

The above review suggests that the ability of the Democratic Party and COPE to aggregate their constituencies declined over time as they became more diverse socially, economically, and residentially. White ethnic suburban migration weakened their traditional union and Democratic Party loyalties. Blacks' loyalty to the Democratic Party vacillated as white ethnics fought to control it and as blacks consolidated strength in the Twenty-first District Caucus. Cohorts entering the labor force during the Great Depression and World War II, once the loyal bulwark of unions and the Democratic Party, have now retired or died. Workers who entered the labor force after 1965 have no memory of the New Deal and a once-vibrant labor movement. Today, fewer and fewer persons volunteer to work for labor and the party.

Faced with the changing political environment of the 1970s and 1980s,

COPE had to work harder to maintain party loyalty. The UAW and the Teamsters created separate political organizations, and all unions strengthened their PACs, which shifted more emphasis to job-related issues, those beyond COPE's ability to push. With the possible exception of the UAW and the CWA, neither COPE nor its member unions increased their budgets for political education. In the interviews, despite probing, informants rarely mentioned race, affirmative action, income taxes, zoning, busing, educational reform, housing for the poor, governmental services, health care, crime, transportation, zoning, welfare, or dependency, all the things close to people's daily lives. Officers discussed unemployment and urban development. But the new baseball and basketball stadiums in Gateway and the new downtown shopping mall solved no deeper community problems: the 40 percent of Cleveland residents who live below the poverty line, the 40 percent high-school-dropout rate, welfare dependency, and decaying housing in the crack-ridden Fifth Ward. In short, although Democrats won most of the elections, they and labor failed to address the area's massive problems. In the November 1994 election, party strength was ebbing. It lost two traditional seats in the statehouse and one in the state Senate. Banking on traditional loyalties, their political success was more than they deserved. But how long can they bank on tradition?

8

Cincinnati

Overcoming Tradition

Cincinnati has long had a reputation as a conservative community and a Republican stronghold. The party's success in local, state, and federal elections supports this impression. Since 1931, the metropolitan area has been divided into two congressional districts. A north–south line roughly splits community and suburbs along economic lines. On the east side of the divide, Congressional District 1, changed to District 2 in 1977, contains African-American, middle-class areas of the community, as well as middle-class and affluent suburbs east and northeast of the city center. From 1931 to 1992, except for two terms (1937–1938 and 1965–1966), the district elected only Republicans to the U.S. House of Representatives. On the west side of the divide, District 2, changed to District 1 in 1977, includes African-American and working-class (Over-the-Rhine) districts, lower-middle and middle-class areas, and suburbs west and northwest of the city center. From 1931 to 1964, except for two congressional terms, this district also was Republican; but from 1965 to 1992, except for three terms, the district has voted Democratic.

State legislative representation echoes this pattern. The three state senate seats were occupied by Republicans from the mid-1930s until the late 1960s; since then, by two Republicans and one Democrat. In the assembly (house), Republicans enjoyed a monopoly from the mid-1930s to the mid-1960s; since then, seven Republicans and two Democrats have served. Hamilton County government has been a virtual Republican reserve. For several decades, the suburban middle-class vote has outpaced the city's African-American and working-class vote.

In the city (see Chapter 6 for details), Republican machines dominated city politics until the 1920s, when the Charterites introduced the city manager plan and proportional representation. Up to 1957, when proportional representation was eliminated, Republicans and the Charter–Democrat alliance alternated in dominating the city council. Republicans regained control in the 1960s, but from 1973 to 1985, the Democrats and Charterites "cooperated" to form a majority. A conservative interparty coalition dominated the council for the next five years. Finally, in 1991, a revived Democratic Party elected a council majority and the county auditor for the first time.

THE DEMOCRATIC PARTY AS A COORDINATOR

The Hamilton County Democratic Party competes with the Charter Committee in the city and the Republican Party in all elections. Patronage is virtually nonexistent in city government; the Republicans have monopolized it in the county. Both parties confront the problem of monitoring twenty-six city wards and thirty county communities and townships. The Democratic Party lacks the resources and supporters to monitor the county adequately.

The fifty-six wards and communities presumably have Democratic clubs, but none has a headquarters, and a third or more hold no regular monthly meetings. The party pays the clubs half of their costs for precinct workers on Election Day. Party headquarters occupied three sparsely furnished rooms in an old building just outside the central business district. The staff consisted of two part-time cochairs and a secretary who worked twenty-five hours a week. For almost thirty years, the party had been run by a chair who reputedly regarded it as his private reserve. On his retirement in 1989, he was replaced by cochairs: an African-American and a white. In 1991, they were replaced by the popular ex-member of Congress, Tom Luken.

In 1992, Tim Burke became chair. A central committee of 750 members elected the party's unwieldy executive committee of 150–200 persons. Slightly more than a tenth of its members were union members, about a quarter were blacks, and the remainder were activists in the wards, outlying municipalities, and unincorporated areas. Finances were a constant worry. Two annual fund drives raised $50,000. The chairman's club of thirty-one members each pledged $1,000, and the state party provided $25,000. Labor's declining numbers reduced its party contributions, forcing candidates to raise the bulk of their campaign funds and discouraging many blacks from seeking office because they had great difficulty raising money. With reduced responsibility for fund-raising, the party's main functions were to identify candidates for office, to give them campaign advice, to train their volunteers, and to coordinate the ward organizations and COPE.

Historically, the party contended with a liberal–conservative split and a split over relations to the Charterites. Some Democrats saw Charterites basically as moderate Republicans; others regarded them as true independents and worthy partners needed to advance liberal causes. On occasion, the Charter party showed signs of collapse but somehow it always managed to reinvigorate itself. Democratic Party leaders considered the Charterites irritating, independent, and episodic allies who were more trouble than they were worth.

For years, ward leaders resisted central party control and retained considerable autonomy. Some of them in the conservative, heavily Catholic, German, and Appalachian areas occasionally cooperated with the Republicans to defeat liberal, labor, or black Democratic candidates. In the mid-1960s, some conservative ward leaders threatened to bolt the party because they felt it was dominated by a liberal–labor coalition. They felt especially threatened when liberals insisted that blacks be represented on the executive committee in proportion to their population.

The inability of party groups to establish stable relationships permitted the chair to control the feeble central organization. The influence of ward leaders and labor activists slowly waned after 1960, as did labor's contributions. The city's African-American population seemed to stabilize at about 35 percent, reducing fears that blacks would soon take over the party. Although blacks in the state senate and city council continued to need party support, they increasingly asserted their independence.

Three major groups in the party's liberal wing contended for influence. Liberal professionals pressed for mental health levies, planning and expanding cultural facilities. Labor placed priority on prevailing wages in government projects, organizing government workers, and attracting employment. Blacks emphasized housing and urban development, racial equity, and welfare. The policy divisions were not irreparable, and the three groups agreed that the party could not gain control of city and county governments without stronger, more centralized administration. At the time of the research, they had decided to replace party officials and tighten party discipline.

REPUBLICAN PARTY DOMINANCE

Republican Party headquarters was as busy, spacious, luxuriously furnished, and well equipped as Democratic headquarters was idle, small, barren, and ill furnished. Located in the heart of the central business district, Republican headquarters had a well-appointed conference room, which the party made available to local business groups. A party staff of five employed full-time year-round included an executive director, a political director, and three secretaries. The executive director supervised the Hamilton County Republican Party and the Republican finance committee. The party had a reputation as one of the nation's strongest. President Bush's eight Cincinnati visits during the 1988 campaign attest to the party's influence.

Unlike the Democratic Party's episodic mobilization, the Republican Party was continuously active in raising funds, handling inquiries, maintaining contact with ward and precinct leaders, planning events, and screening possible candidates. The party had strong ward, township, and suburban organizations capable of supplying the necessary volunteers at election time. Many were older well-educated women experienced in organizational work. The party monopolized county patronage and had a strong presence in state politics. It brought a large state office building to the city and obtained plentiful funding for the University of Cincinnati, the city's largest employer. Republican officials felt that the Democratic Party was poorly organized and that its leaders had a defeatist attitude. Were it not for labor's electoral machine, which was much better than the party's, the party would be unable to win any city election.

Republican leaders felt optimistic about the party's future. The black community was no longer a single constituency; some of its leaders were abandoning traditional Democratic allegiances. Almost half of union members were Republicans, and the party could attract more. Organized labor already supported some Republican candidates (e.g., unbeatable judges and county officials). Blacks and union members were beginning to understand that everyone profits from Republican policies that reward self-reliance and individual initiative. Charterites, less troublesome than the Democrats, were affluent liberal holdovers from a bygone reform era whose hobby of clean local government was no longer needed.

CHARTERITES

The Charterites maintained a small downtown suite of modestly furnished offices with two staff members and a part-time executive director. Their small budget was supported mainly by a few affluent business men and women and professionals. An informant explained that the party did not need a large budget because its main resource was the community respect that its dedicated leaders enjoyed. Many Charter supporters were second-generation Charterites, liberal and well-educated citizens who believed that the party was needed to *preserve* good local government. Their immediate goal was to reinstate proportional representation in elections, which, they felt, would guarantee minorities better representation.

Charter activists had little interest in running candidates for county elections even though they thought that county government was unrepresentative, inefficient, and patronage-riven. They also claimed they lacked resources and volunteers to run a county organization. Critics saw Charter policy as backward; it put resources into city elections, where reforms had taken place, and not in county elections, where they were needed.

Some Charter leaders were aware that others considered the party a historic relic, a private club of old families that wanted to keep alive ancestral legacies of good government. But Charterites insisted that the party was still making contributions: It had recruited more blacks to the city council than either party; it bridged labor, business, and other groups; it still pushed for voting reform (proportional representation); and it had conducted its affairs more openly than the other parties.

Charter influentials knew that many of the party's traditional supporters were moving to the suburbs. The party rarely won a majority of council seats, but it could tip the balance on important issues. The party's future was uncertain unless it recruited a new generation of supporters. For the present, some suburbanites who worked in the city continued to support the party financially because good government was required to maintain a healthy local economy.

COPE AS A COORDINATING PARTY

After World War II, Cincinnati labor developed weak ties to the Democratic Party. Although the AFL–CIO merged in 1955, COPE did not operate locally until 1960, when about 125,000 union members resided in the metropolitan area. The party chair allegedly resisted labor's influence because he feared labor would unite with dissident groups to unseat him. By 1964, his fears were realized. Labor and disgruntled liberals united to replace him in the campaign to elect Lyndon Johnson as president. Labor handled campaign finances and coordinated the drive to register new voters.

Despite fears of labor domination, labor and the Democratic Party worked well together during the 1960s, although some party regulars objected to labor's insistence on occupying executive committee seats and yet reserving the right not to back the entire party slate. During the decade, labor helped strengthen the party's precinct and ward organizations and improved its own organization until it became better than the party's.

A number of events slowed Democratic Party growth. The Charterites, who had all but succumbed in 1960, recovered by 1965, winning three city council seats. For twenty years labor, the Democratic Party, and the Charterites had to cooperate to remain a viable force in city elections. The Republicans strengthened their precinct and ward organizations, which, although stronger than the Democratic organizations since the 1920s, were weakened when traditional supporters moved to the suburbs. In the 1970s, candidates began to raise more of their own campaign funds and rely less on the party. Labor decided on a policy not to dominate the party and refrain from participating in primaries. Party discipline slackened. The UAW's leaving the AFL–CIO in 1968 weakened COPE. The shrinking of the manufacturing sector also reduced union members by about 40,000 between 1970 and 1990. Although the city's black population had grown, labor and the Democratic Party did little to strengthen ward organizations. However, both Republicans and Charterites succeeded in recruiting a few blacks to run for office.

Increasingly, the Democratic Party and labor operated separate electoral organizations, especially in the wards. Liberals became disillusioned with party leadership. Labor, complaining of insufficient representation, increasingly supported some sympathetic Republican candidates. In the 1991 election, COPE endorsed 28 percent of city and county candidates who were not Democrats. In the late 1980s, some liberals, labor leaders, and professionals decided to reorganize the party and change its leadership. To maximize party–labor effectiveness, COPE leaders decided to reorganize COPE.

REORGANIZING COPE

COPE's Cincinnati operations generally resembled Cleveland's but differed in important ways. Both COPEs organized screening committees, operated phone banks, and engaged in registration and voting drives. In both cities, the UAW and the Teamsters were among the largest unions outside COPE. The BTC unions were influential in local politics but maintained a calculated distance from COPE. The Cincinnati COPE's budget was smaller because more locals sent their "hard" money to their internationals. The Cincinnati COPE could spend only $20,000 on an average election. The state COPE provided about $5,000, and $15,000 was raised locally by dinners, dances, and auctions.

In the early 1990s, Daniel Radford, the executive secretary-treasurer of the Cincinnati AFL–CIO labor council, was an active member of the

Democratic Party's executive committee. He and other COPE officials thought that labor's electoral efforts had become ritualistic, and they embarked on a program to improve it to invigorate the party.

In 1990, the central labor body launched the National Association of Working Americans (NAWA), which extended associate union membership to workers not represented by unions where they worked. For a modest fee, they were provided most services available to union members: savings on medical expenses, lower interest rates on loans, a no-fee credit card, lower-cost legal services, lower insurance rates, shopping savings, and union publications. NAWA was designed to broaden support for labor's goals and to compensate in part for losses in union membership. As a local test area, Cincinnati labor hoped to recruit 3,000 to 5,000 members to NAWA, many of whom would be former union members. NAWA was given a delegate on the Central Labor Council, which automatically incorporated NAWA into COPE. COPE identified about four hundred activists who agreed to recruit three members each for NAWA.

In a year, about 2,000 workers had joined NAWA. The newly appointed NAWA director mailed several attractive newsletters to inform members about job issues, local political concerns, and community services. Members who became unemployed by plant closings were referred to a private foundation for advising. NAWA also sought federal grants to help the unemployed.

COPE introduced other innovations to increase labor's electoral strength. It tried to integrate the political organizations of AFSCME and BTC more closely into COPE, and COPE made its phone banks available to the UAW. More important, COPE began to plan electoral campaigns in July rather than October. A retired union member was recruited to work full time on the project. As in Cleveland, lists of local union members, arranged by precinct, were obtained from state and national COPEs. Membership lists were also collated from sixteen unions not affiliated with the national AFL-CIO. The consolidated lists of 60,000 members were matched against the board of elections' voter lists.

Staff members from individual unions and volunteers recruited to operate phone banks and engage in electoral activities made calls to identify voters' political preferences and views on five issues, typically not bread-and-butter ones: health care, child care, jobs, unemployment, and the national debt. Divisive issues like gun control and abortion were avoided. Then, the national COPE sent voters letters that explained the stands of current party candidates on the two most important issues. The voters were again called for their current views. In 1988, about 15,000 letters were generated; more were contemplated in ensuing elections. In the month before the election, each large local was assigned one night at the phone banks. The number of calls made was recorded and published to stimulate competition among the locals.

The practice of reminding members to vote was moved from Election Day to the preceding Sunday. Depending on the election, this switch increased voter contacts from 20 to 66 percent. COPE established four or five neighborhood centers in union halls and recruited about 250 volunteers to walk and talk with members in high-union, high-Democratic but low-turnout precincts. About 120 phones were used at the peak of the campaign to remind members to vote. On election day, some unions sent staff and activists to canvass wards that had many members. Since about 45 percent of union members lived in the city, COPE concentrated its efforts in city precincts, including those in the black wards. COPE leaders estimated that they made contact with 10,000 voters on Election Day. Clearly, the union's presence in the precincts was more visible than the party's.

These efforts appeared to improve the Democratic Party's fortunes. In 1991, for the first time in many years, Democrats elected a majority to the city council. Voting increased in the black wards, and African Americans were elected to state and local offices. An African American, currently president of the Cincinnati AFL–CIO labor council, indicated that labor had done more for blacks than the Democratic Party.

COPE planned to increase its electoral effectiveness in the party. Volunteers were still hard to recruit, and ways had to be found to increase their number. COPE planned to increase officer and activist political training in the locals as well as political communication with members at their workplaces.

Despite such efforts, COPE's relations with the Democratic Party remained strained. The party continued to back a judge who had ruled against the application of prevailing wage rates in public construction. It backed levies for government agencies that resisted unionization. The party's precinct performance was not improving as rapidly as labor's. Voter turnout in the precincts, townships, and suburbs had not increased. A few union officials felt that labor had enough strength to take control of the party, but most of them thought it might be counterproductive. In the meantime, when COPE disagreed with the party's choice of candidates or its position, COPE presented its case directly to voters.

THE POLITICS OF THE BIG TEN UNIONS

The ten major unions in the area together represented about 65,000 members. In most instances, I interviewed the largest locals on the assumption that their leaders were best informed about how the union's political program affected members' political behavior (see Table 8.1).

The Auto Workers

Region 2A of the UAW included southern Ohio, West Virginia, and southwestern Pennsylvania. The Greater Cincinnati CAP council included four UAW locals with about 7,000 members in Hamilton and 5,000 in Clairmont County to the east, placing the UAW among the largest locally. The Ford local, near Batavia, a town about twenty-five miles east of the city center, was the largest in Hamilton County. Its members lived in widely scattered communities. Because of declining membership, Region 2A of the UAW was being phased out and melded into another.

After the UAW reaffiliated with the AFL-CIO in 1980, the regional director recommended that the union not reaffiliate with the local or regional COPE. "Personality conflicts" presumably played a role, but UAW officials acknowledged that they did not want to lose their power base in the party and did not want the UAW's liberalism diluted by joining COPE.

UAW membership declined precipitously after GM closed its Norwood plant in the mid-1980s, although union officials claimed that the loss did not diminish their ability to raise money for political work. The cost of servicing members had declined, and 70 percent of the members of the Ford local elected to take part in the political check-off (see Table 8.1), making about $55,000 annually available for politics. Three percent of the

Table 8.1
Characteristics of Hamilton County Labor Unions
as Reported by Informants, 1991–1992

Union	Members	Check-off (%)	Blacks (%)	Democrats (%)
Auto (UAW)	7,000	70	15	68
Teamsters	6,000	60	15[b]	60
Building trades	13,500	—	10	55[b]
Carpenters	2,500	0	10	50
Electricians (IBEW)	1,100[a]	40	12	70
Steel (USW)	7,500	10	30[b]	52
Communications (CWA)	1,450[a]	0	5	85
Government (AFSCME)	4,200	40[b]	40	55
Teachers (AFT)	3,700	33	10[b]	55
Food (UFCW)	13,000	10	15	60
Service (SEIU)	1,300	45	85	75

[a]For one local only.
[b]Estimated by interviewer.

dues were assigned to CAP, half of which remained with the local. The informant did not reveal the funds available for politics, but they probably exceeded those of any union except the Teamsters.

A member survey during the 1990 election revealed that 68 percent had voted Democratic. UAW officials depicted a very active CAP council. Its screening committee reviewed both Republican and Democratic candidates. It was less inclined than COPE routinely to approve incumbent candidates and more inclined to ignore the Charterites. UAW electoral work typically began after Labor Day, a few weeks after COPE's. CAP sent its members four letters and political flyers with information about candidates and their positions on important issues. This work was largely done by retired members. Just before the election, CAP again called members, using COPE's phone banks. Because the residence of members was widely dispersed, door-to-door canvassing was done only in a few selected areas. Occasionally, CAP cooperated in the labor–party coordinated campaign.

The UAW was more involved in state and national elections than in local ones. Membership mailing lists were sent by the international in Detroit to the locals to facilitate the distribution of political information. CAP and COPE usually exchanged information on the candidates they endorsed. Occasionally, they disagreed. UAW officials acknowledged that the local Democratic Party was weak, especially in fund-raising. The party relied heavily on the UAW, one of its strongest financial backers. Although the party was improving its ability to increase the voter turnout, it still underperformed the UAW and COPE. Without labor's help, the party could not compete evenly with the Republicans, who substantially outspent the Democrats. Despite its heavy dependence on labor, the party managed to limit labor's party influence. In turn, as CAP informants emphasized, CAP was not an arm of the party. It remained independent, backed Republican judges, and invited Republicans (who always accepted) to submit their records to the screening committee.

Even though CAP workers felt that their union was more politically active than any other in the region, they were not satisfied with their political education program. Most members were uninterested in politics, and a minority opposed the union's involvement. Yet enough volunteers were always available for political work, especially when the issue directly affected labor. Divisive issues such as race, affirmative action, gun control, and abortion were avoided, a policy that worked well.

CAP's concern with local welfare and working-class issues was muted. Its office did not display the pamphlets on health, race, taxes, and other issues so conspicuously displayed in Cleveland. Cincinnati CAP officials did not mention participating in the ALERTS, the international's device that alerted locals to flood Congress with letters backing or opposing important bills. Neither did they refer to local issues such as race relations, tax abatement, welfare, educational equality, housing, and crime. Nor would they specify their differences with COPE or the party. In short, CAP lacked the interest and perhaps the resources to monitor political issues in the electoral districts of Hamilton and Clairmont Counties, preferring to concentrate on the explicit instructions from the state and national CAPs.

The Teamsters

The Teamsters' Joint Council 24 included six locals in Ohio and northern Kentucky. Local 100 in Cincinnati, the largest in the state, was housed in a modern two-story building that included a spacious meeting hall and well-equipped offices for the thirteen business agents and staffs. The building was paid for and produced rental income. Before industry deregulation, Local 100 had 13,500 members; today it has 6,000, a decline of 56 percent (Table 8.1). Half of the members were drivers, a quarter were warehouse personnel, and the remainder worked in the public sector. Teamsters' annual earnings ranged from $50,000 to 70,000.

Aware of corruption charges being leveled against top national Teamster officials, local officials described themselves as the "good guys." Their political world revolved around two issues: the disastrous impact of deregulation on the trucking industry and management's drive to replace strikers with nonunion workers. DRIVE's main objectives were to restore industry regulation and press for legislation to prohibit striker replacement. Failure to enact such legislation could reduce current union membership by 50 percent in five years.

Teamsters officials were not modest about their political clout. They boasted of having the country's largest union, largest PAC, most dedicated officers, and most effective political organization. About 60 percent of the members of Local 100 contributed a dollar a week to DRIVE, half of it sent to the national DRIVE and half retained by the local. In a year, the local might raise over $180,000 for political work. This achievement was no accident. Stewards, trained to contact individual members, told them that their jobs ultimately depended on DRIVE's effectiveness. Contacts with drivers were routinely made as they reported at terminals before and after runs.

Although perhaps 60 percent of the Teamsters identified themselves as Democrats, party identification and loyalty were of secondary importance. Thus, the state Teamsters endorsed the Republican Voinovich for governor, while the local joint council backed the Democrat, Celebrezze. In the most recent state election, the local council backed six Republicans and eight Democrats, while in the city elections, it backed only Democrats because they were more prolabor than the Republicans.

The Teamsters saw little need to develop a formal political education program. The local, state, and national officers sent members newsletters which informed them of the union's position on issues and the candidates they should support. This was thought to be sufficient education.

DRIVE had almost no contact with COPE in Cincinnati or Kentucky, and officials saw no need for any. Although COPE and DRIVE generally agreed on candidate endorsements, DRIVE allocated its funds to candidates without consulting others. The Teamsters defended this tactic on the grounds that it had more concrete goals than COPE. Besides, COPE did not support the Teamsters on the regulation of the trucking industry, state laws to certify commercial driving standards, and the fight against privatizing jails, which the Teamster had organized.

Four staff members of the local (president, secretary, treasurer, and organizer) constituted the screening committee. It distributed a newsletter naming the candidates to be supported. The committee also allocated campaign contributions to individual candidates, who normally initiated contacts with the committee and knew in advance that they would be expected to support Teamster interests.

The Teamsters reported that, although they had good personal relations with COPE officers, they held divergent views about the Democratic Party. The Teamsters claimed to be the party's biggest contributor, but they were unhappy with it. The party had become too diversified and too liberal, especially on race. An official commented:

> We're turned off by certain groups in the party. I'd like to see a good southern Democrat come out of the party. Liberalism turns my people off. We like the Democrats'stand for the working class, antiracism, and so forth, but I could never support Mondale. I liked his stand on labor, but I really liked Harry Truman. Our members have jobs that pay $50,000- to $70,000-a-year, but they're turned off by the Democrats.

The Teamsters had no member on the Democratic Party executive committee, nor did they seek a larger party role. Becoming involved in party affairs would simply consume too much time. Unsurprisingly, the union had no contacts with the Charterites. In the words of an officer:

> Teamsters are concerned with money—endorsing a philosophy of the people. If candidates want Teamster money, they know what they have to do. Besides, we are already making an important contribution to the party with the best election organization in the labor movement. We have a better organization than the party, and the party should set out to improve itself. If labor wants a larger voice in the party and in the country, it should follow the Teamsters and choose a few central issues and support those issues with money.

In short, the Teamsters, proud of their independent position, kept a discreet distance from the parties and COPE. Focusing on job issues, they made direct contact with individual candidates and legislators and avoided becoming entangled in labor's welfare and working-class concerns.

The Building Trades Council

In 1990, the Cincinnati BTC represented 12,000 to 15,000 members in the building trades. Membership and resources had declined at least 10 percent after the 1970s, when the American Building Contractors (ABC) targeted Cincinnati in an open-shop drive (Table 8.1). In 1974 and again in 1981, the trades were forced to accept wage reductions that together cut wages by at least 25 percent. The chamber of commerce cooperated with ABC in declaring Cincinnati to be an open-shop city.

Historically, members of the building trades in Cincinnati tilted toward the Republican Party. When the AFL and the CIO merged in 1955, the BTC was not inclined to join COPE. Members of the skilled trades, especially, thought that the AFL-CIO was too closely attached to the Democratic Party. Therefore, for thirty years, up to 1985, the BTC operated independently of COPE, deviating more from its endorsement than even the UAW or the Teamsters. In some elections, the BTC and COPE disagreed on as many as 70 percent of the candidates. However, in the last decade, relations between the two bodies had improved somewhat. In 1980, only one member of the building trades had been on COPE's executive committee; a decade later, there were four. BTC and COPE endorsement disagreements had narrowed to 50 percent.

The success of local builders in the drive of ABC to reduce union membership and wages in the construction industry persuaded some union leaders that BTC should establish closer ties to COPE to protect prevailing wages in the local market. Disagreements over COPE lingered within the BTC but became muted. The BTC's current director occupied a middle position in the dispute. When locals disagreed with him, they simply operated independently. The majority of the BTC unions leaned toward the Democratic Party, but members showed little interest in party or politics. BTC leaders understood that their members had to become more politically active to fend off further business attacks on the trades.

The BTC's director devoted most of his energy to issues before the state legislature, channeling information to the unions, which then decided whether and how they should respond to it. The BTC's screening committee operated independently of COPE, disagreeing on endorsements almost as often as agreeing. BTC members routinely supported

Republican candidates for judge and often differed on other candidates. Thus, IBEW generally supported more COPE-endorsed candidates than the carpenters. In such disagreements, BTC officers remained silent. They also did not take a stand on most local issues but loudly condemned the three local parties for failing to support the BTC's main agenda item: prevailing wages.

Republican members of the BTC were the most frustrated. Not inclined to switch party allegiance, they had to admit that Republicans were unsympathetic to labor, especially on the issue of prevailing wages. The Charterites were regarded as relics of a bygone era, uninterested in organized labor. The Democratic Party was seen as weak and too preoccupied with minority and women's rights to pay attention to labor's main concerns. The Democrats in the BTC thought that labor should not dominate the party but should have enough influence to tip the party toward labor on divisive issues.

A frustrated BTC official shouted:

> The city council is dominated by a bunch of fascists who pay little attention to labor. Perhaps labor should run its own candidates for office. Of course, this wouldn't work in the suburbs. We're too few out there. But we're spread out, and that's an advantage because it links labor to every one.

A BTC member expressed the general view that Washington labor leaders were bureaucrats and not aggressive enough. In the 1980s, they had done nothing to contain the business greed that led to the suppression of labor. But this very suppression was beginning to unite labor and was promoting national prolabor sentiment. Labor had hit bottom and was now on the upswing. In short, the BTC, torn by its members' conflicting politics, probed for rapprochement with COPE. Yet it remained ambivalent about COPE, hoping that gestures of solidarity would suffice to mobilize the support needed to protect union jobs and wages in construction.

The Carpenters

The carpenters best represented political ambivalence and indecision in the building trades. Their district council in the Cincinnati region included three construction locals and a millwright factory local with a total membership of 2,500 (Table 8.1). Earlier, the district had sixteen locals organized around neighborhoods. Many carpenters were second- and third-generation union members. Since 1975, residential construction had become completely deunionized, membership had declined, and locals were consolidated. Blacks made up slightly more than a tenth of the membership; women, 2 percent. Dues, 3 percent of monthly wages plus $17.50, were pegged high because employers did not provide standard fringe benefits.

A Republican union official estimated that 50 percent of its members were Democrats; 35 percent, Independents; and 15 percent, Republicans. His estimate for the Democrats was the lowest reported for any union in this study. He explained that the number of Democratic sympathizers had increased slightly because their wages were falling toward those of industrial workers. Three wage cuts since 1974 had reduced carpenters' wages by a quarter or more. Currently, the carpenters were focusing on three issues: preserving prevailing wages, union protection, and improving the construction market. Union protection was a matter for national legislation, but wages and construction employment were local concerns. The carpenters monitored both public and private construction contracts for their adherence to union wage levels. Success was deemed to depend largely on bluff: convincing contractors that the union had sufficient power to make attacks on union wages troublesome and expensive.

Carpenters' involvement in community affairs had declined over the years. The traditional "walking the courthouse every other week just to keep in contact with local officials" had been discontinued. Carpenters had belonged to the chamber of commerce before 1970 but had dropped out, only to rejoin in 1985. One member served on the city zoning commission. The union had no plans to make contact with the downtown development committee because it would be fruitless to try to influence the small clique of local power brokers who controlled it.

Officers of the local claimed that politics was supremely important to their union; yet they had not developed a political education program. Members could presumably become politically informed by attending monthly meetings (less than 10 percent did) or by reading the local's recently launched quarterly newsletter and the AFL-CIO's monthly newsletter.

The union raised small political contributions—$500 to $3,500 a year—through raffles, auctions, and selling tickets to COPE-sponsored events. The money was spent locally. Contracts contained no political check-off clause. The carpenters' national PAC, the legislative improvement committee, was supported by a 1 percent check-off for all full-time staff members of the local district council, which generated about $6,000 yearly.

For decades, the carpenters operated a screening committee but had recently abandoned it in favor of participating in the BTC and COPE. The local took its turn in operating COPE's phone banks for one evening in the election season, an activity thought to be effective in increasing the voter turnout. On the whole, the officers regarded their political education program as ineffective because they did not discuss issues and candidates with members prior to the election. By that time, members had decided how to vote and resented advice from anyone, including the union.

Surprisingly, our informants thought that the carpenters' political efforts compared favorably with those of other strong programs, including the UAW, USW, CWA, and AFT, and that these unions, in turn, operated stronger programs than the small unions in the BTC, SEIU, and AFSCME. Informants apparently had limited knowledge of other unions' political programs or the Democratic Party. They thought that the local Democratic Party had become weaker because its coalition with the Charterites had collapsed, ignoring the fact that the Democrats had elected a majority of the council without Charter help.

The carpenters had no strong party preferences. The best strategy, they felt, was to endorse an equal number of Republicans and Democrats. One official explained:

> Look, it's often futile to endorse Democrats when they're going to lose. Why back a loser? You have nothing to gain. Better back somebody who you don't like who is going to win because maybe you can have some influence. So most of our local endorsements are Republicans, but national endorsements are more Democratic—90 percent. They make the laws that affect the union. This isn't done on the local level. On the local level, I am a Republican and on the national level, I often vote Democratic. On COPE, I don't make a big thing of party affiliation.

Even at the national level, some carpenter officials felt that labor had put itself in a no-win position by identifying with the Democratic Party. Thus, after Humphrey's defeat in the 1968 presidential campaign, labor's endorsement of candidates led to their certain defeat. But even when Democrats were elected, they forgot about labor. Since labor had neither the talent nor the money to control the Democratic Party, it should not favor any party. Moreover, since labor leaders could not force their party preferences on the rank and file, they should abandon the Democratic Party and endorse electable candidates who would support selected labor causes. The argument continued: National labor leaders were incapable of restoring public confidence in labor. They were too young, radical, and inexperienced. In contrast, the carpenters' national leaders were effective but truly exceptional. Perhaps a conservative labor leader like Lane Kirkland should run for Congress.

To conclude, the carpenters seemed detached and uninformed about local politics, split in party loyalties, and in favor of the traditional AFL formula of party neutrality, rewarding friends, and punishing enemies.

The Electricians

IBEW politics differed considerably from the carpenters'. The IBEW had five locals in the Cincinnati area, one in construction and four in small plants. The building local examined here had 1,100 active members, about half of the total membership (Table 8.1). From 1910 to 1984, the electricians had never conducted a strike. In 1984, the seven largest contractors in the region, refusing to engage in joint bargaining, conducted a moderately successful lockout. The local lost members and finally settled for lower wages, first with small builders and later with some larger ones. The union then inaugurated a "market recovery fund," in which 2 percent of wages were reserved to subsidize builders in exchange for union recognition and collective bargaining.

The strike convinced IBEW officers that they should concentrate on local politics in order to ensure that prevailing wages would prevail in government construction and downtown development projects. Officers convinced about 40 percent of the members to participate in a political check-off of five cents an hour, or about $100 a year. The local had raised about $30,000 for politics in 1992 and aimed to triple that amount in a few years. In the national election, it sent $15,000 to the international in Washington, with the proviso that some money would be returned to finance critical local campaigns. The additional small sums that were raised by dinners and raffles were given not to the Democratic Party, but to local candidates, such as judges and council members.

IBEW's political education program was not highly developed, but the union was politically active. A section of an apprentice-training film was devoted to the importance of politics, and the local had recently launched a four-page newspaper that carried some political information. The local participated on the BTC and COPE screening committee. IBEW took its turn on COPE's phone banks, enlisted volunteers to make yard signs, worked for selected candidates, provided office space for the Democratic gubernatorial and city council campaign, and recruited retiree volunteers to work for a congressional candidate.

IBEW monitored local politics. Its officers visited the courts weekly to plead for members arrested for misdemeanors. They also attended council meetings to push for prevailing wages, especially when contracts with builders were being considered. An IBEW member on the downtown commission monitored compliance with prevailing wage guidelines. Altogether, IBEW's local political involvements exceeded those of most unions, perhaps because one officer dedicated much of his time to politics. Contrary to the carpenters, he underestimated the union's political performance, calling it average, with fund-raising its weakest part.

IBEW officials were well acquainted with other unions' political efforts. The UAW and the Teamsters were thought to have the strongest and best-financed organizations. Even though the Teamsters had a Republican bent and the UAW a strong Democratic bias, both should join COPE. An officer commented, "We should all be together and speak with one voice. We should circle the wagons and get behind the same candidates and programs." He reported that, in the BTC, only the carpenters and the IBEW were moderately involved in politics. The BTC itself was too loosely organized. It needed centralization, a larger budget, more vigorous leadership, and a more innovative program of political action. Finally, he observed that the CWA's once strong program was weakened by internal divisions and leadership turnover. The AFT, interested only in school issues, was really not a union: "Its leaders drive Hondas and Nissans and do not teach students the importance of unionism."

The Democratic Party was regarded as relatively weak but growing stronger. Were it not for labor support, the party would not be able to compete with the Republicans. Yet labor was not well represented on the Democratic Party executive committee, not because party leadership was antilabor but because union members could not find the time to devote to the party. In fact, labor could dominate the party if it chose to, but not enough members were willing to run for office and assume party responsibilities.

One IBEW officer, almost alone among our informants, thought that no single interest group dominated the party. Labor should therefore play the dominant role because the Republican Party, which had once left labor alone, was now determined to undermine it. The Charterites, once allied with labor and the Democrats, was growing weaker and less distinguishable from the Republican Party. If the Charterites collapsed, both labor and the Democratic Party would be stronger.

IBEW officers were among the few who discussed national political issues. They felt that labor should become more outspoken and more visible and should exert more pressure on Congress. A good beginning would be a fight for national health insurance. Labor's national leaders were old and tired. Fresh leadership was needed to rouse a potentially sympathetic public, especially on political "fairness" issues. Chances for success would increase if labor played a more aggressive role in party and national affairs.

In short, unlike the carpenters and the building trades, the IBEW had developed a consistent labor ideology and a program that approached COPE's original purpose: to become an effective tool, mainly through the Democratic Party, to advance the cause of labor and the welfare of the poor and the working classes.

The Steel Workers

The USW district that included western Ohio, Indiana, and Kentucky contained 180 locals with 25,000 members. As part of the national trend, the district had lost more than half its membership since the 1970s. The Cincinnati area now included about 7,500 members in such industries as dairy, baseball bat manufacturing, power plants, and steel. Steel workers had become a minority in the union as it organized other industries to make up its losses of steel workers.

Predictably, officers found that cooperation among locals was declining because they did not share the traditional steel workers' sense of political purpose. Members who identified themselves as Democrats had declined to a bare majority (Table 8.1). Although union officers retained their allegiance to working-class causes, new members had no such interest.

All USW locals, regardless of size, had PACs. Their representatives met periodically with district officers to consider local, state, and national legislation. The thirty to fifty attendees at these meetings included most of the activists who did all of their local's political work.

Only about 10 percent of USW members, mostly officers and activists, participated in the political check-off. At election time, members were encouraged to contribute to local candidates' campaigns. Surprisingly, $30,000 in "hard money" had been raised in the district in the last election, but this averaged only $167 per local, an amount easily raised by officers and a few activists.

USW conducted relatively few activities outside of COPE. It followed the endorsements of COPE's screening committee, took part in the phone banks, and did some door-to-door canvassing on the Sunday before the election. Raising money was much easier than generating political interest and recruiting volunteers. Despite these problems, officers felt that the union's efforts were as fruitful as those of any local union. UAW appeared stronger only because it could raise more money. One informant observed that COPE was more effective and more working-class-oriented before the UAW withdrew in 1968. The local building trades were regarded as relatively influential as they "typically pursue selfish interests." The teachers also played a selfish political game and approached COPE only when they needed its support. COPE's major problem was that it did not sufficiently press the party to pursue working-class interests.

USW officers concurred with the general opinion that the Democratic Party was weak, especially at the county level. Were it not for COPE's superior ability to mobilize voters, the party could not compete. Yet labor could not survive without the party and therefore should not try to dominate it. Responding to the local political climate, USW officers felt restrained in urging their members to support the Democratic Party. The union stressed that endorsement should be based on candidates' records. Therefore, it endorsed some Republican candidates.

USW officers were doubtful that a stronger political education program would convince members to become more involved in politics. Members became complacent and conservative whenever their incomes improved or stabilized. As with striker replacement, members became aroused, but only temporarily, only when their jobs were threatened. Although the officers felt the need for a better political education program to overcome member apathy, they did not know how to improve it. The current economic climate of stagnation seemed to promote political caution, uncertainty, and inactivity.

The USW represented a union with declining and diversifying membership and declining involvement in COPE, the Democratic Party, and politics. Its officers were trying with little success to maintain the union's liberal tradition, but new locals with their more conservative members resisted these efforts.

Communications Workers

Before the Bell telephone system was broken up, the CWA played a leading role in Cincinnati labor politics. Since 1970, automation, work reorganization, and forced retirements reduced membership in the three surviving locals' membership by a third. The introduction of fiber optics technology threatened to reduce membership even more. Cincinnati's CWA, unlike those in Cleveland and Columbus, had not tried to organize other local industries.

The three locals represented different parts of the telephone industry. The first represented Ohio Bell technicians, splicers, and plant linemen; the second, Ohio Bell telephone operator services; the third, long-distance AT & T services. Two Bell locals were covered by a joint bargaining agreement; otherwise, the three locals had little contact. The technicians' Local 4400 selected for study had mostly male members; the other two were predominantly female. Local 4400 had the highest status and exemplified the strongest traditions in the industry.

Local 4400 had been very active politically in the past. One of its retirees currently spent most of his time on COPE affairs. The local's political viability declined with its membership and the retirement of an experienced generation of officers. A current officer estimated that 85 to 90 percent of the members were Democrats, among the highest in this study, an unlikely figure (Table 8.1). Members showed little interest in the local; attendance at membership meetings rarely exceeded 4 percent.

Members showed little interest in politics. Officers monitored legislative and congressional bills that dealt with the industry. Sometimes the international would ask locals to take part in letter-writing campaigns to Congress. Although members seemed more interested in community than national politics, the officers had little knowledge of the local political scene and did nothing to encourage member involvement in it.

The local had no political check-off in its collective bargaining agreement, nor did it raise "hard money" by the usual practice of buying dinner tickets and conducting auctions and raffles. Officers contributed $200 every other year to the Quorum Club of the international in Washington. The local also published a monthly paper; almost all of its news was devoted to job issues and legislative bills bearing on the telephone industry. A local officer once served on COPE's screening committee and a few volunteers helped COPE operate phone banks.

Significantly, CWA had no state-level COPE. Local CWA officers seemed uninformed about the political efforts of other local unions. They knew little about the UAW and Teamsters and were unconcerned that they did not participate in COPE. Despite the near absence of political activity in the local, its officers evaluated the political education program as satisfactory, and were making unspecified plans to improve it.

One spokesman, unlike most officers in other unions, thought that the Democratic Party and labor were well coordinated, and that the party chairman was strongly prolabor and proworking class. He thought that labor was doing a better job mobilizing voters than the party, even though a quarter of union members had not registered to vote. The party's grass roots organization was not as strong as the Republican's, but it performed better than in most communities. The informant was almost alone in thinking that the Charterites were needed because they gave union members more choice. He also thought that at-large representation gave minorities an equal chance of winning elections.

Some leaders were knowledgeable about community issues, like school levies, prevailing wages, tax abatement, and downtown development. Yet they did not know what stance the unions, COPE, or others had taken on them. In sum, political activity of the local had declined, including involvement with COPE, the party, and other unions. A new generation of officers seemed unable to assess the political scene and what the union or labor should do about it.

Government Workers

Cincinnati's regional office of AFSCME's Council 8 included almost 6,000 members in municipal and county governments of six counties and the University of Cincinnati. An additional 2,000 were covered by contracts but were not union members. Seventy percent of those covered resided in Hamilton County. About two-thirds of the members were manual and service workers, and one-third were clerks and professionals. About 40 percent were African Americans; 40 percent were women (Table 8.1). AFSCME officers thought that slightly more than half of their members were Democrats; a substantial minority were Republicans or Independents, not Charterites. Because their jobs were in the public sector, AFSCME members were more interested in politics than most unionists. The union experienced little difficulty in recruiting active and retired members for political work.

AFSCME took full part COPE's electoral activities: candidate screening, phone bank operation, and working with the party in coordinated campaigns. AFSCME also operated its own PAC, Public Employees Organized to Promote Labor Equality (PEOPLE), which paralleled COPE activities. Officers thought that PEOPLE was more effective than COPE or the Democratic Party. The regional office also coordinated a legislative district committee, forty locals that met every three months to monitor local issues and candidates. Its endorsements generally coincided with COPE's, but candidates also responded to AFSCME's special concerns.

Almost a quarter of the locals had a political check-off in their contracts, but additional funds were raised through raffles, dinners, and other devices. Perhaps $100,000 of hard money was raised annually. In state elections, additional support was provided by Council 8 in Columbus. Before and during the campaign, members were given literature that described the candidates and issues which, officers claimed, members read.

The local legislative district committee met often in the months preceding the elections. About two hundred volunteers distributed flyers and campaign signs. Voter information from the board of elections was used to target selected city areas for heavy canvassing. In addition, the union made direct contacts with city and county officials to inform them of the union's concerns.

AFSCME officers thought that their political education organization was superior to that of any other union. It had interested members, enough money, and enthusiastic volunteers. Commenting on the local scene, they observed that the political activities of most other local unions were small, almost invisible. The UAW, the machinists, and the teachers, however, had effective organizations. Although the BTC's electoral work received widespread publicity, it accomplished little outside fighting for prevailing wages. AFSCME had a broader political vision. The decision of the UAW and the Teamsters to remain outside COPE weakened labor's political influence.

AFSCME had special problems because it had to bargain with government officials, often Republicans, whom it sometimes opposed in elections. The union's strategy was to be always civil and balanced in collective bargaining negotiations and to project an image of being moderately liberal and responsible in politics, occupying the middle ground in the Democratic Party. The local party was regarded as less effective than it had been because it suffered from inadequate finances and uninspired leadership. Its precinct leaders seemed unable to motivate nominal Democrats to vote.

AFSCME tended to avoid direct contact with the party. Its policy was to have COPE handle all contacts with the local Democratic Party. AFSCME approached candidates directly, or more often, they first approached AFSCME for support. Currently, labor had some party influence but did not get everything it wanted. Its limited local influence reflected labor's limited influence in the national party, which had become too liberal to be successful. It seemed unable to identify charismatic presidential candidates who held the middle ground.

To conclude, AFSCME had worked out a political formula that both buttressed COPE and yet left room for adroit operation outside it. While AFSCME wanted to be regarded as strongly supportive of labor, it also sought to distance itself from liberals in labor and the party. This policy seemed to work well in Cincinnati's conservative political climate.

The Teachers

Given Cincinnati's conservative political environment, the presence of an AFT local seemed an anomaly. The union represented 3,700 dues-paying teachers and staff in city elementary and secondary schools. Two-thirds were women. The majority lived in the city. The president of the local estimated that a bare majority of members were Democrats, slightly higher than the city average (Table 8.1).

AFT members had little interest in politics save on educational issues. About a third participated in the political check-off program, which raised about $20,000 annually. This reliable source of funds was used primarily in elections for the board of education, the city council, and judgeships. Sympathetic judges to preside over cases that the union might bring against the board of education were important for the AFT. Since some unions backed other judges who sympathized with their interests, tensions between the AFT and other unions were not uncommon. With the possible exception of the building trades, the AFT alone supported an equal number of candidates from both parties. Since AFSCME also represented some school employees, the two unions sometimes cooperated politically. Together, AFT, AFSCME, and the BTC pressed COPE to support more Republican candidates.

In AFT's staff of seven no one was responsible for political education. The staff had problems in recruiting volunteers to work in city and county elections. However, despite being burdened with job issues and grievances, the staff quickly mobilized many volunteers in crises, like tax levy referenda and school board elections. Thus, in a recent drive to pass a school levy, the staff recruited 150 volunteers who made 15,000 phone calls in a three-week period.

The AFT president was on the executive board of the central body and COPE's screening committee. While the AFT took its turn operating COPE's phone banks, differences with COPE were not uncommon. The AFT judged candidates on their educational views, while COPE judged them on broader grounds. In the 1990 congressional race, the AFT did not back the Democratic candidate because he supported a voucher system for school choice. In the gubernatorial race, the AFT supported the Republican, Voinovich, while COPE backed the Democrat, Celebrezze, who, AFT claimed, had no coherent educational policy. In turn, COPE gave the AFT only token support on school levy referenda, forcing the union to assume full responsibility for the campaign. The AFT also opposed the building trades' supporting tax abatement because it would reduce school revenue. The AFT sometimes sought the backing of other public service unions such as the firefighters, police, and AFSCME. When these unions formed a coalition against the building trades and the Teamsters, COPE took no public stand.

AFT contacts with the local Democratic Party were meager. When we asked a spokesperson what he thought of the Democratic Party, he replied, "When did they start one?" He observed later that the party was not as fractured along ward or ethnic lines as in Cleveland but it had not backed black council candidates while the Charterites did. The party was so weak that candidates had to raise their own campaign funds. He also thought that the younger generation of Charterites was liberal and the party should work more with the Charterites. The Democratic Party could become more liberal if labor would take it over by leading a coalition that included civil and gay rights organizations, environmental and consumer groups, and perhaps liberal lawyers. All these groups performed better than the party in mobilizing their members in elections. If liberals learned to be as effective as labor in elections, the party could become strong again.

The AFT formula to invigorate the party contained ambiguities and contradictions. Thus, labor should initiate the formation of a liberal coalition but not dominate it because this might cause a backlash. However, labor lacked the muscle to form or dominate the coalition. Labor should not dominate the party, but it should be less cautious in exerting itself. In a reorganized party, labor should provide more precinct leaders and spearhead national drives to enact legislation, such as national health care, but it should not be too liberal.

In sum, despite their liberal rhetoric, AFT leaders knew that teachers would not support a liberal coalition or its agenda. Indeed, AFT officers refrained from identifying themselves as "liberals" in public debates. They had not thought through the problems of forming and holding together a liberal coalition. The AFT had learned how to pursue its interests effectively but had not learned the IBEW lesson that labor's political strength depends on discipline and the ability of individual unions to pursue their goals without appearing to divide labor.

Food and Commercial Workers

While union membership had declined in the Cincinnati area, the UFCW's had grown with the expanding service sector. Its regional office had jurisdiction over seventy locals in the Cincinnati–Dayton–Springfield area, northern Kentucky, and four Indiana counties. Local 1099 in Cincinnati included 13,000 members who worked in meatpacking, grocery, drug, discount stores, barbershops, and other services. Half were women; 15 percent, African Americans (Table 8.1). Over half worked part time. The spacious and well-appointed district headquarters on the city outskirts housed a large staff, part of which managed the union's health plan.

Officers were uncertain about members' political leanings but surmised they were predominantly Democratic. A 1988 survey by stewards reported much nonregistration and nonvoting, among young part-time workers especially . Most members, uninterested in the union or its politics, clung to their jobs because they desperately needed the union's health plan. To entice new members to learn about union benefits, the local gave a $25 rebate on initiation fees if they attended a meeting at which officers explained the union's economic and political goals. Members were then asked to join the union's active ballot club (political check-off), which would make them eligible for special benefits like lottery winnings. But only 10 percent had joined, mostly stewards, officers, and long-time, full-time workers.

No staff member was formally assigned political education. The union employed no full-time lobbyist at the state capital, but it published a newsletter that contained information about legislation of interest to the union. Officers indicated that the union was more involved in national than local politics because members were employed in too many different industries for officers to monitor relevant legislation. Therefore, the union targeted national issues like minimum wages, health care, striker replacement, and free trade. Yet the international's legislative action committee had never asked the local to pressure Congress to support or oppose any piece of legislation.

UFCW was involved in a dispute with the governor, who proposed to privatize state liquor stores, which UFCW had organized. Here, the union had convinced the Cincinnati Central Labor Council to back a resolution in the city council to oppose the governor's proposal. UFCW officers indicated that they could not motivate members interest in local politics because they were so widely dispersed residentially. In Hamilton County, the UFCW took part in COPE's screening committee and took its turn operating phone banks. The union generally went along with COPE's endorsements.

UFCW leaders had limited knowledge of other unions' political activities. They acknowledged that the UAW was strong but weakened by its separation from COPE. CWA was very active, USW was weakening, AFSCME and AFT were self-interested, and SEIU was the least active. UFCW had so ignored local politics that no candidate, union, or special interest had ever approached it for support. The union had no contact with the Democratic Party or its candidates for office. All party contacts were left to COPE. UFCW officers shared the general view that the party took labor for granted and approached it only for money. They also believed that labor should try not to dominate the party but to maintain a certain "flexibility" to avoid being labeled a "special interest." Labor's political influence would decline as long as its membership declined. For the present, labor should fight to preserve past gains and launch a campaign to educate members.

Despite its exceptional growth, UFCW had become only slightly and ritualistically involved in local labor and party politics. The union had responded to the health needs of its low-paid members, but its leaders did not try to implement locally the national leaders' broader working-class goals, perhaps because they did not know how.

Service Workers

The Health Care Division of SEIU's local in the Cincinnati region serviced about 1,300 members. About 85 percent were African-American women employed in nine private and public nursing facilities (Table 8.1). The local's barren office in a converted school building with several other unions was located several miles from the city center. The local was not readily accessible to the black community. SEIU's Health Care Division and its clerical Nine-to-Five Division had little contact with one another.

Health Care Division membership had declined more than a third after 1970, when employers launched a drive to lower wages. Since starting wages in 1991 were as low as five dollars an hour, the union's main attractions were its retirement and disability benefits.

The business agent, one of three black women officers in this study, indicated that more than 75 percent of the members were nominal Democrats but uninterested in politics, especially local politics. They recognized the importance of union security, unemployment and health insurance, and public support for the health care industry. Because the state and federal government made policies on these issues, members did not understand why they should pay attention to local politics. The main source of political news, if members read it, was the international's journal, mailed to all members.

Local officers, dissatisfied with the union's political education program, had recently decided to improve it. The local had earlier published a magazine which had to be abandoned to cut costs. The new educational program would install PACs in nursing homes that now lacked them. Political topics would be discussed at all membership meetings. Stewards would be trained in the techniques to increase registration and voting.

Currently, members were also supposed to receive political information from the staff at bimonthly meetings held in the nursing homes. Two-thirds of the homes had PAC committees, and 45 percent of their members participated in the political check-off of $2 to $4 a month. The additional $200 to $1,000 raised annually by dances, bake sales, and raffles was dispensed to sympathetic local candidates for office. Together, these funds amounted to more than $16,000 annually, an amount comparable to that raised by much more affluent locals.

Yet, the union's political efforts failed to impress the vast majority of members, who remained politically apathetic, convinced that politics was corrupt and nothing could be done about it. SEIU routinely participated in the central labor council, sometimes had a member on COPE's screening committee, and took its turn at the phone banks. It also contributed to COPE's campaigns to raise funds for candidates for state offices. Although SEIU's officers generally supported COPE and the Democratic Party, they felt that both should take stronger stands on race and equality issues. SEIU had established a local reputation as being more vocal than other unions on these issues. While SEIU's involvement in local politics was limited, its financial contributions were not trivial, and its strong public stand on racial issues made other labor leaders feel uneasy.

SEIU's relative isolation from other unions was reflected in officers' limited knowledge about them, even the UAW, AFSCME, and Teamsters. They thought that the AFT was a progressive union and that the BTC effectively made Cincinnati a good union town. The Fraternal Order of Police (FOP) was noisy and self-serving, as was AFSCME, which had tried to invade SEIU's jurisdiction.

The local Democratic Party was held in low esteem. An officer saw it as a "Who's Who club presiding over their little bailiwicks and calling on labor to do the hard work in elections." While African-American volunteers helped the party on phone banks and electioneering, the party recruited no blacks to run for local offices. Some black leaders had not shown strong party loyalty. A few of them began their careers as Democrats, switched to the Charterites, then switched again to the Republican Party.

Speaking for the black community, an SEIU officer concluded that Democratic Party insiders repeatedly rejected black women and labor members as candidates for office. Many blacks, in turn, were now ignoring the party, devoting more of their energy and money to the state and national party. Yet blacks had no alternative but to support the local party and try to improve it. Perhaps a new generation of black leaders might succeed. Despite claims that blacks avoided local politics, the union was involved in local issues like the fight against closing the state mental health facility, the demand for more police evenhandedness in dealing with African Americans, and the demand that the party appoint blacks to fill city council vacancies.

Despite pessimism over the local scene, black leaders felt optimistic about the national future of labor and the Democratic Party. In a few internationals, a grass roots movement was emerging that would challenge conservative AFL-CIO leadership in Washington. Liberal leaders would emerge to attack the problems of youth, prisoners, the aged, the mentally ill, the disabled, and the sick. SEIU pressed for such reforms in Ohio Democratic administrations, and it hoped the pattern could be repeated nationally.

In sum, although SEIU, as a predominantly black union, had difficulty arousing members to action, its leadership pressed COPE and the party to revive their earlier liberalism and fight for women, blacks, and the underprivileged.

CONCLUSIONS

In contrast to Cleveland, where Democrats traditionally dominated city politics, the Republican Party and the Charterites complicated life for the Democratic Party in Cincinnati. Even though Democrats had made headway electing candidates to the legislature and Congress in recent years, Republicans maintained dominance. In city elections, the Democrats had finally become strong enough to abandon their traditional coalition with the Charterites, but the Republican grip on county government had not loosened. While Republican financial and organizational advantages would persist, the revival of the Charterites depends on the uncertain commitment of its younger generation.

The most important factor in renewing the Democratic Party was the labor council's determination to reorganize COPE and the party. COPE's drive could only have a small immediate impact on the traditional conservatism of members and ward and party leaders. COPE could not assure its liberal members and the professions that the party could win future local elections without the Charterite alliance. Nor could COPE counterbalance the power of downtown influentials or make Democratic Party leaders respond to the black community's demands.

COPE's achievements must be evaluated in the context of a conservative city tradition that permeated the parties, the labor movement, and even the black community. For example, labor leaders felt that labor could not and should not try to dominate the Democratic Party. Radford was probing the "legitimate" perimeter of labor influence. He probably had not yet reached it because other groups in the party had not become alarmed about labor's increasing activism.

Labor's efforts to make the party stronger and more liberal were loosely coupled. COPE faced formidable obstacles in linking these goals. The major political orientations of the major unions, on balance, tipped in a conservative direction. Segmentation theory helps explain how political diversity among the four groups of unions sustained a conservative community political tradition.

Among the ex-CIO unions, only the UAW modestly supported a liberal–labor coalition in the party, but primarily in state and national politics, not locally. The steel workers' earlier position in the coalition was diluted by loss of members in the steel industry, an increasingly heterogeneous membership, and politically inexperienced leaders. The communication workers had also suffered losses of members and leaders and dilution of its liberal tradition. Thus, all three traditionally liberal unions had suffered membership losses and a decline in ideological intensity. Their coalition, now nominal, was an empty shell.

The ex-AFL unions retained their job-oriented political tradition. The Teamsters' near total preoccupation with their industry's problems isolated them from COPE and partisan party politics. The BTC, relatively weak and split like COPE itself, cooperated with business to support the local growth machine and monitored the prevailing wages situation. The carpenters' job-conscious unionism was expressed in their minimalist approach to politics. While the IBEW supported the BTC's limited goals, it was more involved in the liberal politics of its international. It strongly cooperated with COPE and pressed it and the party to take a more liberal stance.

The two unions in the public sector approached labor politics differently. Despite liberal rhetoric, the teachers' job-unionism differed little from that of the building trades. In contrast, AFSCME's political formula adroitly supported COPE's aggregating demands while strongly pushing its own agenda, including making an acceptable accommodation with Republican officeholders.

The two service unions also differed in their approach to local politics. Although both ritualistically supported COPE and the Democratic Party, UFCW's leadership seemed unable or unwilling to develop a political educational program for its widely dispersed members, half of whom worked part time. SEIU also had problems meeting its COPE obligations, but its leaders were visibly active. Along with leaders of other unions with black majorities (e.g., the laborers), they kept race issues alive on COPE's and the party's agenda.

In sum, the unions with a more liberal rhetoric included the auto, steel, communication, and electrical workers. AFSCME could generally be counted on to support this informal coalition and COPE. The job-conscious unions that kept a discrete distance from COPE included most unions in the BTC (carpenters), the Teamsters, and the teachers. Service-sector unions had an ideological affinity for the liberal wing of COPE and the party, but they had the least effective political organizations. With improvement, they could tip the balance to the liberals. Last, many small unions not included in this study remained politically unmobilized.

Given the political orientations of the largest unions, Radford had to stress labor–party unity rather than a liberal labor–party coalition. In the 1994 Democratic congressional primary, labor decided to take a stand. While party regulars supported the incumbent, David Mann, COPE and many African Americans backed his black challenger, William Bowen. Mann had voted for the North American Free Trade Agreement (NAFTA), which organized labor strongly opposed. Mann narrowly defeated Bowen in a low primary turnout. The near upset demonstrated labor's growing party influence, but it also underlined the need to improve political education in the locals. In the Novermber election, COPE withheld support from Mann, and he was rounded defeated. In the Republican sweep, the Democratic state senator of twenty-two years was defeated, but a couple of House Democrats managed to retain their seats.

My interviews revealed that some officers still did not know their members' party preferences and political beliefs (see Table 8.1). Officers were also unaware of other unions' political activities. Lacking this knowledge, they overrated their own programs. Yet, compared to the past, progress had been made. Almost all leaders reported that they now had more political contacts with one another than before.

Thus, despite declining union membership in the Cincinnati area, COPE had made recent strides in strengthening itself and the Democratic Party. Given the community's historical conservatism and the traditional strength of the Republican Party, COPE's achievements were noteworthy. In Cincinnati, the limited rewards for labor's political efforts were less than labor deserved.

9

Columbus

Comfortable with Tradition

Research accessibility in Columbus made possible a deeper penetration of the labor–party system than in Cincinnati and Cleveland. I was able to examine the politics of different locals of the same union and the political organization of teacher and police unions that did not belong to the AFL-CIO.

The political tradition of Columbus was closer to Cincinnati's than to Cleveland's. From the Civil War to 1930, Republicans overwhelmingly dominated city, county, and congressional politics. A Democrat occupied the congressional seat from 1931 to 1939, but the Republicans then recaptured and held it for more than a half century. In the early 1970s, a second congressional district was created in the metropolitan region (see Figure 6.1). Except for one term (1982–1984), that seat was held by a Republican. Typically, Republicans won their seats by a two-thirds margin or better.

In the state assembly, the picture differed somewhat. Democrats captured all four seats in 1931, but lost them in all subsequent elections until 1949. After 1950, the seats were contested, but the Republicans captured three or all of them until 1975. Thereafter, the seats tended to be evenly split between parties. Democrats captured the two state senate seats in 1931 but then all but yielded them to Republicans until 1950. In the ensuing twenty years, the Democrats sometimes won a seat, but after 1971, the parties tended to split them equally. Although in 1990 the county registered more Democrats, Republicans more than held their own in county and state elections.

Over the past century, Columbus elected only five Democratic mayors but elected a Democratic majority in the council from 1965 to 1990. Typically, Democrats won city elections by a 60 percent majority, while Republicans won by the same margin in the county. Burgeoning suburban population favored Republicans. In the city, Democratic voters were concentrated in the African-American neighborhoods, the university district, and working-class districts in the south and west parts. The line separating the two congressional districts split African American and working-class areas, disfavoring the Democrats (Figure 6.1), and the at-large city elections restricted black representation on the council. Yet, with a plurality of registered Democrats in city and county, Democrats had to admit that they were less efficient than Republicans in electing mayors and county commissioners.

THE MIGHTY REPUBLICANS

Despite its dominance, the Franklin County Republican Party did not rest on its oars. Its executive director, an experienced campaign organizer, had held office for fifteen years. The party occupied a suite of well-equipped offices close to the city center. The staff, consisting of an executive director, a full-time fund-raiser, and three secretaries, worked full time year round. The executive committee had representatives from the 133 wards; a third were women, and almost a tenth were African Americans. Wards were organized into twenty-six Republican clubs. The party's small central committee named the candidates for office. Although it had internal disagreements, the party presented a public face of harmony.

A newspaper reporter, a long-time observer of local politics, observed,

> The Central Committee has been shrewd in selecting candidates who have wide appeal. They avoid country club types and select candidates for Mayor like Lashutka, Watts, Kasich, and Casey. My parents are traditional Democrats, but in the last five elections, they voted for a Democrat only once. It's the same for the Italians and Irish with Democratic roots.

Although Columbus ethnic groups were not large, their proclivity to vote Democratic was being slowly eroded by the Republican Party, whose leaders realized that the strongest barrier to local hegemony was the black Democratic caucus. In eighteen years, the Republicans ran three blacks for the city council, and they lost. Recently, the party supported some black women for the council and the legislature who, despite broad appeal, did not win.

The party has also made progress in eroding labor's loyalty to the Democratic party. The executive director observed,

> Organized labor works in two cycles. In even-numbered years [election years], they put on their donkey suits and wear them all zipped up. In odd-numbered

> years, they try to be a little more impartial and work with us to an extent. We are making a number of inroads. ... To begin with, we have good solid issues that speak to the rank-and-file, issues like taxation, ending this welfare state claptrap, and so on. And some of the union leadership are coming around.

The building trades, apparently the first unions to build bridges with the Republicans, wanted judges who would not automatically issue injunctions against picketing, judges who would be lenient with members charged with misdemeanors. Some building-trades officers, the Teamsters, and the Columbus Educational Association (CEA) were registered Republicans. Even the UAW recently supported a Republican for mayor.

Republican leaders, believing that union officers lack member support, saw officers as self-serving because they focus on union issues (bargaining, strikes) where they play the dominant role; members are more interested in issues like taxes, welfare costs, government services, quality of education, and employment. A few union leaders know that only Republicans can help unions because only officeholders have something to give. Congressional Republicans, not Democrats, brought defense contracts to the city. Republican, not Democratic mayors increased the number of unionized firefighters, police, and government workers.

As a source of party vitality, patronage had shrunk considerably, although some survives in county and state government. Thus, forty-seven employees of two county commissioners were contributing 2 percent of their pay to the party. In 1993, the party's executive director resigned over a charge that this practice violated legal guidelines on patronage. The Republicans sought to decrease patronage going to the state Democratic Party. They successfully led a drive to eliminate the patronage that state deputy registrars for auto licensing gave the Democratic party—allegedly 10 percent of their earnings. When the party lost this source of revenue, it became more dependent on labor for income. More important than patronage for the Republican Party was its ability to reward supporters and volunteers by putting them in contact with its well-developed business network.

Republican leaders claimed that their party was financially stronger because it worked harder at raising money from small and large contributors. However, the party's fund-raising role was declining as candidates raised more of their own expenses. The party was concentrating on providing better campaign services: conducting focus groups, polling, and giving advice on campaign literature and advertising. Recently, candidates were advised to make more contact with individual voters and rely less on meetings and mass media. The executive director said, "You can't win with just TV ads. You've got to combine it with grass roots door-to-door work. We've done that, and that partly explains why we've won fifty-four of the seventy-four elected offices in the county."

Republicans acknowledged Democrats' built-in advantage with labor volunteers and phone banks. They were more effective in state and national than in local elections where labor did not solidly back Democrats. Moreover, large voter turnouts no longer favored Democrats. The 1984 presidential election had the largest turnout in history, and Republicans won the presidency. The Republican Party won more races because it was more united than the Democrats. Their liberal leaders alienated the rank and file; their party fights reinforced the public image that "the party is made up of a bunch of losers who can't deliver."

THE WOBBLING DEMOCRATIC PARTY

The Franklin County Democratic Party had elected a chair with strong prolabor sentiments. COPE leaders acknowledged this but felt that she confronted difficult problems, some of her own making. The chair and COPE agreed that the party was in perilous shape, but they did not agree why. Labor was the major financial contributor, but it had only 8 percent of the two hundred seats on the executive committee. The chair felt that labor's declining numbers were partly responsible for the party's declining revenues and voter loyalty. Labor countered that the party was poorly organized; it consistently lost elections despite a plurality of registered Democrats in the county.

Party headquarters consisted of a two-room suite in an office building located two miles from the city center, staffed by a chairperson and a secretary. The offices lacked the disorderly stacks of literature, wall maps, typewriters, tables, and duplicating paraphernalia usually seen in party headquarters. A month before the 1990 election, the chair, who was also the executive director, was encumbered with countless campaign details, many of which could have been handled by a larger staff or volunteers. The week after the election, the phone at party headquarters was disconnected, and the party, deeply in debt, was evicted for failure to pay rent. The director sought help from a Republican businessman who provided office space at reduced rent.

In 1994, the party had a debt of $60,000. While mass media costs were rising, party revenue had declined 50 percent because of reduced patronage and contributions from labor. The financial crisis was exacerbated by changes in the flow of money. Labor began to contribute directly to a candidate's campaign, rather than have the party disburse labor funds. Labor also contributed more money to the better-organized state party. The chair had to devote more time to raising funds than to organizing campaigns. Candidates hired fund-raisers who competed with the party for the same sources but felt that the party should continue to pay for TV ads. Since Columbus is the state capitol, contributors increasingly approached legislators and governmental officials directly, rather than ask the party to make the contacts. Finally, state employees felt little loyalty to the local party.

The Democratic Party chair controlled the sample and absentee ballot programs, which cost $35,000 per election. She also controlled the campaign master calendar, mailing and voter lists, and the get-out-the-vote campaign. Yet she could not withhold voter lists from the candidates, especially since she could not offer them services from the shrinking pool of volunteers. The party depended increasingly on labor for space, phone banks, and other forms of aid. The chair did not reduce party headquarters expenses in time, but established new funds: The $1,000 Club, The $150 Chairman's [sic] Council, The Goal Club with its $10 party dues, dinners, and fund-raisers. Increasingly, the chair turned to business for contributions, appealing to Republican business people on the grounds that their support was needed to maintain a healthy two-party system locally.

The party's aggregating role was reduced by the independent stance taken by several labor PACs and candidates' increasing control of the campaign. The chair could not convince labor members on the party screening committee to back *all* candidates, especially judges and county commissioners, rather than Republicans who had supported labor in the past. Labor's failure to back more than 75 percent of party candidates strengthened the widespread belief that the party was faction-ridden. Even when labor members of the party screening committee agreed with its choices, they could not guarantee that labor's screening committee would comply—for example, COPE, CAP, DRIVE, PEOPLE, and BTC, OEA, FOP (police), and the firefighters—forcing the overworked party chair to make separate contact with these organizations.

If all the candidates and PACs turned to the party at the beginning of the campaigns, it could have coordinated their efforts. Whatever its deficiencies, the party had the best data on party performance in precincts and wards. Thus, although all candidates and PACs needed party advice on where to invest their contributions and energy, they failed to exploit it. Individual efforts to increase voting turnout in some districts actually swelled the Republican turnout. Some districts required a strong effort in the primaries; others did not. Some districts, once Democratic, had turned Republican and were unlikely to change. Monitoring electoral performance was poorest in the suburbs and was probably the major source of the party's recent weakness.

Party leaders felt that labor wanted more influence, but it had no agenda. Although labor was a major contributor, it did not represent most of the Democrats in the other constituencies: African-Americans, Young Democrats, women, liberals, old-guard ward leaders, social services, and volunteers. The main party suffered from deep cleavage between moderates, conservatives, and pragmatists, on the one hand, and liberals and blacks, on the other. Labor was split but tilted toward the pragmatists, more numerous and more united. Some elections had been won with little labor support; the pragmatists were not inclined to respond to labor's grumbling. When groups failed to agree, the chair made decisions. This subjected her to charges of being autocratic, but few people dared challenge her because she was difficult to replace. Applicants were scarce after the previous chair was removed for failure to obtain required signatures to put a Democrat on the ballot for mayor. When the chair resigned in 1994, the executive committee claimed it had found only one qualified candidate.

Some activists said that the party lacked vitality because, unlike Cleveland, the prosperous Columbus region lacked burning issues. This charge has little evidence to support it. It might apply to some suburbs, but not to the city or region, which suffered from problems relating to race relations, economic development, crime, housing, taxation, educational equity, urban development, unemployment, poverty, homelessness, and metropolitan services: transportation, water, and waste disposal (see Chapter 6). The party's failure to confront them troubled several constituencies.

Although labor supported the party, it also brought the party problems. Most important was its inability to ensure that a sturdy majority of members would support party candidates and agenda. Labor even failed to mobilize members to vote against antilabor Republican legislators, and it occasionally refused to endorse liberal black Democrats. Labor was so divided ideologically and in party support that it contributed to the party factionalism that it denounced.

In 1994, when the executive committee met to appoint a new party chair, labor opposed a request by blacks and others to delay the choice until more candidates could be considered. The sole nominee was a businessman who had voted Republican in the 1980s and had not registered as a Democrat in the primaries of 1984, 1986, and 1988. In a rare show of unity, the UAW, Teamsters, and AFL-CIO supported the candidate, who some dubbed the labor candidate. Labor was also accused of skirting party intermediaries in its lobbying in the legislature.

Table 9.1 summarizes a party official's views of the ideology and party support of twelve major unions, hardly a labor bloc. Liberal ideology and strong party support rarely occur together (see the exception, AFSCME). Some conservative unions (UAW) strongly supported the party, while others (Teamsters) did not. Some liberal unions (CWA, SEIU) were too weak to help the party, while some large conservative unions (building

Table 9.1
Party Cooperation and Ideology of Unions in Columbus, 1990

Union	Party cooperation	Ideology
Auto workers (UAW)	Very helpful	Conservative
Teamsters	Least helpful	Very conservative
Building trades	Declining helpfulness	Very conservative
Steel workers (USW)	Helpful, state level	Conservative
Police (FOP)	Sometimes helpful	Conservative
Firefighters	Sometimes helpful	Split
Teachers (CEA)	Sometimes helpful	Fairly liberal
Government (AFSCME)	Helpful	Liberal
Communications (CWA)	Weak	Liberal
Food workers (UFCW)	Helpful	Very liberal
Civil serivce (OCSEA)	Most supportive	Liberal
Service workers (SEIU)	Weak	Liberal

trades) were unwilling. Other unions maintained distance from the party (police and firefighters). Notably, some labor leaders did not reflect members' ideology or party preference (CEA and OCSEA).

COPE'S ACCOMMODATION STYLE

Of the 80,000 union members in the Columbus region in 1990, only 50,000, or 63 percent, were in COPE-affiliated unions. Absent were the UAW, Teamsters, CEA (Columbus Educational Association), police (FOP), firefighters, and others. From 1970 to 1990, labor lost more than 20 percent of its members in the automobile, glass, paperboard, steel, and aircraft industries. The growth of government unions slowed the decline but augmented the unions' ideological mix. These changes further weakened labor's already weak party influence.

Top officials of the county AFL-CIO had been involved in local politics for many years. Traditionally, the executive board acted as COPE and screening committee. All candidates from both parties were invited to present résumés and be questioned on union and community issues. Previously endorsed incumbents were reendorsed without systematic review. Endorsements for state and federal offices were sent to the state COPE; those for local offices were presented at central body meetings to which about 70 percent of the locals sent delegates. Typically, endorsements were accepted and communicated to members. Some candidates were invited to speak at a "candidates' night" meeting.

COPE did not become involved in primary elections for fear of offending unendorsed winners. COPE's officers felt they should support a "fair number" of Republicans because 40 percent of the members were Republican. Moreover, it made little sense to endorse Democrats who were inevitable losers, especially when their Republican opponents had proved to be good friends. A high official commented, "Look, I'm a dyed-in-the-wool Democrat, but I'm not dogmatic or stupid. We have good relations with every officeholder. Everyone in office will call us back. No one snubs us."

COPE leaders believed that Columbus had the state's best get-out-the-vote organization, surpassing Cleveland and Cincinnati. COPE began operating its bank of fifteen phones two to three weeks before election day. In local and state elections, calls were not targeted to local areas but were made to all members and the public. However, most of the work was done on Election Day. About four hundred marginal precincts were usually selected for special attention. Four voting centers were strategically located and supervised by union members who were local residents. From four to five hundred volunteers canvassed the neighborhoods twice to ensure that all qualified persons voted.

COPE officials wanted to extend their canvassing over a longer duration, but the state COPE insisted that it be done only on election day. Data on union members were obtained in the traditional way. Locals sent membership lists to their internationals, which, in turn, sent them to the Washington COPE. It consolidated the lists and returned them to the state COPE, which then sent them to Columbus. Local officials complained that the lists were poor; 20 percent of the addresses were wrong, and some dead and transient members' names had not been removed. Obviously, the internationals were the source of the inaccuracies, but Washington did not let local COPEs gather and consolidate data from their locals.

Local COPE officials thought that the UAW and the Teamsters did not join for fear of losing control of their PAC money, a needless concern because COPE's policy let locals spend the funds they raised. COPE and the UAW reportedly met regularly to review candidate endorsements; agreements were the rule. COPE spent its limited funds ($1,500) largely on phone banks. Unlike in Cleveland and Cincinnati, the Columbus COPE had little problem recruiting volunteers for phone banks and "walking the precincts."

Two COPE officials were on the Democratic Party executive committee and its vice chair was a union member. Almost all labor informants agreed that labor was underrepresented on the committee. The party chair was prolabor, but she was unable to discipline the committee. It was dominated by old-timers who, unionists claimed, were financially irresponsible, spending money on party headquarters rather than on campaigns. In response to the alleged chaos, several unions reduced contributions to the party and sent them directly to the candidates, who in turn increasingly turned to labor to mobilize the vote, recognizing that COPE had a better electoral machine than the party.

COPE did not support Democratic opponents of long-time Republican members of Congress Chalmers Wylie and John Kasich, even though they were clearly antilabor. For twenty-six years, no "serious" Democrat candidate could be found to oppose Wylie, whose COPE voting record was typically near zero. COPE also supported several Republicans for the city council to the consternation of council member Jerry Hammond, an influential black Democrat. Labor also supported school levies and worked with the president of CEA, a registered Republican. In short, labor's failure to support party candidates consistently illustrates the party divisions that labor so deeply lamented.

COPE also vacillated on local issues. It opposed tax abatement for downtown construction but supported other concessions to attract business. It opposed a special tax for a convention center in a referendum, but proposed a hotel-bed tax that was ultimately passed. It did not support a tax referendum to extend public transportation but later supported a similar referendum that won. Labor made its offices available to a Democratic candidate for the legislature but also endorsed "Republican" candidates for the board of education.

Labor probably contributed more energy to public service than to politics. Thus, an officer of the central labor council was on the board of COTA, the public transportation system. He and the council president were United Way board members and a union member was its campaign manager. Labor annually presented the George Meany Award at a well-attended dinner to the person who had contributed most to the community; all labor–management committees in the area were invited. Labor took part in Operation Feed, the most successful in the nation. It spent $8,000 annually for a public fireworks display at Cooper baseball stadium. A unionist was president of the Cerebral Palsy Foundation and the Metropolitan Human Services Commission. In short, labor presented itself as a responsible and contributing community member in the hope that local leaders would accept it as a legitimate part of the system.

THE POLITICS OF THE BIG TEN UNIONS

Turning to the activities of the city's main labor unions, I first examine the unions outside COPE, but inside the AFL-CIO: the UAW, Teamsters, and BTC. However, in Columbus, other unions were outside both COPE and the AFL-CIO, including the teachers in the NEA and its local affiliate, the Columbus Education Association (CEA), the Fraternal Order of Police (FOP), and the Ohio Civil Service Employees Association (OCSEA), part of AFSCME. Their politics are described in the section dealing with public sector unions.

Auto Workers

As in the other cities, local UAW officers in Columbus resisted being interviewed and urged me to talk to better-informed officers in the *regional* CAP council. Interviews revealed that they were much better informed about state and national politics than about the local political scene. The Democratic Party chair assured us that *local* UAW CAP officers were actively involved in and knowledgeable about local politics; we therefore interviewed them.

UAW membership in the area had declined more than that of any union. Employment in auto and airplane manufacturing fell from more than 30,000 to 3,000 between 1970 and 1992 (Table 9.2). One of the two surviving locals, McDonell Douglass Aircraft, died with the plant's closing in 1993; the future of GM's Fisher Guide parts plant remained cloudy. Nonetheless, the UAW still had more members than any other local in manufacturing.

Columbus CAP officials thought that UAW members were returning to the Democratic Party. Perhaps half now identified themselves as Democrats, a third as Independents, and a fifth as Republicans. Although Independents lowered union involvement in the primaries, about 70 percent of the members usually voted in general elections. The local CAP council screened candidates for local and state offices and sent its recommendations to the state body, which routinely confirmed them, almost half for Republicans.

Contrary to reports from COPE informants, CAP officers indicated that they did not routinely inform COPE on UAW endorsements, but met occasionally, "to ensure that all labor was moving in the same direction." UAW locals sent half of their "hard money" to the regional CAP and kept half for local politics. Because of high member participation in the political check-off, the UAW probably raised more money per capita than any other local union. In the aerospace plant, almost 90 percent participated. On the conservative assumption that half of the current members gave three dollars weekly, the locals raised more than $250,000 annually. Since UAW locals contributed large sums to both party and candidates, many politicos considered the UAW politically the most influential union.

Table 9.2
Characteristics of Unions in Franklin County, as Reported by Informants, 1990

Union	Membership	Check-off (%)	Blacks (%)	Democrats (%)
Auto (UAW)	3,000	90	20[a]	55
Teamsters	5,000	65	5[a]	60
Bldg. trades (BTC)	10,5000	—	10	33
Carpenters	4,000	5	5	55
Electricians (IBEW)	950	0	10[a]	75[b]
Factory IBEW	3,000	0	30	60[a]
Steel workers (USW)	950	5	65	85
Communications (CWA)				
Marketing local	300	0	20	55
Service local	2,600	?	60	65[a]
Clerical local	1,300	?	60	65
Technical local	1,900	?	20	50
Government				
OCSEA	10,000	0	20	60
ODOT chapter	1,300	0	20	45[a]
Teachers (OEA)	4,800	0	10[a]	40
Police (FOP)	2,500	0	7	60
Food (UFCW)	13,000	40	30	70
Service (SEIU)	350	1	90	95

[a]Guessed.
[b]Reported, but unlikely.

UAW locals cleared membership lists with the international in Detroit even for national elections that were supposed to be coordinated through COPE. For state and local elections, CAP made contact with its members via mail, not through phone banks. Members received sample ballots, a bimonthly newspaper, and literature on the endorsed candidates. Leaflets were distributed at plant entrances, and candidates occasionally greeted workers as they left. The Congressional District Action Committee in Washington allegedly issued ALERTS to local activists to make contact with Congress on "key" legislation. No informant reported being so contacted, perhaps because the two local members of Congress were hopelessly antilabor.

UAW officials believed that CAP was more efficient than COPE because CAP did not need to persuade other unions to cooperate. CAP refused to join COPE presumably because COPE would moderate the UAW's liberal politics, an unlikely outcome given the UAW's record of Republican endorsements. Some UAW members had no objection to joining COPE but left the decision to top union officials.

CAP officers reported being deeply involved in such local issues as taxes, urban growth, education, and council elections. Not infrequently, they opposed both COPE and the Democratic Party. Unlike in Cleveland, the Columbus UAW backed tax abatement for downtown and industrial development on the grounds that local jobs were needed in the non-governmental sector, and that Columbus had to compete with other communities for jobs. CAP backed Republican Greg Lashutka for mayor, while COPE backed the black councilman, Ben Espey. When some black UAW members charged their officers with racism, they insisted that Lashutka was the better candidate; the racially balanced CAP council had endorsed him. Thereafter, CAP became cautious in taking stands on racially sensitive issues, such as school busing and neighborhood and alternative schools.

Although the UAW strongly supported the Democratic Party, union officers believed that it needed restructuring. It could not solve its financial problems after it lost patronage income. Ward leadership was crumbling; the party was failing to attract volunteers. The party was losing the loyalty of Democratic candidates who no longer could count on its financial support. During the campaign, the party proved incapable of coordinating TV, advertising, and newspaper publicity.

CAP officials did not agree that the party's executive committee had denied labor more seats; labor itself had limited its seats for fear of being accused of dominating the party. Although both the UAW and COPE had developed a better electoral organization than had the party, neither currently engaged in door-to-door canvassing because their members were too widely dispersed. COPE officers insisted they still engaged in canvassing. Perhaps reflecting on a past when many UAW members engaged in active politics, current officers indicated that politics was no longer fun because personal contacts between the party, union, and voters had declined. Younger members had few union and party contacts and were suspicious of both.

UAW officers did not see themselves as part of the party's problem. They preferred to be independent of COPE, bypassed the party, were reluctant to assume party responsibilities, gave to individual candidates, and supported almost as many Republican as Democratic candidates. UAW officials defended their position on three grounds. First, since Democratic candidates did not strongly identify with the party, it made little sense to give the party all of its funds. Second, the UAW could not endorse more Democrats unless the party identified better ones than the Republicans. Third, most local elections (auditor, judges, commissioners, and mayor) were not based on the "philosophical" issues of state and national elections. A UAW official said,

> Locally, we don't vote on party issues. How can the county auditor vote on a party issue? Locally, you go for the individual. If we have a problem before the judge, we do *not* want the case to be fixed. We want to tell the judge what type of union member and citizen they are, what kind of work record they have. Then the judge can understand a worker's made a mistake and he gets a better picture of the person. Part of the chairman's job is to put up a good candidate, so we don't give the money to someone else. We always tell her to tell us who they're going to put up there, and we'll tell you if we'll support them.

In short, the Republican environment of Columbus had moderated the UAW's working-class ideology to a point where it was more conservative than that of several other local unions. Despite this, UAW leaders felt that labor and the Democratic Party had a brighter future, that labor had hit a low point, and that unions could convince their members to support Democrats in the presidential election.

The Teamsters

Columbus Teamsters were in a state of transition. A long-time president had recently retired; new leaders were immersed in administrative affairs. While the local's membership had declined with industry deregulation, it had not fallen as much as elsewhere. The local of 10,000 members had split in two. The over-the-road and construction locals each had about 5,000 members. The construction local was part of BTC and COPE; the transportation local analyzed here remained independent. About 75 percent of its members resided in the Columbus area.

Conversations with Teamsters centered on two related themes: the fight for honesty in Teamsters affairs, and the drive to break away from the Cleveland joint council. Rightly or wrongly, the public viewed the Cleveland council as being associated with the ousted corrupt national leadership. A newly created joint council that would include locals from Columbus, Akron, and Dayton would enable local Teamsters to gain the public respect they deserved. An officer explained:

> Our goal is to represent our members. This is our top priority. Our rapport with our members is great, due to X's honesty. That is what the Teamsters need: honesty. Not a corrupted background, but clean. We want a clean name.

Creating a new council was also justified on the grounds that the Cleveland's joint council was not well acquainted with unique problems in Columbus, the state's largest city. The new council would use the money that it now sent to Cleveland to organize more local companies.

The new Teamster officers in Columbus had not paid much attention to local politics. They spent most of their time in administration, mending fences with members, and preparing for up-coming elections. An officer commented:

> I would like to see improvement in cooperation within the local; then I could spend more time with politics. We could spend more time on it if it wasn't for inner politics. Every three years we have to run again. Power plays in the local take away time we can spend with our members. They are spread out and the changing work schedules make it difficult for them to attend meetings when we discuss local politics.

Current officers depended on the retired president to handle local politics and to inform them about it. He had introduced the new officers to local politicos and city council members. The local had no political education program. Members received the international's magazine, which contained some items on the union's positions in national affairs. The Teamsters' state PAC, DRIVE, sent all members annually two bulletins that summarized state and national issues important to the union and provided data on legislators' records. Officers of the local made up the screening committee, reviewing all candidates for local judgeships, city council, county commissioner, and state legislative posts. The past president provided background material on all candidates, many of whom he knew on a first-name basis. The endorsements were then communicated to the members.

Despite the limited political involvement of the local's officers, members were urged to participate in the political check-off of a dollar a week. The local led Ohio with an estimated 60 to 70 percent participation, much higher than in Cleveland and slightly higher than in Cincinnati. Presumably, the local annually raised an estimated $150,000 for political work. Thus, even with a sparse political program and low officer involvement in politics, the Teamsters had local influence because they had access to local officials and contributed significantly to their campaigns.

Officers estimated that perhaps 60 percent of their members were Democrats, and 40 percent were Republicans (Table 9.2). But parties were not important. Politics was a matter of building interpersonal relationships with politicos and of pursuing concrete objectives in local, state, and national affairs. Thus, as elections approached, candidates from both parties approached the local for donations and support. These were ignored unless the candidates paid a personal visit. An officer explained:

> Basically, our relations with politicians are this: They need us and we need them. If someone is in bad with the unions, then naturally we won't hold hands with them. Personal appearance means a lot more than fliers. This is what we are trying to do, personal contact. We talk to people personally. You know that the only way to a politician's heart is through the pocket. Since we have this

> good rapport with the past president, we have good contacts with different politicians in town.

Teamster legislative concerns focused almost exclusively on transportation: lower taxes on business to permit trucking firms to survive, more regulation to decrease competition in the industry, and more safety regulations to reduce injuries. Laws that permitted longer trucks, heavier loads, and wider roads would also improve industry competitiveness with railroads. These concerns bore little relation to party politics. While the Democratic Party seemed to be more interested in workers than the Republicans, the candidates had to be evaluated in terms of the issues they supported. Labor's influence on parties now depended on its ability to clean up its own house.

In short, the Teamsters' internal politics in Columbus focused on erasing a public conception of the union as corrupt and becoming independent of the Cleveland joint council. Its involvement in local party politics was shallow, interpersonal, and oriented to industry welfare.

Building Trades Council

The BTC had about 10,500 members in central Ohio, most of whom lived in Franklin County. Its largest unions were the carpenters and electricians, sheetmetal workers, plumbers, and laborers. Membership decline began in the 1970s and leveled off in the 1980s, with half of construction workers now unionized. The steady growth of business and government construction locally had moderated membership decline. About a third of the members were now regular employees of establishments, and two-thirds were at transient work sites.

The BTC represented the most conservative Columbus unions. Its officers estimated that members were split evenly between Republicans, Democrats, and Independents. Officers claimed that the BTC best achieved its aims when it supported friends regardless of party. It tended to support Republicans in local elections and Democrats for governor, state senators, and the president. Their estimate that 90 percent of the members supported Dukakis and Clinton, Democratic nominees for president, seems highly inaccurate. For many years, the BTC supported Republican member of Congress Chalmers Wylie, even though he had an almost perfect antilabor COPE rating. A member explained, "On key votes that are important to us in the BTC, he's been very supportive, although perhaps on every other issue he may be antilabor." Informants were not able to specify these "key" issues.

BTC operated a loose and decentralized organization. Each union contributed a member to the screening committee. Although it tried to arrive at consensus, individual unions could and did make different endorsements. The BTC did not send endorsements directly to members; rather, each union sent its revised BTC endorsements to its members. The BTC engaged in no electoral work or political education. It provided member unions with their membership list rearranged by districts that candidates represented. Locals distributed flyers and yard signs and operated phone banks.

Monetary support for candidates was loosely "centralized." In the words of a BTC officer:

> The benefit of being a council is evident when it comes to money. If the candidate gets money from one union, then people might think he's beholden to that one union. With us, if a candidate asks for $1,000, I'll call up each of our affiliates and say, "I need $100 from you." So it shows that the money came from the electricians, the carpenters, and so forth, so it doesn't look like he's owned by a single group. The public impact is better.

Local politics was more important to the BTC than state and national politics. Because the building trades engage in organizing ongoing building projects, they often appear before judges on charges of illegal picketing and distributing leaflets. The BTC therefore endorsed judges who didn't automatically issue injunctions against them. The decline of union labor in residential housing increased the importance of government construction. The BTC actively supported the omnipresent construction proposals of the state government and university, endorsing any candidate who backed prevailing wages.

BTC members did not regard employers as adversaries, even though the "people in charge of this city have deliberately tried to steer the city away from unions." BTC joined employers in pressing for downtown development, and they supported a special tax to build a downtown convention center, shopping mall, and sports arena. They also supported tax abatements for new businesses, taxes to maintain the mass-transit system, and larger budgets for vocational education. Reluctant to evaluate the political activities of other unions, a BTC official explained that it approved of unions that had "similar growth objectives for the community" like AFSCME, Teamsters, and teachers (CEA).

In BTC philosophy, like that of the Teamsters, party loyalty was unprofitable and individual candidate loyalty was a good investment. Although local parties sought BTC support, officers advised their members not to assume party leadership positions. Experience had proved that the Democratic Party, taking the BTC for granted, was interested only in its contributions and volunteers. The party had not only neglected the trades, it supported causes that alienated members: abortion rights, gun control, and civil rights. Therefore, the BTC no longer supported Democrats unless they supported the building trades:

> What we have to offer a candidate is our loyalty. Once we endorse someone, we're not going to throw them over for the next candidate that comes along. And we promote that idea to the candidates. They know that, and they actively seek our endorsements.

In a city where political elites acknowledged their antiunionism, the BTC maintained the AFL's traditional philosophy of avoiding party entanglements and evaluating candidates on their commitment to building-trades interests.

Carpenters

About 4,000 carpenters in the Columbus area were organized in factory and construction locals. The factory locals had a few carpenters and had abandoned apprenticeship programs. Two construction locals, with about 2,000 members, were selected for study (Table 9.2). Membership had declined almost by half since the 1970s, forcing the union to accept a "market recovery wage" at 70 percent of the earlier rate. Membership had stabilized in the late 1980s, but in the 1990s, the union's TARGET fund still subsidized builders who bid against nonunion competitors.

Currently, perhaps more than half of the carpenters worked on public projects, the remainder on large industrial-commercial projects. All government and university contracts accepted the prevailing wage scale, and union officials placed great importance on protecting this labor market niche. They insisted, but would not explain, that political influence was also important in nongovernment construction.

The carpenters engaged in little direct political education. Their locals had six delegates on the county AFL-CIO central body, and one district council member served on the AFL-CIO executive committee. Since central bodies required locals to pay a fee for taking part, about a third of the locals in the state did not affiliate, but all belonged to the BTC. A state lobbyist for the carpenters estimated that 75 percent of the Columbus carpenters were Democrats, but local officers estimated a bare majority.

Because the dispersal of construction sites limited political contacts between officers and members, almost all of the political work was done by about twenty agents, staff members, and officers. They endorsed candidates and sent recommendations to their district council, BTC, COPE, and eventually to the members. The officers also raised money to support candidates, invited them to address the membership, distributed yard signs, and operated phone banks. Annually, about $30,000 was raised through political check-offs and contributions. In a recent council race, the carpenters raised money, recruited volunteers, and made their phones available to the black candidate whom the UAW opposed. In other races, it made its forty phones available to the AFL-CIO and made thousands of stakes for yard signs.

The carpenters considered themselves deeply involved in the community. They contributed their labor to community projects, named representatives to the city charter review committee, made recommendations to the zoning board, and monitored city contracts for adherence to prevailing wage rates. They supported downtown development, changes in zoning to accommodate new businesses, and the chamber of commerce's development committee. Carpenters thought that their political organization was a model for other unions, like the construction trades, OCSEA, AFSCME, the teachers, the police, and the firefighters, all unions that were heavily involved in government. Unions which emphasized national issues were thought to be weak in local politics.

Over the years, the carpenters had endorsed more Republicans than Democrats for local offices (especially for judges and county commissioners) on the grounds that Republicans were more supportive. Moreover, the Democratic Party was disorganized, while the Republicans were efficient and "avoided being all things to all people." Despite their low involvement in the Democratic Party and COPE, carpenter officials thought that labor should have a stronger voice in the party, especially in monitoring incumbents' records. Espousing a doomsday logic, they concluded that Republican attacks on labor and prevailing wages were a good thing. They had pushed labor into a corner and forced it to fight back. The future looked promising.

In short, in local politics, the carpenters did not embrace labor's affinity for the Democratic Party, and they kept a measured distance from COPE. While they favored COPE and the party at the state or national level, they maintained their traditional job-oriented policies.

The Electricians

The IBEW had about 7,500 members in six locals in the Columbus area. Four were "inside," permanently attached to firms, and two were in construction. We interviewed officers of the two largest construction locals and the largest factory local. Apart from the monthly BTC meetings of the construction locals, the six locals had little contact with one another.

The largest construction local's membership of 950 had grown slowly over the years. Notably, it had never conducted a strike because all problems with management were resolved through the council on industrial relations. An officer of the local insisted that three-quarters of the members were Democrats and that the union placed the highest priority on involving them in politics. Union registrars had registered over 95 percent of the members. The local distributed a newsletter that contained local political news, and the international's journal summarized national issues. The IBEW also devoted a large section of its apprentice program to politics. Despite these efforts, communicating political issues to members proved difficult because they moved constantly from one construction site to another. They remained uninterested in politics. The percentage who voted fell far short of the percentage registered.

The IBEW initiated a few political activities. Its BTC and COPE representatives routinely informed members of screening-committee endorsements and sent them election materials. The local contributed money to IBEW's donation of twenty scholarships to Ohio State University. However, the local raised very little "hard money" for electoral purposes. After an intensive drive, perhaps a majority of the members would contribute two dollars, about $800 of which was sent to Washington. The union sponsored a Christmas party for local politicians. An official reported:

> We make no discrimination by race, creed, or party. About 100 show up for lunch and cocktails. This is good public relations, especially for judges. We don't expect them to be on our side, but at least they should hear our side.

The IBEW did not become involved in the community or work with local business or other unions to attract construction projects. The union's major operation was making contacts with the city council, the county commissioners, and the university's board of trustees to urge them to sign contracts only with union employers. Despite these modest efforts, IBEW officials thought their political program was strong, perhaps weaker than AFSCME's and the USW's, but equal to the carpenters'.

Apart from responding to requests for money, the IBEW had little contact with the Democratic Party. Union officers "disagreed with the party's philosophy" and emphasized that its candidates were generally inferior to the Republicans'. The local had backed the last Republican candidate for mayor. Yet officers estimated that they supported only 5 percent of the Republican candidates, an unlikely figure given that they believed that the Republicans had superior candidates.

With respect to national politics, IBEW officers thought that Republicans were undermining the laws that protected labor. However, "since the Democrats did no better than the enemy," young members were disenchanted with a system that was not working for them. The interview concluded with the question, "What should be done?" They answered,

"We should go back to the old system. Gompers was right. He didn't believe in parties. Reward your friends and punish your enemies."

The IBEW factory local had almost 3,000 members, down from 10,000 in the 1970s. About 30 percent were black, and its president was a woman. Although the local was three times the size of the largest construction local and a larger proportion of the members of the factory local lived in Columbus, it was even less active politically. It distributed a newsletter that contained Democratic candidates' paid political advertising. The small sums raised for campaigns were sent to its Cincinnati headquarters. Officers admitted that their political education program was "not very good," but they had no plans to improve it.

The local routinely cooperated with COPE. Fifteen staff members with no volunteers did what was expected: attended COPE meetings, operated phone banks for a night, distributed COPE's handbills, and followed COPE's endorsements. No member served on COPE's screening committee; one officer apparently did not know what it was. Members were not advised on candidate preferences nor urged to become involved in community issues because "COPE takes care of those kinds of things." Officers were uninformed about local unions' political strength, were unaware that the Teamsters belonged to the AFL–CIO, and that the UAW had endorsed the Republican candidate for mayor. They claimed to be disassociated from their liberal international, and they were.

Yet, local officers thought that COPE was an effective political agency and that the IBEW's contribution to it was excellent. Contrary to most informants, they thought that the Democratic Party was very effective, that labor strongly influenced it, and that labor had a stronger electoral machine. In short, the IBEW's factory local was even less involved in politics than the construction local. It routinely cooperated with COPE; was uninformed about labor, party, and local politics; and did not try to influence the politics of its potentially liberal members.

Steel Workers

Columbus had ten USW locals; the union organized one for every employer. We selected a large local in a steel fabrication plant. It had 950 members, down from 1,500 in 1970. Located opposite the plant, the local's hall contained a meeting room and three offices. The president, son of a former president, was the sole paid officer, and he had no secretary. About two-thirds of the members were African Americans, and 80 percent identified themselves as Democrats (Table 9.2). They had little interest in politics or the Democratic Party.

The president realized that politics was important for union survival, but he had not developed a political education program. He attended meetings of the state USW legislative committee and COPE. The union accepted COPE's endorsements, participated in its phone banks, and convinced some of the stewards to distribute voter registration forms before elections. The local held three membership meetings in a single day, one for each shift, but attendance rarely reached 10 percent. Voter registration was routinely mentioned at these meetings. An occasional leaflet on the bulletin board and political news in the international's magazine completed the union's political education efforts. Aware of their ineffectiveness, officers planned three improvements: to include politics in stewards' training, publish a regular newsletter with political information, and encourage political check-offs. The local had already inserted a check-off clause in the last contract and had enlisted fifty members. Compared to the past, these plans looked promising.

USW officers evaluated other unions' political efforts by their visibility at state house rallies and in the United Way. The largest unions were considered the most active: AFSCME, OCSEA, UFCW, CWA, and the Building Trades Council members. USW officers had little contact with the UAW and the Teamsters, which, they insisted, should become part of COPE. COPE already had a better electoral machine than the party. With UAW and Teamster cooperation, it would be even stronger.

Despite few contacts with the local Democratic Party, officers had strong convictions about it. It courted too many special interests: abortion rights, gay rights, gun control, and race. The party was prolabor but fragmented. Labor should not take over the party, but it rightfully expected more returns. Since labor was partly responsible for party factionalism, it should give money directly to the party rather than the candidates, which would make the party more responsive to labor. Labor also had to do more organizing to make up for its dwindling numbers, and it should be more united.

Thus, the USW in Columbus had supported the strikers against Greyhound and the mass transit authority (COTA), but most unions failed to exhibit solidarity. Labor had sufficient numbers to be potentially decisive in local elections, but the unions did little to educate members about local politics. In sum, USW leaders had a sophisticated political vision but insufficient resources to realize it or communicate it to other unions.

CWA: A Microcosm of Labor's Diversity?

The research design called for interviewing officers of the ten largest unions in each city. While this would be adequate if the unions were homogeneous, some were internally so heterogeneous that no single local could adequately represent them, especially unions that had amalgamated with other unions or had organized other industries to make up for membership losses, like UFCW, USW, or CWA. To consider the potential political consequences of member heterogeneity, I selected the communication workers (CWA). Three of its four Columbus locals were in the telephone industry. I identify each local by its dominant characteristic. The service local at Ohio State University had organized janitorial, cafeteria, and housekeeping workers. The marketing local handled telephone marketing and sales for AT & T. The clerical local included clerks and operators at Ohio Bell and AT & T, while the technical local at Ohio Bell represented installers, technicians, telephone maintenance workers, clerical workers, and printers.

The marketing local had only three hundred members; the other three had between 1,300 and 2,600. Almost all members of the marketing local were women; in the other three, about half were women. Blacks made up about a fifth of the members in the marketing and technical locals, and three-fifth in the service and clerical locals (Table 9.2). Unlike Cleveland's, the locals had no political contacts with each other, apart from occasional meetings of the union's state legislative committee.

The political leanings of the four locals, as reported by the officers, varied with racial composition. The technical local, with the fewest blacks, was evenly split between Reagan Democrats and Republicans; marketing tilted toward the Democratic Party; the clerical and the service locals, with most blacks, were mainly Democratic. Members of all locals had little interest in politics except for one event: the mayoralty race between an African-American Democrat and a white Republican. Three-fifths of the members of the service and clerical locals were black, and they were interested in the outcome.

All informants indicated that politics was supremely important to their union's survival, but this conviction bore no relation to their political efforts. All locals received the international's publication, and three of them published newsletters with some political news. Three locals had a political check-off clause in their contracts. The small marketing local had no COPE committee. The black woman president did little except urge members to register to vote.

The locals' relationship to COPE best captures their politics. After a period of absence, the marketing local had recently joined COPE but did nothing more. The service local had withdrawn from COPE the previous year. Its PAC assumed all COPE functions: a registration drive, screening and endorsing candidates, and campaigning. It campaigned for two Democratic candidates, a black for mayor, and a white incumbent for the state assembly. The clerical local took its turn on COPE's phone bank because its members were skilled operators. Finally, the technical local cooperated in all of COPE activities: raising money, participating on the screening committee, phone bank operations, and related activities.

Officers of the four locals had limited knowledge about other Columbus unions' political activities. They agreed that perhaps AFSCME was strongest; the Teamsters and building trades were effective, but self-interested. Officers of the service and clerical locals thought that the UAW was strong, but antiblack because it backed the Republican white candidate for mayor.

Appraisals of the local Democratic Party were also disparate. An officer of the clerical local on the party's executive committee thought that the party was very effective, prolabor, and heavily influenced by labor. Officers of the technical local thought that the party leaders were good but subjected to cross-pressures from too many interest groups. The party's problems were lack of good staff and organization, not financial. Leaders of the service and marketing locals thought that the party's problems were primarily financial. No one could suggest what the party should do to become stronger or what labor should do to increase its party influence. Except for the marketing local, the others endorsed an occasional Republican. Only the technical local did not back the black candidate for mayor.

All informants had little knowledge of community issues or what labor should do about them. They preferred to discuss the problems facing labor as a whole (like strike replacement) or the industry (like telephone monitoring). When pressed to discuss local issues, officers of the service and clerical locals mentioned black community problems like garbage removal and educational choice. In discussing labor's future, all informants thought that labor's decline had ended and that its future was promising. Officers of three locals thought that the national labor leadership should be replaced because it had lost touch with the rank and file. Blacks in the service and marketing locals wanted labor to be more aggressive and radical and perhaps revive the civil rights movement.

This overview of the politics of four locals demonstrates the hazards of generalizing about unions with heterogeneous members. The locals' racial composition best predicted their politics, but this bore little relation to their political efforts. Attempts by internationals to press political programs on their locals may bear little fruit, especially when locals make no effort to communicate with one another directly or through COPE.

AFSCME: The Search for Grass-Roots

Three AFSCME affiliates in Ohio together had over 100,000 members, one of the state's largest internationals. Because Columbus is the state capital, I assumed that the union's local political involvement would be strong. However, identifying informants on the local scene proved difficult, not because they were unwilling to cooperate, but because the union's structure discouraged local politics.

A lobbyist for AFSCME Council 8 described the state organization. AFSCME had three councils or affiliates. Council 8 represented municipal, county, and state university employees. In 1982, the Ohio Civil Service Employees' Association (OCSEA) affiliated with AFSCME as a separate council. Its contracts covered state employees and nonprofit hospitals. In 1983, the Ohio Public School Employees (OPSE) joined AFSCME, representing nonteaching school personnel, librarians, and mental health workers. Collaboration among the three organizations was infrequent and ad hoc. Council 8 and OPSE were represented in Franklin County Central Body; OCSEA was not.

I sought out local officers of the three AFSCME affiliates, but they were not organized geographically as "locals." AFSCME Council 8 had a tiny unit, politically invisible, in the City of Columbus. I decided to interview officers of OCSEA Local 11, but it turned out to be a state body with 37,000 members. The informant portrayed OCSEA's state operations. I asked for names of officers who knew Columbus area politics, but no one coordinated OCSEA's politics locally. The union was divided into 155 "chapters," based primarily on occupational and agency groups. Because many government employees worked in the Columbus area, some chapters included many local residents. I selected the largest chapter, the Ohio Department of Transportation (ODOT). By chance, all of my informants (AFSCME, OCSEA, and DOT) had worked for ODOT. Below I summarize the political operations of the two state bodies (AFSCME Council 8 and Local 11 of OCSEA) and the "local" ODOT chapter.

Although AFSCME was well represented in the Columbus AFL-CIO central body, it devoted most of its money and energy to its legislative district committees (LDCs). Ohio was divided into twenty LDCs, sixteen of which were county units. Franklin County was one of these units. LDCs endorsed candidates for the legislature and local communities; Council 8 endorsed state and congressional candidates. LDCs made their endorsements earlier than COPE in the hope of influencing it. They generally succeeded, although occasional disagreements arose. Council 8 in Columbus operated its bank of twenty phones (compared to fifteen for COPE) to make contact with members in the first five days of October. It then turned its phones over to COPE for the coordinated campaign. The weekend before the election, Council 8 again phoned members; on Monday and Tuesday, it again passed its phones to COPE. AFSCME officials estimated that 80 percent of its members supported its endorsements, in contrast to 62 percent for labor as a whole.

Curiously, AFSCME's main problem was members' low voting turnout. Locally, more than half its members were women and about a fifth were black. Surveys revealed that state employees' registration rate was lower than that of federal and municipal employees. Nonvoting was especially high in Franklin County, where many state employees resided. Consequently, AFSCME concentrated on registration drives. In the last election, Council 8 provided $25,000 to spur local registration by door-to-door canvassing. Although these efforts were "nonpartisan," AFSCME concentrated on a few neighborhoods with Democratic leanings, often African-American.

In statewide races, AFSCME mostly supported Democrats, but in local ones, it endorsed more Republicans. The union was less successful in Franklin County than elsewhere in turning out the vote, marginalizing its effect on local elections. Unless AFSCME, OCSEA, and OPSE decide to coordinate their campaigns, government employees are not likely to have decisive local effects. On the state level, AFSCME spent more money on politics than any union except the UAW. Yet AFSCME officers recognized that money alone did not ensure victory. More volunteers were needed to vitalize the Democratic Party and labor's contribution to it.

OCSEA

In 1938, Local 11 of OCSEA had sixty members; it grew to 37,000 by 1990. It joined AFSCME in 1983 but retained much autonomy. OCSEA's bargaining units were organized by occupation and agency like the state employees board. Clerks were organized across agencies. Department of transportation employees belonged to a single bargaining unit. Over half of OCSEA members were women, and a fifth were black (Table 9.2). The president estimated that perhaps 60 percent were Democrats, but party affiliation was not critical to the union's main concern: improving negotiated contracts. For that, the union needed good relations with state legislators, the governor, administration, and bureau officials, especially in the office of collective bargaining.

The importance of politics was so obvious to members that an elaborate political education program was not needed. The president said:

> We don't have to work hard to make members conscious of the importance of politics. We have a bright, educated, and talented membership with plenty of volunteers to do almost anything we want to do. They write articles for our newspapers, prepare leaflets and pamphlets, and participate in registration and voting drives.

Not a member of COPE, OCSEA had its own PAC, PEOPLE, which was supported entirely by dues. It performed all the functions of COPE.

The organization restricted its activities exclusively to state politics. Its 10,000 members in central Ohio were not advised on local and county issues, even though AFSCME members worked in these governmental units. Both organizations maintained Columbus lobbyists but, surprisingly, did not coordinate their lobbying or campaign efforts.

Nor did OCSEA develop ties to the Democratic Party. Union officers thought that the party, poorly organized, made only feeble efforts to raise money. Its inadequate voter registration drives resulted in a low turnout. The African-American turnout was especially low because the party neglected the black community. Yet OCSEA officers were not motivated to improve matters. Their outlook was summarized by an officer:

> Look, we have no permanent friends politically, only permanent interests. Republicans don't do much for labor [locally], so we don't do much for them. We do what we need to do because we have lots of activists and volunteers. Nationally, we are very liberal.

Working outside the party system, OCSEA supported sympathetic candidates regardless of party. Occasionally, officers spent small sums for local Democratic events, like buying dinner tickets to demonstrate sympathy for labor and the party, but they did not become involved in community, labor, or statewide issues unrelated to the union's bargaining goals. OCSEA regarded itself as the most effective union in state politics. It exemplifies an industrial union devoted to bread-and-butter issues on the state level and weakly committed to labor's agenda in national affairs.

ODOT of OCSEA

OCSEA's twelve districts included 155 chapters. The Columbus ODOT chapter of 1,300 members, the largest chapter in the largest district, had a full panoply of officers: president, vice president, and executive board. It had some professional, skilled, and technical members, but the large majority were clerks. About 20 percent of the members were African Americans. Membership meetings were held every other month, normally drawing twenty-five people, less than 2 percent of the membership.

Contrary to the views in OCSEA, ODOT officers felt that, although OCSEA was Democratic and liberal, local ODOT members tended to be Republican, conservative, and politically apathetic. A female officer commented:

> Politics is important to the union, but the members don't recognize it. They are more interested in personal affairs of their families, shopping, and going to the hairdresser. All they care is what the union is doing for them. We bargained so that they could get their birthdays off, but they take this for granted and do not realize that it was due to the work of the union.

Apparently, the chapter engaged in little political education. It collected no money for political campaigns, and its quarterly newspaper contained little political news. The same people, mostly officers, took part in political activities. They were the "volunteers" who operated phone banks and distributed postcards for members to mail to state legislators urging them to support particular bills. District 6, which included all the agencies in the area, invited candidates to address them, including those for the city council. Yet, the district did not contribute to their campaigns.

Chapter officers thought that their political efforts were not fruitful and that the union's strength was based in other communities and on its strong lobby. Local members could not be motivated to participate in union or party affairs. An older officer commented, "The workers have lost memory of what the union movement was all about. These kids have been brought up on milk. All they ask is, 'What have you done for me lately?"' He then observed that the local Democratic Party was so ineffective that it drove voters into the Republican Party. Like many other informants, he observed, "Maybe we need more bad times. Voinovich (the Republican governor) is the best thing that happened to our membership. The tougher he gets, the more our people get aroused. If he runs again, he'll get smashed." (He ran again in 1994 and won by a wide margin.)

This overview of AFSCME, OCSEA, and ODOT shows that a large and uncoordinated union can be relatively successful in its statewide political efforts by evading local party attachments and by building a strong lobbying organization. Because of its large size, it can involve a few activists in many localities who together constitute a sizable political corps. Thus, top leaders see a politically active membership; local officers see apathy and indifference. Because AFSCME limited politics to narrow occupational goals, its affiliates had developed a fairly robust political organization without a strong grass roots organization.

The Teachers

Columbus's AFT local of 530 members represented not teachers but employees in Franklin County Children's Services. An officer reported that the union was not involved in politics because it was restricted by state law, a point not raised by other AFT locals. Actually, the law prohibited teachers from holding party offices and patronage jobs but permitted them to get out the vote, register voters, run in nonpartisan elections, display signs, make voluntary contributions, attend rallies, and wear political buttons. Since AFT officers were employed by the union and not the government, they could engage in any political activity, but they did little more than take a turn on COPE's phone bank.

Since the Ohio Educational Association (OEA) was the major teacher bargaining unit in the Columbus area, I substituted it for AFT. OEA bargained with school boards and organized some school support personnel in competition with AFSCME. Ohio law permitted OEA to use membership dues for campaigning, a sum that approached $100,000 in state campaigns. The union was organized on an assembly and senate district basis. All locals in a given district had seats on district committees, called E-PACs. Senate district committees comprised three house district committees. About 60 percent of E-PAC members were women, but very few were black women. A survey showed that 40 percent of OEA members were Democrats; 40 percent, Republicans; and 20 percent, Independents (Table 9.2).

The Columbus Educational Association (CEA), OEA's largest and strongest local, included a senate and three assembly districts. Each district committee had its own screening committee. At elections, OEA activists, along with the union's one hundred labor-relations consultants, operated the phone banks. With its large financial resources, staffs, activists, and lobbyists, OEA projected an image of power even though officers admitted that their political operations were less than satisfactory.

Officers also realized that many, if not the majority, of members did not follow district and state committee endorsements. Thus, in 1991, the majority did not follow OEA's endorsement of Democratic gubernatorial candidate Celebrezze. Republican Voinovich won handily. OEA officers complained that even though teachers were well educated, they were as politically apathetic and naive as most union members. Apart from school levies and board of education races, teachers had difficulty discerning how politics might affect larger educational and national issues.

On educational matters, OEA had minimal contact with the AFT, no contact with AFSCME, and little contact with other local unions apart from asking for support in local levies, which was generally forthcoming. However, COPE did not support OEA's call for increased state taxes for education.

OEA's approach to parties was pragmatic. Although it usually gave more money and volunteer support to Democratic than to Republican candidates, it did not make permanent party commitments. Thus, in the 1984 state campaign, it supported no Republicans for the senate, but in the 1988 campaign it supported more Republicans than Democrats. In return, Republicans supported OEA's demand for a state professional standards board, which AFT opposed. OEA depended heavily on its lobbying in the legislature, where it was generally perceived as powerful.

In sum, OEA's political behavior resembled OCSEA's. It developed an independent political organization that concentrated on state politics. Highly focused on occupational goals, it relied heavily on lobbying, making only transient ties with local unions and parties. Despite lack of rank-and-file support, it projected an image of enormous political influence when it mobilized its large staff and resources.

The Police

A newspaper reporter who had observed local politics for years thought that the Fraternal Order of Police (FOP) was the most influential local union because candidates competed hardest for its endorsements. The local lodge had 2,500 members, 1,400 in Columbus. About 95 percent were white males. A FOP official reported that a quarter of the police were completely apathetic politically; the remainder became interested when issues directly affected their welfare. The state and national FOP leadership had little success involving members in larger concerns.

Since the police had contacts with the mayor, council, courts, and public, they were aware that local politics affected their welfare. The city council determined the size of the force and its equipment, salaries, and pensions, and the judges determined the disposal of criminal cases. The election of favorable candidates visibly promoted police well-being. A FOP official observed that police were, by nature, a conservative lot and not interested in party politics. Yet, because candidates were linked to parties, the police had to make party choices. These were made entirely in terms of perceived occupational benefits. The monthly newsletter provided information on the issues being raised in the department, council, city hall, and courts. When elections approached, the lodge president appointed a committee of ten to screen candidates for city and state offices. After interviewing them, the committee made recommendations at a monthly membership meeting. Incumbents were always rescreened. Endorsements were made almost exclusively on the basis of candidates' position on law enforcement and police welfare issues. These did not always fall into a clear party pattern because candidates' positions varied on the size of the police budget, gun control, police conduct, civilian review boards, pension rights, and racial equity in hiring. Once made, the endorsements were supported by about 70 percent of the members. Over the years, 60 percent of the endorsements were for Democrats, but in most elections, the FOP endorsed candidates of both parties. In 1994, the retired former FOP president ran as a Republican for the county commission and won handily.

Using dues money for its PAC, the FOP raised little "hard" money for candidates or parties. It made small contributions to both parties by buying breakfast and banquet tickets. FOP did not have to spend much money to advertise its endorsements because the candidates who were endorsed widely publicized it on TV and radio and in newspapers.

When unendorsed candidates won elections, the police respectfully cooperated. Because officeholders typically wanted to be reelected, they tried to compromise differences with the police. The FOP, avoiding entanglement in such local issues as liquor store privatization, school board elections, prevailing wages, and tax abatement, did not collaborate with COPE or other public-sector unions. FOP officers thought that their political program was more effective from 1970 to 1985; it had become less so because of budget constraints and race relations controversies.

In short, the FOP represented a pure case of AFL bread-and-butter unionism, avoiding party entanglements and rewarding friends on the basis of their support of police interests. The policy was effective because crime was an important public concern and candidates from both parties competed on almost equal terms for FOP endorsements.

Food and Commercial Workers

UFCW Local 1059 in Columbus supervised forty-three counties stretching from Toledo to Columbus and south to northern Kentucky. The local included 13,000 members in grocery, discount, and drug stores as well as meatpacking and hairdressing. About 85 percent of the members were women, 40 percent of whom worked part time. In the Columbus area, blacks were about a third of the membership (Table 9.2). The union's health and welfare insurance attracted workers who might otherwise seek employment in nonunion firms. A staff of twenty-one workers and four organizers occupied a large, well-equipped new building at the city's eastern edge.

Union leaders recognized the importance of politics, and they tried to involve members. Twenty-five dollars of the initiation fee was rebated if new members attended an orientation meeting where officers explained the importance of political participation. They convinced about 40 percent to join the active ballot club, an annual five-dollar check-off that made $25,000 available for local politics. The local also published a bimonthly news letter that listed names of candidates endorsed by the union. Finally, the local conducted annual surveys to determine the position of its members on important union and public matters.

UFCW members were predominantly Democrats. To achieve their political purposes, officers needed only to convince them to vote. But they faced formidable problems. Member turnover was high, members were widely dispersed in many communities, and members were feebly integrated into the union and their neighborhoods. Volunteers could not be identified to fill vacancies in the central labor bodies and their COPEs.

Politics was left mostly to officers and staff. In Columbus, they sat on COPE's screening committee, took part in its phone bank, and gave money to it, the party, and local candidates. They evaluated these efforts as being as strong as any union's, including those of AFSCME, UAW, and the building trades. In contrast to widespread opinion, UFCW officers thought that the local Democratic Party was rebuilding, that the labor movement was growing, and that labor was becoming more aggressive politically.

Because the Columbus local had such a large staff, it could readily mobilize one hundred activists to take part in political rallies, phone banks, candidate dinners, and other events. Given its membership size, the UFCW's political contribution of $25,000 for politics was modest, but it was regular and concentrated in a few cities. The local's Columbus headquarters enabled officers to make easy contact with lobbyists, party leaders, and state legislators. But the union's ability to mobilize a large member turnout to vote for liberal Democrats was quite limited.

Service Workers

The Columbus district of SEIU, Local 47, had three to four hundred members, made up mostly of part-time workers in nursing homes, hospitals, and building maintenance services. Owing to an antiunion drive by new owners of various facilities in 1982, membership had declined 50 percent and then stabilized. About 90 percent of the members were blacks; 70 percent were women (Table 9.2). Wages in the industry were barely above the legal minimum.

The president, a black male, occupied a small office with neither secretary nor modern office equipment. He recognized that the legal protection of unions was especially important to his union and the members' well-being. Yet they were not interested in politics because they thought they suffered the same fate regardless of the party in power. Occasionally, they voted for a black city official who, they thought, might be able to do something to improve their neighborhoods.

SEIU had no political education program outside steward training, where the importance of government regulations in the health industry was reviewed. The district newsletter had to be discontinued for lack of funds. Politics was sometimes discussed in membership meetings at work sites, but attendance was typically very low. The president contributed to the president's club, but he raised no money for COPE. The president and three delegates attended meetings of the central body, and the same four operated COPE phone banks and distributed leaflets. Contacts with other unions were few. The delegates generally accepted COPE's endorsements of candidates except when it failed to endorse a black whom they thought was qualified.

Because members of SEIU were overwhelmingly Democrats, they typically supported the party's candidates if they voted, except for some Republican judges who were allegedly more favorable to labor. However, the Democratic Party typically did not approach the union for support. The president commented:

> There is too much division in the party leadership. The party has drifted away from its labor roots. Labor was the most effective tool that the party had, and the politicians have got away with it and they think they own the party. No, we shouldn't dominate the party, but it should work more with us. People believe we run the party even though we don't. I don't think we should dominate the party, but we should be a vital part of it. We should have more voice. They should let us be heard and understand the needs of working men and women.

SEIU's members were aware of black community problems: housing and neighborhood deterioration, crime, unemployment, school board fights, low-quality education, and abusive police behavior. Yet they did not become involved in these issues because they were preoccupied raising families and scrambling to make a living. The president's sense of futility extended to everything: Unions were becoming less influential, the media had indoctrinated people with the idea that labor leaders are corrupt, labor can not resist management because the NLRB is stacked against it, labor leaders are inadequate:

> The national leadership is getting to be too business-oriented. The local guy is being tuned out of the process. They [leaders] look like corporate types, like businessmen at the top—rather than like labor types at the top.

His solution was to make education a top priority in the schools. Students should be taught about labor's historical contributions, so that they would be ready to fight for their unions when they became workers. How this educational program might be implemented was not specified.

In conclusion, although SEIU was a growing and liberal union nationally, it had suffered a decline in Columbus. Wages in the industry were not much above the minimum. The union was small and had little or no influence on labor's politics. Feelings of powerlessness among its officers prevented them from engaging the problems of the black community.

CONCLUSIONS

Columbus represents a case where labor had accommodated to historic Republican Party domination. Only a slight majority of members in most unions identified themselves as Democrats. Almost all labor leaders complained that members were politically apathetic, but the leaders had developed no programs to combat the apathy. They criticized the Democratic Party for being weak and unresponsive to labor but had not considered ways to improve matters. Labor contributed to party weakness by giving money to candidates directly, not funneling it through the party. Labor also failed to mobilize members to vote against antilabor Republican congressional incumbents and backed many Republicans for local office. Seeking local respectability, labor probably contributed more to community projects than to local politics.

Political cleavages among and within the unions were even larger than expected. The ex-AFL unions seemed locked into a pre–World War II mold of job-oriented unionism. The Teamsters ignored COPE and both parties and supported only candidates who backed its industry-oriented objectives. The BTC also circumvented COPE and decentralized its political work to its conservative members. Thus, the carpenters, who were formally in COPE, supported more local Republicans than Democrats. The IBEW's construction local had shallow ties to COPE and the party, and its officers formally endorsed Gompersian nonpartisan ideology.

The ex-CIO unions were too politically fragmented to conform to the traditional CIO pattern. The UAW, by making large contributions to candidates for state and national office, was a major party player. Its independence from COPE weakened it, and its political conservatism weakened the liberal wings of COPE and the party. The small USW locals retained their liberal ideology, but their modest resources constricted their political efforts. Their active lobbyists in the state capital supported the Democratic Party, lending the locals an appearance of strength. The factory local of the IBEW was even less involved in politics than its construction local. The CWA's four locals varied greatly in their political ideology and in their support of COPE and the Democratic Party. The racial composition of the locals best predicted their political orientation, but not the extent of their involvement in COPE and the party. Because the locals did not coordinate their political efforts, CWA lacked political influence commensurate with its membership size. In short, the ex-CIO unions had a weak political education program, disagreed ideologically, and failed to congeal into a liberal coalition in COPE or the party.

Columbus's four public-sector unions had developed somewhat parallel but uncoordinated political styles. AFSCME had enough resources to support COPE and the Democratic Party and yet mount a stronger effort on its own behalf in state politics. OCSEA, equally strong in state politics, developed a pattern similar to the Teamsters'. It largely ignored COPE and the Democratic Party and pursued the bread-and-butter politics of sector unionism. The ODOT local chapter of OCSEA routinely followed state directives and remained passive in local politics. The teachers in OEA were not in the AFL-CIO, but their behavior resembled OCSEA's. Despite its meager grass roots activity, OEA's strong lobby in state government projected a public image of local political strength. In contrast, the police (FOP) were deeply involved in local politics, and both parties competed on almost equal terms for its endorsement. In sum, although the public-sector unions varied in ideology and political involvement, they tended toward sector bread-and-butter unionism.

The two service unions, SEIU and UFCW, also differed almost as much as the public-service unions. SEIU was a small, liberal, weak, and despondent player in COPE and the party. UFCW's staff was large and active enough to make the union a visible player in COPE and party affairs, despite its modest grass roots support. Clearly, the industrial, service, and public sector unions in Columbus did not form a liberal coalition within either labor or the party. Neither did the craft unions, Teamsters, and non-AFL-CIO public-sector unions form a conservative coalition.

Four conclusions may be drawn about union politics in Columbus. First, the Democratic Party was too disorganized and financially weak to exploit its advantage of having a majority of registered voters. Second, the Republicans had penetrated all unions to varying degrees, loosening labor's allegiance to the Democratic Party. Third, the major unions varied in their commitment to COPE and the Democratic Party, contributing to their factionalism. Fourth, the typology of craft, industrial, public-sector, and service unions was only weakly corroborated in the city's conservative climate. Political ideology and behavior in the locals of the same union varied almost as much as among the unions themselves, raising doubts that the union is the appropriate unit for political analysis. In short, given the main unions' insistently fragmented approach to politics, the political weakness of Columbus labor was what it deserved.

Social science predictions are perilous. In the spring of 1994, the Democratic Party's executive director resigned. The Teamsters, UAW, and AFL-CIO on the party's executive committee, in a rare instance of unity, agreed with old party regulars on a replacement. Blacks and liberals on the committee called for a delay to consider additional nominees. The majority coalition refused. Whether this labor–party coalition will endure and revive the party remains an open question.

In the November 1994 election, the Republicans maintained their historical control of the two congressional seats. A local black Democrat won a state senate seat, but Democrats lost a long-held seat in the state house and won only two of the seven for the region. An ex-Democratic council member won the contest for judge of the court of appeals. The reorganized party showed no improvement in its historical performance.

10

Labor–Party Relations in Three Cities

Relations between labor and the Democratic Party have been changing ever since the New Deal. Below, I describe the main changes from 1960 to the present. Then I examine the current efforts of the Democratic Party and COPE to aggregate interest groups behind the party in each of the three cities. After tracing the impact of each city's political culture on the political behavior of individual unions, I evaluate the effectiveness of the party's and labor's electoral systems in the three cities, comparing their patterns to Greenstone's community typology.

THE LABOR–PARTY NEXUS

When Greenstone (1969) studied labor politics in the early 1960s, labor and the Democratic Party had achieved a substantial amount of cooperation. The AFL and the CIO merged their political organizations into COPE in 1955. Among the major unions, only the mine workers (UMW) and the Teamsters remained outside the AFL-CIO. The UMW had disaffiliated from the CIO in 1942, and the Teamsters had been expelled from the AFL-CIO in 1957. By 1960, the UMW was losing many members, which weakened its political voice. Charges of corruption were forcing the Teamsters to the political periphery of the labor movement.

When this study began in 1990, organized labor and COPE had undergone important changes that affected their relationships to the Democratic Party. The UAW, which left the AFL-CIO in 1968 and returned in 1981, had not melded its political arm (CAP) into local COPEs. The Teamsters, reaffiliated in 1987, had attained some respectability but had not merged their political organization (DRIVE) into local COPEs. The teachers, police, firefighters, and other municipal unions had grown in size and become more politically active. Government and service unions had grown in size and political strength, while industrial unions had suffered losses in membership and influence. Many AFL-CIO unions had strengthened their PACs and reduced their contributions to COPE. Thus, compared to the 1960s, labor's political arms had become more numerous, more diversified, and more decentralized.

Greenstone was preoccupied with pluralism's main concerns: how interest groups were aggregated, the extent of their aggregation, and identification of groups that dominated the aggregation process. These concerns framed his analysis of labor–party cooperation in Detroit, Chicago, and Los Angeles. I found that the labor–party systems in Cleveland, Cincinnati, and Columbus differed considerably from Greenstone's 1960s profiles of Detroit, Chicago, and Los Angeles. In Cleveland, the city that has most consistently supported the Democratic Party since the 1930s, labor's major political organizations remained uncoordinated. No union or combination of unions resembled the UAW's 1960s challenge in Detroit: how to operate the Democratic Party that it dominated. Strong, centralized Democratic Party machines had declined everywhere since the 1960s. Not surprisingly, in no Ohio city did labor face the dilemma that it faced in Chicago in the 1960s: how to accommodate to the powerful party machine. While the labor–party systems in Cleveland, Columbus, and Cincinnati in the 1990s suffered from the disorganization apparent in Los Angeles in the 1960s, the patterns differed in each Ohio city. Greenstone's three cities and the three Ohio cities in this study undoubtedly differed even in the 1960s. And it may well be that the patterns in the two sets of cities are more similar today. Very likely, the patterns that Greenstone described had changed in the direction reflected in the three Ohio cities.

National changes in labor–party relations since the early 1960s (see Chapter 3) were clearly evident in all three Ohio cities. Many respondents reported that the party's organization had weakened and that party patronage and loyalty had declined. The campaign organizations directed by candidates had become stronger, grass roots politicking had declined, and reliance on mass media for campaigning had increased. The changes were more apparent in Columbus and Cincinnati than in Cleveland, where the Democratic Party remained more successful.

Increasing suburbanization, declining ethnic neighborhoods, and growing urban black populations had eroded party efforts to reach all voters. Simultaneously, COPE's voting strength had declined because of declining union membership, which reduced the size of the volunteer corps, while the increased residential dispersion of members simultaneously reduced COPE's ability to reach them. These trends had proceeded farthest in the Cleveland area, somewhat less in Cincinnati, and least in Columbus. Moreover, urban areas were experiencing more economic and social dislocation. The increasing social heterogeneity of union members reduced their consensus on the connections between local, state, and national issues. Unable to cope with these changes, labor leaders concluded that their members were losing political interest and had become more conservative. But the leaders themselves were subject to the same forces that had changed their members. Leaders had become more socially heterogeneous and were losing a common perspective on the ways to link local, state, and national issues.

THE PARTY AS COORDINATOR

A party's electoral success depends on its ability to coordinate and aggregate the interests and resources of potential constituencies. Both the Democratic Party and COPE may be examined for their success in this area. The party must coordinate many groups, including labor, ward organizations, patronage recipients, candidates for office, government officials, financial backers, unorganized voters, ethnic and racial groups, business and professional associations, and single-interest groups such as firms, teachers, women, youth, and religious organizations. COPE, as a party, must aggregate and coordinate the interests of its constituent unions and unions outside COPE as well as the groups to which union members belong, groups defined by sex, race, ethnicity, neighborhood residence, and the like.

Table 10.1 presents estimates of how the parties in the three Ohio communities ranked in their ability to coordinate interest groups. The table's first seven items refer to participants in the political-governmental system; the last eight refer to other constituencies. Central party control refers to a party chair's capacity to coordinate groups; the greater the chair's independence, the greater the potential for party discipline. Ward leaders' ability to withhold cooperation weakens centralized coordination. The more patronage that is available to the chair, the higher the chair's potential to attract supporters. The more candidates control their campaign organizations, the weaker the party's aggregating potential. The more access party leaders have to governmental officials, the greater the party's aggregating potential. Finally, the less opposition the party faces from other political parties, the easier its aggregating task.

Surprisingly, the Democratic Party leader in Columbus experienced the least interference in running the party and the least opposition from

Table 10.1
Aggregating Capacity of the Democratic Party in the Three Cs

Items	Cincinnati	Cleveland	Columbus
Party			
Party leaders' independence	Moderate	Low	High
Ward leaders' independence	Moderate	High	Low
Patronage	Low	High	Moderate
Financial support	Moderate	High	Low
Candidates' dependence	Low	Moderate	High
Access to government officials	Low	Moderate	Low
Republican Party challenge	Moderate	Low	High
Party Supporters			
Ethnic political power	Moderate	High	Low
Black political power	Moderate	High	Low+
COPE cooperation	High	Moderate	Low
UAW cooperation	Moderate	Moderate	High
Teamster cooperation	Low	Low	Low
Teachers' cooperation	Moderate	Moderate	Low
AFSCME-OCSEA cooperation	Moderate	Moderate	High
Liberal professional support	Moderate	Moderate+	Moderate−

ward leaders and exercised the most control over campaigns; access to patronage and government officials was moderate. Cleveland's party leader was the weakest because he had the least control over ward organizations and less access to patronage and city officials than council members and ward leaders. Cincinnati's party leader had little access to patronage and government officials and moderate access to ward organizations.

When groups cooperate outside the party, they increase the party's aggregating power. The main groups include white ethnics, blacks, COPE, the UAW, the Teamsters, the teachers, and, to some extent, AFSCME and professional groups. The relatively weak race and ethnic organizations in Columbus strengthened the party leader's hand, just as strong race and ethnic organizations weakened it in Cleveland. In Cincinnati, the party leader's strength was in between, but closer to the Cleveland situation. Of the three labor electoral organizations (COPE, UAW, and Teamsters), COPE helped the party most in Cincinnati and least in Cleveland. The UAW strengthened the party leader most in Columbus, less in Cleveland, and least in Cincinnati. The Teamsters operated outside the system in all three cities but probably were closest to the party in Cleveland and most distant in Columbus.

Cleveland's party received the most funding from nonlabor groups.

In Columbus, nonlabor groups contributed the least. Liberal professionals supported the party most in Cleveland, less in Cincinnati, and least in Columbus. The party's aggregating task is made easier when Republican opposition is weak. Obviously, the Republicans were weakest in Cleveland. Even though the Cincinnati Democratic Party confronted opposition from both Republicans and Charterites, the Democratic challenge was stronger in Cincinnati than in Columbus.

The above analysis supports several conclusions. First, because the aggregating process is multidimensional, estimating its effectiveness is risky. Second, Cleveland's party seemed to be strongest in its aggregating potential, followed by the party in Cincinnati, and then the party in Columbus. Third, the complex patterns of aggregation may not result in a typology as clear as Greenstone's. Fourth, competition for control of a party may not be decisive in weakening its electoral effectiveness. Thus, ethnic groups and blacks fought to control the party in Cleveland, yet the party managed to win elections. Fifth, party cooperation may not be related to the financial contributions that groups make to it. Thus, although the UAW, COPE, and the teachers cooperated only moderately with Cleveland's Democratic Party, they contributed more resources than the more cooperative groups in Cincinnati and perhaps in Columbus. Finally, the ability of the opposing party to aggregate groups and resources must be considered. One party may aggregate better, but its resources may be slimmer. Cleveland's Republican Party was probably better coordinated than the Democratic Party, which, however, had more organizational resources.

LABOR'S AGGREGATING APPARATUS

COPE was designed as an umbrella organization to coordinate the political activities of its member unions. Like political parties, it faced the problem of aggregating diverse interest groups. How well was COPE organized to perform this task? How well did it perform in the three cities?

COPE's initial liability was that it could not speak for all labor because more than a fifth of union members belonged to unions outside COPE: the UAW, the Teamsters, the teachers in the OEA, the police (FOP), and the firefighters. Also excluded from COPE were an undetermined number of AFL-CIO unions that paid no dues to the Central Labor Body. As a COPE spokesperson said, "You have to pay to play." Therefore, in assessing the aggregating potential of labor for the Democratic Party, one must consider at least six or more labor organizations and their relationships. Coordinating these organizations is a formidable task.

Figure 10.1 summarizes relations among labor's main political organizations. Clearly, they do not constitute an integrated social system. First, as indicated, an undetermined number of unions and locals are completely outside the system. Second, all COPE members presumably coordinate their political activities through COPE, which then presumably handles labor's relationships to the party. However, most unions establish PACs that duplicate, supplement, or even oppose COPE's activities. Most conspicuously, the Building Trades Council (BTC) pursues its own political agenda. Its individual members approach the parties and candidates directly and define their relations to COPE. AFSCME, representing a variant on this pattern, has the resources to support COPE stoutly and to maintain a strong organization outside it which, however, dwarfs AFSCME's contributions to COPE. AFSCME also approaches the parties and candidates directly. Third, the UAW and the Teamsters operate strong political organizations completely outside COPE, and they, too, approach parties and candidates directly. OCSEA, a part of AFSCME, operates outside COPE and behaves much like the UAW. The UAW occasionally informs COPE of its candidate endorsements, which tend to be similar. The Teamsters do so less often; their endorsements deviate more from COPE's. Thus, four big

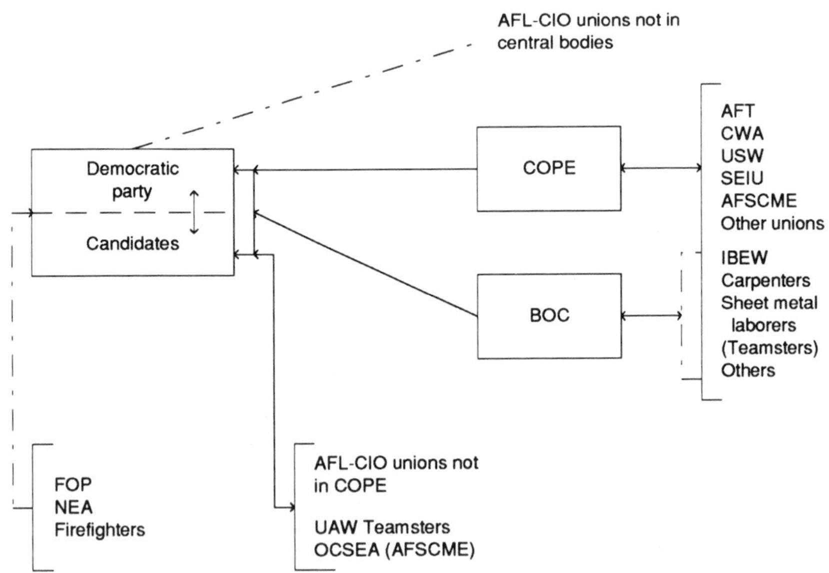

Figure 10.1. Local union–party system.

unions (the UAW, Teamsters, AFSCME, and OCSEA) whose resources approach the size of the party's and exceed those of COPE approach candidates directly. Fourth, the NEA, FOP, and the firefighters rarely make contact with COPE; they deal directly with the candidates and avoid the parties.

Labor's political organizations could hardly be coordinated less rationally. Some locals do not engage in politics. Six of the largest unions and BTC escape COPE's aggregating net altogether: the UAW, Teamsters, BTC, NEA, OCSEA, FOP, and the firefighters. Most unions spend more money for their PACS and lobbying activities than they give to COPE. Their major resources are not funneled through COPE. Party leaders must make contact with COPE and the independent unions outside it, as well as strong unions in COPE. This highly disjointed system has no mechanism to pool resources and personnel to exert maximum influence on the Democratic Party, candidates, or the broader society.

A comparison of party and COPE organizations reveals that the party remains the main "coordinator" of local interest groups. Labor organizations make contact with members as voters, but as a whole, labor has no ward structure and makes only episodic contact with ethnic and racial political machines. Neither does labor make systematic contact with business and professional interest groups that might support it and the party. Finally, labor rarely raises campaign money outside its own ranks (see Table 10.2).

Table 10.2
COPE's Aggregating Capacity in the Three Cs

Items	Cincinnati	Cleveland	Columbus
Internal cooperation	High	Moderate	Low
Number of volunteers	High	Low	Moderate
Financial Resources	Moderate	High	Low
Conscious political strategy	High	Moderate	Low
Ties to the UAW	Low	Moderate	Low
Ties to Teamsters	Moderate	Moderate	Low
Ties to teachers	Moderate	Moderate	Low
Ties to AFSCME and OCSEA	Low	Low	Moderate
Ties to municipal unions	None	Low	None
Relations to Democratic Party	High	Moderate	Low
Access to wards	Moderate	Moderate	Low
Access to black community	Moderate	High	Low
Access to suburbs	Low	Moderate	Low
Community issue involvement	Moderate	High	Low
Ideological viability	Moderate	High	Low

The party, in contrast, makes contact with all groups: voters, ward organizations, ethnic and racial organizations, candidates for office, legislators, labor's political organizations, and individual unions, businesses, and special-interest groups. The party also tries to oversee fund-raising and political campaigning. At best, labor represents an uncoordinated subsystem of the larger and also uncoordinated party system. Candidates for office make contacts that are broader than labor's, often paralleling those of the party. Moreover, candidates rarely coordinate their organizations. Only the party organization is all-embracing and enduring. The conclusion is inescapable: Without fundamental restructuring, labor must play a subordinate aggregating role in the party.

COPE's Strength in Three Cities

COPE's strength in Cleveland, Columbus, and Cincinnati may be analyzed with the same categories used to estimate the party's aggregating strength. COPE deals with four relationships: unions inside COPE, labor bodies outside COPE, and political parties and interest groups in the community. Considering COPE's internal operations, Cincinnati unions cooperated the most, provided the most volunteers, and gave COPE moderate financial support. The Cincinnati COPE also worked hardest to devise a strategy to become more influential politically. Cleveland's COPE made up for its fewer volunteers by generating more money. Its unions cooperated moderately well, and COPE worked reasonably hard on its political strategy. Columbus's COPE occupied the lowest position along these dimensions, except that it had relatively more volunteers than Cleveland.

Cleveland's COPE managed best with respect to Democratic party constituencies, wards, the black community, and suburbs. Despite disagreements with the party, COPE developed the strongest ties to the wards, the black community, and the suburbs. Its superior suburban performance resulted from its decision to establish two suburban COPEs. Its stronger ties to the black community simply reflected COPE's larger black membership. In contrast, until 1994, COPE's party relations in Columbus can be best described as "sulky." Its ties in the wards and the black community were poorly developed. COPE's relations to the party were closest in Cincinnati; its political ties in the wards and suburbs were less developed than in Cleveland but more ample than in Columbus.

In no community did COPE develop strong ties to other labor political organizations like CAP, DRIVE, PEOPLE, FOP, and the municipal unions. Cleveland's COPE probably had more contacts with all of them. In Columbus, only the powerful AFSCME kept in close touch with COPE even though it favored its own PAC. Cincinnati's COPE developed the leanest ties with the other labor political organizations.

Finally, COPE's greater involvement in Cleveland community issues reflected the ideological heritage of its major unions, especially of the USW, CWA, UAW, and the building trades. COPE's restricted involvement in Columbus issues reflected the higher priority that its largest unions placed on occupational concerns. Cincinnati's COPE occupied a middle position.

In sum, Cincinnati and Cleveland COPEs ranked about the same in their aggregating profiles, but their areas of strength differed. The Columbus COPE, though increasing its strength, ranked lower in most areas. The main aggregating strength of Cincinnati's COPE was its determined drive to resolve internal disputes and develop a stronger Democratic Party. Cleveland COPE's aggregating strength reflected its superior suburban organization and the greater inclination of large unions in and outside COPE to "speak out for labor." It also had more receptive audiences in the wards and the black community that were inclined to support the Democratic Party. Columbus COPE's main strength was that it recruited a relatively large number of volunteers and it received solid support from the powerful AFSCME. Although the political environment in Columbus was as conservative as in Cincinnati, Columbus's COPE aggregated its constituents less successfully because their divisions, like the Democratic Party's, were accepted as a fact of life. As I concluded from the case studies, the supportive Democratic tradition in Cleveland enabled COPE to be more successful than its efforts deserved. Since Cincinnati's formidable conservative tradition impeded COPE's strong aggregating efforts, its rewards were less than it deserved. Since COPE did not recently try to overcome Columbus's conservative tradition, COPE received the returns it deserved.

COMMUNITY IMPACTS ON INDIVIDUAL UNIONS

How much does local political tradition, culture, or context affect the political orientation of different unions and their locals? If all unions and their locals behave the same way in all three communities, it is fair to conclude that community tradition, culture, or context has no effects. If unions respond differently according to their type (craft, industrial, public-sector, and service), and if their locals respond differently in the three communities in a particular hypothesized direction, then community tradition, culture, or context has an effect. I analyzed variations in responses of the unions and their locals to three concerns: labor solidarity; involvement in local class, welfare, or ideological issues; and support for the Democratic Party.

I predicted that the building trades and Teamsters would respond uniformly in the three communities by placing little emphasis on the three concerns because their AFL heritage downplays union solidarity, welfare or class issues, and party loyalty. On the other hand, industrial unions should place greater emphasis on these three concerns. The more liberal the political tradition of a community, the greater the emphasis a given local should put on these concerns. A conservative community tradition should depress the intensity of the responses. Thus, locals of industrial unions in Cleveland should place greater emphasis on labor solidarity, class issues, and party support than locals in Cincinnati and Columbus. Unions in the public sector should display moderate concern for union solidarity, ideology, and party loyalty. A conservative community culture would push locals of these unions toward the traditional AFL pattern. Service-sector unions resemble industrial-sector unions in their political rhetoric, but not in political activism. A conservative community context should depress expressions of concern in the three areas. I examine the case for each union.

Ex-AFL Unions

The Teamsters, BTC, Carpenters, and IBEW represent ex-AFL unions. Few differences appeared for the Teamsters in the three cities. All Teamster leaders expressed reservations about developing close relationships to the Democratic Party and COPE. They all endorsed the pre–New Deal AFL philosophy of concentrating political efforts on advancing the welfare of the industry. Their interest in state and federal legislation was largely limited to transportation. Perhaps responding to the louder political rhetoric in Cleveland, the Teamsters projected an image of being tougher, stronger, more aggressive, and more prolabor (undefined) than other unions. They avoided discussing corruption in the international. Responding perhaps to the conservative climate in Cincinnati and Columbus, the Teamsters emphasized their responsible leadership and yearning for public respect. In Columbus, the Teamsters seemed the most isolated from local politics. As predicted, community political context had little bearing on Teamster politics.

Community context had some impact on BTC politics. Although Cleveland's BTC differed with COPE on some local issues, the two bodies maintained regular ties. The BTC felt sufficiently strong to publicly reveal its preference for Democrats and yet maintain relations with the chamber of commerce and business groups interested in downtown development.

While BTC members varied in their support for Democrats, they all raised "hard" money for consensual candidates. Cincinnati's BTC had traditionally remained independent of COPE, but the antiunion drive of local contractors forced the BTC to approach both COPE and the Democratic party cautiously. Yet party splits among its members inhibited the BTC from making its preferences public. In Columbus, the BTC maintained a distance from COPE that seemed to satisfy most of its conservative unions. Its decentralized structure permitted members to consistently support downtown development, conservative Republican members of Congress, and nonparty entanglements. In no city did the BTC become involved in issues other than community growth and downtown development. Thus, community tradition had little impact on BTC politics, but the small local differences were in the expected direction.

The responses of the carpenters paralleled those of their BTCs. In Cleveland, the carpenters generally supported the Democratic Party and participated in COPE. They endorsed business growth, raised money to support Democratic candidates, and were cautious about becoming involved in nonconstruction issues. In Cincinnati, the carpenters had reduced their political and community involvement over the years, and they balanced Republican and Democratic endorsements. Yet they supported COPE stoutly. The Columbus carpenters seemed less split and discouraged, and they largely limited their political participation to the BTC. Reflecting the local political environment, they endorsed more Republicans than Democrats. Again, while the city differences were small for the carpenters, they were in the expected direction.

The IBEW was more active politically than the carpenters in all three communities, and its patterns reflected community traditions. In Cleveland, the IBEW raised "hard" money through a check-off system. It participated in COPE, routinely followed COPE's endorsements, engaged in electoral activities, and supported the Democratic Party. Unlike the BTC, Cincinnati's IBEW committed itself to the programs of COPE and the Democratic Party. IBEW members participated in the political check-off, supported COPE's recommendations and activities, backed the Democratic Party, and promoted labor's community interests. In Columbus, the IBEW nominally supported COPE but initiated almost no political action, raised no "hard" money, and had little contact with the Democratic Party. It sought local respectability and opted for Gompers's approach to labor politics. Perhaps the liberal influence of the IBEW's industrial locals made the construction locals more active politically than the BTC and the carpenters in all three communities. Differences in involvement in community issues, COPE, and the party were in line with theoretical expectations, with Cleveland the most involved and Columbus the least.

The Ex-CIO Unions

The UAW in Cleveland was stronger, more disciplined, more active, and more ideologically aggressive than in the other two cities. Columbus's UAW was least developed along these lines. Cleveland's UAW was also most involved in community and national issues and, despite disputes with the Democratic Party, supported it strongly. The UAW's refusal to support the Republican Voinovich for mayor increased its isolation from COPE and other labor leaders. Despite its declining fortunes, the UAW still had sufficient members and resources to sustain an effective independent political organization.

The scenario differed in Cincinnati and Columbus. Because the Columbus UAW provided the deficit-ridden Democratic Party with relatively more financial support than it did in Cincinnati, the UAW in Columbus was a more visible player despite unaggressive and conservative leadership. In Cincinnati, UAW membership was so dispersed geographically that it remained more isolated from both COPE and the Democratic Party, diminishing its political visibility. Since differences among UAW locals were relatively small in Cincinnati and Columbus, the prediction of community influence is supported.

The USW stood almost alone in agreeing on the "proper course" for political action in the three communities. USW officials clung to the ideology of labor's heyday. Labor should be committed unfailingly to working-class interests; it should unite solidly behind COPE and the Democratic Party; and the UAW must return to COPE. Cleveland's USW most closely clung to the traditional pattern because it could still rely on a core of steel workers to lead the effort. It was almost the only union that worked intimately with the black Twenty-First District Caucus. Yet the officers found it increasingly difficult to transmit their faith to a diversifying membership.

In Cincinnati, USW officers looked back to a period when more members were identified with the working class, labor, and the Democratic Party. The union was experiencing difficulty in maintaining its traditional political appeal to members in its new locals and found it harder to recruit COPE volunteers and arouse political interest. Political involvement, not finance, was the officers' chief obstacle. In Columbus, the USW's political education program had collapsed, and the locals were planning to rebuild it. Officials had to confront the fact that keeping the faith in politics, labor, and the party was not enough. In short, support for a liberal political ideology, labor solidarity, and party loyalty was highest in Cleveland, only a past memory in Cincinnati, and an aspiration in Columbus. This pattern fits theoretical expectations.

Like the USW, the CWA's membership was declining and becoming more diversified as the union expanded into other industries. The Cleveland locals tried to maintain their traditional liberal activism in the face of rising member apathy and conservatism and jurisdictional disputes with other unions. Its past policy of creating a liberal coalition outside COPE had failed and forced the union to return to COPE to try to make it and the Democratic Party more liberal. Cincinnati's CWA had not tried to organize new industries. Having lost their traditional liberal leaders, the telephone locals also lost their political vitality. In the face of declining membership, officials tried to maintain their ties to COPE and the Democratic Party while they worked on plans to become more politically active. The four Columbus locals reflected different patterns. Not profiting from a coordinating council, as in Cleveland, the Columbus locals varied from no contact with COPE and the Democratic Party to moderately strong attachment. The high concentration of blacks in two locals encouraged officials to voice their objections about local issues involving blacks. The impacts of industrial change on the CWA's membership had challenged its officers' ability to implement the union's traditional liberal ideology. In Cleveland, although bruised, they still experienced some success; in Cincinnati, officers struggled to recover the lost tradition; in Columbus, no pattern appeared for the four locals. In sum, community context had a discernible effect on issues, party support, and labor solidarity, being highest in Cleveland, lowest in Columbus, and in between in Cincinnati. The prediction is partially confirmed.

Public Sector Unions

AFSCME Council 8 and its major affiliates, OCSEA and APSE, were powerful organizations, but their political arms operated almost independently. The three organizations strongly emphasized their sector objectives and invested their large resources in state government concerns. In all three cities, they successfully recruited volunteers and raised money to support favorable candidates. While OCSEA avoided entanglement with COPE everywhere, AFSCME Council 8 supported it but invested more in its PAC. Party involvement varied locally. AFSCME supported the Democratic Party most in Cleveland even as it criticized party failure to respond to working-class issues. While AFSCME leaders in Cincinnati leaned toward the Democratic Party, they were careful not to project an image of being too liberal. In Columbus, the union endorsed slightly more Republicans than Democrats for local offices. In Columbus, OCSEA revealed no concern about ideological issues, associating with COPE, or working with the local party. The union was so large that it could recruit an effective volunteer corps almost solely from its officers or staffs. Although community political culture had more impact on Council 8 than on OCSEA, it affected them both.

Although Cleveland and Cincinnati teachers belonged to the AFT and Columbus teachers to the OEA, the politics of both unions were similar. Both unions concentrated on state educational issues, avoided making permanent party commitments, and withheld allegiance to COPE. Although their party preferences expectedly reflected local party strength, the preferences did not determine the unions' political strategies. Thus, the AFT in Cleveland and in Cincinnati backed Republican Voinovich for governor in 1990, while the Columbus teachers backed the OEA endorsement of Democrat Celebrezze. Cincinnati's AFT had developed stronger ties to COPE and the Democratic Party than Cleveland's, and predictably, the Columbus chapter of the OEA maintained distance from both. In short, the teachers were committed to job-conscious unionism; unexpectedly, community political tradition had little discernible influence.

Service Sector Unions

The headquarters of UFCW locals, which covered large geographic areas, were located in each city. The members, mostly women, lived in widely dispersed communities. The impressive headquarters projected an image of a wealthy and influential union, but none of the locals seemed to have the resources or the ability to develop even a small political education program. Officers routinely participated in COPE, generally followed its recommendations, and supported the Democratic Party financially. Community context seemed to have had little or no effect on politics.

In all three cities, SEIU members were predominantly black women. Although the locals varied in size and occupational composition, they differed little in political organization and orientation. While officials had convinced a third of the members to participate in the political check-off, the union had neither the personnel nor the resources to develop a political education program. Local leaders were aware of the strong liberal stance taken by their international, but they simply could not translate it into practice. They ritualistically followed COPE's recommendations and supported the Democratic Party. However, the membership remained detached from both because, in their eyes, neither union nor party did much to support the black community's political causes. Community context had little effect on the political activities of the locals.

In summary, among the ex-AFL unions, the community context was absent for the Teamsters, small for the BTC and the carpenters, and modest for the IBEW. As expected, community context had most impact in Cleveland and least in Columbus. The ex-CIO unions had retained residues of their traditional ideology, party support, and labor solidarity, being strongest in the UAW, followed by the USW and CWA. The pattern was strongest in Cleveland and weakest in Columbus, with Cincinnati in between. Public-sector unions showed less consistency than expected. All embraced sector-conscious unionism, but the pattern of AFSCME's Council 8 fell between those of the ex-AFL and ex-CIO unions. The council supported the party and COPE yet maintained a discrete distance. OCSEA's pattern resembled that of the ex-AFL unions, but community political traditions exerted influence in the expected direction. The pattern for teachers unions also resembled the traditional AFL pattern even more than OSCEA's; no consistent community impact was apparent. The patterns for the service sector unions were similar. Although their locals were not deeply involved in issues bearing on race, they were recognized locally as important political actors because they could mobilize large staffs and a few activists for political rallies and events. This was more true of the UFCW in Columbus, where demonstrations at the state capitol received wide publicity. Community effects were unimportant.

Overall, community political traditions had little effect on craft and service unions, but for different reasons. Traditions had most effect on the industrial unions and an intermediate effect on some public-sector unions.

CONCLUSIONS

The data suggest that industrial and residential changes in metropolitan regions and changes in their political organizations altered labor politics differently in each city. Even though Cleveland experienced the most change, labor's loyalty to the party since the 1960s was reduced the least. However, changes in the area's ethnic and racial composition, as well as suburbanization, diminished the organizational efficiency of both COPE and the Democratic Party. Cincinnati experienced almost as much change as Cleveland, but the vitality of COPE, the party, and labor–party relations fluctuated considerably over the period. Although the metropolitan area of Columbus grew the most, party, labor, and labor–party relations remained relatively unchanged.

Massive changes had occurred in labor's membership composition and political organization. COPE's tasks became the most complex and least manageable in Cleveland because its metropolitan region had changed the most. COPE decentralized to cope with the problems of suburbanization, but it failed to repair its relations with the Democratic Party and the black community. The UAW and Teamsters outside of COPE complicated the ability of the party to respond to labor's interests. Faced with similar but less drastic metropolitan change, Cincinnati's COPE tried to repair its divisions and strengthen its bonds to the Democratic Party. The Teamsters played their traditional independent game, while the UAW shifted more of its resources to state and national politics. In Columbus, COPE, the UAW, and the Teamsters continued on their independent ways and were unable until recently to cooperate to meet the economic problems of the battered Democratic Party.

In the three cities, COPE did little to aggregate nonlabor groups and liberals behind the Democratic Party. While the party remained the main aggregating vehicle, individual candidates increasingly eroded this role. The party in Columbus suffered the least interference because, even in its weakness, groups did not compete to control it. However, labor and party regulars recently took steps to repair the situation. The party remained strongest in Cleveland because labor and other groups provided more resources and because blacks and white ethnics episodically consolidated enough strength to dominate it. Labor and political liberals revived the party in Cincinnati; whether the revival will stabilize is unclear. The party's central organization remained supine in all three communities. Groups occasionally tried to dominate it, but none succeeded in coalescing the diverse constituencies.

Labor politics in the three cities bore little resemblance to Greenstone's community typology. In no instance did labor dominate the party. In no city did the party machine dominate labor's political organizations or compete with them. In all cities, coordination of party and labor organization had weakened. Importantly, the class and welfare issues that had played such an important role in Greenstone's analysis of labor politics became minor themes in the three Ohio cities. Although community differences in this area persisted, they did not fall into a neat pattern. Both labor and the party varied in their aggregating capacity and ability to mobilize constituencies. The number of electoral organizations had grown and had become smaller in size and more independent. Three cases are too few to allow one to arrive at a reliable typology, if one can be drawn. However, in any typology, race must play a much more important factor in party and labor relations than in the past. How race will affect their relations is still unclear.

Finally, community political traditions influenced the politics of ex-CIO unions the most and influenced ex-AFL and service-sector unions the least. The pattern is mixed or may be emerging for the public-sector unions. These findings—pointing to greater variation than Greenstone described for Detroit, Chicago, and Los Angeles—will be analyzed later.

11

Labor, Community, and State Politics

Labor's political efforts must finally be evaluated by its ability to influence the political behavior of union members and governmental bodies. In the preceding chapters, I examined labor's community operations to accomplish these ends. This chapter explores the effectiveness of these operations in a state election.

Early studies (Campbell et al. 1964; Scoble 1967) showed that organized labor influences but does not determine the political behavior of its members because they, like other citizens, are subject to many influences emanating from their family traditions, religious affiliation, ethnicity, race, and community attachments. Since the 1960s, relatively few scholars have studied the sources of political influence on labor union members (see the reviews in Form 1985, Chs. 9, 10; Masters and Delaney 1987b). Yet, enormous changes have taken place in the size and social composition of labor membership and in the organization of politics (see Chapter 3).

In charting the changes in union members' political behavior and attitudes from 1952 to 1988, Asher, Ripley, and Snyder (1991) concluded that labor leaders lack information about labor's political influence. The authors therefore conducted a statewide survey of the political behavior and attitudes of union and nonunion members in the 1990 Ohio gubernatorial election. The authors graciously gave me access to their data, which enabled me to compare organized and unorganized workers in the metropolitan areas of Cleveland, Columbus, and Cincinnati. The data permitted an analysis of (1) the community political climates of the three metropolises; (2) differences in attitudes, beliefs, and political behavior of union and nonunion voters; (3) political differences of union members in three communities; and (4) COPE's impact on union members' political behavior.

What should one expect to find in each of the four areas? With respect to political climates, the data in previous chapters suggested that the survey would show Clevelanders to be more liberal in political beliefs and Cincinnati and Columbus respondents to be more conservative. Cincinnati voters were expected to show more variation than Columbus voters because Cincinnati had the Charterites, a larger percentage of blacks, and a more politically aggressive labor movement. The greatest political polarization was expected to appear in Cleveland because it had fewer "independents" than the other two cities. Given the looseness of party loyalty in the United States, cross-party voting was expected, especially if favorite sons and daughters were running for office.

In comparing the politics of union and nonunion respondents, small differences were expected to appear in Columbus and Cleveland because Cleveland was historically as Democratic as Columbus was Republican, while Cincinnati's recent politics suggested more political diversity due to the presence of the Charterites and labor's drive to vitalize a unified labor–party coalition against the Republicans. Because Cincinnati's heritage was Republican, evidence of diversity depended on labor's success in denting Republican domination.

In exploring political diversity among union members, Cleveland unionists were expected to be the most homogeneous and most likely to follow labor's recommendations. Columbus unionists were expected to be less homogeneous and least likely to heed union advice. Cincinnati unionists were expected to occupy an intermediate position, but closer to that of Columbus than to that of Cleveland.

It is difficult to predict how union members might perceive the political influence of COPE and other labor organizations. Given the segmented nature of labor's political organizations in all three cities, members should perceive labor's influence as relatively small. COPE's recent reorganization in Cincinnati might make union members more conscious of labor's efforts. Cleveland's reputation as a strong union city might also lead members to attribute some political influence to labor. The routine political efforts of Columbus labor should make them least visible to union members.

THE POLITICAL CONTEXT OF THE ELECTION

In the 1990 election, the state's top administrative officers were on the ballot, including the governor, the lieutenant governor, the attorney general, the auditor, the secretary of state, and the treasurer. All assembly, or house, seats were being contested, half of the senate seats, and two Ohio Supreme Court seats. Prior to the election, the Democrats controlled the house, and Republicans, the senate. Although this pattern was expected to persist, the outcomes for the executive offices and the supreme court were uncertain.

The Democratic nominee for governor was the state's attorney general, Anthony Celebrezze; the Republican nominee was George Voinovich. Both had been active in Cleveland politics. Voinovich had just served two terms as mayor and had received organized labor's support (see Chapter 7). In the 1990 state election, all major unions except the Teamsters had endorsed Celebrezze and all other Democratic candidates except for an incumbent supreme court judge. The unions also endorsed 94 of 99 Democratic house candidates, and 13 of 17 Democratic senate candidates. Since labor strongly backed the Democratic Party in all three cities, its community stance was not a variable in the analysis.

Voinovich, the Republican candidate for governor, decisively defeated Celebrezze, 56 to 44 percent. The Democrats elected the auditor, but not the secretary of state. Since these three offices, plus a Democrat and a Republican from the assembly, constituted the reapportionment board that was to redraw state legislative districts based on the 1990 census, the Democrats lost the majority on that board. Expectedly, the Republicans captured both congressional districts in the Columbus area, the Democrats took two of the three Cleveland districts, and the parties split the two Cincinnati districts. In the state assembly, the state senate, and the municipal elections, almost no changes occurred.

Overall, the election represented the stable party patterns documented in Chapters 7, 8, and 9, with the notable exception that the Republican Voinovich won in Cleveland. After labor twice endorsed Voinovich for mayor, it then supported Celebrezze for governor. Many union members could not understand why Voinovich was such a good choice for mayor but not governor. To be sure, Celebrezze had also been mayor of Cleveland, but Voinovich's tenure was more recent. In Cincinnati, Robert Taft, the Republican candidate for secretary of state expectedly won, aided perhaps by his family's local political reputation.

THE OHIO SURVEY

Asher, Ripley, and Snyder (1992) designed two surveys, one for union members and another for a random sample of Ohio voters. The two surveys were identical, except that the union survey included additional questions on the political activities of the respondent's union in the election and the member's evaluation of them.

The common content of the two interviews included the following topics:

- Warmth or coldness (thermometer questions) toward U.S. political groups, including the political parties, labor, big business, the women's movement, Congress, the U.S. president, the U.S. Supreme Court, whites, and blacks.
- Position on important issues facing Ohio, including legalized gambling, legalized abortion, government health insurance, and affirmative action. Also, questions on how labor leaders and fellow workers felt about these issues.
- Interest in government, party preference, political ideology, sources of political information, whether the respondent had registered to vote and voted.
- Voter choice for major administrative and legislative offices.
- Approval or disapproval of union political activities: endorsement of candidates for office, donating money to candidates, and engaging in voting and registration drives.

In addition to the above, union members were asked:

- Name of union, length of membership, importance of union, and attendance at meetings.
- Importance of various reasons for belonging to a union.
- Union political activities in the last election, including participating in phone banks, distributing literature and yard signs, registering voters, donating money to candidates, endorsing candidates, meeting candidates, and work at party headquarters.
- Respondent's participation in union electoral activities.
- Union impact on the politics of respondent and fellow workers.

The surveys, conducted in November and December 1990 after the election, used a procedure that ensured adequate representation of adults with unlisted telephones; 790 interviews were conducted for the random sample of the state's adult population. The union sample of 798 interviews was derived from a weighted combined list of union members in the Ohio COPE, the Ohio Educational Association (OEA), and the Ohio Civil Service Employee Association (OCSEA) (see Asher et al. 1991). Because the Teamsters and the UAW did not furnish membership lists to COPE, the representation of liberal and conservative union members may have been reduced. There is no way of knowing the extent to which they canceled one other. To derive the subsamples for the Cincinnati, Cleveland, and Columbus areas, zip codes of the respondents' residences were combined to approximate, as closely as possible, the COPE boundaries for Hamilton, Cuyahoga, and Franklin Counties. The remainder of cases were divided by zip codes into "Other Metropolitan Areas" and "Residual Areas." The former combined the metropolitan areas of Akron, Youngstown, Canton, Dayton, and Toledo. The sample sizes of the five groups (three counties, other metropolitan, and the residuals) were large enough to make statistically reliable comparisons (see Table 11.2).

The random sample of the state included 190 union members. To maximize the number of union respondents in the three cities, I decided to combined the union sample and the subsample of union members in the random sample, if their responses on the substantive interview questions were similar. Significance tests were possible on 115 of the 120 survey items. Differences at the .05 level were found on only seven items. Since the items did not concentrate in any content area, I combined the two samples.

When the responses of the combined union sample were compared to those of the nonunion sample, 29 of 80 appropriate comparisons differed statistically; an additional eight approached significance. Thus, for two-fifths of the questions, union and nonunion responses tended to differ enough to call for detailed comparison. But first, I compare the responses of the three community random samples to probe whether the results conform to the political traditions or cultures described in earlier chapters. To save space in presenting tabular materials, I sometimes combine response categories. However, the significance tests were calculated on full distributions. Unless otherwise stated, all reported differences were statistically significant at or below the .10 percent level.

COMMUNITY POLITICAL CULTURES

Random sample data documented known attributes of the metropolises. Cleveland and Cincinnati reported higher percentages of blacks and Catholics than Columbus. Columbus respondents were slightly better educated and earned slightly higher family incomes, and more were currently employed. The samples differed little in sex composition and residential patterns. Over half lived in suburbs, almost one-quarter lived in the central city, and another one-quarter lived in rural areas. The Cleveland sample expectedly reported a slightly higher proportion of union members.

When the city samples were compared for the 66 items with sufficient numbers to apply tests of statistical significance, responses on 25 (38%) of the questions differed. While not clustering neatly, they generally depicted expected differences. Thus, in the "thermometers" questions, about 70 percent of the Columbus and Cincinnati area residents felt "cold" toward the Democratic Party versus 53 percent of Cleveland's (see Table 11.1). Almost two-thirds of Cleveland residents felt cold toward labor unions in contrast to three-quarters in the other two cities. Equal proportions (60 percent) in all cities felt cold toward big business. About one-half of Cincinnati and Columbus residents felt cold toward the women's movement versus about one-third for Cleveland. Cleveland and Cincinnati respondents were closer to each other than to Columbus on their feelings toward the Republican president, the U.S. Congress, and the U.S. Supreme Court. Columbus expectedly tilted more toward the warm pole on these items. In general, as expected, Cleveland and Columbus, respectively, represented liberal and conservative poles, Cincinnati was in between, but closer to Columbus.

Similar community patterns appeared on national political issues (data not shown). Larger percentages of Cleveland respondents supported abortion rights, a government plan for universal health care, and legalized gambling, but small community differences were smaller on support for affirmative action for blacks. No community pattern appeared in estimates of where labor leaders stood on these issues. Expectedly, more Clevelanders, almost two-fifths, identified themselves as Democrats, compared to one-fifth for the other two cities. Surprisingly, a larger percentage of Cincinnati and Columbus residents (70 percent) thought that labor leaders were Democrats than in Cleveland (56 percent). The pattern held in attributing political liberalism to union leaders; 50 percent of the Columbus and Cincinnati respondents thought they were liberal or very liberal compared to 36 percent in Cleveland. Again, more of the Cincinnati and Columbus respondents than Clevelanders thought that labor leaders were Democrats: 70 and 56 percent, respectively. Thus, Clevelanders tended to see labor leaders as being more like themselves in politics, while the respondents in the other cities saw them as more liberal and more inclined to be Democrats. Since small community differences appeared in ideological self-placement (liberal, moderate, or conservative), apparently ideology is not a good indicator of party identification (see Miller 1992).

In Columbus, the percentage of respondents voting for the Republican candidates for governor, secretary of state, and attorney general was about the same, suggesting that they voted a straight party ticket. Cincinnati support for the Republican candidate for secretary of state, Taft, was equal to that of Voinovich, the Republican candidate for governor, while support for the Republican candidate for attorney general was 10 percent lower. Community loyalty to the Taft family name helped Robert Taft. In Cleveland, loyalty to Voinovich, the Republican ex-mayor, boosted his

Table 11.1
Percentage of Union and Nonunion Members Registering "Cold"[a] on Political Items in Three Ohio Cities and Other Metropolitan Areas,[b] 1990

	Cincinnati		Cleveland		Columbus		Metropolitan areas	
Items	Union	Random	Union	Random	Union	Random	Union	Random
Democratic Party	.52**	.70	.40**	.53	.55	.68*	.49***	.61
Republican Party	.67	.58	.73	.73	.73	.60	.73***	.63
Labor unions	.43***	.74	.30***	.64	.41***	.73	.29***	.61
Big business	.67	.62	.70	.59	.62	.57	.72**	.65
Women's movement	.39	.52	.44	.35	.32	.46	.45**	.49
U.S. Congress	.70	.70	.68	.72	.59	.66	.67*	.72
U.S. president	.38	.50	.51	.51	.52	.44	.50	.48
U.S. Supreme Court	.44	.61	.46	.50	.49	.44	.46*	.47
Whites	.45	.49	.47	.40	.47	.52	.43	.44
Blacks	.58	.57	.57	.54	.57	.61	.57*	.54
N	71	112	126	153	94	116	472	373

Source of data in this chapter's tables: Asher, Ripley, and Snyder (1992).
[a]"Cold" defined as less than 50 degrees on a thermometer of 0–100 degrees.
[b]Akron, Canton, Dayton, Toledo, and Youngstown zip code areas.
*$p < .11$.
**$p < .05$.
***$p < .003$.
Four quartiles were used for statistical calculations, with the two lower ones collapsed for this table.

vote for the governorship, but his advantage did not help other Republican candidates. Thus, the vote for the Republican candidate for attorney general was 30 percent lower than that for Voinovich.

Only small community differences appeared in levels of political interest, registration and voting rates, and sources of political information (radio, TV, newspapers, family, friends, coworkers, and labor unions). The major sources of political information were TV (80 percent) and newspapers (90 percent). Importantly, about three-quarters of the respondents in all three cities indicated that labor unions and co-workers were not important sources. A clear majority felt that family, friends, and radio were not important sources. Yet over four-fifths in the three cities indicated that newspaper endorsements of candidates had no influence on their vote, and about seven-tenths, that labor's endorsements had no influence.

Yet almost two-fifths of the respondents in the three cities reported that labor unions *greatly* influence American life and politics, and an additional 45 percent felt they had *some* influence. While consensus was almost universal that unions could urge their members to register and vote, three-fifths of Cleveland respondents (slightly less in the other cities) disapproved of unions' endorsing candidates for office. About half thought it was permissible for labor to contribute money to political candidates.

In sum, while the responses revealed city differences, they were not as large as anticipated, especially for party voting and sources of political information. Clevelanders were the most liberal and Columbusites the most conservative. Clevelanders put less political distance between themselves and labor leaders than did respondents in the other two cities. Both Cleveland and Columbus seemed to have more homogeneous political climates than Cincinnati, a matter that will be examined later.

UNION AND NONUNION VOTING PATTERNS

I compare union and nonunion voters for Columbus first because the fewest differences were expected there. The two samples differed only in race and employment status; the union had higher percentages of blacks and the employed. No differences appeared for sex, education, religion, marital status, income, residence, and social class identification. For the responses to 51 substantive comparisons for which there were enough cases, significant differences appeared for 19 (37 percent) of the items, mostly in the electoral arena. Union members felt warmer toward the Democratic Party, labor unions, and the women's movement, and colder toward the Republican Party (Table 11.1). A larger proportion of the unionists identified themselves as Democrats, voted for Democrats especially when endorsed by labor unions, supported a government-sponsored health plan, and felt that unions influence the nation and its politics.

No differences appeared between the two samples on political issues such as legalized abortion, affirmative action for blacks, and legalized gambling; on feelings toward big business, Congress, the president, the Supreme Court, and blacks and whites; on political ideology, political interest, registration and voting rates, political knowledge, sources of political information, strength of party identification, and effect of newspaper endorsements on voting; and on the appropriateness of unions' registering voters, endorsing candidates, and contributing money to individual candidates. In short, union members differed from their fellow citizens primarily in the area of partisan party politics, but not on most substantive political matters. In this relatively homogeneous conservative community, union membership exerted a visible influence mainly on party preference and voting.

Since Democrats dominated Cleveland politics as much as Republicans dominated Columbus politics, the responses of union and nonunion samples should be as uniform as in Columbus, but in a more liberal direction. Of 53 comparisons, only 14, or 26 percent, differed, suggesting that the Cleveland samples were even more alike than the Columbus pair. This held even though the Cleveland samples differed more in their social characteristics. The union sample contained relatively more male, employed, married, Catholic, and higher-income workers; no differences appeared for race, education, and residential patterns.

On the thermometer questions, the union sample was warmer toward the Democratic Party and labor unions, while the nonunion sample was slightly warmer toward big business (see Table 11.1). Relatively more union respondents had registered, voted, and voted for Democrats. A larger percentage were interested in politics and thought of themselves as Democrats. Finally, relatively more respondents in the union sample thought that union leaders were liberal and felt that it was alright for unions to endorse political candidates, that union endorsements influenced their votes, and that unions influenced American life and politics.

No differences between the samples were found for feelings toward the Republican Party, Congress, the president, the Supreme Court, whites, and blacks; for the issues of legalized abortion, national health care, affirmative action for blacks, and legalized casino gambling; and for the propriety of unions' registering voters and donating money to candidates for office. In short, compared to Columbus, more of Cleveland's union members favored the Democratic Party and unions than the general population, but in the context of the local political culture, Cleveland's respondents were more homogeneous than Columbus's.

The Cincinnati samples differed widely in social characteristics. Relatively more union members were male, married, white, Protestant, employed, better educated, lived in rural areas, and had higher family incomes. In social characteristics, the Cincinnati samples differed most; the Columbus samples, least. While the Cincinnati samples differed in 20, or 38 percent, of the 53 items (as in Columbus), half of the differences in Cincinnati barely reached the required level of statistical significance.

On the thermometer questions, Cincinnati unionists, compared to nonunion respondents, clearly felt warmer toward the Democratic Party, labor unions, the women's movement, the Supreme Court, and the president (see Table 11.1). More identified themselves as liberals and Democrats, and as interested in politics. More had registered and voted in the last election. Although a larger percentage of union members voted for the Democratic candidates, only for the attorney general was the difference statistically significant. Also, more of the union respondents approved of union-sponsored registration drives and candidate endorsements, and more admitted that such endorsements positively influenced their voting. Finally, more unionists agreed that unions influenced American life and politics.

The Cincinnati samples did not differ in support for major issues: legalized abortion, a government-sponsored health plan, affirmative action to support blacks, and legalized casino gambling. Responses of the samples were also similar for party loyalty, political ideology, and how union leaders and fellow workers felt about the major issues. In sum, even though more of the union members supported the Democratic Party and unions and expressed more liberal feelings on the thermometer questions, the two groups were alike on political issues and were not deeply split on party voting. These results reflected Cincinnati's cross-cutting political traditions.

In a comparison of union and nonunion samples in the three cities, the Columbus samples were the most alike in social characteristics and showed the fewest differences in political attitudes and behavior. The Cincinnati samples were least alike in social characteristics, but they differed as much as the Cleveland samples in political attitudes and behavior. These findings corroborate the expectation that the Cleveland and Columbus samples would be more homogeneous than Cincinnati's. However, in all cities, higher percentages of union members were prounion, identified with the Democratic Party, and voted for Democrats. In Cleveland, more of the union members were interested in unions and politics, a situation approached in Cincinnati. In general, these data tend to support observations drawn from the case studies.

THE POLITICS OF UNION MEMBERS IN THE THREE CITIES

Union members in the three cities were compared in (1) social characteristics, (2) beliefs about the importance of unions, (3) political interests and ideologies, (4) sources of political information and their impact on political behavior, and (5) union electoral activities and their impact on members' political behavior.

Union members in the three cities differed little in education, employment status, marital status, and occupation. Expectedly, a higher percentage of Cleveland than Columbus unionists were Catholic, belonged to manufacturing unions, and had been union members longer. The Columbus sample had the highest proportion of blacks, the highest percentages in white-collar unions, and the lowest duration of union membership.

Each city displayed a different residential pattern. Columbus had the smallest percentage residing in the suburbs, while Cincinnati had the lowest percentage in the central city; a somewhat higher percentage of Clevelanders lived in suburbs. Cincinnati had the lowest proportion living in the central city and the highest in rural areas. Cincinnati union members had the least education, but the highest family income (Table 11.2). In sum, the three union samples differed little in social composition. Even when statistically significant, the differences were small and unpatterned, suggesting that they had at best a modest impact on political attitudes and behavior.

When respondents were asked to respond to four statements concerning the reasons people belong to unions, agreement with all of the statements were high, and community differences were small. About nine-tenths agreed that unions helped them bargain for money and benefits; about four-fifths believed in the union movement and what it had done for workers in America. A majority agreed that they were members because they worked in a union shop, that membership helped them get along with fellow workers, that unions were very important to them, and that they attended union meetings some of the time (see Table 11.2). Finally, in a thermometer question, three-fifths expressed warm feelings toward labor unions. In short, union members in all three cities were favorably disposed toward unions, with somewhat more of the Clevelanders than the Cincinnatians expressing consistent support.

Respondents were asked how much they followed governmental and public affairs. Cleveland unionists ranked highest, Cincinnati's ranked

Table 11.2
Union Member Characteristics and Importance of Unionism to Members in Three Cities

Characteristics	Columbus (%)	Cincinnati (%)	Cleveland (%)
Union member in household	11	9	16
Union			
AFSCME	16	4	4
Teachers	23	26	26
Steel	1	8	9
Middle-sized	23	26	22
Small	36	35	19
Belonged to union > 10 years	60	69	83
Education			
High school or less	48	55	44
Some college	21	17	28
B.A. or higher	31	28	28
African Americans	18	4	13
Females	44	33	29
Family income less than $40,000	62	54	64
Married	68	80	72
Catholic	19	31	48
Residence			
Urban	32	16	32
Suburban	44	51	53
Rural	28	32	15
Importance of union membership			
Union helps me bargain	84	93	92
Believe in unionism	77	79	86
Membership is legally required	57	59	61
To get along with fellow workers	47	63	55
Attends union meetings	51	63	63
Feels warm toward unions	60	57	70

lowest, with Columbus in between. The interviewers were asked to estimate the respondent's level of information about politics and government. More of the Cleveland sample ranked very or fairly high. A somewhat higher percentage of the Cleveland sample had registered to vote, but the percentage voting in the last election was about the same in the three cities (see Table 11.3).

Earlier data suggested that Cleveland union members were the most liberal, but the data barely supported this expectation. Almost two-fifths in all three cities refused to identify themselves ideologically. Of the remainder, about one-third identified themselves as liberal. Somewhat more of the Cleveland unionists identified themselves as moderates, more Cincin-

Table 11.3
Political Interest, Ideology, Party Identification, and Voting Behavior of Union Members in Three Cities

Items	Columbus (%)	Cincinnati (%)	Cleveland (%)
Follows politics most of the time	48	42	59
High level of political information	37	37	45
Registered to vote	85	81	93
Voted in last election	89	83	88
Political ideology			
Liberal and somewhat liberal	37	36	32
Moderate	33	16	41
Conservative and somewhat conservative	30	48	27
Party identification			
Republican	16 (27)[a]	22 (38)[a]	9 (17)[a]
Independent	38 (23)	35 (15)	39 (13)
Democratic	37 (50)	37 (47)	50 (70)
Other	9	6	2
Public issues			
Unemployment and lack of jobs	13	6	16
Favor legalized abortion	60	48	62
Favor national health plan	49	42	59
Affirmative action for blacks	64	44	65
Favor legalized gambling	32	27	38
Party vote			
Democratic governor (Celebrezze)	56	43	53
Democratic secretary of state (Brown)	63	36	60
Democratic attorney general (Fisher)	55	41	65
Democratic treasurer (Withrow)	60	29	60
Democratic auditor (Ferguson)	63	52	59
Supreme court justice (Douglas)	40	45	26
Supreme court justice (Jones)	23	14	27

[a]Recalculated with leaners included in the categories.

natians as conservative. Columbus unionists split almost evenly between liberals, independents, and conservatives (see Table 11.3).

Despite Ohio's severe unemployment at the time of the survey, only 6 percent of Cincinnatians mentioned it as an important problem, about half the rate of other cities. Even though a higher percentage of the Cleveland sample was Catholic and of the Columbus sample Protestant, larger proportions supported legalized abortion than in Cincinnati. Cincinnati unionists were the least sympathetic with governmental affirmative action for blacks; half supported it in contrast to seven-tenths in Cleveland (Table 11.3). As noted above, unionists in all three cities differed little in warmth toward whites and blacks, but both the Cleveland and the Cincinnati samples were colder than the Columbus sample toward the women's movement. Overall, ideology was loosely coupled with position on public issues. Cleveland unionists were somewhat more liberal; Cincinnatians, more conservative; and Columbus in between.

City differences in party identification were more marked than ideological and issue differences. In no city did a majority of the union members identify themselves as Democrats, although as expected, the proportion was highest in Cleveland (Table 11.3). When independent "leaners" were added to the parties toward which they leaned, Cleveland's Democratic tradition asserted itself, with 70 percent identifying as Democrats and barely one-half in Columbus and Cincinnati, a lower percentage than most union leaders estimated in my interviews. When Republican "leaners" were added to Republican identifiers, they represented the largest minority in Cincinnati (38 percent), compared to 27 percent for Columbus, and only 17 percent for Cleveland. The proportion of independents and leaners was highest in Columbus.

Small city differences appeared in the thermometer questions: 40 percent in Cleveland felt "cold" toward the Democrats; 50 percent in the other cities. Over eight-tenths of Clevelanders felt "cold" toward the Republican Party; about seven-tenths in the other cities (see Table 11.1). In these party questions, the Columbus pattern tilted toward Cincinnati's.

If voting follows party identification, Cleveland's unionists should have supported Democratic candidates the most. This was not the case in the 1990 state election. Although almost 90 percent of the respondents said they voted, their responses to voting questions suggested that the rate was closer to 70 percent in Cleveland and 60 percent in the other two cities.

Of the five major races, Cleveland unionists reported the highest support for only one Democrat (attorney general); they supported the other four at about the same rate as Columbus unionists (see Table 11.3). For all five races, Cincinnati unionists ranked lowest in support of Democrats; in fact, only one Democrat, the auditor, had majority support. Although the reliability of such small samples is shaky, the data showed that about 60 percent of the unionists in Columbus and Cleveland supported Democrats, and about 40 percent in Cincinnati.

To conclude, the data reveal a rather loose coupling between Democratic Party preference and voting behavior, especially in Cleveland and Cincinnati. Surprisingly, even though barely half of Columbus members identified with the Democratic Party, they supported it more than Cincinnati members did. As suggested, favorite sons on the ballot loosened the connection between party identification and voting. Apparently, many Columbus union members, like Janus, faced two ways: toward the Republicans locally and toward the Democrats statewide.

Scholars know little about how unions influence their members' political decisions. While voters may not know how they make up their minds to vote, their perceptions of the process are informative. The survey asked respondents to judge the influence of various sources of political information on their voting, including the mass media (newspapers, television, and radio), institutions (church and union), and interpersonal networks (family, friends, and co-workers). In an open-ended question, interviewers asked respondents to name the most important source of information that helped them decide to vote the way they did. About two-fifths in all three cities mentioned the daily newspaper, and one-fifth mentioned television. Labor unions, political parties, pamphlets, and past records of candidates were named by fewer than one-tenth.

Later in the interview, respondents were asked to identify the various sources of political information that helped them decide on how to vote: TV, newspapers, radio, labor unions, family, friends, and co-workers. Again, newspapers and television were the overwhelmingly choice; community differences were small (Table 11.4). About one-half indicated that, after newspapers and TV, all other sources were not very important. Overall, labor unions ranked fifth or sixth in relative importance. Less than one-fifth thought that unions were very important (2 percent in Cincinnati!); about a third, somewhat important; and about half, not important. A sympathetic interpretation of these findings suggests that labor unions are

Table 11.4
Sources and Importance of Political Information for Union Members in Three Cities (%)

	Newspaper	TV	Radio	Family	Union	Friends	Coworkers
Very important							
Columbus	37	26	9	12	15	8	5
Cincinnati	47	35	6	15	2	4	2
Cleveland	43	27	10	16	21	7	8
Somewhat important							
Columbus	41	46	48	40	33	38	41
Cleveland	40	44	46	37	39	33	37
Cincinnati	49	53	45	34	31	37	32
Not important							
Columbus	21	28	43	48	51	53	54
Cleveland	13	21	48	48	60	63	61
Cincinnati	9	19	44	49	48	56	61

as much a source of political information as family, friends, co-workers, and possibly radio.

Respondents were asked whether their newspapers and unions endorsed candidates for office and whether the endorsements influenced their votes. Not surprisingly, almost all respondents who read newspapers (about three-quarters) indicated that their newspaper had endorsed Voinovich, the Republican candidate for governor. About 60 percent of respondents knew whether or not their union had endorsed candidates; about three-fourths of these reported that the union did, presumably Celebrezze, the Democrat. When asked whether newspaper endorsement would make it more or less likely that they would vote for the candidate, over four-fifths in each community replied, "No difference." In a similar question on union endorsement, about two-thirds indicated, "No difference."

While only 10 percent indicated that a newspaper's endorsement would increase their likelihood of voting for a candidate, over 20 percent indicated that the union's endorsement would do so (see Table 11.5). When asked directly whether the union endorsement did, in fact, influence their vote, almost 40 percent of the Columbus unionists responded affirmatively, in contrast to about 20 percent in Cleveland and Cincinnati. They estimated that the union's effect was "moderate" (see Table 11.5). To conclude, although we do not have a comprehensive view of how different sources of political information influence voting, from the respondents'

Table 11.5
Newspapers and Union Sources of Political Influence for Union Members in Three Cities (%)

	Columbus	Cincinnati	Cleveland
Effect of newspaper endorsement on vote			
More likely to vote for candidate	8	10	10
Less likely	10	5	5
No difference	82	84	85
Effect of union endorsement on vote			
More likely to vote for candidate	27	21	31
Less likely	8	10	4
No difference	64	68	65
Union endorsement influenced views	38	21	19
Effect of labor union on vote			
No effect	69	69	64
Big and moderate effect	25	19	28
Small effect	6	12	8

view union influence, while not major, is greater than that of newspapers and other known sources.

ASSESSING LABOR'S ELECTORAL EFFORTS

Little is known about how union members respond to union efforts to influence their politics. Labor unions typically do eight things to reach members: urge them to register to vote, remind them to vote, endorse candidates for office, distribute political literature, distribute yard signs, collect donations to support the party and candidates, invite members to meet candidates, and involve members in party activities. Respondents were asked whether their unions engaged in these activities, whether they became involved, and whether their union's activities influenced them.

On average, almost half of the respondents did not know whether their unions engaged in the eight activities (see Table 11.6). Averaging the responses to the eight questions of those who presumably knew, 61 percent said that their unions did not engage in the activities. When the "don't know" and "did not engage" responses are combined, *four-fifths of union members were not aware of a union's political action program.* Whatever the actual situation, the political activities of labor unions were not reaching most members.

Member awareness varied according to type of political activity. Slightly more than two-fifths reported that their unions endorsed candidates and distributed literature, but less than 15 percent on average were

Table 11.6
Union Electoral Activities Reported
by Union Members in Three Ohio Cities (%)

	Total sample			Informed respondents	
Activities	Yes	No	Don't know	Yes	No
Endorse candidates	46	13	41	78	22
Distribute literature	42	20	37	68	32
Meet political candidates	17	39	44	30	70
Distribute yard signs	10	42	48	19	81
Phone bank participation	15	37	49	29	71
Register voters	17	33	50	34	66
Raise campaign money	19	30	50	39	61
Work at party headquarters	6	34	59	16	84

aware of the other six activities (see Table 11.6). Only 15 percent indicated that their unions participated in the highly publicized phone bank program.

Among those who were aware of their union's political activities, about seven-tenths reported that their union endorsed candidates and distributed literature, and the average for the remaining activities was 28 percent. Less than 40 percent reported that their union engaged in registration drives and drives to raise campaign money. These low figures may explain why 80 percent of the respondents reported that unions were not an important source of political information and that union endorsement made no difference in how they voted (Tables 11.4 and 11.5). Cleveland reported the highest percentage of union participation in all eight activities; Cincinnati, the least; and Columbus, a midpoint in between. This order held for every activity. Given the small number who reported on union activities, a detailed analysis by community is unwarranted.

Respondents were also asked whether officers invited them to participate in any of union political activities. On average, less than 5 percent were asked to participate. Only 16 percent reported that they had been asked to contribute money for campaigns. Among those informed about their union's activities, the invitation to participate was much higher. The average for the activities was about 20 percent, varying little by community. Almost two-fifths were asked to place yard signs and help raise money. About two-thirds of those asked to contribute money did so. The data, sparse as they are, suggest that when unions asked members to participate in political activities, the response was quite favorable.

REGRESSION ANALYSIS OF VOTING FOR THE UNION'S SLATE

A regression analysis was run for the factors that influenced voting for the slate of seven union-endorsed candidates. The variable was regressed on nine independent variables: party identification, political ideology, race, income, social class identification, religion, union membership, sex, and city. The results were not expected to differ much from past studies of support for the Democratic Party because five state candidates were Democrats and two were "nonpartisan" judges. The main question is the extent to which union membership and community influenced Democratic voting independent of other factors.

Thirty percent of union and forty-six percent of nonunion respondents reported not voting; the actual figures are probably higher. Thus, the data that apply to less than two-thirds of the combined samples reveal nothing about the political inclinations of a sizable minority of potential voters.

The first analysis combined union and nonunion samples. Sex and social class were eliminated from the equation because they had no effect. Unless otherwise indicated, I report only statistically significant results with probabilities of 5 percent or lower. Predictably, Republican and Democratic Party identification exerted the strongest influence; nonwhite, liberal ideology, conservative ideology, and union membership exerted smaller but significant effects. No community effect was evident, except that Cincinnati's negative beta approached statistical significance.

When the equations were run separately for each community, slightly different patterns emerged. In Cincinnati, *only* Democratic Party identification and liberal ideology had effects; union membership did not. For both Cleveland and Columbus, Democratic and Republican Party identification, as well as union membership, had effects. Also, for Columbus, nonwhite status had a positive effect and Protestant affiliation a negative effect. Cleveland's voting pattern seemed least differentiated; its adjusted variance was 0.318. The Columbus pattern was most differentiated, and its adjusted variance was highest at 0.500. Cincinnati's fell in between at 0.429. In all three communities, party identification exerted the strongest and about equal effect, considerably stronger than union membership. The standardized beta for union membership was not significant in Cincinnati and was positive and higher for Columbus than for Cleveland.

The above pattern emerged stronger in a separate analysis for union members. In both Cincinnati and Cleveland, the *only* variable associated with support for the union slate was Democratic Party identification. In Columbus, only nonwhite status had a positive effect; identification with the Republican Party, no party identification, and conservative ideology all had negative effects. The above patterns were slightly altered for nonunion members in each city. In Cincinnati and Cleveland, only Democratic Party identification exerted strong independent influence, and in Columbus, only Republican Party identification exerted a negative influence. In the other metropolitan communities in the state, for both union and nonunion respondents, only party identification and nonwhite status exerted independent positive effects.

CONCLUSIONS

Comparisons of the random samples in the three cities revealed differences in political climates, but they were smaller and less coherent than expected. Cleveland apparently had the most liberal political climate; Columbus, the most conservative; and Cincinnati, in between.

In Cleveland, the fewest differences appeared between union and nonunion samples in political attitudes and behavior. Differences between Columbus's samples were greater for social characteristics, but not for political behavior. Thus, both communities were internally homogeneous in their liberal and conservative tilts. Union–nonunion differences in social characteristics were largest in Cincinnati, but they had only marginal political consequences. The overall effect of union membership in the three cities was to slightly increase voting turnout, marginally increase support for Democratic candidates, and encourage sympathy for organized labor. It seemed to have relatively less impact on ideological identification or positions on important political issues. These findings do not depart materially from those of earlier studies.

Without historical data, COPE's effect on the voting behavior of union members can only be surmised. The lack of coordination among labor's political organizations in the three communities led me to expect a modest effect, at best. Although Cincinnati's COPE recently engaged in the most comprehensive political education effort, in the 1990 state election, it still seemed insufficient to counterbalance the Republican sympathy of many of its members. COPE's activities in Cleveland and Columbus had not changed recently. Despite Cleveland's strong labor tradition, COPE could not convince 40 percent of union members to solidly support its electoral endorsements and remain constant in their natural party inclinations.

COPE's inability to do better in Cleveland and especially in Cincinnati probably reflected the presence of local politicos on the Republican slate. Without a favorite son on the ticket, despite the strong Republican environment, Columbus's union members supported the Democratic slate as strongly as Cleveland's. The social divide between union and nonunion members was greatest in Cincinnati, but it seemed to have little impact on voting behavior. Although the divide was smaller in Columbus, party identification, ideology, race, and income seemed to have some political consequences. These findings do not suggest that COPE has been able to increase political discipline among its members.

Almost all union officials interviewed in the three cities indicated a strong commitment to politics and a strong desire to politically educate the membership. This survey revealed that union members ranked unions far behind newspapers and television as sources of political information. Yet candidate endorsement by unions influenced member voting more than newspaper endorsements. Why and how this occurs is not clear.

One of the most important findings is that well over one-half of the union members either were unaware of their union's political activities or reported that their union did not engage in political activities. Simply put, most union officials think they have a political education program, but most members are not aware of it. Undoubtedly, union officials and a few activists do become hectically involved in electoral activities during the brief campaign period. They probably define this exhausting activity as their union's political education program, and they think it reaches most members. The message that does reach a minority apparently has little content beyond "Support the party."

The data also show that unions involve very few members in electoral and party activities. Yet the limited union efforts appear to produce fairly favorable results. This suggests that political education and political involvement programs could be much more effective if unions took them more seriously, which apparently they cannot or will not do. If labor does so poorly in local and state politics, how well does it do in national politics? In the next chapter, I examine labor's relations to the national Democratic Party, and in the following chapter, I examine labor's legislative success in Congress.

The question arises whether labor learned anything from the 1990 election. In the gubernatorial election of 1994, the Republican Voinovich again ran for governor. As part of the national Republican sweep, the entire Republican slate won all of the statewide offices. Voinovich defeated the COPE endorsed Democratic nominee for governor in all three metropolitan areas. Voinovich's vote in Cuyahoga County was 2.6 greater than his opponent's; in Hamilton County, it was 3.9, and 2.9 in Franklin County. For the first time since 1972, the assembly moved to Republican control. With a Republican governor and both state houses dominated by Republicans, the future for labor in Ohio looked dim. As part of the Republican tide in the U.S. Congress, Ohio lost four Democratic seats. Insofar as labor contributed to the weakening of the party, it still had much to learn.

III
Labor in National Politics

12
Bargaining in the Democratic Party

For better or worse, labor almost irrevocably committed itself to the Democratic Party in the 1930s. Up through the 1950s, the party needed labor as much as labor needed the party. Tensions between the two, apparent from the start, increased steadily, almost reaching a breaking point in the 1970s. Since then, relations have settled into a fluctuating pattern of symbiotic cooperation. Both labor and the party, representing coalitions of local, state, and national organizations, continue to try articulate their organizations as elections approach (Mayhew 1986). Bargaining between the these two coalitions has been a continuous process from the beginning, a process which is little understood. This chapter tries to gain insight into some aspects of that process.

The research in Cleveland, Columbus, and Cincinnati showed that, no matter how strong or weak the Democratic Party and no matter how much or how little labor contributed to it, labor–party relations remained strained. Party leaders publicly minimized differences, but they did little to placate labor. Democratic defeats in the 1990 and 1994 Ohio gubernatorial campaigns underlined the party's concern: Labor lacked discipline. Yet the party could ill afford to forgo labor's financial and electoral support. Mutually dependent, labor and the party seemed permanently locked in an uncomfortable embrace. In the interviews, both labor and party informants explained that, whatever their local relations, the two closely cooperated at the national level, which was what really mattered. This chapter examines their claim by analyzing labor–party relations since the New Deal.

Although segmentation theory suggests that the many cleavages within labor and within the party, as well as those between them, reflect their external environment, there is no reason to believe that the external environment is less turbulent at the national than at the local level. In Europe, labor–party relations are more stable because they are institutionalized and legally legitimized. In Britain, the labor movement sponsored the Labour Party, which began as an arm of the movement. In Italy and France, left-wing parties sponsored or captured parts of the labor movement (Sturmthal 1973, p. 3). In the United States, labor–party relations are less structured and therefore more subject to change. In the parliamentary system, a victorious party may include a labor or labor-oriented party in the governing coalition. In the American Party system, labor's relations with the party remain in flux outside the government. Relations are more dynamic as both parties bargain to maximize self-interest.

This chapter first examines the organizational features of COPE and the Democratic Party, the goals they try to realize, and the inevitable problems they encounter in trying to realize common and separate objectives. This is followed by a history (1932–1994) of labor's attempts to influence the party choice of presidential nominees and favorable planks in party platforms. Then, applying segmentation theory, the analysis examines how changing national issues change the bargaining strength of labor and the party. A theory of sunk investments helps to explain why labor remained attached to a party that seemed incapable of fulfilling labor's basic legislative demands. The analysis ends with a description of labor's tactics in this unfavorable bargaining situation.

LABOR AND PARTY BARGAINING ORGANIZATIONS

Coleman's (1990) rational choice metaphor applies to labor's bargaining with the party. The metaphor posits organizational actors who calculate the costs and benefits of particular options and bargain to maximize short- and long-term interests. Examining alternative means to attain valued ends, they select the most effective and efficient course.

As experienced bargainers, labor leaders designed a political organization to attain defined objectives. They organized COPE, a hierarchy of political organizations from every local in the community to the nation. They systematically trained members at each level of organization, teaching them critical political skills: how to mobilize the electorate, lobby, and build coalitions. They recruited a staff of lawyers and lobbyists to influence legislatures. They organized activist networks to exert pressure on legislators to pass or defeat major bills. They developed coalitions to increase labor influence in the party and in legislatures.

Although the AFL regularly favored the Democratic Party as early as the Wilson administration in 1912 (Greenstone 1969, p. 33), only a few unions publicly aligned with the party until a decade after the New Deal was launched. In 1943, the newly formed CIO unions created political action committees (PACs) to support Democratic candidates, and the AFL soon followed suit. Not until 1955, when the AFL and CIO merged, did labor create an integrated political organization, COPE, to support the party. Although the AFL–CIO proclaimed nonpartisanship then, as today, COPE has never endorsed a Republican presidential candidate, and few Republicans take labor's nonpartisan claim seriously.

For most purposes, COPE may be thought of as a party operating parallel to the Democratic Party. All locals are expected to organize COPEs to educate members on political affairs. The locals send representatives and money to the city central body that organizes communitywide COPEs. State AFL-CIO bodies also organize COPEs. Finally, the internationals support the national COPE. All these COPEs are supported by dues, contributions, and financial investments which add up to millions of dollars.

In addition to the COPEs, individual unions support their own PACs and staffs to shape, lobby, and monitor legislation in state legislatures and the U.S. Congress. Legislative goals are defined in resolutions passed at state and national conventions (Cornfield 1989b). Federal laws specify that dues can be spent in federal elections only to educate members, not to influence the public. Voluntary contributions, apart from dues, can be spent for almost any political purpose, such as supporting parties and candidates and educating the public. Voluntary contributions, or "hard money," may be raised by the political check-off. Although check-off participation varies by local and union, millions of dollars are raised annually. Most of this money is sent to state or international bodies that decide whether to return it to locals on request, to individual candidates, to the AFL-CIO COPE, or to other groups.

The preceding chapters described how COPE operates locally, directing political information to members through training sessions, leaflets, brochures, and newspapers. Local, state, and national COPEs screen and recommend candidates for office to the membership. COPE names candidates to Democratic Party executive committees at county, state, and national levels. Labor delegates to party conventions report convention proceedings and make recommendations to the membership.

These activities are minuscule compared to the efforts to mobilize members to vote. On or before Election Day, COPE, as well as many union locals, call members urging them to vote for endorsed candidates. While labor officials may exaggerate the scope and effectiveness of these efforts, they involve thousands of volunteers who make millions of calls to members, reminding them to register and vote.

The basic party units are local precincts, which are combined to form ward, village, city, and county organizations that are articulated in various ways to the state and national party. Leaders at each level are elected or selected in primaries. Their main functions are to raise money and organize campaigns. The larger party units have executive committees with elected and appointed members. Members and delegates meet periodically in caucus or convention to select or elect candidates for office and to propose legislative goals in party platforms. State and national party directors are typically paid employees who supervise small office staffs that raise money and help candidates organize campaigns. In recent years, candidates have created their own electoral and fund-raising organizations, thus weakening party control. The party is supported by contributions from citizens, appointed governmental employees, and special-interest groups.

ARTICULATING LABOR AND PARTY STRUCTURES

Unions and parties have parallel and singular organizational features. Both (1) are organized at local, state, and national levels and are loosely coordinated; (2) are run by elected officers; (3) conduct conventions to hammer out legislative objectives; and (4) screen candidates for nominations; (5) solicit contributions to finance campaigns of candidates; (6) use volunteers to mobilize voters at elections; and (7) have difficulty disciplining volunteers.

Certain organizational features differ. Unions are unevenly dispersed; the party is organized nationwide. Member ties to unions, quasi-involuntary, endure as long as the employment relationship; party ties (registration, voting, contributions) are voluntary. Union dues payment, typically universal except for a very few who ask the employer to withhold the part spent for political education, supports full-time officers and staffs; parties support small staffs with irregular and uncertain contributions from individuals and interest groups, which means that officials must try to balance competing interests. Union officials must also respond to competing interests, but the range is smaller. Finally, while unions offer only the satisfactions of social participation, attending union events, and aspiring to office, the party can offer some patronage and material enticements to its workers.

On balance, labor's political structure is superior to the party's. Unlike party leaders, labor officials are in constant contact with members. Labor can recruit volunteers for political work more easily than can the party; union officers, aspirants to office, and office staffs form a corps that gives time and money to politics. Most union locals have a headquarters with a meeting hall, full-time executives, clerical staffs, and equipment (duplicating machines, phones, computers) that can be used for political work. These facilities are usually superior to those in most local Democratic Party headquarters. Labor can send political messages to members more easily and more often than the party can to voters. COPE has a steady income; the party relies on voluntary contributions. Labor's political appeals to members are targeted on visible gains; party appeals, except to organized interest groups, are amorphous and disparate.

However, the party's broader and larger constituency permits top officers to control their organizations more easily. Unions have independent financial and organizational resources that permit them to ignore top COPE leaders. Thus, when the UAW, Teamsters, miners, and other unions withdrew from the AFL-CIO and COPE, they could still function politically.

Political Goals of the Party and Labor

Nationally, the party's main goal is to attract enough voters to elect a president and a congressional majority. Party leaders make vague ideological noises in order to attract almost any group, even opposing ones. Because no single interest commands the loyalty of a majority of voters, party leaders must attract enough to create a majority. Leaders try to satisfy as many groups as possible and yet project the impression that none of them has captured the party and determined its policies. Party leaders are most influential when no group has a majority on the executive committee or a majority of convention delegates. No matter how large labor's financial and organizational contributions to the party, it cannot become dominant without arousing an opposing coalition of business, education, ethnic, racial, gender, regional, or other groups.

Party leaders' ability to make decisions is enhanced when no group can claim to speak for the party. In bargaining with groups, party leaders must consider (1) their constituency size; (2) the resources they bring the party; (3) the group's voting discipline; (4) the party's immediate need to build or maintain a margin of victory in elections. These elements are not fixed over time; party leaders take calculated risks in temporarily favoring some groups over others.

Organized labor's goals are narrower than the party's: to pass laws favorable to organized labor, to press for legislation important to its major internationals without appearing to oppose other interests, and to promote the consumer interests of organized and unorganized workers. Their priorities are clear: (1) to repeal the 1947 Taft-Hartley Act and other legal restrictions on labor; (2) to pass laws that make it easier for organized labor to expand and prosper; (3) to enact laws that protect striking workers; (4) to enact legislation restricting foreign trade that undercuts wage levels; and (5) to expand general welfare: national health care, Social Security, and consumer welfare. Presidential candidates and party platforms are supported to the extent that they respond to these priorities.

In return for supporting the party, labor also wants its help in disciplining the president and elected Democrats to pass labor's agenda. Because this goal has not been achieved, labor wants more voice in selecting nominees for president and Congress, a larger delegation to the party convention, and more representation on the executive, platform, and other committees. These are negotiable goals that party officials can satisfy, at least in part.

At the same time, most union officials claim they do not want to dominate the party or make it into a labor party, which would be counterproductive in forging a majority party. However, they want a party that responds to labor interests *commensurate* with labor support. This demand seems reasonable. Since World War II, labor has been the party's largest financial supporter, and labor operates the largest electoral machine of any interest group (Cotter et al. 1984, p. 140). Party failure to respond adequately has fueled labor's sense of grievance, of being short-changed and underappreciated.

Labor's Party Dilemmas

In America's two-party system, parties enjoy a maximum chance of enacting their programs when they control both houses of Congress and the presidency. From 1932 to 1990, the Republicans held this advantage briefly: in 1953–1956 under Eisenhower and in 1981–1985 under Reagan. The Democrats held the advantage nearly four times as long: in 1933–1947 under Roosevelt and Truman; in 1960–1968 under Kennedy and Johnson; in 1976–1980 under Carter; and in 1992–1994 under Clinton. Republicans had the advantage for about eight years; Democrats, for thirty-one years; and neither, for seventeen years. In short, for somewhat more than half the time, labor enjoyed the optimal situation of a Democratic president and Congress.

Why was labor not more successful (see Chapter 13) in getting key labor legislation passed in this period? Basically, labor needed enough liberal legislators from nonsouthern states to form a congressional majority, which rarely happened. The early New Deal was an exception. Southern Democrats had not yet allied with northern Republicans to oppose liberal legislation. Labor faced strong obstacles in electing liberal Democrats in areas where it had few members and little influence in the local party. It could only contribute money, not an electoral organization.

Labor often faced the almost impossible task of supporting a presidential nominee who was strongly prolabor but who was not perceived by the public as *the* labor candidate. Labor also confronted disputes between conservatives and liberals in its own house and in the party. Although unions agreed on what was good for labor as a whole, they split on many other issues, such as equal opportunity for blacks and women, foreign policy, taxes, tariffs, items in the federal budget, and social welfare. Within the party, other groups have always differed with labor both on labor issues and on issues on which labor itself was divided. Thus, splits occurred within labor, within the party, and between labor and the party.

Historical drifts muddle neat definitions of political liberalism and conservatism. As I show below, labor sometimes confronted hard choices: either to support presidential candidates weak on labor but acceptable on other issues and to other groups or to back strongly prolabor candidates less acceptable on other grounds and to other groups. Labor also faced the dilemma of when to support presidential candidates. If endorsed before the convention, the candidate risked being labeled as *the* labor candidate. Before the 1968 convention, party leaders consulted labor informally about presidential nominees' acceptability. Labor formally backed candidates only after nomination by the convention. After 1968, changes in the rules governing convention representation forced labor to consider identifying preferred candidates before the convention. Labor also decided to get direct representation on the platform committee.

LABOR'S INFLUENCE IN PARTY CONVENTIONS: 1932–1992

I examine each Democratic Party convention, 1932–1992, for labor's stand in the context of major issues facing the party, interest groups, and the nation. The data are derived largely from the *Congressional Quarterly Inc.* (1987), which presents profiles of candidates and party platforms since 1831. Segmentation theory suggests four predictions: (1) The more labor was divided internally, the less would be its influence on party decisions; (2) the less party leaders controlled conventions, the less would be labor's influence on party decisions; (3) the more labor's internal divisions coincided with party divisions, the less would be labor's influence on party decisions; and (4) the less labor made common cause with traditional liberal constituencies, the less would be labor's influence on party decisions.

During Franklin Roosevelt's four presidential campaigns, 1932–1944, labor lacked a coordinated political machine. Before 1936, some unions still wanted a labor or socialist party, but most union officials feared that if they did not support Roosevelt, the Republicans would win. When Roosevelt was first nominated in the 1932 convention, the party platform did not call for protective labor legislation (*Congressional Quarterly 1987*, p. 85). Although most labor officials were pro-Democratic, they maintained an official nonpartisan stance.

At first, Roosevelt had little interest in labor, and he responded to it in ad hoc fashion. Skocpol and Amenta (1985) revealed that he belatedly supported legislation to protect unions. He agreed to support Section 7a of the National Industrial Recovery Act (NIRA) and the National Labor Relations Board (NLRB) only after strong congressional support for the acts had consolidated. Even so, labor credited his administration with passing protective labor legislation and unemployment and old age insurance. Labor's Nonpartisan League, formed in August 1936, coordinated efforts to support Roosevelt's bid for a second term. The league and the AFL's Nonpartisan Political Campaign Committee were already quarreling over legislative targets, the nominee, and the endorsement of other candidates (David 1951, p. 105).

The 1936 Democratic convention nominated Roosevelt for a second term. The party abolished its two-thirds rule on nomination, which weakened southern influence and strengthened the urban–labor–black coalition. Roosevelt now recognized that he needed strong labor support. The party platform briefly affirmed the importance of the NLRB, and Roosevelt conducted his only strong antibusiness campaign (Lash 1984, p. 191). Labor's Nonpartisan League, under the growing domination of the CIO unions, openly supported Roosevelt, but some AFL leaders held back (see Table 12.1). In 1937, the AFL expelled the CIO unions, which then took an even more open partisan stance. The 1940 convention quickly nominated Roosevelt for a third term, but the approval of labor's favorite candidate, Henry Wallace, for vice president, proved contentious. However, the platform again supported federal unemployment benefits and other welfare legislation. The CIO unions endorsed Roosevelt's nomination more openly than did the AFL unions. The Republican platform opposed the federalization of welfare but proposed a constitutional amendment for equal rights for women.

Labor leaders increasingly recognized labor's dependence on the Democratic Party and began to build a support organization toward the end of Roosevelt's third term. By 1943, sensing a conservative swing, especially in the party's southern wing, the CIO launched its PAC, and the AFL patched up dissension in its Nonpartisan League (Table 12.1). By this time, labor and the party had mobilized a large working-class vote. To stanch the conservative tide, another large turnout was needed.

In the 1944 Democratic convention, a tired Roosevelt was nominated a fourth time, but the conservative southern block solidly opposed his liberal vice president, Henry Wallace. While Roosevelt withheld a decision on a running mate, the CIO endorsed Wallace and the AFL backed Harry Truman (David 1951, p. 107). Before finally deciding on Truman, Roosevelt ordered his advisers to "Clear it with Sidney [Hillman]," the influential president of the Amalgamated Clothing Workers, founder of the CIO, and an ardent Roosevelt supporter. Truman was selected. Republicans seized on Roosevelt's statement as proof that organized labor controlled the Democratic Party. Despite Hillman's declaration in 1944 that the CIO-PAC was not linked to either party, convention events and the electoral campaign clearly demonstrated that both the CIO and the AFL had become major players in the Democratic Party. From that time to the present, labor has confronted the dilemma of acknowledging its political muscle while simultaneously denying that it controls the party.

Importantly, while the 1944 Democratic Party platform backed women's rights and civil rights, issues that would later prove divisive, it did not stress labor rights. Although Roosevelt won handily, his majority was the smallest in four campaigns, and although labor's support was still strong, its turnout was the lowest on record. Almost 36 percent of union members did not vote (Table 12.2).

On Roosevelt's death in 1945, Truman became the president of a nation at war. He promised to extend New Deal gains through the "Fair Deal," but he confronted a Republican-controlled Congress in 1946 and failed to make headway on his program. Preoccupied with postwar reconstruction problems, he exuded no great warmth for organized labor. He did veto the antilabor Taft-Hartley Act in 1947 but Congress overrode the veto (Table 12.1).

At the 1948 Democratic convention, Truman confronted a deeply divided party. Several southern conservatives, irked by Truman's Fair Deal and angered by his executive order to end racial segregation in the armed forces, bolted the party to form the State's Rights Party, with Strom Thurmond as presidential nominee. Some liberals, angered by Truman's Cold War tactics toward the Soviet Union and by his failure to push Fair Deal legislation, also bolted the party and formed the Progressive Party, with Henry Wallace as nominee. Although Truman was the unenthusiastic party choice for president, most of organized labor worked hard to elect him. The Communist-dominated unions, later expelled from the CIO,

Table 12.1
Presidential Candidates, Endorsements, Events, 1932–1988

Year	Candidates[a] Democratic–Republican	Type of labor endorsement[b]	Important events
1932	*Roosevelt*–Hoover	Unofficial	NLRB, 1935
			Social Security Act, 1935
1936	*Roosevelt*–Landon	Nonpartisan	AFL expels CIO, 1937
		League endorses	Fair Labor Standards Act, Minimum Wage, 1938
1940	*Roosevelt*–Wilkie	Some CIO unions endorse	Fair Employment Practices Act, 1943
			CIO-PAC formed, 1943
			Smith-Connally Act, 1943
1944	*Roosevelt*–Dewey	CIO–PAC endorse, AFL unofficial	Taft–Hartley Act, 1947
1948	*Truman*–Dewey	CIO unions endorse	Third Party, Wallace, 1952
1952	Stevenson–*Eisenhower*	Unofficial COPE endorse	Green dies. Meany AFL president, 1952
			AFL-CIO merge, 1955
1956	Stevenson–*Eisenhower*	COPE endorse	Teamsters ousted, 1957
			Landrum-Griffen Act, 1959
1960	*Kennedy*–Nixon (Johnson)	COPE endorse	Equal Pay Act, 1963
			Civil Rights Act, 1964
1964	*Johnson*–Goldwater	COPE strong endorse	Vietnam policy split
1968	Humphrey–*Nixon*	COPE strong endorse	Democratic Party split, new rules, 1969
			UAW quits AFL–CIO, 1968
			OSHA and postal unionization, 1970

1972	McGovern–*Nixon* (Ford)	COPE neutral, liberal unions endorse	Labor enters primaries, 1972
			Liberal unions revolt COPE, 1972
			Watergate, 1972–1974
			Labor Reform Act, 1974
1976	*Carter*–Ford	COPE endorse	LCCH launched, 1976
			NEA wins Education Department, 1977
			Humphrey-Hawkins Full-Employment Act, 1978
			Kirkland becomes AFL–CIO president, 1979
1980	Carter–*Reagan*	COPE endorse	Anderson forms third party
			Reagan breaks PATCO union, 1981
1984	Mondale–*Reagan*	COPE early endorse	AFL–CIO push for party delegates
1988	Dukakis–*Bush*	COPE endorse	UAW returns to AFL-CIO, 1981
			Teamsters return to AFL-CIO, 1987
			Democratic party rules relaxed
1992	*Clinton*–Bush	COPE endorse	Mine workers return to AFL-CIO, 1989
			Self-imposed party A.A. guidelines
			NAFTA passed, 1993

[a]Italics denote the victor.
[b]Except where noted, after 1956, AFL–CIO endorsed the party candidate after the election.

Table 12.2
Presidential Vote of Union and Nonunion Members, 1944–1992 (%)[a]

Election	Members: Democratic	Members: Republican	Differences	Not voting	Voting Democratic: Nonmembers	Voting Democratic: Difference
1944[b]	44	20	24	36	31	13
1948[b]	55	13	43	32	25	30
1952	42	33	9	25	26	16
1956	45	33	12	22	26	18
1960	48	26	22	25	33	14
1964	69	12	57	19	49	20
1968	38	26	11	35	30	9
1972	30	43	8	26	24	7
1976	52	25	27	23	32	20
1980	36	29	7	35	25	11
1984	43	29	15	28	27	16
1988	43	30	13	27	30	13
1992[c]	55–	24–	12–			

[a]Miller and Stokes (1989).
[b]NORC (1944, 1948), for union households.
[c]American Enterprise (1993). Nonvoting excluded from calculation. Voting for Perot, 21 percent.

backed Wallace. The Democratic Party platform called for the repeal of the odious Taft-Hartley Act and the enactment of equal pay legislation.

Truman's surprising victory over Dewey cheered his labor supporters, who claimed credit for it (David 1951, p., 109). Indeed, labor support for the Republican candidate was the second lowest in history (see Table 12.2). Nonetheless, events proved that the party and labor, as well as the nation, were swinging in a conservative direction. The beginning of the Truman era probably represents the end of labor's brief "free ride." From 1933 to 1947, labor probably got more party support than it gave. Thereafter, labor probably gave the party more than it got.

Truman's term of office was dominated by foreign affairs: the economic reconstruction of Europe, the containment of Soviet threats, and the Korean War. At home, his domestic program did not fare much better with a Democratic than previously with a Republican Congress. His administration was plagued with charges of corruption and accusations that Communists had infiltrated the U.S. State Department. Late in his term, he alienated labor by ordering the government to seize and run the steel mills in order to break the steel workers' strike which, he felt, threatened the nation's economic recovery. The U.S. Supreme Court declared his executive order unconstitutional. In 1951, a constitutional amendment was ratified that limited presidents to two terms. Although Truman was eligible to run in 1952, he chose not to.

By the 1952 convention, both labor and the Democratic Party were torn by internal strife. Half of the CIO's forty unions were charged with being Communist-led. Among the largest were the longshoremen, the electrical workers (UE), the UAW, the USW, and the United Mine and Mill Workers. Stepan-Norris and Zeitlin (1989, p. 506) estimated a lower number of Communist-led unions because in 1950 the CIO had placed only eleven internationals on trial on the charge that their leaders "parroted a pro-Soviet line." Several unions were expelled from the CIO. Deprived of some of their most active political workers, the CIO and some AFL unions came to the Democratic convention sobered and subdued. Yet the labor caucus with one hundred delegates, was instrumental in blocking the presidential nomination of Alben Barkley, a southerner who had White House support (Pomper 1963, p. 152). On the third ballot, a divided convention finally settled on Adlai Stevenson. Labor strongly backed him and convinced northern delegates to join it. Stevenson had not run in any primary, and the convention was free to select any candidate. Labor was happy with the platform, which called for the repeal of the Taft-Hartley Act, enactment of fair labor standards, higher minimum wages, and equal pay legislation.

Although the liberal Stevenson was a witty and eloquent campaigner, he was easily defeated by the popular general, Dwight Eisenhower. Labor maintained its traditional level of support for the Democratic candidate but could not dissuade a third of its members from voting for Eisenhower, the highest party defection ever recorded except in the McGovern–Nixon race in 1972 (Table 12.2).

Stevenson, nominated a second time to run against Eisenhower, won on the first nomination ballot with strong labor support. The party platform remained strongly liberal and prolabor. Although the labor turnout for Stevenson was larger than in the previous election, one-third of union members again voted for Eisenhower, who won handily (see Table 12.2).

Eisenhower's administrations, 1952–1960, were relatively prosperous. He terminated the Korean War and launched a vast federal highway program. Although Republicans dominated both House and Senate from 1953 to 1956, Eisenhower was a moderate. His administration undertook the largest expansion of Social Security coverage since the New Deal and also raised the minimum wage. Labor needed unity to maintain its political influence. In 1955, a combination of forces led to the reunification of the AFL and the CIO and the creation of COPE (Table 12.1). The CIO's expulsion of Communists left it more conservative and palatable to the AFL. And the AFL's more open support of the Democratic Party made it more acceptable to CIO leaders. The conservative drift in the Democratic Party, the nation, and the Congress was threatening labor's gains. Although labor had committed itself to the Democratic Party, it continued to label its policy "nonpartisan."

At the 1960 Democratic convention, John Kennedy won the presidential nomination on the first ballot. Labor's effort to stop Lyndon Johnson's nomination as vice president failed because party leaders wanted to conciliate the South (Pomper 1963, p. 105). As at all conventions since 1944, delegates fought over southern representation and civil rights planks. The Republican platforms had been generally stronger on civil rights and equal rights for women. The Democratic convention's rules committee had strengthened northern representation, which favored labor. The long party platform was strongly prolabor. It opposed right-to-work laws, approved of the Fair Employment Practices Commission, urged raising the minimum wage and extending coverage, and proposed that pensioners retain all of their earned income, that health care for the aged be extended, and that a policy to encourage economic growth of 5 percent a year be adopted. The convention reflected labor's growing strength in the party. Quadagno's (1992, p. 620) careful study of labor unions and racial conflict concludes that 1960 marked the high point of labor influence in the Democratic Party, but in that election, the black vote, rather than the labor vote, emerged as critical in tipping elections in the party's favor.

Even with the strongest union support since the Roosevelt era, Kennedy narrowly defeated his Republican opponent, Richard Nixon. Kennedy received 48 percent of the labor vote and Nixon only 26 percent (Table 12.2). Kennedy faced a conservative Congress that successfully resisted most of his economic program. Confronted with raging inflation, he urged labor to restrain wage demands; it reluctantly complied. His administration faced civil rights crises and confrontations with the Soviet Union in Berlin, Cuba, and Vietnam. Some unions resisted his civil rights reforms but supported his foreign policy.

After Kennedy's assassination in 1963, Lyndon Johnson became president. He had more success with Congress, quickly pushing through a legislative program on civil rights, educational aid, tax reform, and poverty reduction. The 1964 Democratic convention predictably nominated Johnson on the first ballot. The undebated moderate "unity" platform essentially duplicated the 1960 planks on economic and labor issues: repeal of the Taft-Hartley provision on state right-to-work laws, support for civil rights without quotas, and guaranteed employment.

Johnson overwhelmingly defeated the conservative Goldwater with 61 percent of the vote, the highest popular vote in U.S. history. In the largest labor turnout ever recorded, Johnson received more support than any candidate on record: 69 percent versus 12 percent for Goldwater (Table 12.2). This election was the high tide of labor support for the Democratic Party, even though labor had had only modest delegate strength at the convention (Table 12.3). Johnson's victory was so overwhelming that labor's turnout probably had only marginal impact on its party influence.

In Johnson's War on Poverty, the building trades were pressured to admit more blacks to their apprentice training programs. The 1964 Civil Rights Act gave government the right to intervene in union affairs. The NLRB ruled that union discrimination was an unfair labor practice; the U.S. Justice Department was given the right to intervene in union affairs to enforce the act. The building trades resisted these "intrusions" and fought directives from the Office of Economic Opportunity and implementation of the U.S. Department of Labor's training programs. By 1965, the 3.5 million members in the construction trades, the strongest block in the AFL-CIO, threatened revolt from the Democratic Party (Quadagno 1992). The legislative record (see Chapter 13) reveals that labor did only slightly better under the Kennedy–Johnson administration than in earlier ones. Johnson tried to extend the domestic War on Poverty, but the Vietnam war increasingly dominated his agenda. The AFL-CIO's constant support of Johnson's foreign policy provoked mounting criticism by a few union leaders and several liberal groups.

Table 12.3
Delegate Composition,
Democratic National Conventions (%)[a]

Characteristics	1968	1972	1976	1980	1984	1988
Union members	—	16	21	27	25	25
Union officials	4	5	6	5	—	—
Women	13	40	33	49	49	48
Blacks	5	15	11	15	18	23
Under thirty years	3	22	15	11	8	4
Lawyers	28	12	16	13	17	16
Teachers	8	11	12	15	16	14
First convention	67	83	80	87	78	65
Protestant	—	42	47	47	49	50
Catholic	—	26	34	37	29	30
Jewish	—	9	9	8	8	7
Liberal	—	—	40	46	48	43
Moderate	—	—	47	42	42	43
Conservative	—	—	8	6	4	5
Median age	49	42	43	44	43	46

[a]Mitofsky and Plissner 1980; Plissner and Mitofsky 1988.

The 1968 Democratic convention in Chicago was torn over the issue of disengagement from the Vietnam war. Street violence against the administration's war policy clouded the convention atmosphere. Johnson had decided not to seek renomination; his vice president, Hubert Humphrey, became the favorite candidate. Eugene McCarthy and George McGovern tried to rally antiwar forces but failed. Labor officials, who made up only 4 percent of the delegates (see Table 12.3), backed Humphrey and the administration's policy of negotiating peace in Vietnam. Humphrey won the nomination, but the party remained deeply divided. The platform perfunctorily summarized liberal economic objectives but, surprisingly, did not elaborate a program for labor. Signaling increasing controversies on policy within the AFL-CIO, the UAW disaffiliated. McGovern had chaired a party reform commission that subsequently changed party rules to favor the representation of women, blacks, youth, and other groups as delegates (Plissner and Mitofsky 1988). An undercurrent of racial division and conflict over the Vietnam war pervaded the convention and the subsequent campaign.

The Republicans nominated Richard Nixon. Some southerners defected from the Democratic Party to launch the American Independent Party, nominating George Wallace for president. Because Nixon had been involved in drafting the odious Taft-Hartley Act, COPE did everything possible to defeat him, but it could not mobilize as much member support as in the Johnson campaign. Wallace attracted considerable support from white skilled workers, especially in the building trades. Only 38 percent of union members voted for Humphrey, the lowest support for a Democratic presidential nominee since the 1932 election, and also a low point in the labor turnout. Labor's division and apathy may have accounted for Humphrey's narrow defeat.

Nixon's administration kept pressure on the building trades to open their apprentice programs. In 1969, the secretary of labor announced that all government contracts would fall under the Philadelphia plan, which set union targets and timetables for minority hiring in construction. The AFL-CIO publicly opposed the plan, but it ultimately worked (Quadagno 1992, p. 628). Facing seemingly uncontrollable inflation, Nixon's administration instituted wage and price controls in 1971, which he knew would hurt labor more than it would business. Yet, trying to attract Wallace Democrats, Nixon sponsored some favorable labor legislation. In 1970, he signed the Postal Reorganization Act, which put postal workers under NLRB jurisdiction, and he approved of the strongly labor-backed Occupational Safety and Health Act (Goldfield 1987, p. 86).

When the Democratic convention began in 1972, COPE was determined to back Humphrey again. Meanwhile, the party's commission on rules, under McGovern's influence, issued the first convention rules ever written. Labor anticipated that these rules would drastically alter delegate composition. Because most delegates were now chosen in primaries rather than by state conventions, labor entered many primaries. Predictably, delegate composition changed drastically. Women and blacks tripled their 1968 representation and delegates under thirty years old increased sevenfold, mostly at the expense of party officials and House members, who had been automatic delegates under the old rules. Labor officials were 4 percent of the delegates in 1968; in 1972, all labor delegates made up 21 percent. Women's representation rose from 13 to 40 percent; blacks', from 5 to 15 percent; and voters under thirty, from 3 to 22 percent (Table 12.3). Although labor was not underrepresented, without the cooperation of the newly expanded liberal delegation it could not determine party choices. However, labor's delegate strength turned out to be unimportant because the primaries had decisively determined the nominee.

Before the 1968 convention, McGovern, strongly urging withdrawal from Vietnam, drew support in the primaries especially from the young and the liberals. Humphrey had won the nomination in the previous convention without entering primaries. The new rules signaled that the old party leaders and labor could no longer dominate the convention. Humphrey withdrew from the race; McGovern won on the first ballot. The platform had the strongest and most detailed prolabor planks ever proposed, covering labor–management relations, labor standards, farm labor, and occupational health and safety. It also called for income redistribution, tax reform, welfare rights, and equal rights for women. The Washington AFL-CIO voted to remain neutral in the campaign. Nixon's reelection majority was one of the largest in history, surpassed only by Johnson's in 1964. In a stunning reversal of party support, 43 percent of union members voted for Nixon versus 31 percent for McGovern (Table 12.2). In eight years, labor support for the Democrats had swung from the highest to the lowest on record.

The 1972 convention marked the low point of labor influence because labor was so divided internally and also from the party's liberal coalition. In terms of rational choice theory, the stand of the AFL-CIO's top leaders seems inexplicable unless one assumes that they thought foreign policy more important than union goals and party influence. Labor's stand on foreign policy marked its abandonment of liberal party allies and basic union goals. Although Humphrey lost the nomination, McGovern was as strongly prolabor. Five major unions publicly acknowledged this, defied the stand of top labor leadership, and supported him. AFSCME, CWA, IAM (machinists), UE (electrical workers), the oil and chemical workers (OCAW), and other unions formed an anti-Meany labor coalition in support of McGovern. The UAW, Teamsters, and mine workers (UMW), already outside the AFL-CIO, joined the dissidents. Together, they made up about one-fourth of the nation's union members. COPE's electoral structure remained idle in many places. In one stroke, Washington labor lost the sympathy of many liberals, who thenceforth defined it as parochial and conservative.

The Nixon administration continued to pressure the skilled trades to train blacks; all government training agencies were consolidated into the Comprehensive Employment Training Act (CETA) in 1973. Opposition by the skilled trades had been essentially undermined. By 1974, the country was in recession, and labor was suffering a hemorrhage of members. Inflation, economic recession, foreign competition, and an aggressive antiunion drive by employers rapidly reduced labor's numbers and financial resources. Fortunately for labor and the Democrats, Republican fortunes had also deteriorated. Although Nixon had wound down the Vietnam war, his administration's involvement in the criminal break-in at Democratic Party headquarters at the Watergate forced him to resign midway in his term. Vice President Gerald Ford succeeded him.

By the time the Democrats convened in 1976, the rules commission had relaxed the implicit delegate quotas for women, blacks, and the young, reducing their representation 20 percent or more from that at the previous convention; labor's representation rose from 21 to 27 percent (Table 12.3). Carter, who had garnered a majority of the delegates in the primaries, came to an informal understanding with the women's caucus and the NEA. The latter's delegate strength had increased from 8 to 12 percent. Labor did not actively court Carter, but he responded to its convention strength and selected its favorite, Walter Mondale, as his running mate.

Carter's platform, avoiding concrete and controversial issues, focused on broad goals that satisfied wide-ranging interests, including labor's. Splits within labor and the party were partly bridged. COPE backed Carter, as did the Labor Coalition Clearing House (LCCH), the unions that, in addition to the NEA, had supported McGovern in the previous election. This time the coalition of COPE, LCCH, blacks, women, and liberals held, and Gerald Ford was narrowly defeated. Many union members returned to the fold; over half voted for Carter, a quarter for Ford, and a normal 23 percent did not vote.

Carter proved to be politically moderate, even conservative. He paid his debt to the NEA by establishing a Department of Education, and he signed a watered-down Humphrey-Hawkins full-employment bill in 1978. Although he won some diplomatic triumphs, he lost popularity as the economy worsened. The Humphrey-Hawkins bill, intended to reduce unemployment to 4 percent by 1983, seemed inoperative. The Arab oil embargo, double-digit inflation, unemployment, rising trade deficits, and an unresolved hostage crisis in Iran marked the end of Carter's term.

At the 1980 Democratic convention, women and blacks obtained delegates proportionate to their number, and labor garnered a 32 percent repesentation, its highest ever (Table 13.3). Although Edward Kennedy challenged Carter's renomination bid, Carter had again won a majority of delegates in the primaries. Kennedy failed to alter the convention voting rules, and Carter was renominated. Kennedy then fought to replace Carter's moderate platform with stronger liberal planks dealing with the economy. He largely succeeded. Even though Kennedy attracted much labor support, most labor delegates backed Carter who retained labor's favorite, Mondale, as the vice presidential nominee. COPE routinely went along with party choices.

The Republicans had earlier nominated Ronald Reagan as their candidate. John Anderson, a Republican, unable to secure his party's nomination, declared himself an independent candidate and launched the National Unity Campaign with Patrick Lucey, former Democratic governor of Wisconsin, as his running mate. They built a platform to attract disgruntled liberal Democrats and moderate Republicans. Apparently, the ticket attracted more Democratic than Republican dissidents. Labor discipline weakened. Despite COPE endorsement, the Democratic ticket attracted only 36 percent of union members; 35 percent failed to vote, and 29 percent supported Reagan. Reagan won impressively over a still-divided Democratic Party. Its defeat was worse than in the Nixon–McGovern campaign. Republicans controlled the presidency and both Houses from 1981 to 1985.

The election portended deeper troubles for labor and the Democrats. In 1981, Reagan fired all striking members of the Professional Air Traffic Controllers Organization (PATCO) after the union defied his order to end the strike. He substituted nonunion controllers, thereby destroying one of the few unions that had backed him in the election. The next year, unemployment soared to its highest level since 1940. Congress then passed the largest tax cut in history and increased military expenditures to outpace Soviet military growth. The trade deficit widened, manufacturing employment declined, and the unions lost even more members. Labor lost more NLRB certification elections than ever before, while union decertifications increased (Goldfield 1987, pp. 159, 211). Toward the end of Reagan's first term, unemployment began to fall.

A sobered AFL-CIO gathered to reappraise its political strategy. To regain more influence in the convention, the delegate strength of women, blacks, and antiwar activists had to be reduced. Lane Kirkland, president of the AFL-CIO, wanted to return to the caucus system and the earlier convention practice, when key party influentials consulted labor on candidates before the convention (Barbash 1984, p. 19). Since this policy could not be quickly realized, AFL-CIO leaders decided to back a prolabor presidential candidate in the primaries and not to wait for the convention's choice. COPE urged unionists to enter the 1984 primaries and declare their support for individual candidates. Most of labor's 573 convention delegates and 179 alternates favored Walter Mondale, and the AFL-CIO formally endorsed him. COPE surveys indicated that many members who had previously supported Reagan were now inclined to support Mondale. However, Hare (1984) claimed that only 30 percent of the rank and file were consulted, and that they were evenly split between John Glenn and Mondale.

Labor's delegate strength at the 1984 Democratic convention dropped from 32 to 25 percent, while women and blacks maintained their strength (Table 12.3).[1] Senator Gary Hart competed strongly, but Mondale, accumulating the support of 55 percent of the delegates, won nomination on the first ballot. He selected Geraldine Ferraro as the vice presidential candidate. Unlike at the previous convention, a seemingly united party agreed on a liberal platform that supported the goals of labor, blacks, feminists, the poor, and environmental groups. The union plank called for the repeal of Taft-Hartley, laws to strengthen the building trades' picketing rights, a revision of bankruptcy laws that let employers escape union contracts, and measures to protect the automobile industry. Labor's influence on party choice and platform had clearly manifested itself. In the election, however, the Reagan–Bush ticket dealt the Democrats one of the worst defeats they had ever suffered. Although 43 percent of union members supported the Democratic ticket, 30 percent voted Republican; 27 percent did not vote (Table 12.2). Washington labor had miscalculated Reagan's popularity with the rank and file.

During Reagan's second term, the NLRB's decisions continued to turn against labor, and union membership continued to slip (Goldfield 1987, Ch. 5). However, the economy improved and unemployment abated. In contemplating its strategy for the 1988 convention, the AFL-CIO brooded over charges that Mondale had lost because many voters had labeled him "labor's candidate." The readmission of the UAW and the Teamsters to the

[1]Hare (1984) reported that Charles Manatt, chair of the Democratic National Committee (DNC), offered the AFL–CIO an unprecedented thirty-five seats, as well as seats on the rules committee. Kirkland responded by contributing $2.5 million in union PAC money to the DNC, a third of its total 1983 budget.

AFL-CIO meant that labor could be more united in electoral work. COPE again encouraged members to vote in the primaries and to back candidates of their choice; 525 (73 precent) of labor's 751 convention delegates committed themselves to Michael Dukakis (*AFL-CIO News* 1988). Labor had increased its delegate strength over 1984 by 178, stabilizing at 25 percent of the total. The AFL-CIO's executive board decided not to endorse a candidate before the convention. Maintaining a neutral facade, President Lane Kirkland said:

> Labor's participation in the selection of presidential candidates doesn't mean that the Federation wears the collar of any political party. If the Republicans had shown comparable interest in attracting the support of workers, more of our members would be going to New Orleans for the GOP convention. And that would vastly improve that gathering too (*AFL-CIO News* 1988).

Dukakis and Lloyd Bentsen were selected to lead the Democrats. Endorsing a typical platform that appealed to liberals and organized labor, they received COPE's formal endorsement after the convention. Democratic campaigning was desultory. Despite efforts to convince voters that the party was moderate, the Bush–Quayle team succeeded in defining it as dominated by irresponsible liberals and big spenders. The Democratic team was soundly defeated. COPE turned out an average performance: 43 percent of union members voted for the Democratic slate and 30 percent for the Republican. However, the voter turnout was the lowest since 1932. Even so, Democrats received 21 percent of the Electoral College vote, the highest since Carter's first campaign in 1976.

The Bush presidency was marked by momentous international events: the Soviet Union's collapse, intervention in the Iraq–Kuwait conflict, crumbling of the Yugoslav state, and intervention in chaotic Somalia to end the famine. When the presidential campaign began in 1992, the outlook for a Democratic victory looked bleak, but lingering unemployment and the mounting national debt emerged as the most important issues. Republicans were torn by attacks from ultraconservatives and the religious right, while the Democrats managed a show of unity.

Washington labor decided not to support any candidate in the primaries but encouraged members to back liberal candidates, most of whom were winnowed out in the early primaries. Bill Clinton, appealing to centrists, won a majority of the delegates and was nominated on the first ballot. The NEA and the AFT were among his early backers. Clinton selected the popular Albert Gore as his running mate. The Democratic Party platform included planks on workers' right to strike without danger of losing their jobs and aid for workers unemployed because of the adverse effects of international trade agreements. COPE officials were worried about Clinton's stance on foreign trade, but they officially backed the Democratic ticket after the convention.

Clinton and Gore conducted a vigorous campaign that focused on reducing unemployment with a coherent economic recovery program. While they accepted the support of blacks and labor, they maintained enough distance from both to convince many voters that such interests were not paramount. Appealing to moderates and avoiding liberal rhetoric, they attracted some Reagan Democrats and independent voters. The Bush–Quayle team conducted a confused campaign that skirted economic recovery issues. Ross Perot entered the campaign late as an independent. Making the reduction of the national debt the main issue, he attracted a fifth of the electorate, but his votes were not sufficiently concentrated geographically to win any Electoral College delegates. Clinton garnered only 43 percent of the popular vote, but the Democrats won a substantial majority in the Electoral College.

Clinton appointed Robert Reich, a prolabor academic, as secretary of labor. He quickly removed some labor restrictions, such as rehiring the air traffic control workers fired when Reagan dissolved their union, PATCO, in 1981. Clinton introduced a national health care bill which was ultimately shelved, and he appointed a commission on the future of labor–management relations, which seemed to stall. In 1993, confirming labor's fears, Clinton pushed the North American Free Trade Agreement through Congress against fierce labor opposition. An angry AFL-CIO withdrew its annual contribution of about $2 million from the party's NDC. Early in 1994, labor resumed payment in exchange for a stronger advisory panel to the DNC (*Wall Street Journal* 1994). Later in the year, Clinton appointed William Gould as chair of the NLRB, and Democrats took control of the board for the first time in a decade (Salwen 1994).

LABOR–PARTY SEGMENTATION

For sixty years, from 1932 to 1992, labor's influence varied in shaping the party's platform and in selecting party presidential candidates. From 1932 to 1947, the party needed labor's electoral support. Democrats initiated prolabor legislation almost without the asking (Skocpol and Amenta 1985). After World War II, the national tide turned against the Democrats. Other party groups, especially southerners, constricted the party's liberal and prolabor stance.

Labor leaders' inability to convince union members to remain loyal to the party after 1948 partly explains labor's fluctuating influence. Marini

(1992) called this the "levels problem," the inability of officers to imbue the rank and file with tenacious allegiance. While the levels problem is endemic to all voluntary organizations, it is less severe in the early stages of social movements, when members envision success if they fully support their leaders. This was labor's situation from the early 1930s to 1950. As soon as high returns on collective bargaining became routine, member support for leaders' political recommendations slackened. Equally important, labor officials became ensconced in party circles, making decisions based more on preserving party solidarity than on advancing union goals and advancing the program of the liberal coalition.

In sixteen presidential elections from 1932 to 1992, labor's position in the party varied considerably. In the first four elections, labor obviously favored Roosevelt but had not yet organized an electoral machine strong enough to be an important player in party decisions. Only in Roosevelt's second campaign in 1936 did a *segment* of labor, the newly formed Nonpartisan League, explicitly endorse him. In that year, the unions in the league were expelled from the AFL, and they formed the CIO. In 1940, labor's endorsement of Roosevelt for a third term was a foregone conclusion because he had the widespread support of the urban working class.

In July 1943, the CIO launched the PAC, labor's first full-blown grass roots political organization. It had a full-time staff of 135; national, regional, and local offices; and a sizable budget raised by voluntary contributions. In short, it was organized to mobilize the CIO's 5 million members to register and vote in the 1944 election (Kroll 1951, p.118). Not until the 1944 Democratic convention, when Roosevelt ran for a fourth term, did labor delegates confront an important party issue: the choice of Truman or Wallace as vice president. Divided at first, they went along with Truman, the party's "choice." Thus, in the first four conventions, although labor played a relatively minor role in party affairs, rewards were high: an accommodating president, protective labor legislation, and Social Security legislation. The party had successfully elicited the support of labor, urban ethnic groups, and the industrial working class. Labor had not yet developed an integrated electoral machine, but most of its members, along with the majority of urban workers, needed little persuasion to support the party. In short, labor's party contributions were relatively small and its returns relatively large, almost a free rider situation (Olson 1965). Contrary to Marxist theory, the party had politically organized the working class, rather than the other way around (Greenstone 1969, p. 37).

Paradoxically, once labor began to operate a fully integrated electoral organization to support the party, rewards slackened. The history of labor, party, and liberal coalition splits over sixteen conventions confirms the segmentation hypotheses stated above. Within the house of labor, the CIO was expelled from the AFL in 1936. Lewis led the mine workers out of the CIO in 1942. The CIO expelled six major Communist-led unions in 1949–1950; the AFL-CIO expelled the Teamsters in 1957. The UAW quit the AFL-CIO in 1968. The AFL-CIO split over the McGovern nomination in 1972; six of its unions joined the UAW to form a coalition to support McGovern while COPE stood by. In 1976, the coalition, joined by the Mine Workers and the NEA, formed a coalition (LCCH) to coordinate political activity outside COPE. The Teamsters stood by. After the election, the NEA pulled out of the coalition. All these divisions within labor paralleled the breakdown of the liberal coalition and the loss of party control by traditional leaders. Together, the three divisions brought about the low point of labor's bargaining position in the party.

Most of the breaches within labor were eventually repaired but never completely healed. The CIO later recaptured most "red" union members they had expelled. The AFL and CIO merged in 1955. The UAW returned to the AFL-CIO in 1981; the Teamsters, in 1987; and the Mine Workers, in 1989. But on returning, the errant unions retained independent political structures, especially at local and state levels. Thus, throughout this sixty-year period, labor rarely spoke with one mighty voice. Dissident unions often traveled parallel paths, but they wasted resources, presented to party leaders a picture of disarray within labor, and permitted party leaders to neglect labor's major concerns.

As hypothesized, party splits exacerbated divisions within labor. Labor confronted such splits in at least four conventions. Henry Wallace's bolt from the party in 1948 to form the Progressive Party coincided with the ejection of the Communist-led unions from the CIO. George Wallace bolted the party in 1968 to create the American Independence Party. While COPE strongly supported Humphrey, many conservative union members defected to support Wallace, and many did not vote. The election had the lowest union voting turnout on record (Table 12.2). In the 1972 campaign, labor's influence in the Democratic Party receded to its lowest point. The AFL-CIO's decision not to endorse McGovern, the party's choice, resulted in the defection of a rump group of unions to work for McGovern. Moreover, more union members voted for the Republican than for the Democratic candidate, and nonvoting was the second highest of all elections. In the 1980 election, Anderson split the Republican Party and attracted enough liberal and labor votes to defeat Carter and elect Reagan. In short, in sixteen presidential elections, labor confronted ten major splits, six within its own house and four within the parties. All of the party divisions coincided with splits within labor.

Segmentation between labor leadership and the rank and file is revealed by variation in member compliance with COPE endorsements for president (Table 2.2). To be sure, in twelve of thirteen elections, more union members voted for the Democratic than for the Republican candidate. When more members voted for the Republican nominee (Nixon over McGovern), COPE was officially neutral. Member support for the Democratic presidential nominee in thirteen elections varied 38 percent, from 31 percent in the McGovern–Nixon contest to 69 percent in the Johnson–Goldwater campaign. Officer support for Humphrey was especially strong in the 1968 campaign against Nixon, but member support was the second lowest of all elections.[2] Surprisingly, although labor support of Carter against Ford in 1976 was tepid, member support for the moderate Carter was second only to the support they gave Johnson.

The percentage difference in member voting for one party over the other varied in the elections from 7 to 59 percent, an average defection from the Democratic Party of almost 20 percent. In a comparison of union and nonunion Democratic voters, union support on average was more than 14 percent higher (Table 12.2). Controlling for occupational composition, union membership probably increased its Democratic support from 5 to 10 percent above what it would normally be. Nonvoting rates are equally important. In thirteen elections, union member nonvoting varied from 19 to 36 percent. This 17 percent spread could well have affected some election outcomes.

Changes in party rules changed the composition of convention delegates and labor's influence in the party. Paradoxically, labor's favored status in the party occurred early, when it had the fewest delegates. When labor's delegate strength peaked at 32 percent in 1980, its earlier informal influence on the party and its leaders had been undermined by the new party rules on delegate composition.

In 1990, union members made up about 9 percent of the adult population. Since systematic data on party delegates became available in the 1960s (Table 12.3), labor's share of convention delegates has been higher than its proportion in the adult population. The same held for blacks, whose delegate strength increased slowly after the 1960s to approximately equal labor's by 1988. I roughly estimated the number of voters that labor could assure the party since the 1930s. While that number always exceeded the black turnout, the difference began to decline in the late 1970s. By 1992,

[2]Wolfe (1969), in a study of elections from 1948 to 1968, claimed that union workers' incomes increased faster than those of nonunion workers, and that union members' working-class consciousness declined over the period. The distinctiveness of the union compared to the nonunion vote declined over this period. In a comment, Hamilton (1973) observed that the income trend depends on the years selected for comparison and that the change in union members' party identification was due to changing occupational composition. Manual union members changed much less than white-collar members.

the average estimated labor turnout for the party was about 500,000 more than that of blacks (U.S. Bureau of the Census 1993, p. 4). Because labor generally had more potential Democratic voters than blacks did, labor leaders felt relatively underrepresented. However, blacks' more reliable support of the party and the growing number of black legislators probably gave blacks an advantage in party circles. Lawyers, teachers, and women became more strongly represented in the party convention during this same period, demonstrating the advantage of recent investors (see Table 12.3).

Labor's party role also changed in this period. Early on, labor thought of itself as the center of the party's liberal coalition. As women, blacks, teachers, and youth groups secured more convention seats, labor not only softened its liberal rhetoric, but it played a lesser role in coordinating liberal interest groups (see Chapter 13).

Because American parties are not clearly split along ideological lines, parties in office try to attract constituencies in the opposing party even at the risk of alienating some of their own members who have no other place to go. Thus, two Republican presidents signed the most important legislation favorable to labor since the New Deal: extension of the Social Security Act under Eisenhower and the Occupational Safety Act (OSHA) under Nixon. The antilabor Taft–Hartley and Landrum–Griffen Acts were passed under Democratic presidents (see Table 12.2). While labor support of the Democrats seemed to be in its best interests, some previously committed Democratic members became convinced that they did as well under the Republicans. Low unemployment and inflation in late Reagan and early Bush years drained labor support from the Democrats. Republican soft-pedaling of civil rights also attracted some conservative white union members.

CONSTRUCTING AND DECONSTRUCTING A POLITICAL MACHINE

Labor's original tilt toward the party antedated World War I. The AFL's official nonpartisan stand became increasingly difficult to maintain in the face of Republican hostility. Even before Wilson's first administration in 1912, Democrats were more favorably disposed than Republicans toward organized labor, immigrants, blacks, and marginal urban groups. Although these groups had a party affinity, their voting turnout was low. Democrats could become the majority party if they could increase these groups' turnout.

After the Democratic triumph in 1932, Congress passed the NIRA in 1933 and the NLRA in 1934, protecting labor's right to organize. In 1935, it passed the Social Security Act, which included unemployment, old age, and disability insurance. Under NLRB protection, union militancy steadily increased union membership during the Great Depression and World War II. This record convinced most leaders that labor's welfare would be best served by forging a permanent association with the Democratic Party.

Yet, as early as 1936, when Roosevelt was reelected the first time, some labor officials sensed that the party's prolabor program was threatened by southern conservatives. During the war in 1943, the CIO unions expelled from the AFL invented the PAC to help finance campaigns of prolabor Democrats who would repeal the Smith-Connally Act, which restricted wartime strikes and union contributions to political campaigns (Calkins 1952). The CIO's PAC was labor's first political organization that explicitly and openly favored the Democratic Party.

Within two years after War II, in 1947, the apprehensions of an antilabor backlash were confirmed when Congress passed the Taft-Hartley Act over President Truman's veto. The act restricted certain union practices and allowed states to enact laws permitting workers in organized plants not to join the union. Within the year, the AFL launched its PAC equivalent, Labor's League for Political Education (LLPE). Finally, in 1955, when the AFL and CIO merged, they merged their two political organizations into COPE. After the Democrats first gave it legal protection under the NIRA in 1934, labor took fully twenty-one years to launch COPE, a unified political instrument to back the party.

For thirteen years, from 1955 to 1968, COPE operated as labor's political machine. Disagreement over the AFL-CIO's political policies increased until 1968, when the UAW decided to disaffiliate. It created its own political organization as had the miners (UMW) when they withdrew from the CIO in 1942 and the Teamsters when they were expelled from the AFL-CIO in 1957. Other unions not affiliated with the AFL-CIO, such as the railroad brotherhoods, electrical workers, postal workers, police, and others, also operated independent political organizations. During the 1960s, the NEA became a union in all but name, and it also maintained an independent political organization. In short, although most of organized labor remained faithful to the Democratic Party, labor's ability to bargain with the party wavered with its ability to speak with one voice. As much as a third of organized labor remained outside COPE at one time or another.

When the UAW returned to the AFL-CIO in 1981, followed by the Teamsters in 1987, and the mine workers in 1989, COPE seemed to reach a high point of formal political unity. But labor was weakened by membership losses and by the decisions of both the UAW and the Teamsters to maintain their PACs separately from COPE at the local and state levels.[3] In sum, the consolidation of labor's political organizations in support of the party was slow in coming, their degree of unity varied over time; unity now is almost as low as it ever was.

From the New Deal years to 1968, labor bargained informally with party leaders on the acceptability of presidential candidates. Labor was consulted on its wishes prior to the national conventions, and it typically endorsed the party's choice after the convention. This system was satisfactory as long as the party chair and the executive committee more-or-less controlled the delegate composition of the convention. However, in the late 1960s, women, blacks, the young, and others forced the party to undertake reforms to increase their convention representation. Rules were changed to reflect the voting strength of these groups (*Congressional Quarterly, Inc.* 1987). Eager to maintain its influence, labor sought to increase its delegate strength. However, the rules committee gave other groups more delegates even though they brought the party fewer resources. As an early, large, and long-term investor in the party, labor felt short-changed; rewards were being given to recent and smaller investors. Why did labor endure this inequitable situation for more than two decades?

A THEORY OF SUNK INVESTMENTS

A theory of sunk investments may help to explain labor's decision to remain loyal to the party. Labor's early decision to support the Democratic Party openly was based on the party's national success and the quick rewards it brought labor despite labor's small investments in it. Then returns began to decline. Labor leaders assumed that the trend would change, especially if it strengthened the party. In view of labor's earlier rewards, increasing the investments made sense. But continued loyalty incurred a number of long-term costs (Davis 1986, Ch. 2).

The earlier AFL policy of rewarding individual friends, punishing individual enemies, and avoiding party attachments approached a free-market model where investments can be moved about almost at will. Resources were committed to individual candidates as long as they protected the interests of individual unions. This strategy worked quite well when labor's economic goals could be attained in local labor markets. Labor combined a skill monopoly in local markets with an ability to buy

[3]These unions permitted their local and state PACs to decide whether they wanted to join COPE, but few did.

some political protection to *prevent* government intervention in labor–management disputes. At the turn of the century, unsurprisingly, labor often backed Republican candidates (David 1951, p. 93).

This situation slowly changed as the economy became national in scope. During the New Deal, CIO unions adopted a national political focus because their members worked in industries with national markets. The CIO's objective was not to prevent government interference in labor–management affairs. On the contrary, it sought government protection to reach its own and working-class goals. To obtain these objectives, labor needed the support of a national majority party.

When labor first cast its destiny with the Democratic Party, the cost of operating an electoral machine was relatively small. Labor invented the PAC to help finance the campaigns of favored candidates and created an electoral machine to supplement the party's local patronage machines. Labor hoped that the combined labor–party machine would give the party a permanent prolabor tilt, but that never materialized, producing a dilemma with no ready solution.

Labor became the major contributor to the Democratic Party *after* it organized COPE in 1955, twenty years after the New Deal. Returns were higher when investments were low and were lower after 1955, when investments were increasing. Rational choice theory suggests that investments should be withdrawn when returns decline. Faced with such low returns, why did labor continue to invest?

Shifting its investments to the Republican Party was not a solution to labor's dilemma on two grounds. First, as a new but not sought-after investor in the Republican Party, labor would have had even less voice than in the Democratic Party. Second, labor would need to forge alliances with older and stronger investors who did not need labor.

Because Democratic Party leaders were aware of the situation, they could entice new investors at the risk of disaffecting older ones, like labor. This was the case when the party first courted labor; the party offered labor bargain rates to invest. Labor ultimately became the party's largest shareholder, but labor did not control the majority of shares. In such a situation, party managers had the flexibility to offer smaller potential investors inducements at bargain rates. To some labor leaders, this tactic appeared to be callous opportunism.

A liberal minority faction proposed different tactics: Delay labor's agenda and support those of the new players in the expectation that they would later back labor's primary agenda. This faction lost to those who had a more guarded stance toward passionate liberal social movements (civil rights, women's equity, and peace). The stance confirmed the suspicion of many liberals that labor was dominated by a self-serving conservative old guard (Form 1990a, pp. 344–6). At the same time, many lower-level union officials and followers felt that top leadership had lost touch with their job–union concerns and were giving race–gender–welfare–foreign-policy matters higher priority. Thus, while top labor leadership did not speak loudly enough in support of the liberal coalition, for many local leaders, it spoke too loudly and not enough on core labor issues.

POLICY OF STASIS

Under these conditions, top labor leaders turned to damage control, preserving the party's commitments to protective labor legislation. Labor continued its practice of trying to influence candidates' selection and monitoring their performance once they were elected. However, labor's regional concentration resulted in uneven influence in state parties, in legislatures, and in the Congress. In the East, the Middle Atlantic, the Midwest, and some parts of the West where membership was more concentrated (Goldfield 1987, p. 118), it was able to preserve past gains. In the South, parts of the West, the Mountain States, and the suburbs, small towns, and rural areas where labor had fewer members, COPE was weak, and local party leaders could recruit successful campaigners even when they were antilabor. COPE's policy, therefore, was to provide financial support for some prolabor candidates in such areas where they had a chance of winning. In short, labor was the largest investor in the national party, the major investor in some state parties, and a minority investor in certain regions. Overall, labor was too scattered to be able to consolidate its resources to influence the national party decisively.

To my knowledge, no one has systematically analyzed the regional party impact of ex-CIO, ex-AFL, public, and service unions. Ex-CIO unions in the manufacturing sector have been associated with the Democratic Party's liberal wing and its social welfare coalition. These unions are probably more concentrated geographically than the ex-AFL unions, such as the Teamsters and the building trades. Although ex-CIO unions still represent the liberal wing of the party and labor, in the 1970s and 1980s they suffered the greatest losses in the metropolitan areas of the East and the Midwest (Goldfield 1987, p. 140), weakening the voice of liberals in COPE and the Democratic Party, where they earlier had greatest strength.

Many ex-AFL unions and the Teamsters, on the other hand, are more dispersed geographically because they function in local markets. They have retained more ties to the local Republican Party and have been reluctant to build coalitions with liberals, minorities, and women (Quadagno 1992). While the supporting evidence is scant, membership in ex-

AFL unions (carpenters, plumbers, teamsters) seemed to have declined less than in the major ex-CIO unions (steel, garment, rubber, textiles). Given their local orientation, moderate ideology, and geographic distribution, ex-AFL unions have probably had marginal impact on the strength of the local Democratic Party and even less on the national party. Public-sector unions are strongest in large cities and state capitals, while the unions of teachers, police, and other municipal workers have a wider geographic distribution. Their ideology falls somewhere between those of the ex-AFL and ex-CIO unions. However, the local political linkages between these unions are weak; they form no bloc to strengthen the local Democratic Party. Even though they form no bloc in support of the national party, individual unions can exert considerable influence on it. Together, the public-sector unions have a moderate influence on the party's liberal wing.

Service unions appear in scattered metropolitan areas nationwide. They have not contributed strongly to the electoral strength of the local Democratic Party but have contributed to it financially. On the national level, they have supported the party's liberal wing, again, largely financially.

Depending on the relative size of these four union types, where ex-CIO and service-sector unions are large, the local Democratic Party should be stronger. In large metropolitan regions and state capitals, public-sector unions provide added strength to the party. Because, the party can aggregate the strength of the four types of unions better nationally than locally, the ideological tilt of the national party can be more liberal than the tilt in most local communities.

CONCLUSIONS

Labor's influence on the Democratic Party is structurally constricted by the nature of the two-party presidential system. Unlike a parliamentary system, a two-party system does not let labor translate its party influence directly into governmental influence. In addition to this source of segmentation, other sources also weaken labor's party influence. The internationals' tendencies to disaffiliate from the AFL-CIO only to rejoin later eroded labor's party influence. Labor's voice was further weakened when its internal disagreements paralleled the party's. The breakup of the liberal coalition eroded its own and individual members' party bargaining power. When party leaders lost control of the conventions just when labor split internally and with the liberal coalition on foreign policy and affirmative action issues, labor's party influence reached its lowest point.

The limitations of the analysis are obvious. Selecting presidential nominees and influencing party platforms are only two areas of party bargaining. Data are lacking on other groups that seek to influence party decisions. Moreover, I have not been able to measure the depth of the divisions in the AFL-CIO, divisions between it and unions outside it, and divisions in nonlabor groups in the party. Michael Goldfield (1993) suggested that the fruitfulness of analyzing party platforms is limited because they represent only symbolic politics. Bargaining strength is better measured by the passage of legislation. Moreover, the national picture is incomplete. As observed above, labor may be weak nationally but strong in some states and regions. A full analysis of labor's legislative success is beyond the scope of this work, but in the next chapter, I examine labor's political organization in Washington and its legislative success.

Given the complexities of divisions within labor, the party, and other groups within the party, any form of class theory would be too cumbersome to apply. More important, the issues around which the divisions are built are often not class issues, however defined. They deal with simple self-interest, foreign policy, civil rights, and many other issues that do not congeal into a recognizable pattern.

Methodological Note

I know of no way to assess the accuracy of the data on labor delegates to national party conventions. The most extensive source is the CBS News Delegate Surveys conducted at the Democratic and Republican conventions beginning in 1968 (Mitofsky and Plissner 1980; Plissner and Mitofsky 1988). CBS reported sending questionnaires to more than 95 percent of the delegates but did not report the return rate. I could not find information prior to the 1968 convention. CBS reported whether the delegate was a union officer or member in 1968, 1972, 1976, and 1980. Only membership was reported for later conventions. Hare (1984) noted that most delegates were business agents, local presidents, or state federation officers or their sponsors.

In Autumn 1991, I called the AFL-CIO research department for data on delegate representation. The director reported that it kept no systematic records on the topic. The *AFL-CIO News* reported data for the 1984 and 1988 conventions, and the research director provided information for the 1976, 1980, 1984, and 1988 conventions. These numbers were much smaller than those reported by the CBS News Delegate Surveys, which suggests that the AFL-CIO data may not have included delegates from the Teamsters, Auto Workers, Miners, and other unions not in COPE. CBS reported the number of union officials who were delegates for conventions only from

1968 to 1980. I assumed that it did not include union officials in the union member category.

CBS data reported the percentage of delegates who were teachers (Table 12.3). They are about twice those reported by the NEA beginning in 1976. Possibly, half of the teachers in the CBS figures were AFT members. It is unlikely that CBS included teachers in both union-member and teacher categories. An NEA official told me that it had the "largest occupational delegations at both the Democratic and Republican conventions," but CBS polls consistently revealed that lawyers had more. NEA may have had more delegates than any other union, but the totals for all other unions combined were at least a third higher than the NEA figures. In short, apparently neither the AFL-CIO nor the NEA had data on the total number of delegates who were members of labor organizations.

13
Labor Politics in Washington

AFL–CIO Washington headquarters occupies an impressive eight-story white building a block from the White House across Lafayette Square. Along the wall facing the entrance stand two mosaics, fifty-one feet long and seventeen feet high, depicting the struggles of American labor to achieve recognition, status, and influence. The AFL-CIO employs four hundred workers at its headquarters and annually receives $125 million from its 105 union to support the organization. In the Maryland countryside not far from the District, the AFL-CIO operates the George Meany Center for Labor Studies. Its thirty-one faculty and staff members occupy a spacious campus that contains conference rooms, dormitories, and dining facilities. Dominating the campus foreground stands a modern structure that houses the William Green Memorial Archives. In its foyer, a large bronze bust of William Green with arms outstretched invites visitors' attention. The AFL-CIO also operates a small Paris office.

The visible presence of the AFL-CIO in Washington is small compared to its internationals' combined facilities. Sixty unions support Washington offices, some almost as large as the AFL-CIO headquarters. The internationals together employ a minimum of five hundred workers (Masters and Zardkoohi 1988). Their combined annual budget is hard to estimate. Although it probably exceeds $300 million, the total is small when compared to the combined budgets of business, professional, and special-interest organizations (see Nachmias and Rosenbloom 1980, p. 239).

Washington's AFL-CIO is divided into nine departments and twelve standing committees. The departments are organized around trade and industrial groups, such as the metal trades, building and construction trades, industrial unions, and public employees. The standing committees include political education (COPE), legislation, civil rights, organization, education, community services, housing, education, Social Security, economic policy, housing, research, public relations, and safety and occupational health. COPE and the legislation units make up the heart of labor's political efforts. COPE organizes electoral campaigning, while the legislation department supervises lobbying. They work together to evaluate Congress and generate support or opposition to proposed legislation.

This chapter examines three aspects of the AFL-CIO's political activities in Washington. The data were derived largely from interviews with Washington labor officials. The chapter first describes COPE's origin and development and how its leaders perceive labor's relationshipstothe Democratic Party. Then it examines how the AFL-CIO organizes and evaluates its lobbying efforts and its role in the Washington liberal coalition. Finally, it analyzes labor's efforts to influence Congress since the 1940s.

COPE: A VIEW FROM THE TOP

Changing political events in the immediate post–World War II period sobered the fast-growing labor movement. Labor leaders became preoccupied with the rising influence of conservative southerners in the Democratic Party, the passage of the Taft-Hartley Act in 1947, the surge in jurisdictional fights, the increasing pace of charges that employers were bringing against labor before the NLRB, the growing right-to-work movement, and the crescendo of corruption charges being hurled at labor. Yet, because of their growing influence in the Democratic Party, many union officials felt that they could stanch the antilabor tide or even reverse it. Recognizing some weak spots in their political efforts, AFL and CIO officials finally agreed in 1955 to merge their organizational and political resources as soon as possible.

The newly formed AFL-CIO Constitution stipulated that the executive council would formulate the general policies of the now-united organizations. It would meet periodically to reveal labor's stance toward parties and presidential candidates. The council established COPE early in 1956 and assigned it five tasks: to organize members' political education, evaluate candidates for office, evaluate members of Congress, raise funds for electoral campaigns, and mobilize the membership to vote in elections.

The AFL's staff of Labor's League for Political Action and the staff of CIO's PAC were combined to form the new COPE staff, but the two bodies were not functionally integrated. Alexander Barkin, COPE's first director, was asked to supervise a staff of fifty. Its first task was to coordinate state and local bodies to prepare for the 1956 Stevenson–Eisenhower presidential campaign. Hasty preparations were made to increase voter registration and fund-raising, and to mobilize a large vote (see Draper 1989, Ch. 4). Many AFL and CIO unions were unable to merge state and local bodies in time for the election; others seemed unwilling to meet the deadline, December 1957. Even by the 1960 Kennedy–Nixon contest, half the local bodies, especially in the Northeast and the Midwest, had not yet merged (Draper 1989, Ch. 3).

COPE remained decentralized and underfinanced. Washington could not force local and state federations to organize. That depended largely on the internationals' ability to convince their locals to form COPEs, join central and state COPE bodies, and support them with money and talent. Thus, in the 1960s, many locals did not send their membership lists to Washington. Local leaders did not regularly transmit Washington's messages to their members. State bodies did not hire full-time COPE directors. Southern locals, entangled in racial controversy, did not affiliate with their central bodies (Draper 1989, Ch. 5). These problems were partly overcome in the 1970s, but COPE remained decentralized and only occasionally successful in mobilizing locals to cooperate when unionism itself was threatened. Thus, in 1958, when Ohio's AFL-CIO leaders thought that the right-to-work referendum might pass, they energized more local COPEs than ever before or since. But Washington's COPE could not convince state and city COPEs to broaden their struggles to include civil rights and other social issues (Draper 1989, Ch. 5).

COPE continued to urge the internationals to send their membership rosters to Washington in order that they could be consolidated and matched against voter registration data. The data were merged by precinct and sent back to the state and local COPEs to assist them in registration and voting drives. In the 1960s, this mammoth and cumbersome task was inefficient; only 30 to 40 percent of the lists were considered current and accurate. Computerization steadily improved the matching process. By the 1990s, COPE officials estimated that the records were 90 percent accurate. Although this figure is higher than those that local officers reported to me, all levels reported steady improvement in the process. Computerization also speeded the identification of members with no party affinity or voting record in primaries. Sometimes COPE sent them questionnaires to probe their political concerns. Then they were sent brochures on those topics.

By the early 1990s, the COPE staff had not grown much beyond its original size of about 55: 12 to 15 professionals, a field staff of 20, and a clerical staff of 20. The professionals were recruited largely from experienced rank-and-file members with skills in computerizing records, knowledge of state and local bodies' finances, ability to prepare position papers and speeches and evaluate candidates for office, and experience with programs for retired members. By contrast, the internationals in Washington employed an estimated 400 people with these skills.

In the five presidential elections from 1976 to 1992, COPE hired a polling firm to conduct surveys on election night to gauge member turnout. In an earlier voting study, Delaney et al. (1988) estimated that 10 percent more union than nonunion members voted and that COPE endorsements increased the probability of member support by 7 to 12 percent. Over the years, COPE developed stronger relations with local leaders and labor bodies. Although some unions, mainly the UAW and the Teamsters, did not fully collaborate, COPE's present electoral organization is about as efficient as its national directors expect it to be.

Persistent Problems

COPE's original charge included four areas: political education at the workplace and in union meetings, political education of local leaders, mobilization of members to vote, and political coordination with other community groups. Washington COPE could direct little education for grass roots members and leaders, a function best performed by the internationals. COPE concentrated on electoral mobilization and facilitating local cooperation with other constituencies.

By the 1970s, Washington COPE officials realized that the changing face of politics was constricting their ability to confront certain problems. Members' political interests had broadened; labor no longer commanded their primary loyalty. They had become divided over abortion, gun control, affirmative action, and other issues. COPE was limited by law in the amount of money it could contribute to individual campaigns (Wilson 1979, p.35), which restricted its use of television to reach members and nonmembers. Although threats to unionism occasionally solidified member support, during the Eisenhower, Nixon, Reagan, and Bush administrations COPE could not convince its members to support COPE's stand on noneconomic issues. The 1992 presidential campaign proved the importance of economic issues. The Democrats focused on unemployment and economic stimulation. Clinton drew 55 percent of the voting members, a high point of member support considering that the independent candidate, Perot, drew 21 percent (*American Enterprise*, 1993, p. 91).

Membership decline after 1970 did not reduce labor's activities and resources. The internationals gradually raised their dues but reduced their contributions to COPE. The drop in individual voluntary political contributions was offset after 1975 when new legislation allowed employers to install a voluntary political check-off system. By 1980, check-offs had increased labor's discretionary political funds to as much as $24 million annually. Most of the money went to the internationals and perhaps $1 million to the AFL-CIO. Although little documentation exists on the flow of this voluntary giving, member contributions had clearly increased, and the internationals hired more lobbyists in Washington (Masters and Delaney 1985). Some COPE officials claimed that the number of campaign volunteers had also increased, but my observations suggest that the officers were simply devoting more time to political matters.

However, labor's political opponents raised funds far beyond labor's capacity (Saltzman 1987). The opposition relied heavily on the mass media to influence voters, while COPE continued to rely primarily on volunteers to make phone calls. No data are available to determine which technique is more effective. To be sure, labor contributed money to candidates who spent some of it on the mass media, but before the 1992 election, opponents raised three times as much money as the Democrats (Saltzman 1987). COPE officials thought that the mass media influenced their members' political views much more than did their employers, whose influence was never very large or important.

COPE's Coordination Strategies

A source of labor's political strength is its alleged ability to muster volunteers to work with neighborhood, ethnic, and racial groups. COPE leaders reported in personal interviews that members' increased residential dispersal reduced volunteers' ability to make neighborhood contacts. Although direct mailings from Washington and local COPEs partly made up for the decline, COPE had not abandoned neighborhood work and planned to augment it. Along with the legislation department, COPE planned to identify union activists, especially in marginal precincts, who would be urged to make contact with a dozen or more neighbors. Even a few supportive voters might tilt outcomes toward labor-endorsed candidates. However, up to the 1992 election, this plan had not been put into general practice.

While the national COPE kept in contact with blacks and Hispanics through the A. Philip Randolph Institute and the League for Latin American Advancement, COPE did not press local bodies to make political contacts with racial and ethnic groups. Some COPE officials thought such measures were unneeded because the Democratic Party made the contacts. My interviews suggested that neither labor nor the party systematically tried to make contact with local ethnic and racial organizations.

Although the UAW and Teamsters generally maintained separate local and state political organizations, national COPE officials did not consider this a problem. They concluded that both unions and COPE generally endorsed the same candidates; most political outcomes would not be altered even if the internationals were in COPE. Besides, local "umbrella" organizations permitted the two unions and COPE to coordinate their efforts. A COPE informant also suggested that where the UAW and Teamsters are sufficiently numerous, they launch more substantial operations than they would if they were part of COPE. In fact, competition between COPE and the two unions may have a multiplier effect on fund-raising and electioneering. Moreover, UAW and Teamster leaders feel more comfortable working with their own members. COPE officials wanted the Teamsters and the UAW to share their membership lists with COPE so that the AFL-CIO could send literature to *all* union members. COPE officials felt that they knew what the UAW was doing politically but lacked comparable information about the Teamsters.

COPE informants did not mention possible negative consequences of having several labor political organizations. Thus, I found in my interviews that local "umbrella" organizations operated sporadically or not at all. Moreover, the failure to share membership residential data reduced the amount of neighborhood canvassing. The unions' occasional endorsement of different candidates also weakened labor's party influence. Party leaders' work became more burdensome when they had to make contact with several labor organizations and accommodate different demands. COPE could not speak for all labor when the UAW and Teamsters publically disagreed.

COPE Washington officials expressed no need to establish closer political ties with the NEA because the two organizations generally agreed on a political agenda. Moreover, NEA members' broader geographical dispersement increases labor's presence nationwide. Like the UAW and the Teamsters, the NEA has enough money and resources to conduct strong campaigns on its own. Again, this assessment of the NEA failed to consider its independent political goals (e.g., the establishment of an independent U.S. Department of Education), disagreements between the AFT and NEA, competition with COPE for delegates to the Democratic Party convention, and the hostility of many teachers to organized labor.

National COPE leaders realized that state and community COPEs mobilize unevenly for different elections. Many remain semidormant for local elections, more become active during state campaigns, and most mobilize as fully as they can for national elections. Even though labor's national electoral fortunes depend on the performance of local and state COPEs, the national COPE made no systematic effort to evaluate their performance. It simply examined local election results. If the turnouts were high and favorable, this was sufficient evidence that the local COPEs had performed well. If not, they needed to improve. In the words of an official:

> When the election is over, it's over. We don't discuss the returns to money and organizations in detail. There is little continuity in thinking about problems between elections. Things change quickly. We meet problems as they arise. There is little retrospection.

Local COPEs do not report to the national on their successes and failures and plans for improvements. Presumably, they evaluate their own performance. Individual locals rarely send reports to their internationals. National COPE officers assumed that the largest internationals—the UAW, AFSCME, IBEW, CWA, and IAM—had the most effective political organizations. When asked for evidence, COPE officials acknowledged that it was hard to assess their performance, but this was not a serious problem. To conclude, without systematic data on the national performance of COPE and its internationals, not to mention COPE's relations with ethnic and racial groups and the local Democratic Party, COPE could not undertake grounded plans to improve its performance.

COPE'S RELATIONS TO THE PARTY

COPE leaders thought that its electoral organization may be more effective than the Democratic Party's because labor reaches its members more easily and frequently. Relations between COPE and the party are complex and changing. One official described relations as being "like a common-law marriage—on and off again, waxing and waning." Party relations had been moderately good until the 1968 convention, when they deteriorated rapidly. After the 1972 convention, when McGovern lost control of the party, a new chair was elected. Relations with labor began to improve, and they are still improving. Although labor obtained more representation on the party's central committee and on other "key" committees, labor opposed the caucus system for blacks, Asians, women, Hispanics, and others:

> We're opposed to the caucus system. Labor doesn't have a caucus like the farmers' caucus, the black caucus, and so forth. Even though we supply the most talent and money, we do not have a labor caucus.

COPE officials see labor and the party as complementary entities. Since the two organizations are responsible to different constituencies, labor feels that it should not dominate the party, nor should the party dominate it. While other groups may make demands on the party in return for loyalty (e.g., patronage), labor demands nothing of the party except to continue to live up to its liberal tradition. The party did try to pursue a reasonably liberal agenda from 1972 to 1992, but it could not be realized against the strong national conservative drift. In summarizing his views on party relations, a COPE official concluded that labor's posture toward the party has remained constant and unchanging. The party's changing responses to labor were due largely to changes in party leadership, not to changes in labor or the party as a whole.

COPE officers realized that labor and party strength varies from one community to another. In some communities, candidates try to distance themselves from one or both. In the 1990 campaign, the AFL-CIO urged the party to exert more control over candidates and play a stronger coordinating role in the campaign. To avoid giving the voters mixed messages, labor asked the party to emphasize party unity and loyalty in its TV spots, pamphlets, and other materials. In its self-interest, the party responded quickly to labor's threat to withdraw its "soft" money (getting out the vote) from the campaign.

Despite complaints about the party, COPE leaders thought that labor could not influence the party much more than it had. Party relations were generally good but could improve if labor were given a more substantial voice in selecting candidates for the presidency and for key state and local offices. But as Wilson (1979, p. 56) pointed out, labor often failed to agree on which candidates to back.

COPE leaders accepted the idea that labor had to tread carefully in the party, observing that even the legal restrictions placed on labor politicking probably served to forestall charges that it dominates the party. Besides, labor was doing moderately well under the current system. In the 1990 elections, COPE officials estimated that the labor turnout was over 50 percent, 14 percent higher than the general turnout. Over 70 percent of union members voted for COPE-endorsed candidates, and 72 percent of them had won their races.

LABOR'S CONGRESSIONAL LOBBY

In 1990, the AFL-CIO's legislation department employed nine full-time lobbyists and a support staff. About sixty international unions in Washington also employed one or more full-time lobbyists. At any one time, thirty-five to fifty labor lobbyists were available to work on any issue before Congress that was of mutual concern. Yet labor's lobby was small compared to, for example, the oil and gas lobby, which employed five hundred people. Most of the lobbyists in the legislation department were recruited from the rank and file, but recent hires were professionals with lobbying experience on the Hill. Although two or three lobbyists were lawyers, the AFL-CIO legal department reviewed legislative proposals and public statements on them.

The legislation department's broad goals were set by resolutions passed at AFL-CIO biannual conventions. In practice, the thirty-three members of the AFL-CIO executive council met three times a year and culled resolutions to specify legislative targets, forwarding them to the legislation department to be fashioned into bills targeted for enactment. The department's divisions included health, environment, taxes, trade, NLRB, budget and appropriations, and family issues. Sometimes the department pursued some legislative targets on its own which, it felt, would help labor and the public.

Every Monday morning when Congress is in session, labor lobbyists, including many from the internationals, meet to review pending bills roughly divided into "parochial" and "general." The former refer to the internationals' specific concerns, which the legislation department tends to ignore, especially when internationals take opposing positions. For example, the construction trades have favored a coal slurry bill, while the transport unions have opposed it. Masters and Delaney (1987a) interviewed representatives of eight large unions in Washington and discovered no overlap on 41 percent of issues they thought were most important.

On general labor bills, each lobbyist is assigned to make contact with an individual congressperson and his or her staff. Sometimes, a task force is created for a concerted drive on important bills, like strike breaking or restricting labor politics. Disagreements on such issues are infrequent; when they arise, efforts are made to arrive at a common position.

Once a bill has been written, the legislation department monitors its progress on the Hill, which is not difficult because an informal network has evolved between labor and congressional staffs. About 80 percent of the senators and representatives hire a staff labor specialist and the congressional labor committees employ another thirty. Thus, while the AFL-CIO and its internationals maximally employ one hundred lobbyists, Congress employs about four hundred labor specialists, about three-quarters of whom are prolabor. In a sense, Congress employs more labor lobbyists than the internationals and the AFL-CIO combined. Communication between the AFL-CIO legislation department and the congressional labor committees is frequent and two-way. Congressional staffers inform the legislation department on a bill's progress. A labor lobbyist reported, "We know every major and minor issue in detail. We have no lack of information."

The AFL-CIO legislative agenda is highly structured. The executive council classifies the bills it wants Congress to consider over a two-year period (as labor, consumer, health, transportation, and working class) and then prioritizes them. The two-year blueprint avoids bickering over priorities. Some bills are listed mostly because strong internationals insist on them, even though chances of passage are slim. The council meets with key members of Congress to inform them of the agenda. From these conferences, the Hill knows what labor wants, and labor officials obtain a fairly accurate assessment of what is possible.

On some bills (like auto emission standards, highway expansion, mass transport), labor–management cooperation is called for. For example, the UAW, convinced that tighter emission standards would reduce large-car production and increase unemployment, joined management to push for an extension of the target dates. Either party may initiate contacts. Meetings may be held at AFL-CIO headquarters, corporate offices, or on the Hill. Not infrequently, business and labor representatives jointly visit individual members of Congress to demonstrate their solidarity on a bill.

Labor lobbyists mobilize support for bills in two ways. First, after securing commitments from some legislators, the lobbyists approach others whom COPE helped elect but who remain uncommitted. They may be subtly reminded of COPE's past endorsement, but threats to withdraw support are rarely made even on "key" labor issues. This approach provides legislators leeway because COPE is more concerned about their overall performance than their position on a particular bill. If their records are unsatisfactory over a range of issues, COPE will withhold support. If the legislator is nonetheless reelected, the cycle is repeated. Some antilabor legislators have been known to become moderately prolabor as they gained experience with an informal sotto voce bargaining style.

COPE's second tactic consists of mobilizing grass roots support for or against a bill, a tactic not yet fully tested. Labor learned that business was much more successful than labor in generating grass roots pressure on Congress, especially after labor's 1975 defeat on the Common Situs Picketing Bill. In 1981, aping business, labor inaugurated legislative action committees (LACs) as a pilot project, later integrated into the legislation department's general operations. By January 1990, LACs were installed in more than 60 important electoral districts, involving about 400 locals and 6,000 trade unionists. Local LACs typically include 30 to 70 rank-and-file activists who try to meet with their congressional representative four times a year. Members were informed about current congressional events through the biweekly AFL-CIO newsletter *ALERT*.

Three staff members of the legislation department, assigned to train LACs, prepare films on how to interview legislators and make convincing presentations (AFL-CIO memo 1990). Before the actual interviews, members review the legislator's record and prepare questions on his or her view on pending bills.

When important pieces of legislation appear before Congress, the LACs are urged to write or call their representatives and remind them of the earlier conferences. These calls serve as informal pressure and performance monitoring. Labor lobbyists feel that LACs have been enormously helpful in getting legislation passed, more helpful than any device that the AFL-CIO has used in recent years. No important piece of legislation is now offered without activating some LACs. Their efficacy now approaches those of business. COPE's ratings of the performance of individual legislators improved 15 percent after LACs were instituted; by 1991, almost no member of Congress appeared in the 100 percent "wrong" category.

Labor lobbyists reported, perhaps mistakenly (see Tables 13.1 and 13.3) that even though they had no LACs in the 1950s and 1960s, labor's success in Congress was better than in ensuing decades. In earlier decades, when party leaders backed a bill, party discipline ensured passage. Party discipline weakened in the 1970s as individual legislators began to build their own electoral machines. During the Carter and especially during the early Reagan years, labor's legislative successes declined. The legislation department then reevaluated its operations, making them more sophisticated and focused. Individual senators and representatives had to be convinced with data that the passage of particular bills would help them, labor, and the country. Labor also monitored individual legislators' behavior more closely. It so improved that many Washington observers now believe that labor has the best political intelligence in Washington (Halloway 1979; Starobin 1989). Even the House leadership calls labor to check on its estimates of votes on upcoming bills.

The 1990 roster of LAC programs identified sixty-four critical congressional districts, twelve of them Republican. Yet, only forty-two labor coordinators were listed, most of them AFL-CIO field representatives, local COPE officials, or officers of state and local unions. One state listed five House districts but no labor coordinator. California's and South Carolina's single coordinators were each "assigned" five congressional districts; New York's and Ohio's sole coordinators were assigned one each.

Almost a year after Ohio's labor coordinator was named, the LACs had not been activated. My interviews with local labor leaders revealed that they had almost no knowledge about the LACs. None of them mentioned being contacted by an LAC labor coordinator. To be sure, the program was designed to involve rank-and-file activists, not officers. Either the program had not been activated or the officers were uninformed about them, which seems unlikely. One cannot conclude that labor did not mobilize grass roots pressure on Congress. My local respondents reported that, on occasion, their internationals would ask them to make contact with their representatives concerning particular pieces of legislation. Almost one-third of them had visited their representatives in Washington or in their districts.

Labor lobbyists sent House members packets that summarized the voting records of the members of their committees. Some AFL-CIO field coordinators, independent of LACs, organized local campaigns to support or work against House representatives. Locals were sent films which showed them how to influence legislation. Perhaps the LAC program was informally being taken over by local officers because they may have faced problems in involving the rank and file. Whatever the process, locals were becoming more involved in the Washington legislative process.

THE LIBERAL COALITION?

In conversations with COPE officials and labor lobbyists, I inquired about the existence, composition, and effectiveness of a liberal coalition in Washington. The word *liberal* had acquired a negative connotation in the 1988 Dukakis–Bush presidential campaign, and labor representatives now preferred the term *progressive*. They also thought that *coalition* conveyed something more structured than the existing relations. The progressives comprised groups that had a "natural intellectual agreement" on 90 percent of the issues. They did not march in lock step but traveled in parallel directions, making only occasional direct contacts. The main groups in the network or circle (my words) included labor, the civil rights community, women's organizations, consumer and environmental groups, and the Democratic Party.

These groups were said to agree with the Democratic leadership on 60 to 70 percent of the issues. They made contact with one another when they needed help. Typically, bills were written by congressional staff members with the cooperation of one or more of the groups. They meet in a House or Senate member's office to map a strategy. Labor typically initiated action in areas such as national health legislation, family leave, child care, and worker protection.

Labor saw itself as the circle's most powerful and successful member. Labor and the civil rights community together most influenced the Democratic Party because they generated the most grass roots support. Because labor had the most efficient intelligence organization, it tended to inform the circle about the course of bills of common concern.

Labor lobbyists claimed that disagreements within the circle were infrequent and not deep. When they occurred, they were more about tactics than goals. While labor targeted a larger set of related issues, such as taxes and the budget, other groups tended to focus on more limited objectives. To avoid unforeseen obstacles, labor sometimes informed appropriate members of the circle about legislation it proposed to pursue.

The network had achieved considerable success in passing bills of common interest, but it rarely succeeded in passing legislation that affected only unions. Halloway (1979) claimed that the circle did not define labor issues as coalition issues. However, labor lobbyists reported that failures to pass major labor bills did not result from lack of cooperation. At times, cooperation was excellent, as in the push to repeal the Taft-Hartley Act (see Wilson 1979, p. 62). A labor lobbyist reported:

> The fact is that we are outdone and outgunned by business. It simply outlobbies us, especially when they bring many small business groups into the battle. They have more money and a bigger mobilizing machine than we do.

Considering the obstacles, labor feels that it has done relatively well in Congress, even under Republican administrations. It has consistently defeated proposals to weaken labor legislation, such as the Davis-Bacon bill. For over forty years, it fended off the worst effects of the Taft-Hartley Act. It has prevented opposition from solidifying by avoiding battles that could not be won. By cooperating with other progressive groups on general legislation, labor has gained status and respect in Washington.

Moreover, labor has succeeded in getting some important labor legislation passed even under Republican presidents, as exemplified by the passage of OSHA under Nixon. After years of opposition, business realized that the bill would eventually pass because, as in the case of workers' compensation insurance, OSHA was more than a narrow labor bill. Rather than trying to defeat it, management tried to make it more palatable. The same logic applied to the plant-closing bill, which required business to inform workers six weeks ahead of their intent to close a plant. Southern legislators at first opposed the bill until they found that many firms in their districts were closing plants to locate overseas. Then they redefined the bill as a "community welfare" rather than a narrow labor bill. Sometimes splits within business are even greater than within labor. On this bill, the business split favored labor. Many small businesses, labor, and community groups united against big business to pass the bill.

Assessing their effectiveness, labor lobbyists felt that they became more successful as labor overcame internal divisions. The return of the Mine Workers, the UAW, and the Teamsters to the AFL-CIO, consolidation of declining unions, membership stabilization, and the creation of LACs buried some old differences, increased the sense of solidarity, and enhanced feelings of power and optimism.

Labor lobbyists had a few mild criticisms of Democratic Party leadership. They knew that the party is subject to cross-pressures and that its leaders "have to take the heat on some controversial issues, including heat from labor." Relations to the party were likened to "a friendly family fight." Labor's success with the party and Congress did not depend on spending more money. At the time, labor didn't need more lobbying money to gain influence in Washington. The obstacle in the 1980s was the Republican presidency, not Congress. Labor spokespersons were confident that a Democratic president would be elected in 1992 and that labor would then realize more legislative victories. However, the election of Bill Clinton in 1992 did not materially change labor's lobbying power in Congress. Clinton pushed through Congress the North American Free Trade Act (NAFTA) against strong labor opposition. His universal health insurance bill failed to pass despite strong labor support. Strangely, none of my Washington informants commented on labor restrictions by federal bureaus (the U.S. Department of Labor, the National Labor Relations Board) or the courts in Republican administrations (see Wallace, Rubin, and Smith 1988).

Labor, Legislation, and the Liberal Coalition

One way to probe whether labor and progressive groups formed a coalition is to examine how their lobbies rated the voting records of individual members of Congress. Since 1947, COPE annually recorded whether representatives and senators voted "right" or "wrong" on key legislation (AFL-CIO 1947–1992). The Consumer Federation of America (CFA) and the Americans for Democratic Action (ADA), two major lobbies in the "progressive network," evaluated legislators the same way. The Americans for Constitutional Action (ACA), the conservative lobby that opposed the network, also evaluated legislators. CFA presumably put consumer interests first. ADA put priority on protecting lower-income groups and minorities, while ACA emphasized the interests of business and industry.

The four groups did not use the same bills in their evaluations, and the overlap varied over time. According to Barone, Ujifusa, and Mathews (1972, p. xii) COPE consistently avoided bills dealing with defense spending, civil liberties, environment, *consumers*, and the Vietnam war. Of course, it supported bills on full employment, occupational safety, and general labor protection, and also bills dealing with social welfare funding, voting rights, urban problems, and desegregation. ADA backed social welfare legislation, cutting the defense budget, the Philadelphia plan (racial integration of construction trades), and social welfare funding. The

CFA supported bills for product safety, meat inspection, mortgage funding, and railpax (transporting trucks) and opposed funding supersonic transport planes. All three supported funding legal services in the Office of Equal Opportunity. ACA opposed bills favoring unions, social security, government regulation of business and the economy, and social welfare spending.

In 1972, Barone, Ujifusa, and Mathews began to compile the ratings that ten lobbies assigned individual members of Congress. Table 13.1 provides mean approval ratings (percentage of "right" votes) for Republican and Democratic senators for COPE, ADA, and CFA, the three progressive lobbies, and ACA in five-year intervals beginning in 1970. The table provides ratings for each lobby over a period of twenty years, 1970–1990, and the extent to which each lobby's ratings "deviate" from COPE's.

Greenstone (1969, pp. 387 ff.) stressed that labor now speaks for its members and for consumers as a class (see Chapter 2). Data comparing COPE and CFA ratings should indicate the extent to which this thesis is supported (see Table 13.1). The two lobbies rated senators differently in four of ten comparisons. In 1970 and 1990, CFA ranked Republicans sena-

Table 13.1
Approval Ratings of U.S. Senators by Four Lobbies[a] (%)

Year	Party	COPE[b]	CFA[b]	CFA[b] Dev.+	ADA[b]	ADA[b] Dev.+	ACA[b]	ACA[b] Dev.+
1970	Democrats	73	74		57	c	31	c
	Republicans	37	48	c	28	c	62	c
	Total	56	55		43	c	45	c
1975	Democrats	66	70		64		21	c
	Republicans	44	34		37		56	
	Total	58	56		54		34	c
1980	Democrats	68	47	c	60		27	c
	Republicans	27	15	c	29		74	c
	Total	50	33	c	47		47	c
1985	Democrats	75	70		69		25	c
	Republicans	23	25		16	c	72	c
	Total	51	48		44		47	
1990	Democrats	80	78		72	c	20	c
	Republicans	22	37	c	19		76	c
	Total	55	61		47		44	c

[a]Calculated from data provided by Barone, Ujifusa, and Matthews (1972, 1978, 1984, 1988, 1991).
[b]*Abbreviations*: Committee on Political Education, Consumer Federation of America, Americans for Democratic Action, American Conservative Association. Dev. = deviation from COPE percentage. + = Percentage deviation from the COPE rating.
[c]Significant = <.05.

tors higher than COPE did, and in 1980, CFA ranked senators of both parties lower, weakly supporting Greenstone's thesis.

ADA, as part of the progressive network, typically ranked senators lower than COPE did; in four instances, the ratings were statistically significant. In 1970, ADA ranked senators from both parties lower than COPE did, and in 1990, ADA ranked the Democrats lower.[1] In 40 percent of the comparisons, the partners in the progressive network ranked the senators differently from COPE. COPE's ratings for both parties were generally higher than ADA's for both parties, suggesting that ADA downgraded senators more when they failed to support bills favoring lower-income groups and minorities. ACA's ratings expectedly deviated the most from those of the three other lobbies, an almost perfect negative correlation with COPE. All three progressive lobbies strongly favored the Democrats. CFA and ADA ratings also fluctuated more than COPE's, especially for Republicans, pointing to COPE's greater party loyalty. CFA's ratings were generally closer to COPE's than to ADA's, especially for Democratic senators. Obviously, the three lobbies selected enough different bills to arrive at somewhat different evaluations, demonstrating that the progressive network was indeed loose. While they all ranked Democratic senators positively, the variation showed that the lobbies had plenty of room for independent action.

COPE'S RATINGS OF CONGRESS

I examined COPE's rating of members of Congress according to the content of the legislation. Between 1947 and 1953, COPE selected and identified bills as dealing with labor, general welfare, domestic concerns, and foreign relations. After 1953, COPE generally identified bills as dealing with union issues but did not classify the content of other bills it selected.

COPE's ratings provide clues to how well it performed under Democratic and Republican congressional regimes and how well it performed in different legislative areas. COPE officials admitted only limited success in promoting favorable labor union legislation but claimed success in protecting past labor gains and advancing the general welfare of workers and consumers. To examine these claims, I coded the content of all House and Senate bills that COPE listed in its bulletins from 1947 to 1992, relying completely on COPE descriptions of the bills. I coded only the first content area when bills included more than one area. The bills were classified into

[1]Wilson (1979, p. 28) noted that the agreement between COPE and ADA ratings began to decrease after 1960.

Table 13.2
Content Area of Bills Listed by COPE for Senate and House of Representatives for Two Periods (%)[a]

	General labor	Specific unions	Employ-ment	General welfare	Class equity	Foreign	Totals %	Totals N
House								
1947–1968	27	12	—	30	28	3	100	90
1969–1992	39	3	11	27	18	1	99	346
Totals	37	5	8	28	20	2	100	—
N	160	22	37	121	88	8	436	—
Senate								
1947–1968	24	9	5	26	33	4	101	86
1969–1992	33	8	8	29	19	3	100	340
Totals	31	8	7	29	22	3	100	—
N	133	34	30	122	94	13	—	426

[a]*Source*: AFL–CIO, 1947–1992.

six areas: (1) general labor union, (2) specific unions or combination of unions, (3) general economic conditions and unemployment, (4) general welfare, (5) class or equity issues, and (6) foreign relations (Table 13.2).[2]

The bills coded as (1), "general labor union concerns," dealt with labor unions generally, minimum wages, immigration, and workers' health and safety. Some of these bills reappeared in several Congresses, like Taft-Hartley, Davis-Bacon, situs picketing, Hatch Act, OSHA, mine safety, AMTRAK subsidies, minimum wages, PATCO, and postal employees. Bills coded as (2), "concerns of specific unions or combinations," included bills that directly affected the interests of highly unionized sectors, although the bills did not mention unions, like bills for school construction, roads, and housing; bills for defense items such as the B-2 bomber, stealth bomber, ships, and atomic weapons; and bills on tariffs that affect highly unionized industries, such as steel, automobile, shoes, and clothing. Bills coded as (3), "economy and jobs," referred to stimulating the economy, reducing unemployment, job training, reciprocal trade, and youth summer employment. "General welfare and consumer bills," (4), included product safety, consumer protection, energy conservation, pollution control, Social Security, unemployment, old age assistance, urban affairs, general taxation, reve-

[2]Freeman and Medoff (1984, pp. 199, 200) divided legislation evaluated by COPE from 1947 to 1980 into four labor areas and a nonlabor area, roughly half in each. They found that "unions do much better winning general labor and social legislation and protecting their monopoly strength in some sections than they do in winning legislation that enhances overall monopoly power."

nue sharing, aid to education, and judicial appointments. "Class or equity issues," (5), included tax rates, antipoverty measures, affirmative action, civil rights, regulation of excess profits, equal educational opportunity, and such matters. The "foreign affairs category," (6), included such items as aid to Israel, boycott of South Africa, selling of aircraft to Arabia, and Soviet immigration. Foreign trade bills that affected specific unions or levels of employment were classified as (2) or (3). In the analysis, I sometimes combined categories (1), (2), and (3) as "labor bills," and the others as "nonlabor bills."

It should be noted first that the data are limited to the bills that COPE selected. It avoided many bills on affirmative action plans for labor, involvement in the Vietnam war, abortion, gun control, crime, drugs, AIDS, monetary policy, and human rights. Second, the analysis is limited to the fate of bills in Congress. When the president vetoed a bill that Congress did not reconsider, this failure to reconsider was not recorded in the data. Third, some bills dealt with parliamentary tactics. Whenever COPE reported votes on such moves (like tabling, referring to committee), I classified the outcome as a victory or defeat in the appropriate content area. Finally, COPE rated relatively few bills in the first decade (1947–1957). They more than doubled in the following decade and tripled thereafter.

The year 1968 represented an important marker for analyzing labor legislation, the beginning of increasing tension between labor and the Democratic Party, difficult economic times, and a resurgence of Republican strength. Beginning with the 1969 Nixon administration, COPE increasingly reported on bills to lower unemployment and protect jobs from foreign competition. I also encountered difficulty in distinguishing bills to preserve jobs in general from bills to protect specific unions. COPE stressed general job protection and job growth even on bills obviously aimed at protecting specific unions.

The bills are divided into roughly equal periods: 1947–1968 and 1969–1992. In the latter, for both houses, COPE rated 3.6 times as many bills as in the earlier period. The two houses did not necessarily consider the same bills simultaneously because some bills that originated in one house failed to pass and were not sent to the other. However, over two-year cycles, the two houses considered most of the same bills. COPE selected about four hundred bills for each house over the forty-five-year period. Both houses considered more bills in the union and job-economy areas after 1968 and fewer in the class-equity area.[3]

Data in Table 13.2 reveal that about half of the bills that each house considered fell into the first three "labor" categories; of these, over two-

[3]Wilson (1979, pp. 26–29) noted similar trends from 1961 to 1976.

thirds dealt with unions, not jobs or the economy. Almost three-tenths dealt with general welfare, one-fifth with class or equity, and 2 or 3 percent with foreign affairs. After 1968, responding to the adverse economic and political climate, COPE selected relatively more bills in the three labor areas, about the same proportion in general welfare, and smaller percentages with class or equity issues.

COPE's Encounters with Eleven Administrations

Table 13.3 reports on the bills that COPE won and lost in both houses of Congress in presidential administrations from 1947 to 1992. Labor's position won in 62 percent and lost in 38 percent of the 862 bills selected. It suffered more defeats in the Senate (44 percent) than in the House (33 percent). Over forty-five years, Republican presidents occupied the White House for twenty-eight years and Democrats, seventeen years. For the 252 bills that both houses considered during Democratic administrations, labor won 68 percent, and 59 percent of the 610 bills during Republican administrations.

Contrary to its beliefs, the AFL-CIO did no worse on specific labor issues under Republican than under Democratic presidents, with 66 percent wins under Republican presidents and 64 percent under Democratic ones. In the nonlabor arena, labor did worse under Republican presidents, winning only 54 percent, in contrast to 70 percent under the Democrats. Contrary to Greenstone's (1969, p. 374) observations, labor appeared to do better, regardless of administration, as a self-interested lobby than as an advocate for the general welfare (consumers) or equity-class concerns.

Party domination of both houses of Congress and the presidency also affected the outcomes of bills. COPE suffered more defeats during the first Eisenhower administration (1953–1956) when Republicans dominated both houses than in his second term, when Democrats became the majority. Labor also won more victories during the Democratic Kennedy–Johnson administrations (1961–1968) when again Democrats dominated both houses. However, although Carter (1977–1980) also enjoyed Democratic majorities in both houses, labor did not much better than under previous or subsequent Republican presidents. Overall, labor performed better in the Senate than in the House before the Republican era which began in 1972, and better in the House than in the Senate during the Republican era.

Except for one Congress under Truman and one under Eisenhower, Democrats dominated the House for this entire period. In the three labor areas, as opposed to nonlabor ones, COPE defeats decreased steadily in the House from 1947 to 1969, regardless of administration. After 1969,

Table 13.3
COPE's Losses and Wins in the House of Representatives and the Senate for Labor and Nonlabor Bills, 1947–1992 (%)

	House of Representatives						Senate					
	Labor			Nonlabor			Labor			Nonlabor		
Dates	Lost	Won	(*N*)	Lost	Won	(*N*)	Lost	Won	(*N*)	Lost	Won	(*N*)
1947–1952[a]	75	25	4	67	33	3	25	75	4	—	—	—
1953–1956[b]	40	60	5	86	14	7	50	50	4	64	36	11
1957–1960[b]	78	22	9	29	71	14	33	67	9	50	50	18
1961–1964[a]	44	55	9	23	77	13	—	100	12	33	67	9
1965–1968[a]	25	75	8	22	78	18	50	50	4	6	94	17
1969–1972[b]	53	47	17	28	72	18	33	67	15	55	45	20
1973–1976[b]	23	77	30	29	71	31	24	76	33	45	55	31
1977–1980[a]	24	76	37	40	60	45	40	60	35	41	59	34
1981–1984[b]	49	51	37	36	64	28	44	56	27	82	18	44
1985–1988[b]	18	82	33	17	83	23	30	70	27	63	37	32
1989–1992[b]	20	80	30	24	76	17	44	56	27	47	53	15
Totals	34	66	219	32	68	217	33	67	197	54	46	229

[a]Democratic presidents.
[b]Republican presidents.

defeats increased somewhat in the first Nixon and Reagan administrations, but otherwise declined in the Republican era. On nonlabor issues, after some dismal defeats in Truman's and Eisenhower's first administrations, COPE sustained victories at a remarkably high and constant rate (more than 70 percent) in all administrations.

The Senate record was more volatile. In five administrations before Nixon's 1968 sweep, COPE's defeats on labor issues varied from none under Kennedy–Johnson (1960–1964) to half under Eisenhower (1952–1956) and Johnson (1964–1968). In the ensuing Republican era, defeats ran 30 to 44 percent. The record in the nonlabor arena was less volatile. With the notable exception of the Johnson administration, where COPE suffered almost no losses, and Reagan's first administration (1981–1984), where it suffered many, COPE's defeats ranged from 40 to 60 percent. Reflecting its constant conservatism, the Senate defeated a larger proportion of nonlabor than labor bills.

Comparing the records of the two chambers, I found that the Senate defeated a higher percentage of bills dealing with unions in five administrations, and a higher percentage of non-labor bills in seven. Taking a difference of more than 20 percent in defeats as the measure of disharmony, the chambers were disharmonious in six of the eleven administrations, four before 1969 (see Table 12.3). Thus, even though the chambers defeated bills dealing with labor at the same overall rate, their unsynchronized performances impeded labor's influence. The Davis-Bacon Act was an exception; both chambers resisted its repeal thirteen times.

Differences in the defeat records of the chambers on nonlabor bills were larger than 20 points in seven of eleven administrations. The Senate tilted against labor's positions more strongly than the House in seven administrations, the defeats being especially large in the last three Republican administrations. The Senate took more anti-COPE stands in the general welfare and class-equity areas than on strictly union issues. It supported only 42 percent of the general welfare bills, while the House supported 67 percent. On class-equity issues, the Senate supported 48 percent of the bills; the House, 67 percent.

The Senate supported 50 percent of the general welfare measures before 1969 and 40 percent thereafter; for the house, 56 percent and 70 percent. The situation is equally dramatic for bills in the class-equity area. The Senate supported 66 percent before but only 39 percent after 1969; for the House, 72 and 65 percent. Clearly, on most issues, especially those dealing with the general welfare and class equity, the Senate opposed labor's position more strongly than the House both before and after 1969.

Responses to presidential vetoes amplify the above analysis. In the eleven administrations, of the bills favorable to labor, the Senate overrode only four of twenty-one vetoes; the House, nine. On bills dealing with union affairs, the Senate overrode only one of seven vetoes; the House overrode eight of sixteen. On nonlabor issues, the chambers behaved more alike; the Senate overrode four of fourteen vetoes; the House, five of fourteen. The Republican domination of the Senate was particularly difficult for labor between 1981 and 1986.

Senate filibusters were less antilabor than the Senate's performance on vetoes. It invoked cloture on eighteen of the thirty-three filibusters. However, it failed to invoke cloture on three bills most odious to labor: Taft-Hartley in 1947, NLRB reform in 1978, and strike replacement in 1992. Filibusters sometimes worked in labor's favor (e.g., preventing the repeal of the Davis-Bacon bill). Perhaps more frustrating to labor than filibusters were the seemingly endless parliamentary maneuvers to prevent voting on important issues.

REGRESSION ANALYSIS

A regression analysis was conducted on voting "right" and "wrong" for labor on COPE-selected bills, 1947–1990. The independent variables included party, region, chamber, president's party, percentage of Congress Democratic, and period before and after 1968 (see Table 13.4). Although the

Table 13.4
Standardized Regression Coefficients for Congress Voting "Right" on COPE-Endorsed Bills, 1947–1990

Variables		
Party	.589***	.673***
South	−.270***	−.217***
President	−.109***	−.045**
Percentage Democratic	.057***	.008
Chamber	.023***	.009
Period	.010	—
Union density	—	.187***
R^2	.369	.548
Adjusted R^2	.369	.547
N	18,059	2,125

**Sig. = <.01.
***Sig. = <.001.

adjusted R^2 was .369, the results confirmed commonsense expectations. All variables, except "period," were statistically significant for voting "right." Not surprisingly, Democratic Party affiliation made the highest positive contribution, while southern constituency was negative. Republican presidents made a small negative contribution, and percentage of Democratic and House membership made small positive contributions. An equation that included five regions showed that all except the South made small positive contributions. A separate analysis for House and Senate yielded similar results.

In a separate analysis, union density of the state of the member of Congress was added to the equation for the three years for which data were avaiable: 1975, 1980, 1982 (Table 13.4). The adjusted R^2 increased from .369 to .547. While the standardized beta for political party still contributed the most to the total variance, union density of the state contributed almost as much positively as southern region negatively. The betas for Democratic Congress and Chamber of members were not statistically significant (see Table 13.4). Similar results appeared in separate analyses of the House and Senate. The regression analyses suggest that labor may exaggerate the importance of the president's party on favorable legislation and underestimate its goodwill in regions other than the South.

CONCLUSIONS

The operations of COPE in Washington reflected the AFL-CIO's decentralized structure. Although COPE had developed sound plans for political education, their execution depended on the willingness and ability of the internationals to convince their locals to do the required work. They had the resources to discipline their locals, but apparently not the willingness. Consequently, no level of COPE (national, state, city central bodies, or locals) was adequately staffed, financed, and organized for political education.

The internationals seemed sufficiently well organized to pursue their own interests at both the state and national levels. On general labor interests, they performed better at the state level than at the local and national level. If they had been equally effective in pursuing common as well as special interests, COPE would have indeed become a formidable political machine. A comparison of the performance of AFL-CIO LACs with those of internationals illustrates the point. The internationals' LACs were better organized and performed more effectively than the AFL-CIO's. Two years after the AFL-CIO organized LACs, I found little evidence that they were functioning as planned in Ohio, but the LACs of some internationals functioned as planned.

Although COPE's national organization to mobilize voters operated more or less as planned, COPE's hierarchy, from the national, state, city, and local union levels, devoted little or no staff time and money to substantive political education. About a month before elections, with almost no attention to current issues, officers and a few volunteers resurrected the apparatus to urge members to register and vote. Despite contrary evidence, local officers assumed that the larger the turnout, the more favorable the probable outcome. In sum, voter mobilization was episodically and moderately well organized, but political education was not.

Top and local COPE officers shared the view that millions of phone calls at election time constituted their most effective political tool. The mobilization organization had become routinized, and COPE did little to evaluate or improve it. The large sums of money raised by voluntary contributions and the political check-off were given to candidates and the party. Almost none was spent on improving political education or the electoral organization. Officers knew that the purpose of education was to strengthen member commitment to labor and the party; they assumed that a larger turnout would somehow realize this goal.

Labor's relations to the Democratic Party stabilized into a pattern of semidiscontent with no apparent solution to reduce it. On both local and national levels, COPE wanted more influence on party decisions, especially in selecting candidates for office, but it did not want to dominate the party. Yet, COPE had not determined how much more influence it needed or deserved and at whose expense. Nor did it press union members to run for state and national offices. In short, labor wanted to be more influential, but it did not want the reputation of being too influential for fear of a backlash, a truly anomic situation.

The AFL-CIO's legislation department does not face COPE's formidable organizational problems. The lobbyists live in a political environment where the players (Congress and other lobbyists) are known and the rules of the game are clear. Legislative objectives are specified and performance can be measured. However, when labor's lobbyists tried to activate LACs, they encountered labor's amorphous and undisciplined organization. Organizing LACs has a well-worked-out and time-tested procedure, but mobilizing volunteers in the locals to press Congress on important legislation proved difficult. In short, labor's lobbyists have learned their Washington assignments as well as any lobby, and their reputation is undoubtedly well deserved. They lack what COPE lacks: an effective infrastructure.

The bills that COPE selected to rate Congress reveal the extent to which labor is a special-interest lobby, a class-oriented party, or a champion of consumers, as Greenstone contended. Greenstone's (1969, p. 392) illustrations of union, working-class, consumer, pluralistic, and mixed issues did not correspond to my classification of union, consumer, general-welfare, and class issues. His consumer-class bills covered a broad range of concerns, including product safety, Medicare, rent subsidies, quality of life, ecology, sales and income taxes, aid to education, and reapportionment. He classified the Davis-Bacon Act on prevailing wages in government construction and public works bills as "pluralistic issues," and bills dealing with the War on Poverty and voting rights as "mixed" issues! I tried to classify bills according to who profits the most from them. Thus, the Davis-Bacon bill was classified as a labor bill, the War on Poverty and rent subsidies as class bills, and Medicare as a general-welfare bill. Greenstone defined the consumer class so broadly that it included almost everyone, ignoring splits among consumers and the groups which profit most from particular pieces of legislation.

Labor's legislative priorities do not neatly fit any theory. COPE's legislative ratings reveal that it acted as a vigorous lobby for unions as a whole and for internationals in specific union sectors. Half of the bills COPE selected benefited organized labor generally or specific union sectors. The percentage of such bills increased steadily over the eleven administrations from 40 to 60 percent. Some segments of unorganized labor also profited from labor's pursuit of its self-interest, but other segments did not. Some consumers also profited, but again, others did not.

Labor's pursuit of its economic interests sometimes helped lower-income groups, sometimes not. Thus, COPE condemned excess profits of some industries but not of others. It sometimes fought for a tax schedule that favored low-income groups, but it also opposed taxes on fringe benefits that favored organized labor but not less fortunate groups. COPE did endorse legislation that helped the unemployed, union and nonunion alike. It backed consumer legislation when it did not injure segments of organized labor.

I estimate that two-thirds of the bills that COPE used to rate legislators bore on the economic well-being of labor directly and labor as a part of the labor force indirectly. Bills bearing on the "general welfare," as I defined it, were not synonymous with those favorable to the consumer class, as Greenstone defined it. Importantly, COPE did not select *all* bills bearing on consumer and general welfare. Conspicuously absent were bills dealing with drugs, guns, crime, family planning, social control, and other issues. To conclude, labor behaved predominantly as a special-interest lobby as well as a lobby for consumers and other class segments when their economic interests overlapped.

The Black Box of Union Composition and Politics

The more union members resemble the entire electorate, the more difficult it is to trace labor's legislative influence. The task is relatively simple for exclusively labor issues like union protection, collective bargaining, strikes, and industrial relations. It becomes much harder for bills involving affirmative action, health, welfare, consumer protection, and taxation. Labor may be one of several interest groups, sometimes acting alone and sometimes in coalition. Here, Greenstone (1969, pp. 393–408) might have had the causal arrows backward. Rather than labor speaking for union members (and others) as a general consumer class, consumer lobbies and other interest groups may be speaking for themselves and, coincidentally, for segments of labor.

It is even harder to trace labor's political concerns to the changing composition of unions and their members. Thus, while new unions were emerging during the early New Deal, it is not clear that Congress enacted protective union legislation and Social Security legislation in response to the demands of the new militant CIO industrial unions. Some researchers (Jenkins and Brents 1989) claim that the legislation was passed to quell the social turmoil provoked by labor, other workers, and the unemployed. Others claim that labor played a marginal legislative role compared to the strong influence of social scientists, intellectuals, Roosevelt's political advisers, and liberal members of Congress (Skocpol and Ikenberry 1983, pp. 99–122). Still others point to the influence of the liberal corporate elite (Domhoff 1990, pp. 98–105).

Clearly, labor became more involved in political and legislative processes during and after the New Deal. The most active union lobbies in Washington tend to be liberal, while the craft unions are not as heavily involved or as liberal. The data reviewed above do not reveal whether the AFL-CIO's changing composition affected COPE's choice of bills to monitor. They did reveal that labor increasingly focused on bills that dealt with its concrete economic interests, rather than with consumer, general-welfare, or class interests. This may have reflected the declining membership of ex-CIO unions. However, the entrance and exit of the CIO, UAW, the Teamsters, the Miners, and others in the AFL-CIO seemed unrelated to the legislative issues that COPE selected (see Wilson 1979, pp. 32–34). Meany and the Washington hierarchy stayed their course. An alternative explanation might be that labor's basic class and social-welfare agenda was realized during the New Deal and that thereafter fewer such issues remained to be pursued. This position would be difficult to defend when one reviews post–World War II legislation on income tax schedules, poverty, civil liberties, affirmative action, crime, urban decay, and other issues.

Some scholars claim that the growth of "postindustrial" unions would change labor's legislative priorities. Yet the rising membership of AFSCME, UFCW, SEIU, and AFT seems to have had little impact on COPE's legislative concerns. The increasing attention given to union concerns, rather than consumer, class, or general-welfare concerns, fits the thesis that an increasingly heterogeneous labor membership spawned more internal controversies, and that it was easier to concentrate on labor than on welfare and class issues.

Labor's legislative priorities need to be put in context. The bills that COPE selected do not reveal which combination of internationals pressed for them. The bills may have reflected general support or nominal support by many unions as paybacks for past support to one or a few unions. Masters and Delaney (1987a) analyzed the legislative positions taken by ten large Washington unions. Over two successive sessions of Congress, no two unions selected the same set of issues. They varied greatly on both the labor and nonlabor bills selected as well as the pattern of legislative success. They became involved in some issues simply to build and maintain alliances and, importantly, often deviated from COPE's positions. Such variation conforms to the expectation of segmentation theory.

I could not gauge the influence of particular unions on the bills that COPE selected by analyzing their content. Thus, a bill to support school construction may have been supported by one or several unions: the building trades, the AFT, the Teamsters, and even the NEA, which is not in the AFL-CIO. Other unions (United Furniture Workers) may have supported the bill because it would marginally profit their industry, while still others may have supported the bill on general welfare grounds.

If scholars try to assess how organized labor's compositional changes affect its legislative activities, they must design a comprehensive historical study that considers in detail how COPE makes decisions on specific bills, how nonlabor groups work independently or with labor on specific bills, how individual unions act with or independently of COPE, and how various groups decide to testify before congressional committees. Researchers should also consider the resources that individual unions, COPE, and others contribute to legislative and electoral efforts. Such an analysis has been successfully employed in the study of business congressional politics (see Akard 1992).

The questions we pursue are critical. If labor maintains a special-interest orientation with regard to public policy, how does it differ from business? Can it lay claim to still being a social movement? Can labor revive its earlier emphasis on the general welfare and the welfare of lower-income groups in the nation? What must labor do to become more politically effective in its traditional agenda of tying its special interests to those of the less privileged? The next chapter considers these questions.

14

Organizational Reform or Movement Revival?

Many social scientists are pessimistic about the future of the American labor movement. Their pessimism stems from their attachment to a vision of a labor movement that furthers working-class interests through social democratic means. By contrast, most labor leaders and union members see their movement as the way to further their job security and economic well-being. The source of disparity is the tendency of all labor movements to involve an inherent tension between two goals: a union democracy that encompasses the interests of the entire working class or a bread-and-butter unionism that advances the interests of certain occupations. The enormous literature on the American exception reflects the inability of many scholars to understand why American labor leaders, unlike their European counterparts, did not lead the labor movement to create or support social democratic parties dedicated to advancing the power, status, and political power of the working classes (see Laslett and Lipset 1984).

Yet, in the post–World War II era, and especially after the 1960s, several European social democratic labor governments suffered electoral defeats. In Britain, Germany, France, and even in Scandinavia, conservative parties ousted labor governments. Unions also began to lose members. Many European academicians became alarmed about the inability of labor to attain its historic mission. They became convinced that something had to be done to revive the labor movement and return it to its mission of furthering the well-being of the working class (Roberts 1978).

Parallel trends in the United States and Europe currently raise questions about the exceptionalism of American labor. As Zolberg (1986, p. 400 ff.) decisively demonstrated, all labor movements have exceptional qualities because they are embedded in different economic and political environments. The research task is to discover how the inevitable tension between the well-being of the entire working class versus a particular part of it responds to unique features of a national environment and to features that all advanced industrialized nations share (see Griffen, McCammon, and Botsko 1990; Lipset 1977).

This chapter, focusing on the dilemmas that American labor shares with organized labor in other mature economies, addresses several questions: Does American labor retain substantial social movement characteristics, or is it largely institutionalized and incorporated into society? Will organized labor stabilize or continue to decline, or can it be revitalized? If revitalized, will it again become a true social movement with a leadership responsive to broad-based membership? How can labor become more influential politically?

FROM SOCIAL MOVEMENT TO INSTITUTION

Like all successful social movements, labor movements have become institutionalized and part of the legitimate social order. As an institution, labor may stabilize, decline, or be revitalized. Stable or declining institutions are sometimes revived by internal reforms. Less often, they are resurrected by grass roots revolts that become true social movements. A life-cycle sketch of a successful social movement (Jenkins 1985, pp. 10–27) suggests that the American labor movement has passed the social movement stage.

The labor movement first grew when workers responded collectively to common grievances, organized informally, and accumulated sufficient resources to mobilize against employers. Challenging employers, local customs, and the state, workers created enough turmoil so that employers and the state increasingly found the costs of disorder so high that they had to make concessions (Tilly 1984). Social movement knowledge that early union organizers learned was transmitted through geographically structured networks to other workers. Leaders began to work together, organize informally, accumulate resources, create turmoil, and extract concessions from employers and the state (Hedstrom 1994, p. 1177). As organizing techniques were refined, standardized, and communicated, union networks grew. An organizing culture emerged. Local unions pooled resources to create stable alliances. As the movement institutionalized, full-time staff officers organized bureaucracies to handle recurrent problems. Added resources were needed to maintain offices that dealt with a widening array of functions and services.

As the movement grew, unions and sympathetic groups that supported them sometimes challenged entrenched institutions and launched opposition parties (e.g., the liberal and labor parties in Great Britain). In the United States, an existing party sought labor support in a coalition party. In some countries, socialist parties launched labor movements and retained direct control over them. In democratic regimes, labor parties occasionally gained control of governments. In order to maintain a majority, labor parties needed to form coalition parties. Once in power, labor governments often had to compromise with nonlabor groups in the coalition. As compromises piled up, governments eventually confronted demands by militant unions that priority be placed on their demands. When this could not be readily done, party control of the government was threatened. At this stage, labor obviously had passed the social movement stage to become part of a legitimate social order that it sought to preserve.

Observing the behavior of union leadership in Imperial Germany, Michels (1911) formulated the iron law of oligarchy. He observed that as unions grow, their leaders become entrenched in office, take control of growing bureaucracies, devote more energy to politics, court other constituencies, lose track of workers' primary concerns, and finally become an unresponsive oligarchy.

Michels's thesis, which implies that the tension between union democracy and an unresponsive oligarchy inevitably tips toward oligarchy, is not endorsed by many scholars who have conducted case studies and surveys of labor movements (Cornfield 1989a, pp. 1–19). They claim that unions vary in officer turnover. Some even develop formal parties that routinely challenge and replace officers (Lipset et al. 1956), thus resisting the development of a gentrified officer corps indifferent to shop-floor concerns. Union factionalism also results in officer turnover as different interest groups struggle to control their union. Changes in the sex, race, and ethnic composition of members result in challenges of the old leadership and in their replacement. Changes in the organization of work alter shop-floor politics, union politics, and union leadership. As unions organize new industries, invade new territories, and merge with other unions, new opportunities for leadership arise. Cornfield (1993a) proposed a status conflict theory that specifies many of the conditions for union leadership turnover and the ascent of new ethnic groups and women into leadership positions.

However, these notable instances of union democracy do not undermine the generalization that labor movements tend to institutionalize, thus increasing their risk of becoming the kind of oligarchy Michels described. Unions grow, bureaucratize, gain influence, become part of a societal order, stabilize, face challenges by other groups, decline, and die (Hannan and Freeman 1988). When labor organizes most employees in a nation and controls the government for a generation or more, as in Sweden, it ceases to be a movement. When unions become incorporated into governments by fiat or force, they no longer represent a labor movement. Like other institutions, they stabilize until they are eventually replaced by new movements (Olofson 1988).

But this scenario is not inevitable. Unions may not become powerful and integrated into the social order. Business can block labor movement growth. Even when labor institutionalizes, opposing groups can attack it, reduce its influence, and speed its decline. Perhaps the alleged exceptionalism of American labor is explained by the exceptional power of American business to sustain its largely successful attack on labor and the left (see Sexton 1991).

EVIDENCE OF LABOR INCORPORATION

American labor shows many signs of being incorporated into society. Both protected and constricted by law, labor is part of a legal collective bargaining system. It disciplines workers who undertake illegal wildcat strikes, organizes employees at all levels of government, is part of the Democratic Party, has established a quasi-political party (COPE), has invested huge funds in government bonds and private business, has influential lobbies in Washington and all state capitals, cooperates with business lobbies on tariff legislation and subsidies for some industries, has secured state-funded labor research and teaching in public universities, cooperates with schools and employers in training workers, administers federal grants to train unemployed workers and operates apprentice programs, has representatives in many community organizations, belongs to international labor organizations, and takes part in United Nations organizations. In short, while American labor is not formally incorporated into the government and assigned official functions as in some European countries (Western 1993), it has developed many ties to most of the nation's institutions. In terms that are currently unfashionable, institutional labor economists have claimed that U.S. labor has "evolved," "matured," become "responsible and respectable," and "integrated" into a national industrial relations system (Lester 1958, pp. 111–113).

WILL ORGANIZED LABOR DECLINE OR DIE?

Even embedded institutions can decline or die. Some scholars claim that American labor will be seen as a phenomenon that grew and died in the twentieth century. Historically, labor has experienced both rapid expansion and decline. Several times the labor movement was pronounced dead only to reemerge with greater vigor. Small labor movements erupted and collapsed before the Knights of Labor created a national organization in 1879 that lasted for a couple of decades. The AFL challenged the Knights in 1891 and was in turn threatened by the IWW in 1905. The AFL survived attacks and was *the* movement until the 1930s, when it was torn by defections of the Mine Workers and other CIO industrial unions. Merger of the AFL and CIO in 1955 led to still larger central bureaucracies. Internal conflicts later led to the departure of the Miners, the Teamsters, and the UAW, followed by reconciliation, more centralization, bureaucratization, and incorporation into the fabric of society.

Such organizational turmoil led Regini (1992) to claim that labor in advanced capitalist democracies has evolved through three stages: a social-movement militant stage of industrial conflict, incorporation into capitalism's political institutions as a representative of the working class, and a current flexible stage of experimenting in labor–management relations. Somewhat more pessimistic, Touraine, Wieviorka, and Dubet (1987, p. 290) postulated that labor in the West, thoroughly institutionalized, is no longer a working-class movement: It has lost its innovative character. The so-called new social movements (of women, and of civil rights, ethnic, environmental, peace, and consumer groups) have displaced labor as the major agent of societal change.

Obviously, nations vary in the extent to which organized labor is a growing or declining institution. From 1950 to 1980, union members' proportion of the labor force declined in the United States, France, Japan, the Netherlands, and Switzerland; it increased in Sweden, Finland, and Denmark and remained stable in Austria, Germany, Italy, and the United Kingdom (Western 1993, p. 267). In the 1980s, unionization levels fell in fourteen of eighteen advanced capitalist democracies and rose in only one (Visser 1992, p. 18).

The trends have had different consequences in different countries. In the United States, declining membership did not materially reduce the size of the union officer corps, nor did union revenue decline substantially. Indeed, spending for political purposes increased substantially.[1] Except for a few wildcat strikes against union leadership in the late 1960s (Hunnius, Garson, and Case 1973), labor leaders' authority has not been threatened. Episodic disaffiliations of internationals from the AFL-CIO ended in reconciliation. COPE has continued to function as in the past, and labor lobbying has not declined in quantity or effectiveness. The Washington

[1]From 1977–1978 to 1987–1988, total labor PAC contributions in the two-year cycles increased from \$10.3 to 35.5 million, and political expenditures increased from \$18.6 to 70.4 million (Federal Election Commission press releases).

gerontocracy maintains control. In the 1993 AFL-CIO convention, seventy-three-year-old president Lane Kirkland was reelected an eighth time. Thus, labor's institutional apparatus appears to be stable and intact.

Yet a few signs of "deincorporation" have appeared. Declining rates of union certification by the NLRB during the Reagan–Bush years represent a weakening of labor's informal incorporation into state administrative apparatus (Goldfield 1987, pp. 195–215). Although organized labor's wage advantage over the unorganized has persisted (see Chapter 3), givebacks of benefits in collective bargaining and the introduction of the two-tier wage system in the 1980s weakened the earlier "social accord" between labor and some large corporations (Craypo 1990, pp. 12–27). Labor's earlier informal influence in Democratic circles has been constrained by the rising influence of other groups. On the other hand, labor's financial contributions to political candidates and the Democratic Party have held firm or grown; lobbying effectiveness in Congress has not diminished, and labor's involvement in community organizations has not declined. In short, institutional embeddedness has not declined much.

What do the ebb and flow of trade union membership mean? With the exception of the New Deal era, union growth in the United States has been associated largely with wars and economic expansion (Filippelli 1990, p. 141). However, on occasion, spontaneous rank-and-file revolts have challenged and revitalized labor as an institution. The American wildcat strikes of the late 1960s and the 1970s, the events of May 1968 in France, and the Italian hot autumn of 1969 demonstrate that the institution can be destabilized, new goals and values can be introduced, and new patterns of participation can be stimulated (Klandermans and Tarrow 1988). What is the current situation for American labor?

ADMINISTRATIVE REFORM OR REVIVAL?

Some recent studies provide evidence of renewed institutional vigor and administrative reform in American labor. Shostak (1991), whose research is the most extensive in this area, has challenged the thesis that labor is bureaucratic, hidebound, inflexible, and incapable of change. In sixteen case studies, he showed that unions are reforming themselves, innovating, and adapting in every major area. Thus, the UAW cooperated with General Motors in introducing new technology to build the Saturn automobile. The UAW campaigned to prevent or buffer the unemployment effects of plant closings. Labor initiated successful campaigns to increase job safety and reduce work hazards. In one year alone, 1987, unions organized 87,000 new members. In 1988, AFSCME organized clerical, technical, and semiprofessional workers at Harvard University into a single local, and physicians were organized in several hospitals. Labor resuscitated PATCO, the air traffic controllers' union that President Reagan had crushed. In California, unions improved the working conditions of illegal immigrants in the garment industry, organized interracial and interethnic solidarity groups, and secured pay equity for women in many collective bargaining agreements. Labor annually trains 60,000 stewards. In several communities, labor has energized the United Way and provided housing, medical, and counseling services for unemployed workers. Labor has invented a novel program for associate union members. Workers have taken over the ownership of failing enterprises. Labor has increased the number of its delegates to the Democratic Party's national convention. It has solidified a liberal coalition in Washington and made it more influential. Labor has improved its operational efficiency through mergers of small unions.

In 1989, a coalition of progressive labor unions created an organizing institute in the AFL-CIO to recruit and train a new generation of organizers in various cities. Trainees were given a three-week internship followed by an apprenticeship and eventually a job of responsibility in labor. A group of professionals, academicians, and intellectuals have formed the Economic Policy Institute in Washington to devise a strategy to revitalize labor as an institution (Shostak 1991, p. 13).

While Shostak's (1991) data point to institutional reform, Brecher and Costello's (1990) twenty-three case studies of grass roots innovation undertaken by union locals in small and large cities point to a renaissance of labor as a social movement. The cases document how community networks emerge in response to workers' job and community grievances. The contributors to the Brecher and Costello volume see these innovations as workers' response to overly centralized unions, officers' neglect of shop-floor problems, and protests of the institutionalization of labor–management relations. The internationals' regional officers were sometimes the main obstacles to problem solving because they clung to the conservative views of officers who appointed them. Unlike Shostak, the authors interpreted UAW cooperation with GM as dangerous, and labor's cooperation with middle-class Washington liberals as a threat to the labor movement. The authors urged labor to form coalitions with oppressed ethnic and racial minorities, liberal churches, new social movements, and liberal officeholders. In these coalitions, labor should cooperate where it can and not seek to dominate.

Brecher and Costello's (1990) cases exemplify a militant class approach to labor movement revival. In organizing the San Francisco's hotel industry, locals attacked labor leaders for their antiimmigration policy. In

Warren, Ohio, an AFSCME local, determined to organize hospital workers, boldly confronted the police. Dissident locals organized corporate campaigns against antilabor employers by disrupting stockholder meetings, engaging in sit-ins at company headquarters, and boycoting company products. Local unions formed progressive PACs to oust conservative Democratic Party leaders in Hartford. Unions joined local coalitions to elect candidates who were opposed by conservative local Democratic Party leaders. Locals formed a New Directions Caucus inside the UAW to fight officers' class collaboration with management. In several cities, workers spontaneously organized committees to support Hormel packing house strikers. In the Pittston coal strike, workers occupied the mines, defied court orders, and conducted sympathy strikes. In the Eastern Airlines strike, eighty unions organized a Jobs-for-Justice media campaign. Minnesota unions formed an Alliance for Progressive Action with a variety of partners, including peace groups, NEA, gay and lesbian groups, Farmer's Union, Council of Black Ministers, the Catholic Conference, and the Urban Coalition.

Fantasia (1988) also provided evidence of movementlike activities in three case studies of worker revolts: a wildcat strike, an attempt to organize a hospital, and a failed year-long strike at a manufacturing plant. In all cases, workers first sought to gain the support of other unions, business, and other community groups before they acted. Their revolts were motivated not by a sense of class conflict but by a culture of solidarity that emerged in response to grievances. Fantasia suggested that labor officials have lost sight of this basic ingredient of social movements. Labor can renew itself by forging cohesive networks with progressive groups, such as women, minorities, and service and technical workers; by enriching members' cultural life through education; by reviving citywide councils to solidify local ties; by linking with unions abroad to fight multinational corporations; and by acting more aggressively by breaking laws and conducting factory sit downs.

The above cases do not exhaust evidence of movementlike activities. Some visible officials of internationals, like President Winpisinger (1989) of the machinists (IAM), have outlined what labor must do to rekindle the labor movement: organize needy workers, form broader alliances, support nascent liberal movements, promote causes broader than unionism, and fight for democratic controls in workplace, community, and society. Periodically, charismatic union leaders like Dennis Rivera of the Drug, Hospital, and Health Care Employees' Union (Raskin 1990) and Richard Trumka, president of the USW (Tarpinian 1989), have mobilized members to fight against seemingly insurmountable odds. But despite evidence of militancy, vibrant leadership, experiments, alliances, and successes, the prospects of a renewal of the American labor movement are dim. Why?

THE CASE AGAINST LABOR MOVEMENT REVIVAL

Professionals now have both the technology and the resources to create the appearance of a *spontaneous* social movement. They employ organizers skilled in helping workers define their grievances. They accumulate sufficient resources to conduct strikes and support strikers and hire experts to engage in collective bargaining. Today, when workers spontaneously organize unions or when local unions spontaneously organize wildcat strikes, the strikes typically come to the attention of labor officials, who quickly take over control.

Applying the defining criteria of social movements, it can be argued that the American labor movement essentially ended as a social movement when the AFL displaced the Knights of Labor in 1891. Social movements are noted for their spontaneity, generation of grievances, informal leadership and organization, emergence of social solidarity, and local mustering of resources to confront antagonists. When professional organizers help workers define grievances, give them resources and leadership to confront management, and conduct workers' negotiations with management, they are engaging in *institutional expansion*, not in a social movement. On rare occasions when the conditions for a social movement and institutional expansion appear simultaneously, the synergy produces explosive growth. In modern society, institutional expansion typically absorbs nascent social movements.

A truly renewed labor movement may have occurred during the early growth phase of the New Deal era, followed quickly by the CIO's explosive growth. Jenkins and Brents (1989) argued that a synergistic situation existed where government, labor, and business groups agreed to institute welfare state measures to quell the rising social turmoil created by militant workers and the unemployed. Other researchers (see Skocpol and Finegold 1990) insist that union growth was a response to protective labor legislation, which was largely instigated by government leaders and intellectuals. Brody (1985) argued that even the CIO's early growth was not a spontaneous mobilization of an aroused working class, but a coordinated drive by experienced union leaders who temporarily overcame splits among workers in the auto, rubber, steel, and mining industries. Workers became loyal union supporters only *after* their officers secured reliable and predictable work rules through collective bargaining.

Spurts in U.S. union growth since the CIO surge have resulted largely from successful lobbying to enact laws protecting union organizing, rather than from a revitalized movement. Thus, the growth of teacher (NEA) and government (AFSCME) unions in the 1960s resulted from legislation that made public-sector organizing easier. The growth of service unions (UFCW and SEIU) starting in the 1970s was facilitated by the concentration of stores in suburban shopping centers and by the explosive growth of the service sector. Future union growth may occur if legal restrictions are removed (the Taft-Hartley Act), by rapid economic growth, or by external societal turmoil, matters beyond the control of labor and business.

The Brecher and Costello (1990) and Fantasia (1988) case studies are not indicators of a labor movement revival. The cases suggest that different unions form different alliances over different issues in different communities. Worker alliances with community groups are typically temporary because they focus on nonlabor issues. Labor's allies rarely reciprocate and support labor's efforts to expand and grow. In short, local union networks do not deepen and spread, an essential ingredient of a successful social movement.

Revitalization by Fission?

Some impatient liberals believe that a splitting of the AFL-CIO would revitalize labor because the current AFL-CIO top leadership is pragmatic, conservative, defensive, and incapable of undertaking needed change (Brecher and Costello 1990). Liberal unions should defect en masse from the AFL-CIO and rebuild the liberal–labor coalition of the New Deal era, as they did when the AFL expelled the CIO unions. Competition between two organizations, sparking growth in both, speeded up political action. Continued compromises after the merger of the AFL and CIO encouraged the general conservative drift in the body of labor.

In a newly split labor movement, most of the ex-AFL unions (building and skilled trades, Teamsters, others) would remain in the current association. Some ex-CIO unions (UAW, USW, UMW, others) would join the public-sector unions (AFSCME and AFT) and most of the service unions (UFCW, SEIU, CWA, laborers, hotel workers, others) to create a new federation. It would continue to organize with the expanding service and government sectors and become the larger and dominant federation.

Government workers already outnumber manufacturing employees. Service-sector unions include many poorly paid women, part-time employees, and racial and ethnic minorities that have a natural affinity for liberal politics. These groups would receive sympathetic support from passionate social movements and from among racial and ethnic minorities, women, and environmental groups (Form 1990a, pp. 334–6). Such a revived liberal–labor coalition would constitute a formidable political force for change.

The proposal to revitalize by fission has several limitations. Although some unions still subscribe to a liberal agenda, they have shown little inclination to take concerted action. They took some first steps in that direction when they established the Labor Coalition Clearing House (LCCH) in 1972 in opposition to COPE's neutral stand in the Nixon–McGovern presidential campaign. But the LCCH did not endure. The liberal internationals have always been free to cooperate with each other and liberal lobbies, but they have preferred to remain in the AFL-CIO and concentrate on industry concerns, sometimes in cooperation with business. Even liberal officers of the internationals like Winpisinger, Rivera, and Trumka have typically been unable to convince members to work for liberal causes. Finally, the new service unions like UFCW and SEIU who have liberal political leanings have the least politically involved union members. In short, the resurgence of American labor, if it is to come, is likely to come from internal organizational reform, a facilitating environment (e.g., booming prosperity), or a national crisis. Since booming prosperity is unlikely and a national crisis hard to anticipate, internal reform may be the most likely path.

NEEDED REFORMS

The more visionary a proposal to reorganize, the more likely it is that top AFL-CIO leaders will resist it. Proposals with the best chance of enactment are those that reorder current organizational goals in line with currently attainable resources. Although the top AFL-CIO leadership has undoubtedly considered many ideas, perhaps including the ones I propose, the absence of a massive reordering of priorities and resources suggests a strong attachment to the status quo. But labor must chose: Stay the course or undertake bold change. I propose drastic reorganization to achieve three goals compatible with current labor ideology and interests. All current commitments should be dropped or downgraded in order to increase (1) membership, (2) work productivity, and (3) political effectiveness. Attaining each objective requires a different approach but progress in one enhances the other.

Organize

Many observers have urged the AFL-CIO to spend more resources on organizing (Cornfield 1989b; Dickens and Leonard 1985; Goldfield 1987). The obvious reason to place top priority on organizing is that labor itself is partly responsible for its declining membership and it can reverse the trend (Form 1990a, pp. 337–8). A third of the membership decline since 1933 can be traced to reduced spending on organizing (Freeman and Medoff 1984, p. 229). Since spending drives the rate of unionization, increased spending on organizing should take precedence over all other expenditures for several reasons.

First, organizing fits labor's basic goal: Organize the unorganized. Second, organizing and administering labor contracts is what labor does best. Third, organizing produces what workers most want: higher wages and better working conditions. Fourth, most union members define organizing as nonpolitical and therefore legitimate. Fifth, organizing silently contributes to labor's political strength because a larger membership automatically signals greater political potential. Sixth, membership growth will produce more activists and officers among minorities and women, goals that the older officers have resisted. Seventh, government and service sector unions would upgrade the jobs of minorities and women, a goal that has been resisted by some unions dominated by white males. Eighth, a larger membership would reduce income disparities in the labor force as more employers compete in a labor market with higher wage levels. Ninth, public attention would be diverted from labor's political activities to its more acceptable economic role. Tenth, organizing service workers would reduce the burdens of the welfare state.

Discouraging as the current situation may appear for organizing (Form 1990a, p. 337), it holds promise because some of today's conditions parallel those in the early New Deal era. Blacks, Hispanics, impoverished women, and the working poor represent large and perhaps growing constituencies that feel deprived and ignored. Ironically, these groups are more prounion than current union members. Although not as easy to organize as workers in mass-production industries, today's dispossessed are more ripe for unionization than European ethnics were in the early New Deal. Kistler (1984, pp. 98–9), an experienced organizer, believes that the service sector is inherently organizable. Especially in the South and the West, many employees in government, hospitals, schools, insurance companies, nursing homes, department stores, and shopping centers want unions. These groups also seek ways to enter the economic and political mainstream. Whereas a bare majority of union members voted Democratic during the Reagan and Bush era, 80 percent or more of the blacks, Hispanics, and the poor identified themselves as Democrats. These groups are already aware of their deprivations. If labor can mobilize them politically, the welfare state coalition may be large enough to dominate the Democratic Party and Congress.

Wherever industry migrates, unions must follow. Unionization of the South and the West has increased only slightly, but overseas migration of industry and industrial growth in Asia and Africa has largely escaped unionization (Form 1995). Although it may appear to be daunting, successful international collective bargaining is possible, especially among unions in advanced industrialized countries (see Moberg 1993). Enormous innovative efforts are required by labor unions everywhere to meet the challenges of an emerging global economy. Organizing the unorganized involves making huge investments in support of unionizing labor in other countries.

Increase Productivity

In capitalism, the growth of union membership ultimately depends on the growth of productivity. Many manufacturing and service jobs are in the process of regional and international redistribution. With notable exceptions, labor has depended on management and government to keep the economy competitive. Labor resistance to plant closings, immigration, and free trade with low-wage countries has been unsuccessful. Union growth in regionally redistributed industries in the United States has not matched union decline in the industrial East and Midwest (Goldfield 1987, p. 119). To stem geographic redistribution of industry, labor must cooperate with management to increase productivity. Studies have shown that unionized plants tend to be more productive than nonunionized plants. If unionization pays, managers may be less opposed to unions. To be sure, many managers will resist collaboration as an infringement on their authority, and many union members will resist it, fearing unemployment, exploitation, and union busting. Although collaboration has uncertainties and dangers, ultimately American labor will have no choice but to help itself by raising productivity (Bluestone and Bluestone 1992; and especially, Jacoby 1994).

Reorganize COPE

Reorganizing COPE will be difficult. As Redding (1992) argued, simultaneous attention to both economic and political expansion may lead to a situation where one tends to displace the other. My research on COPE revealed that local officers highly overevaluate its effectiveness. The organization was designed to educate members politically and mobilize them for elections. Although local officers reported that they engaged in both, a survey of the Ohio gubernatorial election of 1992 revealed that 80 percent of union members indicated that their unions were not an important source of political information. Members were either unaware of their unions' political efforts or thought they had not engaged in any. Only 15 percent reported that their union had operated phone banks during elections. Both local officers and the rank and file had serious concerns about COPE's relations to the Democratic Party and its catering to liberal groups and causes. The cases suggest that different unions form different alliances over different issues in different communities. Moreover, COPE failed to relate union objectives to community issues that the membership recognized as important, and it failed to educate them on how local and national problems are linked.

A reorganized COPE needs to convince union members of the importance of three basic labor goals: protection of unionism through legislation and political action, the importance of employment growth and job security, and the need for legislation to meet workers' basic health and welfare needs throughout their lives. It is not beyond COPE's ability to teach members the importance of *unionism*, *jobs*, and *security*.

Members can be mobilized to support goals that they understand. While the *national* AFL-CIO failed in its efforts to pass the mild Labor Law Reform Bill of 1977, even with a Democratic Congress and president, COPE effectively mobilized *local* groups in Missouri in 1978 to defeat a right-to-work referendum that, according to early polls, had the support of two-thirds of the voters (Seybold 1990, pp. 71–3). Ohio labor helped defeat a similar referendum. In 1982, Ohio unions rallied behind the Democratic candidate for governor, Richard Celeste, who promised legislation that would make it easier for state government workers to organize and engage in collective bargaining. In 1991, unions rallied behind UFCW to defeat Republican plans to privatize state liquor stores. In short, members supported COPE when it promoted issues they understood and thought to be important. COPE cannot expect members to be loyal to a party that shows little commitment to important labor concerns. Therefore, COPE must convey to the rank and file that labor's loyalty to the party is contingent on party support of member concerns.

COPE has now existed in one form or another for more than fifty years. By this time, it should have identified the structural flaws in its operations. On paper, COPE's organizational design is excellent. It has established responsibilities and reporting lines from each local to the community, state, and nation. However, as I have shown, the organization does not function most of the time. Apart from routine reports that officers deliver in meetings of locals and central bodies, COPE rarely operates *as an organization* from one election to the next. Just before elections, officers and a few activists engage in a burst of activity. Exhausted by the ordeal, they do little until the next election, when they repeat the cycle. Titular officers of COPE and chairpersons of COPE committees are normally too preoccupied with other duties to engage in political education between elections. Also, the evidence shows that COPE has not redesigned its tactics and organization despite enormous changes in political parties, campaigning, and the residential distribution of its members.

Clearly, if COPE is to function as designed, it needs full-time paid officers at the local level who have the status and resources of other major officials. Each city central body could support one full-time educational officer for every 1,000 members. Unions dues of a dollar a week per member would provide the initial support. State COPEs would conduct periodic training for these local officers on how to prepare reports on local political issues and how to inform the membership of them. Members would receive at least one such COPE communication every month. The central body could also involve retired union members who have had experience with COPE. The Cincinnati central body showed that having even one retired person working full time significantly added to COPE's political education program. A larger group of retired volunteers, working with a full-time paid staff member, could markedly improve member political education.

Members are now well trained to perform major union functions such as monitoring contract compliance, filing grievances, writing reports, and organizing United Way campaigns. COPE officers can be equally well trained to provide members with the political information they need. The message is simple: a legislative program to promote unionism, economic growth, and economic security. Others may be appended later.

American unions must eventually participate in managing enterprises and contributing to their vitality and growth (see Bluestone and Bluestone 1992). Both management and labor may resist this evolutionary objective of industrial democracy, but it must be confronted, and the sooner, the better. Officers need to explain to members that this project is directly related to labor's three fundamental goals of protecting unionism, promoting employment growth and job security, and passing health and welfare legislation. Finally, more labor leaders should run for public office. Why this is an exception in the United States remains a mystery. The Black Caucus in Congress is very influential. A labor caucus would have an equal opportunity for influence.

CONCLUSIONS

Responding to the inherent tension between the well-being of the entire working class versus its own well-being, organized labor in the United States has tended to move toward the latter. This has resulted in a long-term decline in the appeal of unionism to many groups and has left working-class efforts to improve social welfare without a rudder. Currently, it would benefit both bread-and-butter unionism and social welfare efforts were the major unions to engage in reforms that would attract members and the sympathy of outside supporters.

The advantages of the program I have suggested are obvious. Because its goals are close to unionism's basic principles, they do not appear partisan and are acceptable even to members who hold different political philosophies. The program is not expensive and can be realized with small additional resources.

AFL-CIO leaders in Washington cannot impose the proposed reorganization on the internationals, which must ultimately bear the burden of the implementation. However, even partial compliance by a limited number of internationals would bear fruit. Officers of internationals must be convinced that the current situation is critical. Labor must reorganize or decline. It does not have much time, probably not more than a decade or two. In that time, a new generation of AFL-CIO leaders will replace the present one.

The main obstacles to labor growth are within labor itself, and its legislative goals are not beyond reach. Legal restrictions on labor can be loosened. Its bargaining position in the Democratic Party can be improved, perhaps by prudent withholding of support when appropriate. COPE's electoral organization can be improved. Members will become more militant when they are encouraged to participate in basic decisions (Griffen et al., 1990). Stronger coalitions will be built when labor demonstrates that their interests will coalesce over time (Rohrschneider 1991)

The institution of American labor will not die, but the labor movement will not be revived. Labor politics will remain uncoordinated and often divided, like the politics of the Democratic Party to which it is attracted. The centrifugal forces in labor politics may increase, but core concerns will continue to bind members loosely. If the vitality of the institution of labor is restored by splitting the AFL-CIO into competing units, so be it. Labor's common goals will better be realized when it builds a more disciplined electoral organization, even with fewer members. Even if a smaller labor organization adopts the political formula I propose, it will become a stronger national political force. Labor is too much a part of the American society to wither and die. A new generation of leaders will be more eager to reorganize labor's institutions. Then, although labor may remain divided, it will stumble on as it has in the past, renewing its vitality.

Appendix A
Interviewing in Cincinnati, Cleveland, and Columbus

Because most current information on local labor politics is qualitative, speculative, and difficult to replicate, I tried to gather data systematically. I report my efforts to provide readers with a context to evaluate the findings. These methodological observations even inform some of the substantive issues.

Most of the information I needed had to be gleaned from personal interviews with people who were familiar with at least part of the local political scene or who were themselves engaged in politics. For each city, I arranged interviews with the following persons: (1) presidents of the county central labor body, who were, by virtue of their office, chairs of COPE; (2) officers of the ten largest national unions who were responsible for the political education of their members; (3) officers of large locals of the same union; (4) executive directors or other officers of the county Democratic and Republican Parties and, in Cincinnati, the Charterites; (5) an African American informed about politics in the black community, including its connection with organized labor; (6) a journalist responsible for reporting local political news; (7) a political scientist acquainted with local politics; (8) state and regional union officials responsible for integrating COPE efforts; and (9) AFL-CIO officials in Washington who knew how COPE and labor lobbyists worked. Altogether, I conducted about one hundred face-to-face interviews, which typically lasted from one to two hours. Sometimes, two or more informants were present at the interview.

Officials of the following national unions were interviewed in each city: Teamsters, National Educational Association (NEA) or American Federation of Teachers (AFT), United Food and Commercial Workers (UFCW), American Federation of State, County, and Municipal Employees

(AFSCME), United Automobile Workers (UAW), United Steel Workers (USW), Service Employees International Union (SEIU), Communication Workers of America (CWA), the International Brotherhood of Electrical Workers (IBEW), and the Carpenters. Because the building trades constituted almost 15 percent of AFL-CIO membership in 1990, I also interviewed officers of the Building Trades Council (BTC), which included all of the building trades. Although membership in the ten unions in each city did not correspond exactly to their national size, they were among the largest local unions. I inadvertently omitted the IAM.

Regardless of union size, the research required interviews with UAW and Teamster officials because their unions operated political organizations that were independent of COPE. When both unions rejoined the AFL-CIO in the 1980s, they reserved the right to retain their local political organizations and did so in all three cities. Even though the building trades (carpenters, brick layers, electricians, laborers, painters, plumbers, sheet metal workers, and others) belong to COPE locally, they conduct much of their politics through the BTC. Although the NEA is not in the AFL-CIO, it was included in the study because it operates a political organization. The same applies to the FOP (police). In large cities, blacks maintain a political organization that may operate as a formal caucus of the Democratic Party. In short, this research called for obtaining data on eight or more interacting political organizations: the Democratic Party, the Republican Party, COPE, UAW, Teamsters, NEA, BTC, and the black caucus of the Democratic Party.

This complex of organizations does not include those of the police, firefighters, and some civil service employees. Nor does it include individual candidates' campaign organizations. Business, professional, and other groups also create political organizations independent of the parties. I am not aware of research that has systematically examined the relationships among all of these organizations in an American city. While organized labor runs one of the largest "private" political organizations, perhaps approaching the size of the Democratic Party, the combined occupational (business and professional) and nonoccupational (ecology, gender, social welfare, religious, ethnic) political organizations are probably larger, richer, and more influential than either COPE or the parties. Thus, this research examined only one important slice of the local political complex: the labor–party nexus. Although the number of unions studied is limited, they include over half of the union members in each area and the most politically active unions. I depended heavily on the data that informants provided, many of which I could not independently validate. On the whole, they received me warmly and tried to answer even the toughest questions.

INTERVIEWS

Typically, I telephoned respondents for an appointment and briefly explained the purpose of the interview. Sponsorship by the Center for Labor Studies at the Ohio State University provided easy access to the presidents of the AFL-CIO central bodies, which organize COPE locally. Although I constructed formal interviews with specific questions, I conduct them as informal conversations. If I inadvertently omitted some questions, I followed up with telephone interviews. Most locals belong to the central body and COPE.

In the initial interviews with the COPE presidents, I asked for the names of officers in the Democratic Party, the chief officers of the main local unions, and the names of black political influentials. Cooperation was excellent. Only two union officials were initially suspicious, but they eventually cooperated fully.

COPE, the Democratic Party, the UAW, the Teamsters, the BTC, the ten unions, and the black caucus are the main organizations in the political system I examined. The system's ability to mobilize support for the party depended largely on how well its component organizations worked together. Therefore, the interviews were designed to obtain information about how each organization functioned to attain its goals and how each cooperated with other organizations in the system.

The interviews with Democratic Party officers asked about the party's internal operations and how it worked with COPE, the unions outside COPE (UAW, Teamsters, NEA), the individual unions, and the black community. The interview with COPE officers asked about COPE's organization and its contacts with th Democratic Party, unions outside COPE, and other groups such as the black caucus. Interviews with officers of the individual unions and occupational associations sought data on their political organizations and how they meshed with COPE and the party. BTC officials were asked about the functions of the council, relations to member unions, COPE, the political parties, and other organizations. Black leaders were asked about their contacts with the party, COPE, and individual unions, and how they evaluated the relationships. Newspaper reporters and local political experts were asked for their views about the relations among the main actors in the local political system. Because of space limitations, I do not reproduce the interviews. However, I summarize the main content areas for the coordinating organizations (the political parties, COPE, and BTC) and for the individual unions inside and outside COPE. For the other organizations (race, ethnic), I report the areas that were added to the general interviews.

Interviews for Party Leaders

1. Historical trends in party effectiveness in the city and suburbs, especially with respect to white-collar and manual workers, ethnic groups, women, and labor unions.
2. Organization and resources of the local party: size of headquarters and staff, sources of financial support, precinct and ward organization, and labor union financial and volunteer support for the local, state, and national elections.
3. Trends in party patronage in the city and county and its importance to various groups.
4. Services the party provides for voters, candidates, officials, and labor unions.
5. Trends in financial support and volunteer services for the party from various local groups, including labor.
6. Present and past relationships with COPE: number of union delegates on party committees; party monitoring of labor's screening committees; disagreements with COPE and methods of resolving them; and evaluation of COPE's relations to the party and other party supporters.
7. Party relations with UAW, Teamsters, and teachers.
8. Electoral mobilization efforts of the party, COPE, black political organizations, individual candidates, and others.
9. Comparison of party and COPE effectiveness in voter registration, voter turnout, candidate support, recruiting volunteers, and raising money.
10. Problems the party confronts in coordinating activities of COPE, African-American political caucuses, and other labor and citizen groups.
11. Desired changes in relations to COPE and organized labor.
12. Responses to labor's complaints about the party.
13. Reasons for the weaknesses of the Democratic Party.
14. Effects of recent changes in campaigning (mass media, etc.) on party functions and its relations to organized labor.
15. Assessment of the future.

Interview for the Black Political Organizations

This interview focused on relations with the Democratic Party and was adapted to the situation in each city:

1. Trend in black voting, percentage registered, and percentage turnout by sex and ward.

2. Democratic Party organization in local areas; number of black representatives on the party's executive committee, identity of local political influentials; and amount and type of patronage.
3. Trends in electing blacks for public office; political factions and caucuses loyal to individual black politicos.
4. Evaluation of the Democratic Party, officeholders, and labor unions in helping the black community.
5. Labor's help in registering blacks and mobilizing voter turnout; relations to organized labor and specific unions.
6. Observations on relations between the party and organized labor, especially with respect to racial issues.

Interview With COPE Officials

1. Description of COPE's local organization: size, number of full- or part-time workers; use of consultants; fund-raising activities; relations to member unions; and comparisons of COPE's effectiveness with that of the Democratic Party.
2. Assessment of trends in COPE's effectiveness in educating union officers about local, state, and national politics.
3. Relative effectiveness of the political education programs of individual unions.
4. Assessment of trends in COPE's efforts to reach nonunion voters, including racial and ethnic minorities, women, unorganized blue- and white-collar workers, urban and suburban voters, and non-COPE unions: UAW, Teamsters, NEA, police.
5. Impact of declining membership on COPE's financial resources, political activities, and effectiveness.
6. COPE's relationships with the Democratic Party: influence on the party compared to other groups on the party's executive committee, providing labor candidates for office, screening candidates for office, and providing funds and volunteer help.
7. COPE's effectiveness in dealing with other groups in the Party before, during, and after electoral campaigns.
8. Relative effectiveness of the party and COPE in electoral activities.
9. Evaluation of labor's relationships with the party: areas of agreement and disagreement, methods of conflict resolution, needed changes, and ideas about shaping the party's policies.
10. COPE's policy priorities in local, state, and national elections: (a) recent involvement in local issues, sources of opposition and cooperation, and relative success; (b) the same for state issues; and

(c) the same for national issues. Does labor have targeted programs for different levels of government?

11. Changes COPE wants in relations to the party and its own organization. Concerns about relations to the Republican Party.
12. The future of labor politics in the United States.
13. Should labor consider an entirely new type of relationship with the Democratic Party?

Interview with Officers of Individual Unions

1. Informant's union career.
2. Brief local history of the union, including changes in size, race, and sex composition; occupational composition; dues structure; accuracy of records; and residential spread of members.
3. Estimate of member identification with Democratic or Republican Party.
4. Level of member interest in local, state, and national politics.
5. Description of the political education activities directed to members; dues, money, and personnel dedicated to political education and action.
6. Strength and weaknesses of the political education program.
7. Amount and type of union participation in COPE activities, such as the screening committee, phone banks, registration, and voter turnout drives; disagreements with COPE policies.
8. Political activities outside COPE; evaluation of their effectiveness and those of COPE.
9. Local unions with the most and least effective political programs; attitudes toward UAW and Teamsters for staying out of COPE.
10. Effectiveness of the local Democratic party and its leadership; comparison of COPE and party electoral effectiveness; extent of labor influence in the party; evaluation of the party's response to labor; ideas for improving relations between labor and the party; and ideas about changing the nature of ties to the party.
11. Contacts with the party outside COPE.
12. Proportion of endorsements of Republican candidates and evaluation of the party's relations to labor.
13. Amount, nature, and evaluation of direct union contacts with local governmental agencies and officials.
14. Community issues and projects important to the union in recent years and union involvement in those projects.
15. Agreements and disagreements with other unions on political issues and projects.

16. Amount, nature, and evaluation of contacts with the local NEA and AFT.
17. Trends in labor's national and local political influence and reasons for the trends.
18. Evaluation of the international's political effectiveness.
19. Prediction of labor's future political influence.
20. How to increase labor's political influence.

For the UAW and the Teamsters, I used essentially the same interview as above but altered some questions that referred to COPE and added questions on their relations to other labor unions on local issues.

For the interview with BTC officials, I added questions to the interview for individual unions: the involvement of BTC and the individual trades in attracting governmental and private building projects to the area, cooperation with business in attracting building projects, BTC's stand on tax abatement and other subsidies to attract building projects, conflicts with other unions on local projects, and relationships of individual trades to the Republican Party.

PROBLEMS OF DATA GATHERING AND INTERPRETATION

The attempt to understand labor's involvement in the political systems of the metropolises presented a number of unanticipated problems. I was largely dependent on participants in the system for information. As I learned more about the system, the questions became more focused, and I could sense whether the information I was receiving was accurate and complete. Toward the end of the interviewing, I had a good grasp of what was going on.

I decided first to approach informants of the large coordinating organizations and then their component units. For example, I first interviewed COPE officials and then officers of the individual union; first, the BTU officials and then the member unions; first, the Democratic Party officials and then the black caucus leaders and others.

The problem was to identify the best informants. In the first telephone contacts, my graduate assistants or I identified ourselves, briefly described the project, and asked for the name of the person most informed about the union's political activities. Most often, it was the president of the regional organization or the largest local; other positions included the business agent, union lawyer, legislative lobbyist, secretary-treasurer, and administrative assistant to the president. Roughly, a quarter of the interviews were conducted with two or more informants present. Three informants were black women, three were white women, four were black men, and the remainder were white men. Although the informants varied in their ability to provide detailed answers, all were cooperative, and only two seemed grossly uninformed or misinformed.

A nagging concern in qualitative research involves the adequacy of the sample. Although COPE, the UAW, and the Teamsters include most of the AFL-CIO locals, they do not voice the political concerns of all unions. In 1989, the unions I selected represented over 60 percent of the national membership. Very likely, they were also the most politically active. In the interviews, we asked informants to identify the most politically active unions. Only the Fraternal Order of Police was absent from the initial sample. Interviews with representatives of smaller unions revealed that their political involvement was typically small. Because union membership size and political action often go together, the sample probably slightly overrepresents labor's political involvements in the three cities.

Whose views do the union informants represent? How well informed are they about union politics? For some informants, the answer is clear. Presidents of the AFL-CIO county central body have typically been involved in labor politics for a long time. They are responsible for administrating COPE and should be able to speak confidently about its activities. When a large union, such as the UAW, has several locals in a metropolitan region, and their political work is coordinated through a regional CAP council, its full-time director is likely to have a good grasp of the union's political activities and a moderate grasp concerning the activities of its locals, which tend to be large and to have well-developed programs. Similarly, spokespersons for the BTC should also be well informed about its political activities and those of its member trades because they meet often to consider a wide range of issues.

Officials of individual unions confront different problems. For example, UFCW locals cover large geographical areas, sometimes two or three states. Officers of these locals find it difficult to monitor politics throughout the region. They cannot be expected to have an intimate knowledge of the union's political involvements in all communities. They concentrate on one or two principle cities and have limited knowlege about the others.

Several locals of a union in a given city may be coordinated by their headquarters, which may be located in another city. Typically, informants at headquarters are better informed about politics in that city than in the "hinterland" cities. The researcher then must locate reliable informants, typically officers of individual locals. The number to be interviewed depends on the number of locals and how they coordinate their politics. When several occupationally homogeneous locals are in the same industry, they tend to be covered by a master collective-bargaining agreement.

Because this tends to bring them together politically, it may suffice to interview officers of one or two locals.

I found that communication among locals of the same union was generally sparse. It was almost nonexistent when the locals were industrially and occupationally diverse. Thus, USW locals in the same city were found in manufacturing, the service sector, and the public sector. Two or more CWA locals were found in the telephone industry, in education, and in other sectors. The occupational, industrial, sex, race, and other characteristics of these locals differed enormously. They were not covered by the same contracts, did not communicate with one another, and were not politically coordinated by their headquarters or COPE.

Even locals in the building trades and the Teamsters varied. The IBEW and the carpenters had "inside" factory or production locals and "outside" construction locals. Some Teamster locals in construction belonged to the BTC and COPE, while over-the-road locals belonged to neither. Thus, some large unions in a city may have several locals in different industries but do not develop a common political program and have little political influence. The researcher must gauge how much effort to spend to get detailed information that may add little to first impressions.

Unions vary in the extent to which their members reside in the central city of a metropolis, satellite cities, or suburbs. Union members with low skills and in poorly paid jobs tend to reside in central cities; members of unions with higher wage patterns tend to scatter residentially. Offices of unions and locals are also scattered because they tend to locate close to work sites. This raises an important question: How do the researcher and union informant generalize about politics in the crazy-quilt government jurisdictions of the metropolitan region?

Cleveland's COPE council confronted the problem by establishing separate COPE councils for the city and the southeast and southwest regions. We interviewed informants from all three councils. They also found it difficult to describe the situation in individual communities in their jurisdictions. Moreover, union members were residentially scattered, and few participated in the politics of the communities in which they worked. Informants commented sparsely on politics in the several municipalities, preferring to focus on statewide and national politics.

Cincinnati is surrounded by a cluster of small cities and suburbs that vary widely in socioeconomic characteristics, while Columbus's contiguous suburbs tend to be more uniformly affluent. Hamilton County (Cincinnati) COPE officials paid some attention to mobilizing voters in communities that had more union members, but they could provide few details. Franklin County (Columbus) COPE concentrated mostly on Columbus. To be sure, COPE activists in all three cities made contact with their members through phone banks, but their knowledge of politics outside the central cities was limited. Thus, it appears that, whatever the distribution of union members over the metropolitan region, COPE and union informants focused primarily on the political situation in the central city. This was the information they shared with the researcher.

Finally, except for a few union officials who work full time as lobbyists in state government or as district directors of political education programs, most union officials, whatever their titles, spend little time on politics. Unions staffs are preoccupied with emergencies and administrative demands. As elections approach, they spend more time on politics but return to administrative affairs right after the elections.

Only a few researchers have asked local union officials to generalize about union and party politics. Their ability to do so varies enormously and seems unrelated to their formal education. They rarely survey their members or gather systematic data on union political activities. Sometimes they cannot recall the most fundamental information, such as the relative size of the union locals, the amount of money raised by COPE in the most recent election, the activities that make up their political education program, the number of unions or locals that take part in the COPE council, or the number of union members on the Democratic Party executive committee. They are reluctant to gather data for researchers, who must rely on what officials provide in interviews. Although officials know a great deal about their unions, their knowledge needs to be brought to the surface by intense interviewing. An interviewer's ability to ask the appropriate questions increases with his or her background knowledge of labor politics.

Appendix B
Important Historical Dates

Presidential candidates[1]	Year	Significant Events
Hoover–Smith (1928)	1931	Davis-Bacon Act
	1932	Norris-LaGuardia Act
Roosevelt–Hoover 1932	1933	New Deal launched Social Security legislation NIRA
Roosevelt–Landon (1936)	1936	Wagner Labor Act
	1936	CIO formed inside AFL
	1938	CIO expelled from AFL
	1938	Fair Labor Standards Act for Minimum Wages and 40-Hour Week
Roosevelt–Wilkie (1940)	1940	40-Hour Week Act
	1942	Mine workers leave CIO
	1943	CIO-PAC formed FEPC established Smith-Conally Act
Roosevelt–Dewey (1944)	1947	Taft-Hartley Act
Truman–Dewey (1948)	1949–50	CIO expels 11 Communist unions
Stevenson–*Eisenhower* (1952)	1952	Meany elected president of AFL
	1954	McCarthy Un-American Activities, Supreme Court school desegregation

[1]Winners are italicized.

Presidential candidates	Year	Significant Events
	1955	AFL-CIO merger, COPE formed
Stevenson–*Eisenhower* (1956)	1957	Civil Rights Act
		Teamsters expelled from AFL-CIO
	1959	Landrum-Griffin Act
Kennedy–Nixon (1960)	1960	Racial sit ins
	1962	Federal employees given right to organize
	1963	Equal Pay Act
Johnson–Goldwater (1964)	1964	Civil Rights Act
		Gulf of Tonkin Resolution
Humphrey–*Nixon* (1968)	1968	UAW leaves AFL-CIO
	1969	Anti-Vietnam demonstrations
	1970	Occupational Safety, Health Act
McGovern–*Nixon* (1972)	1972	Senate passes Equal Rights Amendment
	1975	Vietnam War ends
		Highest post-war unemployment
Carter–Ford (1976)	1978	Full Employment Act
	1979	Lane Kirkland succeds Meany as president of AFL-CIO
Carter–*Reagan* (1980)	1981	Reagan fires all PATCO union members
		UAW rejoins AFL-CIO
	1982	Highest unemployment since 1940
		Equal Rights Amendment defeated
Mondale–*Reagan* (1984)	1987	Teamsters rejoin AFL-CIO
	1989	United Mine Workers return to AFL-CIO
Dukakis–*Bush* (1988)	1991	Iraq War
Clinton–Bush (1992)	1993	Anti-Labor executive orders removed
	1994	NAFTA passed against labor opposition

References

Adrian, Charles R. (ed.). 1960. *Social Science and Community Action*. East Lansing: Institute of Community Development. Michigan State University.

AFL-CIO. 1947–1992. *Report on Congress*. Washington, DC: Legislative Department.

AFL-CIO. 1990. "The Legislative Action Committee Program: Brief History and Materials." Mimeo.

AFL-CIO News. 21 July 1984. "Voter Registration Campaign to Enlist Army of Volunteers." 29:21.

AFL-CIO News. 23 July 1988. "Union Cards Link Delegates in Different Political Camps." 33:30.

Aiken, Michael, and Robert R. Alford. 1970. "Community Structure and Innovation: The Case of Urban Renewal." *American Sociological Review* 35:650–65.

Akard, Patrick J. 1992. "Corporative Mobilization and Political Power: The Transformation of U.S. Economic Policy in the 1970s." *American Sociological Review* 57:597–615.

Alba, Richard D. 1981. "The Twilight of Ethnicity among American Catholics of European Origin." *Annals* 454:86–97.

———. 1990. *Ethnic Identity: The Transformation of White America*. New Haven, CT: Yale University Press.

Aldrich, Howard E., and Peter V. Marsden. 1988. "Environments and Organizations." Pp. 361–92 in *Handbook of Sociology*, edited by Neil J. Smelser. Newbury Park, CA: Sage.

American Enterprise. January/February 1993. "What Voters Said on Election Day."

American Labor Yearbook. 1931. New York: Rand School Press.

Apostle, Richard, Don Clairmont, and Lars Osberg. 1986. "Economic Segmentation and Politics." *American Journal of Sociology* 91:905–31.

Asher, Herbert B., Randall B. Ripley, and Karen C. Snyder. 1991. "Organized Labor and Political Action, Attitudes and Behavior." Unpublished manuscript, Department of Political Science. Ohio State University, Columbus.

Asher, Herbert B., Randall B. Ripley, and Karen C. Snyder. 1992. "Political Attitudes and Behavior of Union Members: The 1990 Ohio Elections." Revised unpublished manuscript, Department of Political Science, Ohio State University, Columbus.

Averitt, Robert T. 1968. *The Dual Economy*. New York: Norton.

Barbash, Jack. 1984. "Trade Unionism from Roosevelt to Reagan." *Annals* 473:11–22.

Barloon, Marvin J. 1987. "Cleveland's Economy." Pp. 360–3 in *The Encyclopedia of Cleveland*, edited by David D. Van Tassel and John Grabowski. Bloomington: Indiana University Press.

Barone, Michael, Grant Ujifusa, and Douglas Mathews. 1972, 1978, 1984, 1988, 1994. *The Almanac of American Politics.* Boston: Gambit.

Bauman, Zigmunt. 1972. *Between Classes and Elites.* Manchester: Manchester University Press.

Baumol, William J. 21 March 1990. "U.S. Industry's Lead Gets Bigger." New York: *Wall Street Journal.*

Bennett, Earl. 1991. "Left Behind: Exploring Declining Turnouts Among Noncollege Young Whites." *Social Science Quarterly* 72:314–33.

Bennett, James. 14 January 1992. "Unions Shrinking, but Richer Than Ever." New York: *Wall Street Journal.*

Berg, Ivar (ed.). 1981. *Sociological Perspectives on Labor Markets.* New York: Academic Press.

Berry, Jeffrey M. 1984. *The Interest Group Society.* Boston: Little Brown.

Blantz, Thomas E. 1970. "Review of Greenstone's, *Labor in American Politics.*" *Review of Politics* 32:410–11.

Bleda, Sharon E. 1979. "Intergenerational Differences in Patterns and Bases of Ethnic Segregation." *Ethnicity* 5:91–107.

Bluestone, Berry, and Irvine Bluestone. 1992. *Negotiating the Future: A Labor Perspective on American Business.* New York: Basic Books.

Bok, Derek C., and John T. Dunlop. 1970. *Labor and the American Community.* New York: Simon & Schuster.

Boryczka, Raymond, and Lorin Lee Cary. 1982. *No Strength without the Union: An Illustrated History of Ohio Workers, 1803–1980.* Columbus: Ohio Historical Society.

Brecher, Jeremy, and Tim Costello (eds.). 1990. *Building Bridges: The Emerging Grassroots Coalition of Labor and the Community.* New York: Monthly Review Press.

Brimlow, Peter, and Leslie Spencer. 1993. "The National Extortion Association?" *Forbes*:73–84.

Brody, David. 1985. "The CIO after 50 Years." *Dissent* 32:457–72.

Buffa, Dudley W. 1984. *Union Power and American Democracy: The UAW and the Democratic Party, 1972–83.* Ann Arbor: University of Michigan Press.

Burnham, Walter Dean. 1982. *The Current Crisis in American Politics.* New York: Oxford University Press.

Calkins, Fay. 1952. *The CIO and the Democratic Party.* Chicago: University of Chicago Press.

Cameron, David R. 1984. "Social Democracy, Corporatism, Labour Quiescence, and the Representation of Economic Interest in Advanced Capitalist Society." Pp. 143–79 in *Order and Conflict in Contemporary Capitalism*, edited by John H. Goldthorpe. Oxford: Clarendon Press.

Campbell, Angus, et al. 1964. *The American Voter.* New York: Wiley.

Campbell, Thomas F. 1990. "Cleveland: The Struggle for Stability." Pp. 109–136 in *Snowbelt Cities*, edited by Richard M. Bernard. Bloomington: Indiana University Press.

Cantril, Albert N. 1991. *The Opinion Connection: Polling, Politics, and the Press.* Washington, DC: Congressional Quarterly Books.

Choldin, Harvey M. 1985. *Cities and Suburbs.* New York: McGraw-Hill.

Clark, Terry N. 1968. "Community Structure, Decision-Making, Budget Expenditures, and Urban Renewal in 51 American Communities." *American Sociological Review* 33:576–93.

Clark, Terry N., Seymour Martin Lipset, and Michael Rempel. 1993 "The Declining Political Significance of Class." *International Sociology* 8:293–316.

Clawson, Dan, and Alan Neustadtl. 1986. "The Logic of Business Unity: Corporate Contributions to the 1980 Congressional Elections." *American Sociological Review* 51:797–811.

Clelland, Donald A., and William Form. 1969. "Economic Dominants and Community Power." *American Journal of Sociology* 69:511–21.

Coleman, James S. 1990. *Foundations of Social Theory.* Cambridge: Belknap Press of Harvard University Press.

Congressional Quarterly Inc. 1987. *National Party Conventions, 1831–1984*. Washington, DC: Congressional Quarterly, Inc.
Cornfield, Daniel B. 1989a. *Becoming a Mighty Voice*. New York: Russell Sage Foundation.
———. 1989b. "Union Decline and the Political Demands of Organized Labor." *Work and Occupations* 16:292–322.
———. 1993. "Integrating U.S. Labor Leadership." *Research in the Sociology of Organizations* 12:51–74. JAI, Inc.
Cotter, Cornelius, James L. Gibson, John F. Bibby, and Robert J. Huckshorn. 1984. *Party Organization in American Politics*. New York: Praeger.
Cox, Kevin R., and Andrew Mair. 1988. "Locality and Community in the Politics of Local Economic Development." *Annals of the Association of American Geographers* 78:308–25.
Craypo, Charles. 1990. "The Decline of Union Bargaining Power." Pp. 3–40 in *U.S. Labor Relations, 1945–1989*, edited by Bruce Nissen. New York: Garland.
Dahl, Robert A. 1961. *Who Governs: Democracy and Power in an American City*. New Haven, CT: Yale University Press.
Dahrendorf, Ralf. 1959. *Class and Class Conflict in Industrial Society*. Stanford, CA: Stanford University Press.
Daugherty, Carroll R. 1941. *Labor Problems in American Industry*. Cambridge, MA: Riverside Press.
David, Henry. 1951. "One Hundred Years of Labor in Politics." Pp. 90–112 in *The House of Labor*, edited by J. B. S. Hardman and Maurice F. Neufeld. New York: Prentice-Hall.
Davis, John Emmeus. 1991. *Contested Ground*. Ithaca, NY: Cornell University Press.
Davis, Mike. 1986. *Prisoners of the American Dream*. London: Verso.
Delaney, John Thomas, Marick F. Masters, and Susan Schwochau. 1988. "Unionism and Voter Turnout." *Journal of Labor Research* 9:221–36.
Department of Labor. 1968–1985. *Monthly Labor Review*. Columbus, OH:State of Ohio.
Doeringer, Peter B., and Michael J. Piore. 1971. *Internal Labor Markets and Manpower Analysis*. Lexington, MA: Heath.
Domhoff, G. William. 1978. *Who Really Rules? New Haven and Community Power Reexamined*. New Brunswick, NJ: Transaction.
———. 1990. *The Power Elite and the State: How Policy Is Made in America*. New York: Aldine de Gruyter.
Draper, Alan. 1989. *A Rope of Sand: The AFL-CIO Committee on Political Education, 1958–1967*. New York: Praeger.
Drski, C. Kenneth. 1985. "Suburban Mobility: The Coming Transportation Crisis." *Transportation Quarterly* 39:283–96.
Durkheim, Emile. (1893) 1964. *The Division of Labor in Society*. Translated by George Simpson. New York: Free Press.
Edwards, Alba. 1943. *Comparative Occupational Statistics for the U.S., 1870 to 1940*. Washington, D.C.: U.S. Bureau of the Census.
Edwards, Richard, Paolo Garonna, and Franz Todtling (eds.). 1986. *Unions in Crisis and Beyond*. Dover, MA: Auburn.
Egger, Charles. 1975. *Columbus Mayors*. Columbus, OH: *Citizen-Journal*.
Eldersveld, Samuel J. 1964. *Political Parties: A Behavioral Analysis*. Chicago: Rand-McNally.
Emery, F. E., and E. L. Trist. 1965. "The Causal Texture of Organizational Environments." *Human Relations* 18:21–32.
Estey, Martin. 1967. *The Unions: Structure, Development, and Management*. New York: Harcourt, Brace, & World.
Fantasia, Rick. 1988. *Cultures of Solidarity*. Berkeley: University of California Press.
———. 1991. Private communication.

Feagin, Joe R., and Robert Parker. 1989. *Building American Cities: The Urban Real Estate Game*. Englewood Cliffs, NJ: Prentice-Hall.

Federal Election Commission. 1978–1988. Press releases.

Filippelli, Ronald L. 1990. "The Historical Context of Postwar Industrial Relations." Pp. 137–72 in *U.S. Labor Relations, 1945–89*, edited by Bruce Nissen. New York: Garland.

Form, William. 1954. "The Place of Social Structure in the Determination of Land Use." *Social Forces* 19:434–40.

———. 1976. *Blue-Collar Stratification: Auto Workers in Four Countries*. Princeton, NJ: Princeton University Press.

———. 1979. "Comparative Industrial Sociology and the Convergence Hypothesis." *Annual Review of Sociology* 5:1–25.

———. 1985. *Divided We Stand: Working-Class Stratification in America*. Urbana: University of Illinois Press.

———. 1990a. "Institutional Analysis: An Organizational Approach." Pp. 257–71 in *Change in Societal Institutions*, edited by Maureen T. Hallinan, David M. Klein, and Jennifer Glass. New York: Plenum Press.

———. 1990b. "Organized Labor and the Welfare State." Pp. 319–42 in *The Nature of Work*, edited by Kai Erikson and Steven Peter Vallas. New Haven, CT: Yale University Press.

———. 1995. "Stratification, Economics, and Demography in a Global Age." *Annales* 4:193–213.

Form, William, and Delbert C. Miller. 1960. *Industry, Labor, and Community*. New York: Harper.

Form, William, and Warren L. Sauer. 1963. "Labor and Community Influentials: A Comparative Study of Participation and Imagery." *Labor and Industrial Relations Review* 17:3–19.

Foster, Emily. 1990. "In the Beginning: A History." Pp. 8–12 in Columbus City Guide. Columbus, OH: CM Media.

Freeman, Richard B., and James L. Medoff. 1984. *What Do Unions Do?* New York: Basic Books.

Galbraith, John Kenneth. 1967. *The New Industrial State*. Boston: Houghton Mifflin.

Geoghan, Thomas. 1992. *Which Side Are You On?* New York: Plume.

Goldfield, Michael. 1987. *The Decline of Organized Labor in the United States*. Chicago: University of Chicago Press.

———. 1993. Personal communication.

Goldthorpe, John H. 1984. "The End of Convergence: Corporate and Dualist Tendencies in Modern Western Societies." Pp. 315–43 in *Order and Conflict in Contemporary Capitalism*, edited by John H. Goldthorpe. Oxford: Clarendon Press.

Gordon, David M. 1972. *Theories of Poverty and Unemployment*. Lexington, MA: Lexington.

Gordon, David M., Richard Edwards, and Michael Reich. 1982. *Segmented Work, Divided Labor*. Cambridge, England: Cambridge University Press.

Gottdiener, M. 1987. *The Decline of Urban Politics*. Newbury Park, CA: Sage.

Greenstone, David J. 1969, 1977. *Labor in American Politics*. Chicago: University of Chicago Press.

Griffen, Larry J., Holly McCammon, and Christopher Botsko. 1990. "Unmasking of a Movement? The Crisis of U. S. Trade Union in Comparative Perspective." Pp. 169–94, in *Change in Societal Institutions*, edited by Maureen T. Hallinan, David M. Klein, Jennifer Glass. New York: Plenum Press.

Hadden, Jeffrey, Louis M. Masotti, and Victor Thiessen. 1967. "The Making of Negro Mayors." *Trans-Action* 5:200–5.

Halloway, Harry. 1979. "Interest Group Politics in Postpartisan Era: The Political Machine of the AFL-CIO." *Political Science Quarterly* 94:117–23.

Hamilton, Richard F. 1972. *Class and Politics in the U.S.* New York: Wiley.

———. 1973. "Trends in Labor Union Voting Behavior: 1948–1968." *Industrial Relations* 12: 113–5.

Hannan, Michael T., and John Freeman. 1988. "The Ecology of Organizational Mortality: American Labor Unions, 1836–1985." *American Journal of Sociology* 94:25–52.

Hare, Marianne. 1984. "Organized Labor and the Mondale Campaign." *Labor Center Review* 1:11–14.

Harrison, Dennis J. 1987. "Labor." Pp. 604–66 in *The Encyclopedia of Cleveland*, edited by David D. Van Tassel and John J. Grabowski. Bloomington: Indiana University Press.

Hawley, Amos H. 1978. "Cumulative Change in Theory and in History." *American Sociological Review* 43:787–96.

———. 1981. *Urban Society: An Ecological Approach*. New York: Wiley.

Hawley, W. D., and James H. Svara. 1972. *The Study of Community Power: A Bibliographic Review*. Santa Barbara, CA: ABC-CLIO.

Hedstrom, Peter. 1994. "Contagious Collectivities: On the Spatial Diffusion of Swedish Trade Unions, 1890–1940." *American Journal of Sociology* 99:1157–79.

Herson, Lawrence J. R., and John M. Bolland. 1991. *The Urban Web: Politics, Policy, and Theory*. Chicago: Nelson-Hall.

Hindness, Barry. 1971. *The Decline of Working-Class Politics*. London: McGibbon & McKey.

Hirsch, Arnold R. 1990. "The Cook County Democratic Organization and the Dilemma of Race, 1971–1987." Pp. 63–91 in *Snowbelt Cities: Metropolitan Politics in the Northeast and Midwest Since World War I*, edited by Richard M. Burnard. Bloomington: Indiana University Press.

Hodson, Randy, and Theresa A. Sullivan. 1990. *The Social Organization of Work*. Belmont, CA: Wadsworth.

Hunker, Henry L. 1958. *Industrial Evolution of Columbus, Ohio*. Columbus: Ohio State University Bureau of Business Research.

Hunnius, Gerry, G. David Garson, and John Case (eds.). 1973. *Workers' Control*. New York: Vintage.

Hunter, Albert. 1974. *Symbolic Communities*. Chicago: University of Chicago Press.

Jacoby, Sanford M. 1994. "Prospects for Employee Representation in the United States." Unpublished manuscript, Los Angeles, University of California.

Jenkins, J. Craig. 1985. *The Politics of Insurgency*. New York: Columbia University Press.

Jenkins, J. Craig, and Barbara G. Brents. 1989. "Social Protest, Hegemonic Competition, and Social Reform: An Interpretation of the American Welfare State." *American Sociological Review* 54:891–909.

Kahn Lawrence M. 1978. "The Effect of Unions on the Earnings of Non-union Workers." *Industrial and Labor Relations Review* 31:205–16.

Kasarda, John. 1980. "The Implications of Redistribution Trends for National Urban Policy." *Social Science Quarterly* 61:373–400.

Katznelson, Ira. 1981. *City Trenches: Urban Politics and the Patterning of Class in the U. S.* New York: Pantheon.

Kerr, Clark, John T. Dunlop, Frederick Harbison, and Charles A. Myers. 1960. *Industrialism and Industrial Man*. Cambridge: Harvard University Press.

Kistler, Alan. 1984. "Union Organizing: New Challenges and Prospects." *Annals* 473: 96–107.

Klandermans, Bert, and Sidney Tarrow. 1988. "Mobilization into Social Movements." *International Social Movement Research* 1:1–18.

Knapp, Vincent J. 1976. *Europe in the Era of Social Transformation: 1700–Present*. Englewood Cliffs, NJ: Prentice-Hall.

Kochan, Thomas A., Harry C. Katz, and Robert B. McKersie. 1986. *The Transformation of American Industrial Relations*. New York: Basic Books.

Kornblum, William. 1974. *Blue-Collar Community*. Chicago: University of Chicago Press.

Kowinski, William S. 16 March 1980. "Suburbia: End to a Golden Age." *New York Times Magazine*.

Kroll, Jack. 1951. "The CIO-PAC and How It Works." Pp. 117–125 in *The House of Labor*, edited by J. B. S. Hardman and Maurice F. Neufeld. New York: Prentice-Hall.

Kweit, Robert W., and Mary Crizet Kweit. 1990. *People and Politics in Urban America*. Pacific Grove, CA: Brooks/Cole.

Lash, Scott. 1984. *The Militant Worker*. London: Heinemann.

Laslett, John H. M. 1972. "Review of Greenstone's *Labor in American Politics*." *American Political Science Review* 66:1040–1.

Laslett, John H., and Seymour Martin Lipset (eds.). 1984. *Failure of a Dream? Essays in the History of American Socialism*. Berkeley: University of California Press.

Lester, Richard A. 1958. *As Unions Mature*. Princeton, NJ: Princeton University Press.

Lipset, Seymour Martin. 1960a. "The Political Process in Trade Unions." Pp. 216–42 in *Labor and Trade Unions*, edited by Walter Galenson, and Seymour Lipset. New York: Wiley.

———. 1960b. *Political Man*. Garden City, NY: Doubleday.

———. 1977. "Why No Socialism in the United States?" Pp. 31–149 in *Sources of Contemporary Radicalism*, edited by Seweryn Bialer and Sophis Sluzer. Boulder, CO: Westview.

Lipset, Seymour Martin, and William Schneider. 1983. *The Confidence Gap*. New York: Free Press.

Lipset, Seymour Martin, Martin Trow, and James Coleman. 1956. *Union Democracy*. New York: Free Press.

Logan, John R. 1976. "Suburban Industrialization and Stratification." *American Journal of Sociology* 82:333–348.

Logan, John R., and Harvey L. Molotch. 1987. *Urban Fortunes: The Political Economy of Place*. Berkeley: University of California Press.

Long, Norton E. 1958. "The Local Community as an Ecology of Games." *American Journal of Sociology* 64:251–61.

Lowi, Theodore J. 1943. "Why There Is No Socialism in the U.S.?" *Society* 22:34–42.

Mackenzie, Gavin. 1973. *The Aristocracy of Labor*. Cambridge, England: Cambridge University Press.

Marcus, Philip. 1966. "Union Conventions and Executive Boards: A Formal Analysis of Organizational Structure." *American Sociological Review* 31:61–70.

Marini, Margaret Mooney. 1992. "The Role of Models of Purposive Action in Sociology." Pp. 21–48 in *Rational Choice Theory: Advocacy and Critique*, edited by James S. Coleman and Thomas J. Farraro. Newbury Park, CA: Sage.

Marks, Gary. 1989. *Unions in Politics: Britain, Germany, and the United States in the Nineteenth and Early Twentieth Centuries*. Princeton, NJ: Princeton University Press.

Martin, Brian D. 1991. "Municipal Reform and Vote Dilution: The Case of Columbus, Ohio." Unpublished manuscript. Sociology Department, Ohio State University. Columbus.

Massey, Douglass S., and Nancy A. Denton. 1987. "Trends in the Residential Segregation of Blacks, Hispanics, and Asians: 1970–1980." *American Sociological Review* 52:802–25.

Masters, Marick F., and John Thomas Delaney. 1985. "The Causes of Union Political Involvement: A Longitudinal Analysis." *Journal of Labor Research* 6:341–62.

———. 1987a. "Union Legislative Records during President Reagan's First Term." *Journal of Labor Research* 7:1–18.

———. 1987b. "Union Political Activity: A Review of the Empirical Literature." *Industrial and Labor Relations Review* 40:336–53.

Masters, Marick F., and Aschar Zardkoohi. 1988. "Congressional Support for Unions' Position across Diverse Legislation." *Journal of Labor Research* 9:149–65.

Mayhew, David R. 1986. *Placing Parties in American Politics*. Princeton, NJ: Princeton University Press.

McCarthy, John D., and Mayer N. Zald. 1987. "Resource Mobilization and Social Movements: A Partial Theory." Pp. 15–42 in *Social Movements in an Organizational Society*, edited by Mayer N. Zald and John D. McCarthy. New Brunswick, NJ: Transaction Books.

McFarlane, Larry. 1971. "Review of Greenstone's, *Labor in American Politics*." *The Historian* 33:504–5.

McWilliams, Cary. 1970. "Review of Greenstone's *Labor in American Politics*." *Political Science Quarterly* 85:689–92.

Michels, Robert. 1911 (1962). *Political Parties*. New York: Free Press.

Milkman, Ruth. 1990. "Gender and Trade Unionism in Historical Perspective." Pp. 87–107 in *Women, Politics, and Change*, edited by Louise A. Tilly and Patricia Gurin. New York: Sage.

Miller, Alan S. 1992. "Are Self-Proclaimed Conservatives Really Conservative? Trends in Attitudes and Self-Identification among the Young." *Social Forces* 71:195–210.

Miller, Warren E., and Donald E. Stokes. 1989. *American National Election Study, 1988*. Pre- and Post-Election Survey Computer File. Ann Arbor: Center for Political Studies, University of Michigan.

Miller, Zane L. 1968. *Boss Cox's Cincinnati*. New York: Oxford University Press.

Miller, Zane L., and Bruce Tucker. 1990. "Cincinnati, The New Urban Politics, 1954–1988." Pp. 91–108 in, *Snowbelt Cities*, edited by Richard M. Bernard. Bloomington: Indiana University Press.

Mills, C. Wright. 1948. *The New Men of Power*. New York: Harcourt, Brace.

Mitofsky, Warren J., and Martin Plissner. 1980. "Making of Delegates 1968–1980." *Public Opinion* 3:37–43.

Moberg, David. 19 December 1993. "Like Business, Unions Must Go Global." *New York Times*. Section F, p. 13.

Muller, Peter O. 1981. *Contemporary Suburban America*. Englewood Cliffs, NJ: Prentice-Hall.

Nachmias, David, and David H. Rosenbloom. 1980. *Bureaucratic Government USA*. New York: St. Martin's Press.

National Opinion Research Corporation. 1944, 1948. Reports.

Nelson, William E., Jr., and Philip J. Merano. 1977. *Electing Black Mayors*. Columbus: Ohio State University Press.

Newspaper Enterprise Association. 1991. *The World Almanac*. New York: Newspaper Enterprise Association.

Noyelle, Thierry J., and Thomas A. Stanback, Jr. 1984. *The Economic Transformation of Services*. Totowa, NJ: Rowman & Allanheld.

Ohio Department of Labor. 1960–1990. *Monthly Labor Review*.Columbus, OH.

Olofson, Gunnar. 1988. "After the Working-Class Movement?" *Acta Sociologica* 31:15–34.

Olson, Mancur, Jr. 1965. *The Logic of Collective Action*. Cambridge: Harvard University Press.

Parkin, Frank. 1979. *Marxism and Class Theory: A Bourgeois Critique*. New York: Columbia University Press.

Pinderhughes, Dianne M. 1987. *Race and Ethnicity in Chicago Politics*. Urbana: University of Illinois Press.

Piven, Frances Fox. 1990. "Why Voter Turnout is Low and Getting Lower." Unpublished manuscript, City University of New York, Graduate School.

Piven, Frances Fox, and Richard A. Cloward. 1977. *Poor People's Movements*. New York: Pantheon.

Plissner, Martin, and Warren J. Mitofsky. 1988. "Making of Delegates 1968–88." *Public Opinion* 11:45–47.

Pomper, Gerald. 1963. *Nominating the President*. New York: Norton.

Quadagno, Jil. 1992. "Social Movements and State Transformation: Labor Unions and Racial Conflicts in the War on Poverty." *American Sociological Review* 57:616–34.

Raskin, A. H. 10 December 1990. "Profiles: Getting Things Done." *New Yorker*.

Redding, Kent. 1992. "Failed Populism: Movement-Party Disjuncture in North Carolina, 1890–1900." *American Sociological Review* 57:340–52.

Regalado, James A. 1991. "Organized Labor and Los Angeles City Politics, and Assessment of the Bradley Years, 1973–89." *Urban Affairs Quarterly* 27:87–108.

Regini, Marino. 1984. "The Conditions for Political Exchange: How Concertation Emerged and Collapsed in Italy and Great Britain." Pp. 125–42 in *Order and Conflict in Contemporary Capitalism*, edited by John H. Goldthorpe. Oxford, England: Clarendon.

———. (ed.). 1992. "Introduction." *The Future of Labour Movements*. London: Sage.

Rehmus, Charles M. 1984. "Labor and Politics in the 1980s." *Annals* 473:40–51.

Reynolds, Lloyd G. 1974. *Labor Economics and Labor Relations*. Englewood Cliffs, NJ: Prentice-Hall.

Richardson, James F. 1987. "Politics." Pp. 775–8 in *The Encyclopedia of Cleveland*, edited by David D. Van Tassel and John J. Grabowski. Bloomington: Indiana University Press.

Roberts, Kenneth. 1978. *The Working Class*. London: Longman.

Roberts, Markley. 1984. "The Future Demographics of American Unionism." *Annals of the American Academy of Political and Social Sciences* 473:64–75.

Rohrschneider, Robert. 1991. "Public Opinion toward Environmental Groups in Western Europe." *Social Science Quarterly* 72:251–66.

Rose, Arnold. 1967. *The Power Structure*. New York: Oxford University Press.

Sabel, Charles F. 1982. *Work and Politics*. Cambridge, England: Cambridge University Press.

Saltzman, Gregory M. 1987. "Congressional Voting on Labor Issues: the Role of PACs." *Industrial and Labor Relations Review* 40:163–79.

Salwen, Kevin G. 8 April 1994. "NLRB Agenda Indicates a Shift Toward Labor." *Wall Street Journal*.

Sassen, Saskia. 1990. "Economic Restructuring and the American City." *Annual Review of Sociology* 16:465–90.

Schlesinger, Joseph A. 1968. "Political Parties: Party Units." *International Encyclopedia of the Social Sciences*. New York: Macmillan and Free Press.

Schwartz, Barry. 1980. "The Suburban Landscape." *Contemporary Sociology* 9:640–50.

Scoble, Harry M. 1967. *Ideology and Electoral Action*. San Francisco: Chandler.

Seidman, Joel, Jack London, Bernard Karsh, and Daisy L. Tagliacozzo. 1958. *The Worker Views His Union*. Chicago: University of Chicago Press.

Sexton, Patricia Cayo. 1991. *The War on Labor and the Left*. Boulder, CO: Westview Press.

Seybold, Peter. 1990. "American Labor at the Crossroads: Political Resurgence or Decline?" Pp. 45–90 in *U.S. Labor Relations, 1945–1989*, edited by Bruce Nisson. New York: Garland.

Shannon, Thomas R., Nancy Kleniewski, and William M. Cross. 1991. *Urban Problems in Perspective*. Prospective Heights, IL: Waveland.

Sheppard, Harold L., Arthur Kornhauser, and Albert J. Mayer. 1956. *When Labor Votes*. New York: University Books.

Shostak, Arthur B. 1969. *Blue-Collar Life*. New York: Random House.

———. 1991. *Robust Unionism: Innovations in the Labor Movement*. Ithaca, NY: ILR Press.

Simmel, Georg. 1950. *The Sociology of Georg Simmel*. Translated by Kurt Wolff. Glencoe, IL: Free Press.

Skocpol, Theda, and Edwin Amenta. 1985. "Did Capitalists Shape Social Security?" *American Sociological Review* 50:572–75.

———. 1986. "States and Social Policies." *Annual Review of Sociology* 12:131–57.

Skocpol, Theda, and Kenneth Finegold. 1990. "Explaining New Deal Labor Policy." *American Political Science Review* 84:1298–1315.

Skocpol, Theda, and John Ikenberry. 1983. "The Political Formation of the American Welfare State." *Comparative Social Research*, Vol. 6. Greenwich, CT: JAI Press.

Starobin, Paul. 2 September 1989. "Unions Turn to Grass Roots to Rebuild Hill Clout." *Congressional Quarterly*.

State of Ohio. 1960, 1990. *Monthly Labor Review*. Columbus, OH.

Stepan-Norris, Judith, and Maurice Zeitlin. 1989. "Who Gets the Bird? How the Communists Won Power and Trust in America's Unions." *American Sociological Review* 54:503–23.

Stinchcombe, Arthur L. 1965. "Social Structure and Organizations." Pp. 142–93 in *Handbook of Organizations*, edited by James G. March, Chicago: Rand-McNally.

Stokes, Carl B. 1973. *Promises of Power*. New York: Simon & Schuster.

Straetz, Ralph A. 1958. *PR Politics in Cincinnati*. New York: New York University Press.

Sturmthal, Adolph. 1973. "Industrial Relations Strategies." Pp.1–33 in *The International Labor Movement in Transition*, edited by Adolf Sturmthal and James G. Scoville. Urbana: University of Illinois Press.

Tannenbaum, Frank. 1965. *A Philosophy of Labor*. New York: Knopf.

Tarpinian, Greg. 20 November 1989. "Pittston: Rebirth of the Unions?" *Wall Street Journal*.

Taylor, Verta. 1989. "Social Movement Continuity: The Women's Movement in Abeyance." *American Sociological Review* 54:761–75.

Tilly, Charles. 1984. "Social Movements and National Politics."Pp. 297–317 in *Statemaking and Social Movements*, edited by C. Bright and S. Harding. Ann Arbor: University of Michigan Press.

Touraine, Alaine. 1986. "Unionism as a Social Movement." Pp. 151–73 in *Unions in Transition*, edited by Seymour Martin Lipset. San Francisco: Institute for Comparative Studies.

———. 1988. *Return of the Actor: Social Theory in Postindustrial Society*. Translated by Myrna Codzich. Minneapolis: University of Minnesota Press.

Touraine, Alaine, Michel Wieviorka, and Francois Dubet. 1987. *The Workers' Movement*. Translated by Ian Patterson. Cambridge, UK: Cambridge University Press.

Troy, Leo and Neil Sheflin. 1985. *U.S. Union Sourcebook*. West Orange, NJ: Industrial Relations Data and Information Service.

Ulaner, Carole Jean. 1991. "Electoral Participation." *Society* 28:35–46.

U.S. Bureau of the Census. 1960. *Census of Population*, Vol. 1, Part 37. Washington, DC.

———. 1961. *Historical Statistics of the United States: Colonal Times to the Present*. Washington DC.

———. 1966. *Statistical Abstract of the United States 1966*. Washington, DC.

———. 1970. *Census of Population*, Vol. 1. Washington, DC.

———. 1975. *Historical Statistics of the United States*, Part 1. Washington, DC.

———. 1978. *Current Population Reports*, Series P-23, no. 72."Selected Characteristics of Travel to Work in 20 Metropolitan Areas: 1976." Washington, DC.

———. 1980. *Census of Population*, Vol. 1, Washington, DC.

———. 1986. *City Government Finances in 1984–5*, Series GF85. no. 4. Washington, DC.

———. 1991. *Statistical Abstract of the United States*. Washington DC.

———. 1992. *Statistical Abstract of the United States 1992*. Washington, DC.

———. 1993. Current Population Reports, P20-466, *Voting and Registration in the Election of November 1992*. Washington, DC.

———. 1972. Bureau of Labor Statistics. Report 417. *Selected Earnings and Demographic Characteristics of Union Members*. Washington, DC.

———. 1985. *Employment and Economy*, Vol. 32. Washington, DC.

———. 1992. *Employment and Economy*, Vol. 38. Washington, DC.

van den Berg, Axel. 1989. *Immanent Utopia*. Princeton, NJ: Princeton University Press.

Vantine, Warren R. 1992. Personal communication.

Visser, Jelle. 1992. "The Strength of Union Movments in Advanced Capital Democracies." Pp. 17–52 in *The Future of Labour Movements*, edited by Marino Regini. London: Sage.

Vogel, Virgil J. 1970. "Review of Greenstone's, *Labor in American Politics*." *Michigan History* 54:258–60.

Wallace, Michael. 1989. "Aggressive Economism, Defensive Control: Contours of American Labor Militancy, 1947–81." *Economic and Industrial Democracy* 10:7–34.

Wallace, Michael, and Arne L. Kalleberg. 1981. "Economic Organization of Firms and Labor Market Consequences." Pp.77–118 in *Sociological Perspectives on Labor Markets*, edited by Ivar Berg. New York: Academic Books.

Wallace, Michael, Beth A. Rubin, and Brian T. Smith. 1988. "American Labor Law: Its Impact on Working-Class Militancy, 1901–1980." *Social Science History* 12:1–29.

Wall Street Journal. 23 February 1994. "Unions Agree to Resume Payment to Democrats."

———. 30 September 1993. "Labor Party in Britain Cuts Union Power."

Walton, John. 1966. "Substance and Artifact: The Current Status of Research on Community Power." *American Journal of Sociology* 71:430–38.

Ware, Norman J. 1935. *Labor in Modern Industrial Society*. Boston: D. C. Heath.

Warren, Rachel B., and Donald I. Warren. 1977. *The Neighborhood Organizer's Handbook*. Notre Dame, IN: University of Notre Dame Press.

Washington Post. 13 September 1987. "U.S. Unions Losing Clout in Shifting Labor Market," Section H.

Waste, Robert J. 1989. *The Ecology of City Planning*. New York: Oxford University Press.

Wattenberg, Martin P. 1990. *The Decline of American Political Parties 1952–1988*. Cambridge: Harvard University Press.

Weakliem, David. 1993. "Class Consciousness and Political Change: Voting and Political Attitudes in British Working Class, 1964 to 1970." *American Sociological Review* 58:382–97.

Weber, Max. 1946. *From Max Weber: Essays in Sociology*, edited by Hans Gerth and C. Wright Mills. New York: Oxford University Press.

Weiher, Gregory R. 1991. *The Fractured Metropolis: Political Fragmentaion and Metropolitan Segregation*. Albany: State University of New York Press.

Weinberg, Kenneth G. 1968. *Black Victory: Carl Stokes and the Winning of Cleveland*. Chicago: Quadrangle Books.

Western, Bruce. 1993. "Postwar Unionization in Eighteen Countries." *American Sociological Review* 58:266–82.

Williamson, Oliver. 1975. *Markets and Hierarchies*. New York: Free Press.

Wilson, Graham K. 1979. *Unions in American National Politics*. New York: St. Martin's Press.

Wilson, James Q. 1973. *Political Organizations*. New York: Basic Books.

Wilson, William Julius. 1987. *The Truly Disadvantaged*. Chicago: University of Chicago Press.

Windmuller, John P. 1974. "European Labor and Politics: A Symposium." *Industrial and Labor Review* 28:3–6.

Winpisinger, William W. 1989. *Reclaiming Our Future*. Boulder, CO: Westview.

Wolfe, Arthur. 1969. "Trends in Labor Union Voting Behavior, 1948–68." *Industrial Relations* 9:1–10.

Wolfinger, Raymond W. 1972. "Why Political Machines Have Not Withered Away and Other Revisionist Thoughts." *Journal of Politics* 34:365–98.

WRHS (Western Reserve Historical Society). 1987. "The Cuyahoga Democratic Party." P. 331 in *Encyclopia of Cleveland*. Bloomington: University of Indiana Press.

Zax, Jeffrey S. 1990. "Election Methods and Black and Hispanic City Council Membership." *Social Science Quarterly* 71:339–52.

Zolberg, Aristide R. 1986. "How Many Exceptionalism?" Pp. 397–455 in *Working-Class Formation*, edited by Ira Katznelson and Aristide R. Zolberg. Princeton NJ: Princeton University Press.

Index

PLENUM STUDIES IN WORK AND INDUSTRY
COMPLETE CHRONOLOGICAL LISTING

Series Editors:
Ivar Berg, *University of Pennsylvania, Philadelphia, Pennsylvania*
and Arne L. Kalleberg, *University of North Carolina, Chapel Hill, North Carolina*

WORK AND INDUSTRY
Structures, Markets, and Processes
Arne L. Kalleberg and Ivar Berg

WORKERS, MANAGERS, AND TECHNOLOGICAL CHANGE
Emerging Patterns of Labor Relations
Edited by Daniel B. Cornfield

INDUSTRIES, FIRMS, AND JOBS
Sociological and Economic Approaches
Edited by George Farkas and Paula England

MATERNAL EMPLOYMENT AND CHILDREN'S DEVELOPMENT
Longitudinal Research
Edited by Adele Eskeles Gottfried and Allen W. Gottfried

ENSURING MINORITY SUCCESS IN CORPORATE MANAGEMENT
Edited by Donna E. Thompson and Nancy DiTomaso

THE STATE AND THE LABOR MARKET
Edited by Samuel Rosenberg

THE BUREAUCRATIC LABOR MARKET
The Case of the Federal Civil Service
Thomas A. DiPrete

ENRICHING BUSINESS ETHICS
Edited by Clarence C. Walton

LIFE AND DEATH AT WORK
Industrial Accidents as a Case of Socially Produced Error
Tom Dwyer

WHEN STRIKES MAKE SENSE—AND WHY
Lessons from Third Republic French Coal Miners
Samuel Cohn

THE EMPLOYMENT RELATIONSHIP
Causes and Consequences of Modern Personnel Administration
William P. Bridges and Wayne J. Villemez

LABOR AND POLITICS IN THE U.S. POSTAL SERVICE
Vern K. Baxter

PLENUM STUDIES IN WORK AND INDUSTRY
COMPLETE CHRONOLOGICAL LISTING

NEGRO BUSINESS AND BUSINESS EDUCATION
Their Present and Prospective Development
Joseph A. Pierce
Introduction by John Sibley Butler

THE OPERATION OF INTERNAL LABOR MARKETS
Staffing Practices and Vacancy Chains
Lawrence T. Pinfield

SEGMENTED LABOR, FRACTURED POLITICS
Labor Politics in American Life
William Form